Sunbelt HOME PLANS

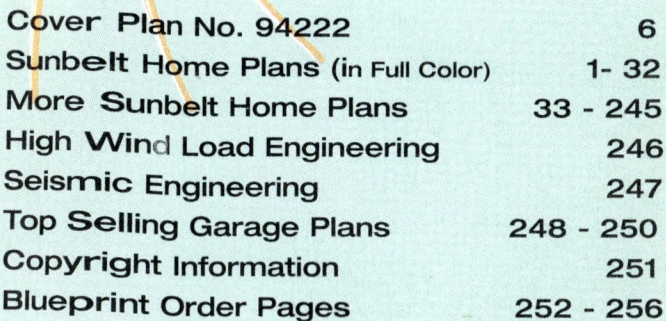

Cover Plan No. 94222	6
Sunbelt Home Plans (in Full Color)	1- 32
More Sunbelt Home Plans	33 - 245
High Wind Load Engineering	246
Seismic Engineering	247
Top Selling Garage Plans	248 - 250
Copyright Information	251
Blueprint Order Pages	252 - 256

Library of Congress No.: 96-77234/ISBN: 0-938708-71-6

Illustration & Back Cover Design by Robert Miles Long

Submit all Canadian Orders to:
The Garlinghouse Company
102 Ellis Street
Penticton, BC V2A 4L5

Canadian Orders Only: 1-800-361-7526
Fax: 1-250-493-7526
Customer Service: 1-250-493-0942

© Copyright 1998 by the L. F. Garlinghouse Co., Inc. of Middletown, Connecticut. Building a house from a design found in this publication without first purchasing a set of home plans is a copyright violation. Printed in the USA. The cover photo may have been modified to suit individual tastes.

Design 94219

Lends Itself to a Corner Lot

Double doors lead to a lovely formal living area, which consists of a living room, dining room, and study, all with decorative ceilings. The living room has a two view fireplace and corner glass looking out to the courtyard veranda. Bookshelves balance an area where a window seat can be placed. The kitchen is open to a bright leisure area and a sunny nook with mitered glass. The leisure room has glass doors to the rear veranda areas. Two bedrooms nearby each contain a walk-in closet and a full bath in between. The privacy from the main living areas and master bedroom results in a great layout. The master suite is off the wing hall way. The suite has a cozy sitting room to the rear views. Through the pocket door, a glamorous full bath has a raised garden tub as its main focal point. Dual vanities have fixed glass above for natural light and a special, dramatic detail. The photographed home may have been modified to suit individual tastes. No materials list is available.

HIGH WIND LOAD ENGINEERING AVAILABLE
SEE PAGE 246 FOR DETAILS

planinfo

First floor	2,986 sq. ft.
Garage	574 sq. ft.
Bedrooms	Four
Bathrooms	3(Full), 1(Half)
Foundation	Slab
Total living area	2,986 sq. ft.

Price Code E

Main Floor

Photography Supplied by The Sater Design Collection, Inc.

Design 94223

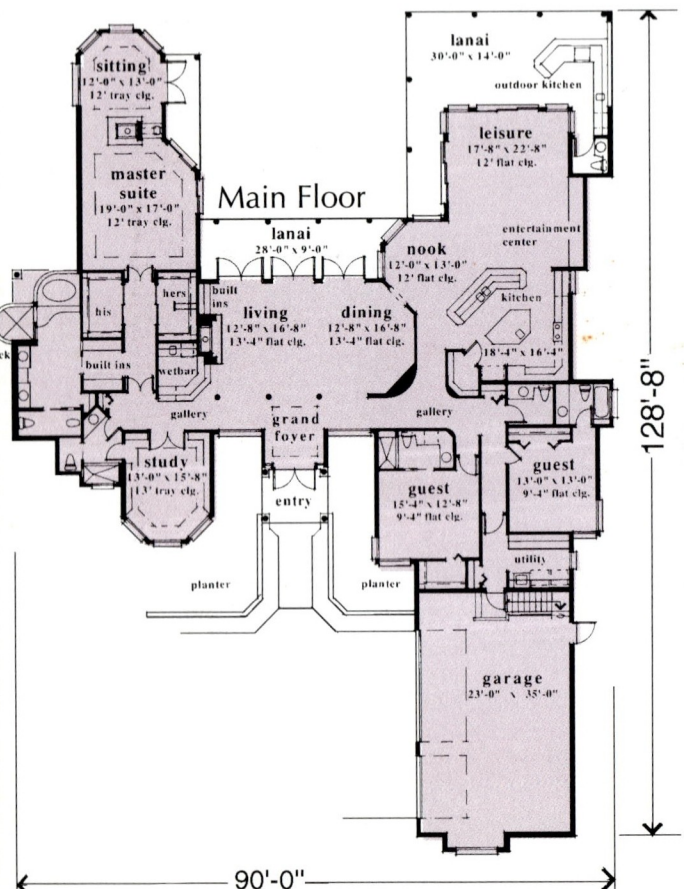

planinfo

Main floor	3,896 sq. ft.
Bonus room	846 sq. ft.
Garage	864 sq. ft.
Bedrooms	Three
Bathrooms	2(Full), 2(3/4)
Foundation	Slab
Total living area	**3,896 sq. ft.**

Price Code F

HIGH WIND LOAD ENGINEERING AVAILABLE
SEE PAGE 246 FOR DETAILS

No materials list available

Grand Statement

The first impression of luxury continues at every turn of this sprawling home. Round columns an quoin detailing make this home and elegant statement. The grand foyer opens to the formal living/dining room which has a fireplace, a wet bar, and access to the lanai through French doors. This room is perfect for those who entertain, formal or informal. To the right of the entry are the informal areas. The secondary bedrooms are full guest suites, each with its own bath. The lanai features another kitchen and powder room for outdoor entertaining. Dominating the other wing is the master suite with two closets, built-ins, a wet bar, and a three-sided fireplace that separates the sitting and sleeping areas. The luxurious bath features a round, glass block shower and a step-up oval tub. A study and a full bath complete the wing, making it perfect for the owners or even another guest suite. This home features an optional bonus dormer room above the garage. The photographed home may have been modified to suit individual tastes.

Design 94209

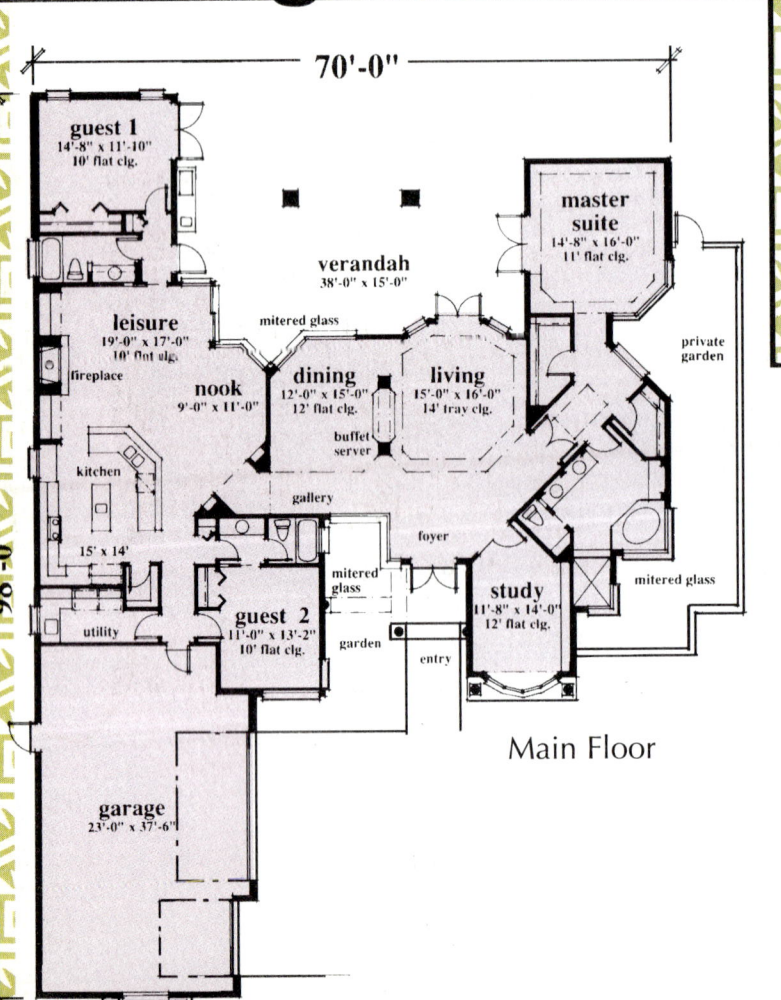

planinfo

Main floor	2,794 sq. ft.
Garage	883 sq. ft.
Bedrooms	Three
Bathrooms	Three
Foundation	Slab
Total living area	**2,794 sq. ft.**
Price Code E	

No materials list available

Main Floor

70'-0"
98'-0"

guest 1 14'-8" x 11'-10" 10' flat clg.

verandah 38'-0" x 15'-0"

master suite 14'-8" x 16'-0" 11' flat clg.

leisure 19'-0" x 17'-0" 10' flat clg.
fireplace

mitered glass

private garden

nook 9'-0" x 11'-0"

dining 12'-0" x 15'-0" 12' flat clg.

living 15'-0" x 16'-0" 14' tray clg.

buffet server

kitchen

15' x 14'

gallery

foyer

mitered glass

guest 2 11'-0" x 13'-2" 10' flat clg.

garden

entry

study 11'-8" x 14'-0" 12' flat clg.

mitered glass

utility

garage 23'-0" x 37'-6"

Street Style

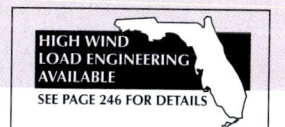

HIGH WIND LOAD ENGINEERING AVAILABLE
SEE PAGE 246 FOR DETAILS

Classic columns, circle head windows and a bow window study give this stucco home a wonderful street presence. The double-arched entryway provides a balanced elegance. The formal living and dining rooms are straight ahead providing one with a captivating first impression of elegance. An arched buffet server separates these rooms. Mitered glass and French doors allow for rear yard views and natural light. Walk through the gallery toward the family areas and the truly convenient part of this home comes to life. An ample kitchen has a walk-in pantry, center island prep sink, an eating bar, and desk space. The open nook is conveniently located for informal family meals. The leisure room provides a peaceful retreat focusing on a fireplace and built-in entertainment center space. Two secondary suites, with full bathrooms, round out the wing. The master wing hosts a convenient study and ample sleeping area, as well as, his'n'her wardrobe closets and an alluring bath. The photographed home may have been modified to suit individual tastes.

Photography Supplied by The Sater Design Collection, Inc.

Photography Supplied by The Sater Design Collection, Inc.

Photography Supplied by The Sater Design Collection, Inc.

Design 94222

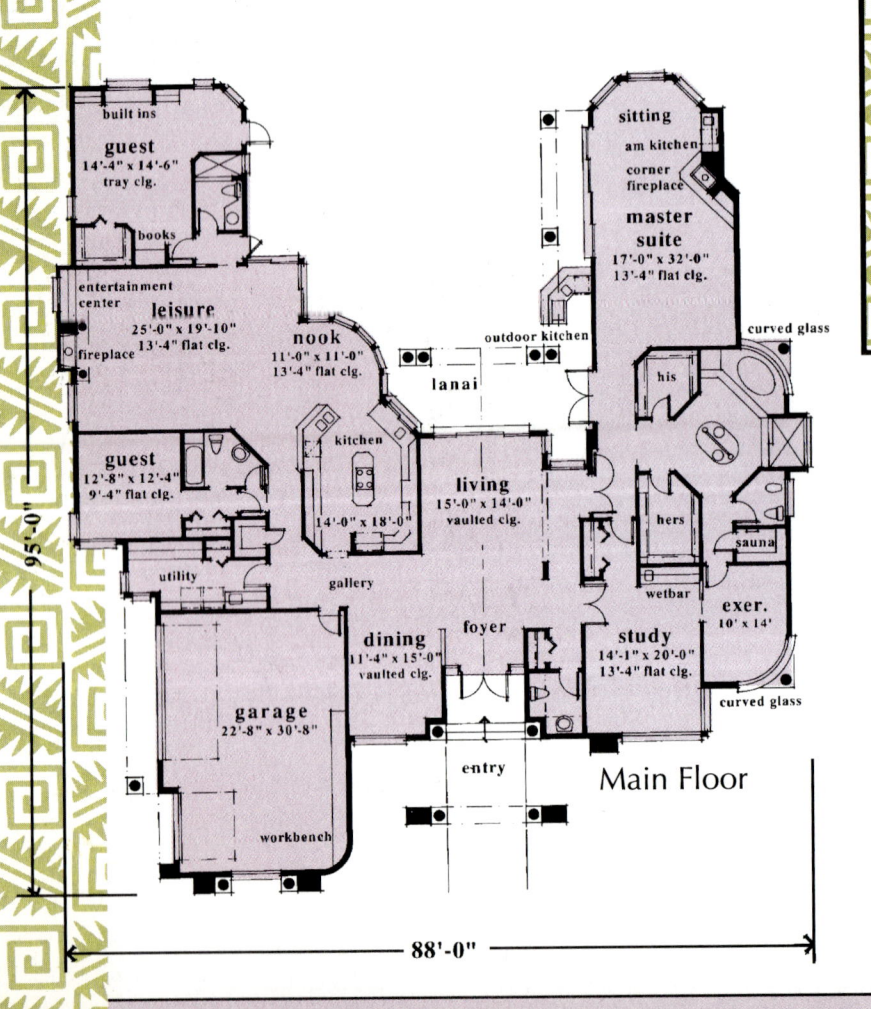

planinfo

Main floor	4,565 sq. ft.
Porch	419 sq. ft.
Garage	757 sq. ft.
Bedrooms	Three
Bathrooms	3(Full), 1(Half)
Foundation	Slab
Total living area	**4,565 sq. ft.**
Price Code F	

No materials list available

HIGH WIND LOAD ENGINEERING AVAILABLE
SEE PAGE 246 FOR DETAILS

Main Floor

- **guest** 14'-4" x 14'-6" tray clg. — built ins, books
- **leisure** 25'-0" x 19'-10" 13'-4" flat clg. — entertainment center, fireplace
- **guest** 12'-8" x 12'-4" 9'-4" flat clg.
- **nook** 11'-0" x 11'-0" 13'-4" flat clg.
- **kitchen**
- **lanai** — outdoor kitchen
- **sitting** — am kitchen, corner fireplace
- **master suite** 17'-0" x 32'-0" 13'-4" flat clg. — curved glass, his, hers, sauna, wetbar
- **living** 15'-0" x 14'-0" vaulted clg.
- **gallery**
- **utility**
- **dining** 11'-4" x 15'-0" vaulted clg.
- **foyer**
- **study** 14'-1" x 20'-0" 13'-4" flat clg. — curved glass
- **exer.** 10' x 14'
- **garage** 22'-8" x 30'-8" — workbench
- **entry**

95'-0" x 88'-0"

Luxurious Living

High ceilings are found in the formal living and dining areas. The arch details showcase beautiful Palladian window detail above the living room doors to the lanai. The gallery leads to the family gathering and secondary bedroom areas. The kitchen, with a cooking island, opens to the round nook and the leisure room. The leisure room has a fireplace and entertainment center area. The spacious master wing area has an owner's study, an exercise room, a captivating bath and a pampering suite. The study has a wet bar area and closet. An optional exercise room has easy access to the master bath. The curved glass corner provides spectacular vistas to the garden area. The exercise room leads to the bath and a private sauna room. The garden tub also has curved glass to the rear and side yard views. The expansive suite has a sleeping space with a bayed sitting area. A morning kitchen, corner fireplace and built-in area make the owner's suite alluring and private. The photographed home may have been modified to suit individual tastes.

Photography Supplied by The Sater Design Collection, Inc.

Design 94220

planinfo

Main floor	3,477 sq. ft.
Garage	771 sq. ft.
Bedrooms	Three
Bathrooms	2(Full), 1(3/4)
Foundation	Slab
Total living area	**3,477 sq. ft.**
Price Code F	

No materials list available

HIGH WIND LOAD ENGINEERING AVAILABLE
SEE PAGE 246 FOR DETAILS

Main Floor

95'-0"
88'-8"

lanai
fireplace   built ins
leisure
23'-0" x 17'-8"
12'-6" flat clg.

nook
10'-8" x 10'-8"
12' step clg.

lanai
30'-0" x 10'-0"

grill
kitchen
wetbar

bedroom
13'-4" x 13'-8"
9'-4" flat clg.

master suite
17'-0" x 20'-4"
14' flat clg.

living
15'-0" x 17'-2"
14' flat clg.
2 view firplace

am kitchen

gallery

dining
17'-0" x 13'-0"
14' flat clg.

utility

bedroom
13'-4" x 12'-0"
9'-4" flat clg.

his
hers
gallery
foyer
entry
planter

study
13'-0" x 15'-8"
14' vault clg.

garage
23'-4" x 29'-8"

8

Look No Further

An angled garage, raised entry and a turret study create an exciting and different streetscape. The entry doors open to the formal living room focusing to the lanai through sliding glass doors and mitered glass corner. A double-sided fireplace is shared with the master suite to the right, a wet bar easily serves the living room, dining room and lanai making this home perfect for family gatherings or entertaining. An island kitchen with an octagon nook has windows spanning all rear views. The leisure room has a fireplace wall with built-ins along the back wall. Optional fixed glass windows above the entertainment center and gas fireplace allow for natural light. The secondary bedrooms have a full bath between them. The study has a peaked vaulted ceiling and cove lighting. The spacious master suite includes a fireplace, a morning kitchen bar, and lanai access. There are two oversized wardrobe closets. A full bath accesses the outdoor area. The photographed home may have been modified to suit individual tastes.

Street Presence

Design 94229

HIGH WIND LOAD ENGINEERING AVAILABLE
SEE PAGE 246 FOR DETAILS

Inside the grand foyer, the plan opens through archways to the formal living spaces. The high stepped ceilings open up the rooms and give them a grand airy feel. An oversized kitchen with a cook-top island and large walk-in pantry make this area perfect for family cooking or entertaining on a grand scale. A bayed leisure room features large windows overlooking the rear yard. The secondary bedrooms, including one full guest suite, round out the family wing. The owner suite area features an extravagant oversized master suite and sitting bay. The bath has a walk-in shower, his'n'her vanity with a makeup space and a garden tub. The second floor layout features a study and a guest suite with their own private balconies. The photographed home may have been modified to suit individual tastes. No materials list is available.

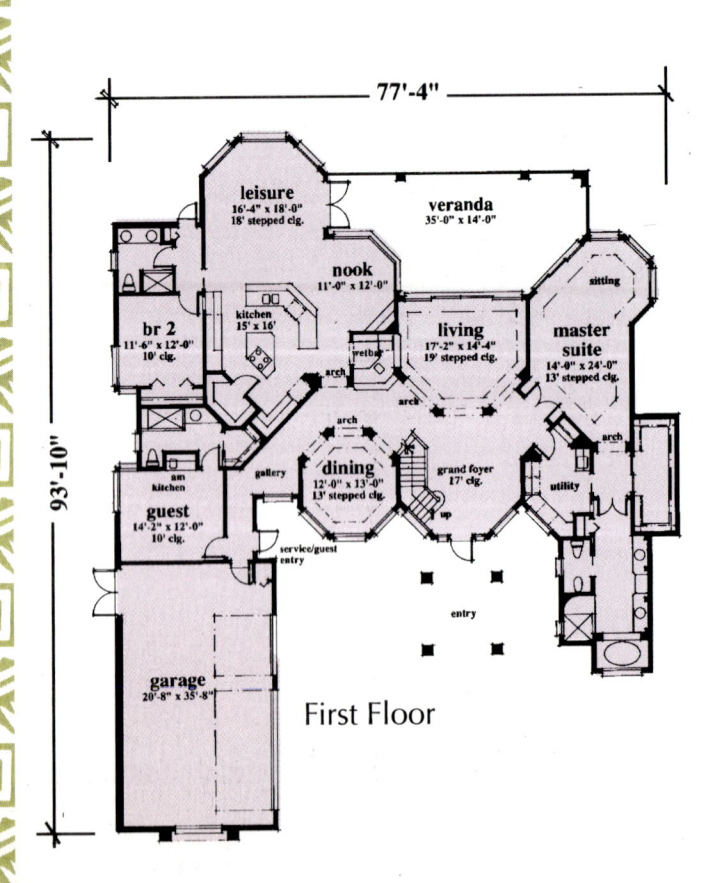

Photography Supplied by The Sater Design Collection, Inc.

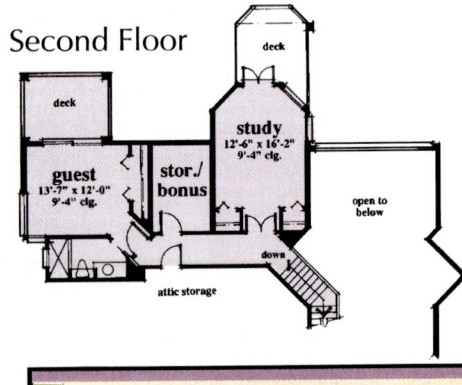

planinfo

First floor	3,092 sq. ft.
Second floor	656 sq. ft.
Garage	785 sq. ft.
Bedrooms	Four
Bathrooms	Four
Foundation	Slab
Total living area	**3,748 sq. ft.**

Price Code F

HIGH WIND LOAD ENGINEERING AVAILABLE
SEE PAGE 246 FOR DETAILS

Dramatic Entry
Design 94205

A dramatic set of stairs leads to the entry of this home. The foyer leads to an expansive living room with a fireplace and built-in bookshelves. A lanai opens off this area and will assure outdoor enjoyment. For formal meals, a front facing dining room offers a bay window. The kitchen serves this area easily as well as the breakfast room. A study and three bedrooms make up the rest of the floor plan. Two secondary bedrooms share a full hall bath. In the master suite, two walk-in closets and a full bath are featured. In one bedroom, a set of French doors offers passage to the lanai. This is a unique raised piling design where the first floor of living space is raised above the garage and bonus areas. The photographed home may have been modified to suit individual tastes.

Photography Supplied by The Sater Design Collection, Inc.

Main Floor

- lanai 58'-0" x 10'-8"
- master suite 13'-0" x 15'-0" 9'-4" stepped clg.
- nook 11'-0" x 9'-4"
- br. 2 12'-0" x 11'-4" 9'-4" flat clg.
- grand room 20'-0" x 18'-0" avg. tray ceiling
- kitchen 11' x 11'
- study 11'-0" x 11'-0" 9'-4" flat clg.
- dining 10'-10" x 15'-0" 9'-4" flat clg.
- br. 3 12'-0" x 11'-0" 9'-4" flat clg.

Ground Floor

- verandah 58'-0" x 12'-0"
- recreation 25'-0" x 35'-0"
- storage
- garage 23'-4" x 24'-0"
- 54'-0"
- 58'-0"

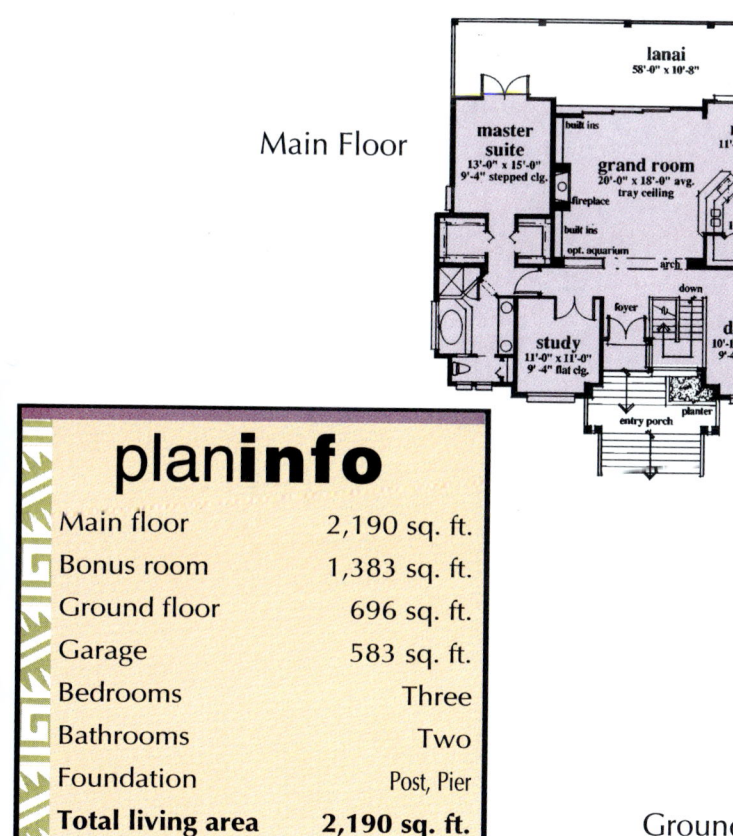

planinfo

Main floor	2,190 sq. ft.
Bonus room	1,383 sq. ft.
Ground floor	696 sq. ft.
Garage	583 sq. ft.
Bedrooms	Three
Bathrooms	Two
Foundation	Post, Pier
Total living area	**2,190 sq. ft.**

Price Code C

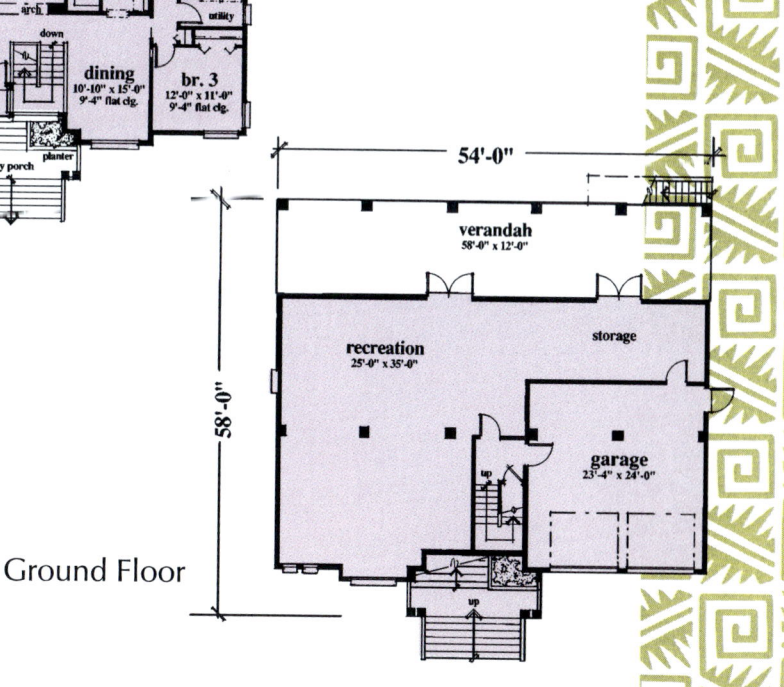

Indoor/Outdoor Living

Design 94204

HIGH WIND LOAD ENGINEERING AVAILABLE
SEE PAGE 246 FOR DETAILS

An abundance of porches and a deck encourage year-round indoor-outdoor living in this classic two-story home. The spacious Great room includes a cozy fireplace and is adjacent to the dining room. Both rooms have access to the screen porch/deck area and are perfect for formal or informal entertaining. An efficient kitchen and nearby laundry room make chores easy. The private master suite offers access to the screened porch and leads into a relaxing master bath complete with a walk-in closet, a tub and separate shower, double vanity and a toilet compartment. A second bedroom and a loft are on the second floor. The photographed home may have been modified to suit individual tastes. No materials list available.

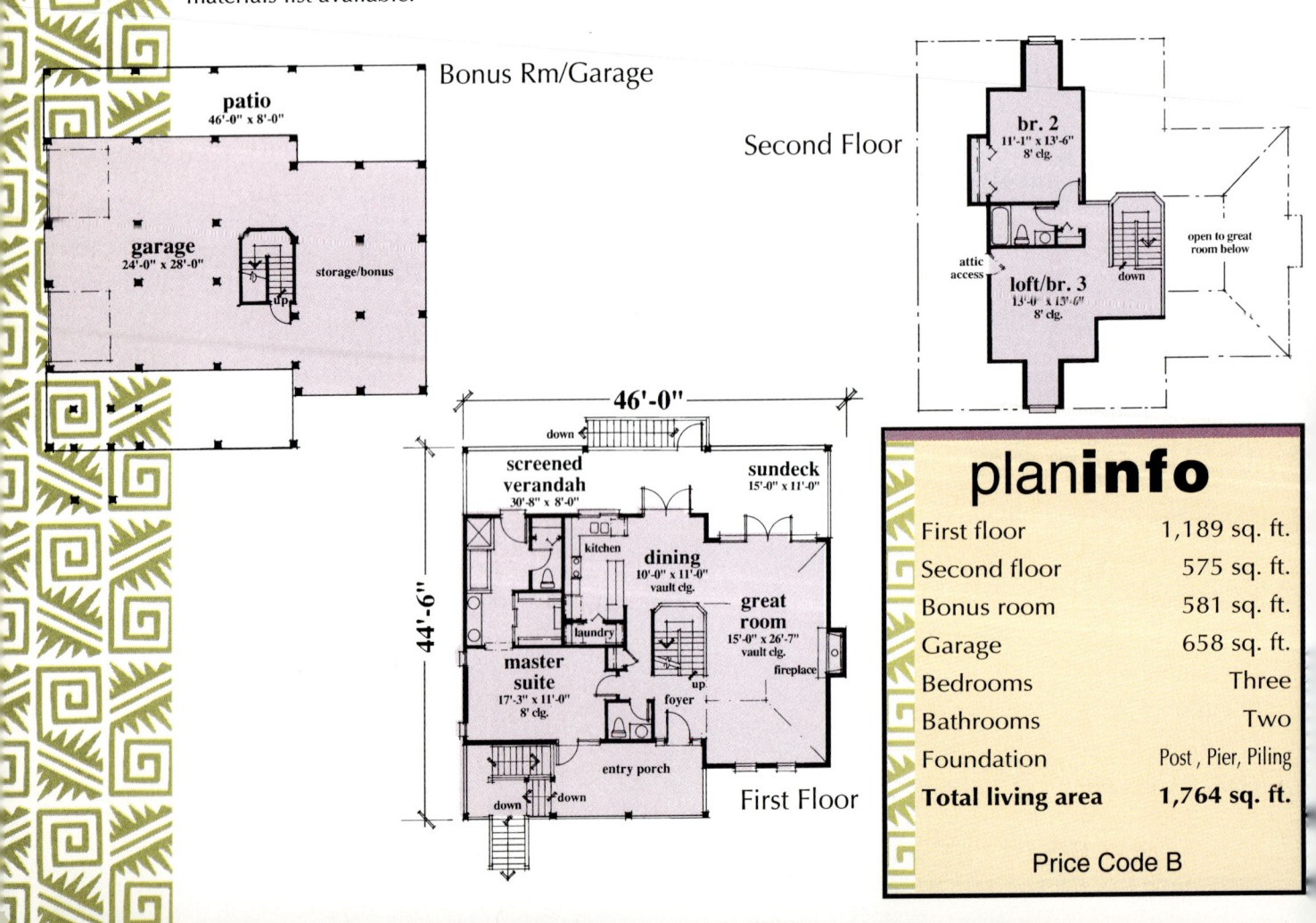

Photography Supplied by The Sater Design Collection, Inc.

Bonus Rm/Garage

- patio 46'-0" x 8'-0"
- garage 24'-0" x 28'-0"
- storage/bonus

Second Floor

- br. 2 11'-1" x 13'-6" 8' clg.
- loft/br. 3 13'-6" x 13'-6" 8' clg.
- attic access
- open to great room below

First Floor

- screened verandah 30'-8" x 8'-0"
- sundeck 15'-0" x 11'-0"
- kitchen
- dining 10'-0" x 11'-0" vault clg.
- great room 15'-0" x 26'-7" vault clg.
- fireplace
- laundry
- master suite 17'-3" x 11'-0" 8' clg.
- foyer
- entry porch

46'-0" × 44'-6"

planinfo

First floor	1,189 sq. ft.
Second floor	575 sq. ft.
Bonus room	581 sq. ft.
Garage	658 sq. ft.
Bedrooms	Three
Bathrooms	Two
Foundation	Post, Pier, Piling
Total living area	**1,764 sq. ft.**

Price Code B

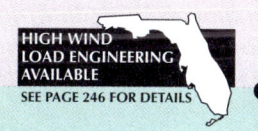

HIGH WIND LOAD ENGINEERING AVAILABLE
SEE PAGE 246 FOR DETAILS

Grand Impression

Design 94214

A three story turret creates a tremendous first impression of the exterior of this elegant design. Siding and the metal roof make a tremendous and elegant statement. On the level above are the main living areas. A dining room with a bay window, a grand room, and the kitchen and nook area are on the first level. The grand room has a fireplace and entertainment center space while large glass doors access the deck. A full length deck adds livability to this level making outdoor gathering convenient. Two family bedrooms to the right of the staircase share a marvelous full bath. The third level is devoted to the master suite. Up the staircase is a cozy sitting loft area with an open railing to below and views out the large glass above the entry. The reading room is off the loft. Double doors lead to the master suite. The suite has a large sitting area. A fireplace is shared by the suite and the bath. The bath has a large tub, a glass enclosed shower, and dual sinks. The outdoor deck is perfect for sunning and the shower access makes it convenient. The photographed home may have been modified to suit individual tastes.

Photography Supplied by The Sater Design Collection, Inc.

Second Floor

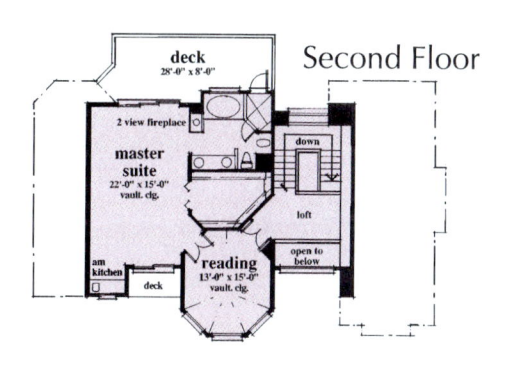

First Floor

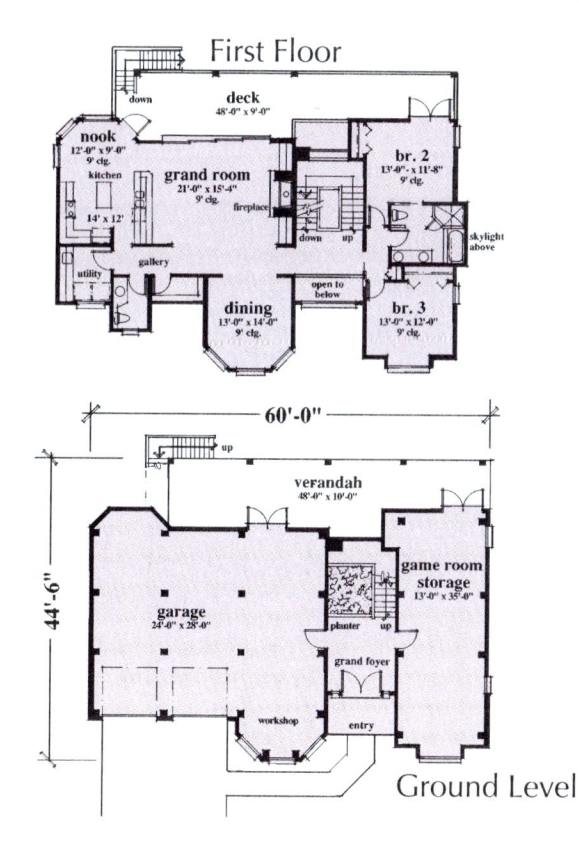

Ground Level

plan**info**

First floor	1,642 sq. ft.
Upper level	927 sq. ft.
Ground level	1,642 sq. ft.
Bedrooms	Three
Bathrooms	2(Full), 1(Half)
Foundation	Pier, Post
Total living area	**2,569 sq. ft.**

Price Code D

Traditional Elegance

Design 94228

HIGH WIND LOAD ENGINEERING AVAILABLE
SEE PAGE 246 FOR DETAILS

The turret stairway, detailed columns and arch top window, give this home a beautiful look from the street. Inside the home, the grand foyer opens up to the formal dining room and overlooks the outdoors. Arches and columns grace the staircase area off the foyer. The right wing of the ground floor features the kitchen, nook, leisure room and utility areas.

Photography Supplied by The Sater Design Collection, Inc.

The wonderful leisure room has a wet bar and built-in entertainment center, perfect for casual entertaining or family relaxing. The master's suite is on the opposite wing with windows and glass doors open to the outdoor rear views. The bath has a his'n'her walk-in closet, garden tub and a walk-in shower. Upstairs are the secondary bedrooms which each have private baths and open to a rear deck. The photographed home may have been modified to suit individual tastes.

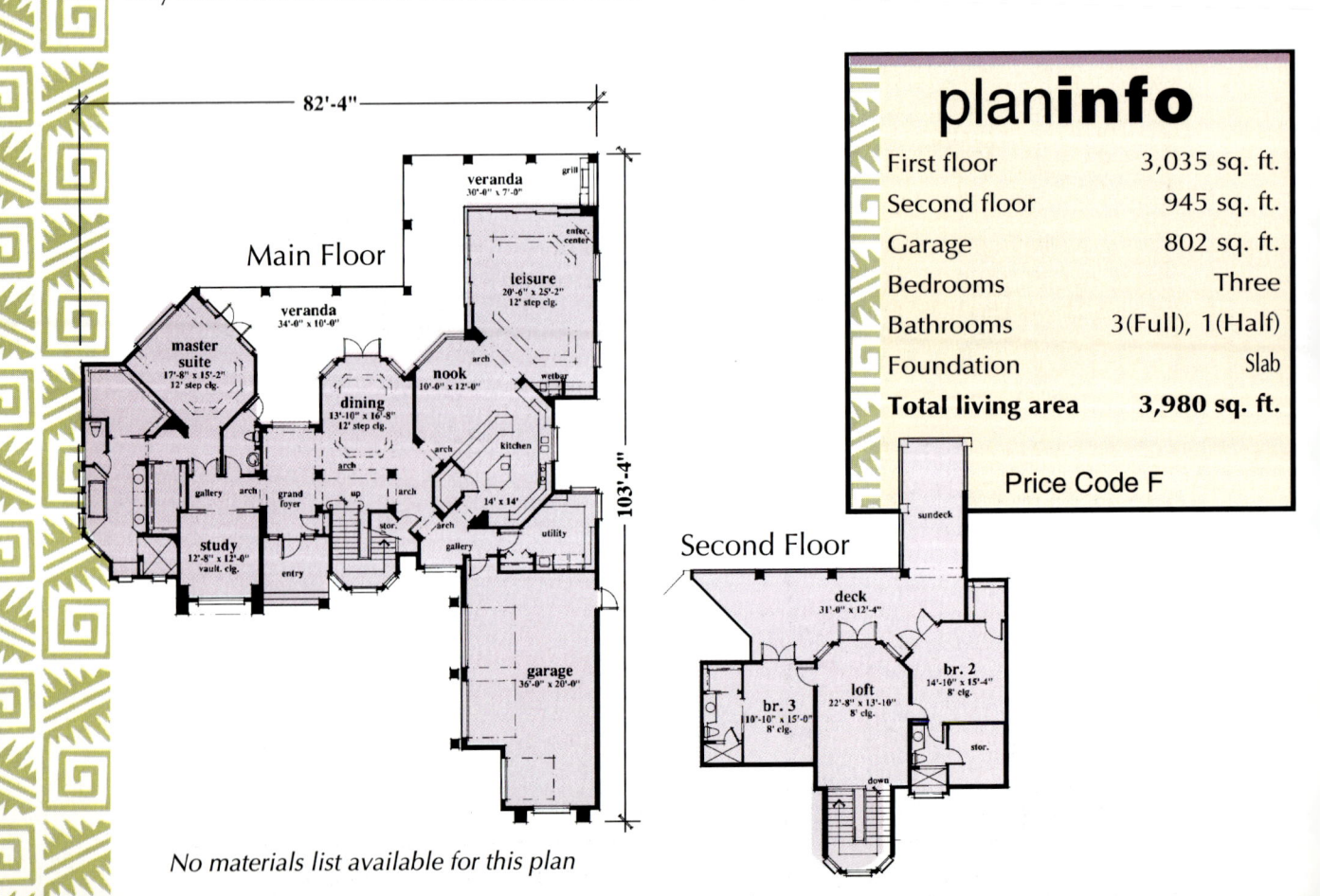

Main Floor

Second Floor

planinfo

First floor	3,035 sq. ft.
Second floor	945 sq. ft.
Garage	802 sq. ft.
Bedrooms	Three
Bathrooms	3(Full), 1(Half)
Foundation	Slab
Total living area	**3,980 sq. ft.**

Price Code F

No materials list available for this plan

HIGH WIND LOAD ENGINEERING AVAILABLE
SEE PAGE 246 FOR DETAILS

Widows Walk

Design 94203

This two-story coastal design is sure to please with its warm character and decorative widows walk. The covered entry, with dramatic transom window, leads to a spacious living room highlighted by a warming fireplace. To the right, the dining room and kitchen combine to provide a delightful place for mealtimes inside or out, with access to a side deck through double doors. A study, a bedroom and a full bath complete the first floor. The luxurious master suite is located on the second floor for privacy and features an oversized walk-in closet and a separate dressing area. The pampering master bath enjoys a whirlpool tub, a double vanity and a compartmented toilet. The photographed home may have been modified to suit individual tastes.

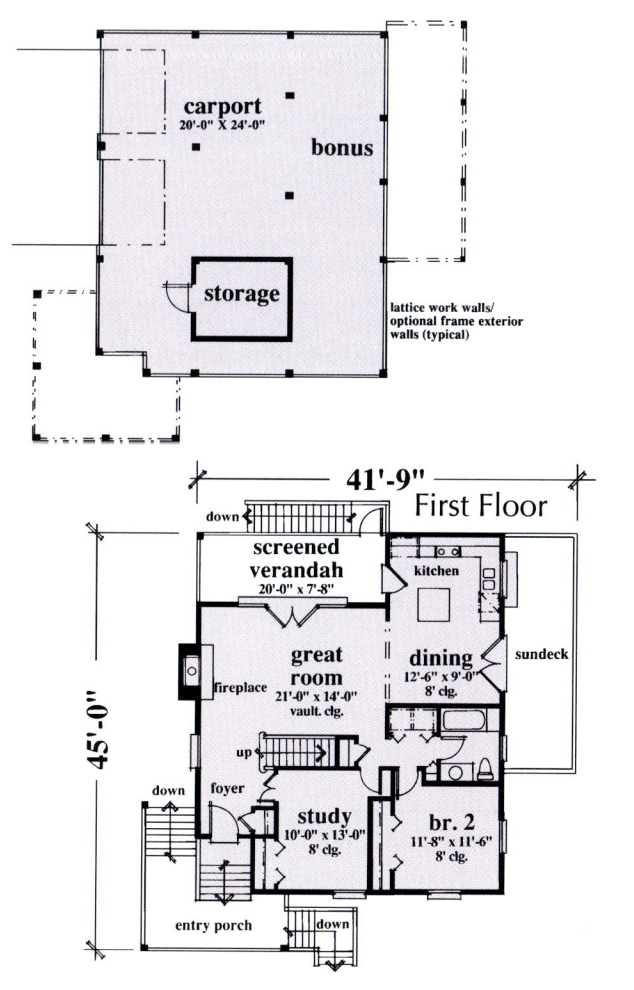

Photography Supplied by The Sater Design Collection, Inc.

carport 20'-0" X 24'-0"
bonus
storage
lattice work walls/ optional frame exterior walls (typical)

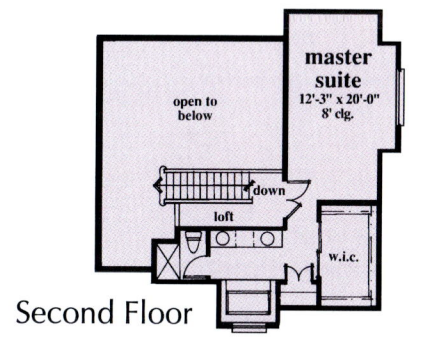

master suite 12'-3" x 20'-0" 8' clg.
open to below
loft
down
w.i.c.

Second Floor

41'-9"
First Floor
down
screened verandah 20'-0" x 7'-8"
kitchen
great room 21'-6" x 14'-0" vault. clg.
fireplace
dining 12'-6" x 9'-0" 8' clg.
sundeck
45'-0"
up
foyer
study 10'-0" x 13'-0" 8' clg.
br. 2 11'-8" x 11'-6" 8' clg.
down
entry porch
down

plan**info**

First floor	1,136 sq. ft.
Second floor	636 sq. ft.
Garage	526 sq. ft.
Bedrooms	Two
Bathrooms	Two
Foundation	Post, Pier, Piling
Total living area	**1,772 sq. ft.**

Price Code B

No materials list available

Coastal Delight

Design 94202

HIGH WIND LOAD ENGINEERING AVAILABLE
SEE PAGE 246 FOR DETAILS

Lattice door panels, shutters, and a metal roof add character to this delightful coastal home. Double doors flanking a fireplace open to the sun deck from the spacious Great room. An adjacent dining room provides views of the rear grounds. The glassed-in nook shares space with the L-shape kitchen. Two secondary bedrooms, a full bath and a utility room complete this floor. The second floor master suite includes double doors to a private deck, two walk-in closets and a grand master bath. The photographed home may have been modified to suit individual tastes.

Photography Supplied by The Sater Design Collection, Inc.

Second Floor
- master suite 17'-0" x 14'-0" vault. clg.
- open to dining room below
- his / hers
- open to living room below
- down / arch

- deck
- lattice work walls/ optional frame exterior walls (typical)
- storage
- carport 28'-0" x 26'-0"
- bonus 13'-0" x 33'-0"
- bonus
- up

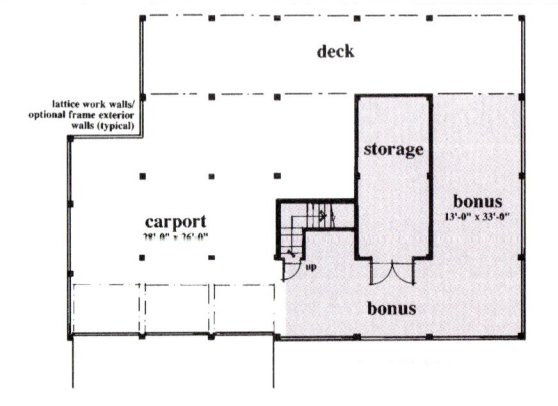

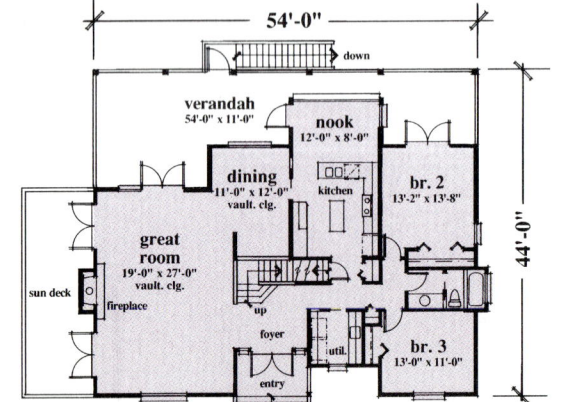

First Floor
- 54'-0" x 44'-0"
- verandah 54'-0" x 11'-0"
- nook 12'-0" x 8'-0"
- dining 11'-0" x 12'-0" vault. clg.
- kitchen
- br. 2 13'-2" x 13'-8"
- great room 19'-0" x 27'-0" vault. clg.
- sun deck / fireplace
- foyer / up / util.
- br. 3 13'-0" x 12'-0"
- entry / down

planinfo

First floor	1,736 sq. ft.
Second floor	640 sq. ft.
Lower floor	840 sq. ft.
Bonus room	253 sq. ft.
Bedrooms	Three
Bathrooms	Two
Foundation	Post, Pier, Piling
Total living area	**3,216 sq. ft.**

Price Code F

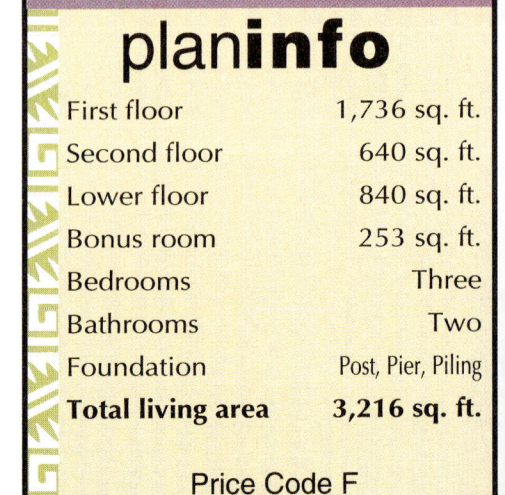

16

HIGH WIND LOAD ENGINEERING AVAILABLE
SEE PAGE 246 FOR DETAILS

Simply Irresistible

Design 94213

Striking exterior detailing and dramatic roof lines add to this home's charm. With three bedrooms and plenty of living area, you're sure to feel at home. Inside, an expansive living and dining area offer flexible living patterns with open rear views. Through sliding glass doors, the living room opens to a rear veranda. There, a grill enhances outdoor dining and gathering. The breakfast nook also accesses the veranda. Through the archway, the kitchen features a large pantry and opens to a family gathering area where a fireplace and built-ins are the focal points. Two secondary bedrooms are on the left side of the home. One bedroom is a full suite with its own private bath that is easily accessible to the outdoor areas. The master suite, bath and owner's study are located on the other side of the house. The study has a bayed window to the front yard. The study can be used for many things including a home office, a nursery and even a third guest suite with its closet space. The suite includes a bayed sitting area with French doors to the veranda. The full bath has his 'n'her vanity spaces, a raised garden soaking tub, and a glass enclosed shower. The ample walk-in wardrobe closet provides a great amount of space for the owners.

planinfo

Main floor	2,854 sq. ft.
Garage	528 sq. ft.
Bedrooms	Three
Bathrooms	3(Full), 1(Half)
Foundation	Slab
Total living area	**2,854 sq. ft.**

Price Code E

No materials list available

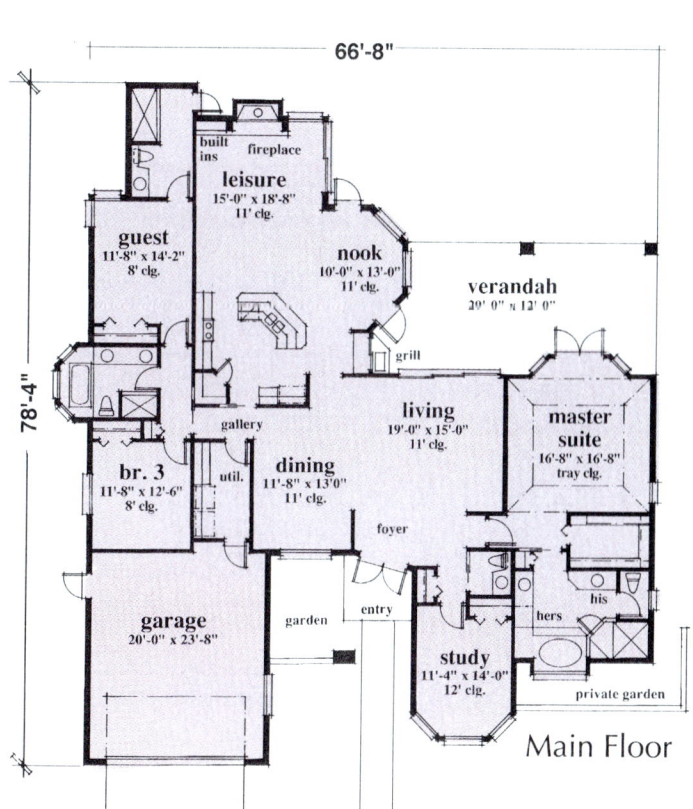

Main Floor

Cozy Traditional
Design 93000

This homey Traditional plan has all the amenities of a larger plan in a compact layout. The ten foot ceilings give this home an expansive feel. An angled eating bar separates the kitchen and the Great room while leaving these areas open to one another for family gatherings and entertaining. The master bedroom includes a huge walk-in closet and a superior master bath with a whirlpool tub and a separate shower. A large utility room and an oversize storage area are located near the secondary entrance to the home. Two additional bedrooms and a bath finish the plan.

No materials list available for this plan.

planinfo

First floor	1,862 sq. ft.
Garage	520 sq. ft.
Bedrooms	Three
Bathrooms	Two
Foundation	Slab
Total living area	**1,862 sq. ft.**

Price Code C

HIGH WIND LOAD ENGINEERING AVAILABLE
SEE PAGE 246 FOR DETAILS

Grand Entrance
Design 94221

The double door entry leads to the grand foyer. Columns and archways grace the view through to the formal living room. A two story ceiling, warming fireplace and three pairs of French doors add to the drama. Down the gallery hallway, the formal dining room faces the outdoor rear views. Toward the front, a guest powder room and full guest suite are easily accessible. An optional elevator adds to the custom touches found throughout. A large gourmet kitchen is well appointed and easily serves the nook and formal dining room. A pass through window serves the outdoor lanai. An impressive informal leisure room has a sixteen foot high tray ceiling, an entertainment center, and wet bar. An octagonal bayed area provides spanning views to the rear. To the right is the owners private wing. A beamed ceiling study has bookshelves and a fireplace. The master suite has a large sleeping area and a sitting room. Large walk-in wardrobe closets lead to the master bath. Upstairs are the guests suites, each with a private bath.

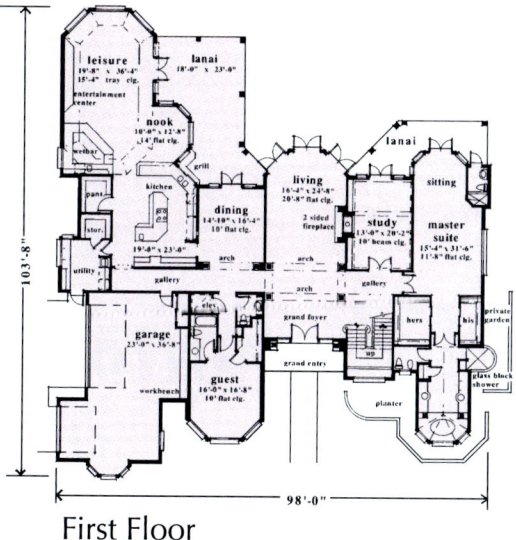

First Floor

Second Floor

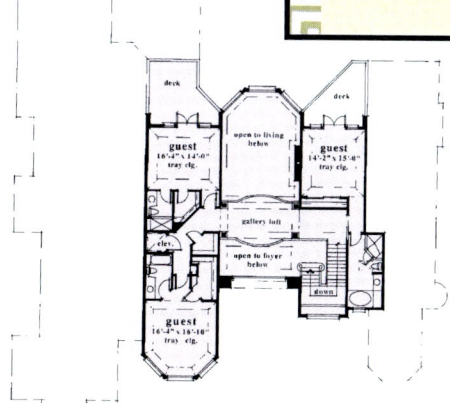

No materials list available for this plan

planinfo

First floor	4,760 sq. ft.
Second floor	1,552 sq. ft.
Garage	802 sq. ft.
Bedrooms	Five
Bathrooms	4(Full), 2(3/4)
Foundation	Slab
Total living area	**6,312 sq. ft.**

Price Code F

Luxury & Convenience

Design 94200

HIGH WIND LOAD ENGINEERING AVAILABLE
SEE PAGE 246 FOR DETAILS

This charming design offers a great deal of luxurious features, unexpected in this size home. The raised entry with double doors and high glass opens up to the foyer area. Large sliding glass doors in the formal provide natural light and outdoor views. The dining room is separated from the foyer and living area by a half wall and column. The large kitchen, nook and leisure room complete the informal gathering areas. Large sliding glass doors giving the leisure room a feeling of outdoor openness. The secondary bedrooms are split from the master wing. The master bath has a large walk-in closet, walk-in shower, private water closet room and a whirlpool tub. The master suite opens to the lanai through sliding glass doors. The large lanai features plenty of room perfect for outdoor entertaining. No materials list is available.

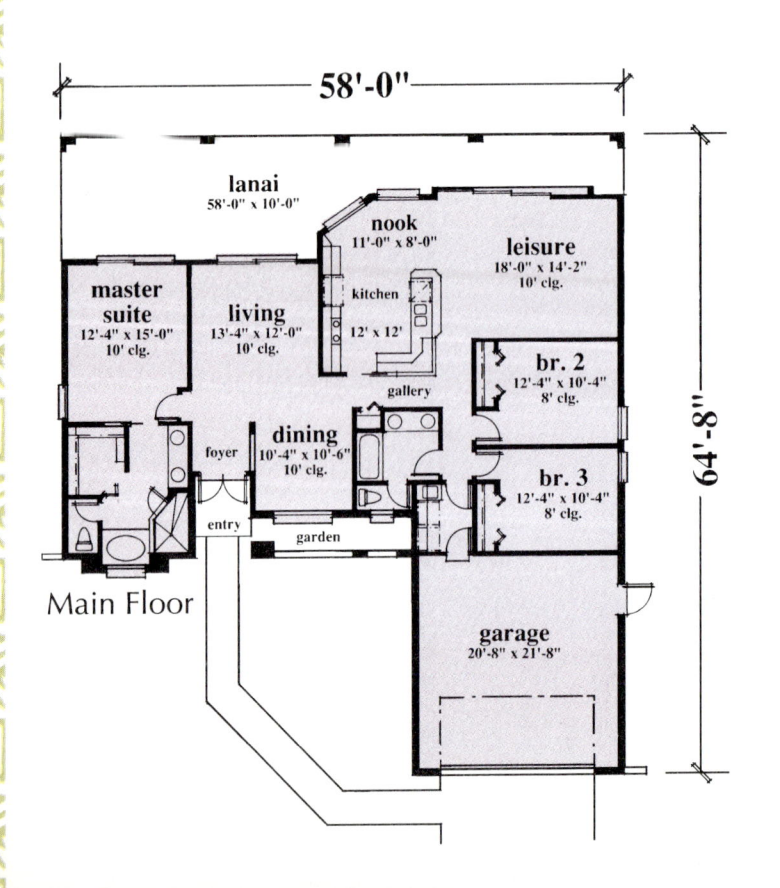

Main Floor

planinfo

Main floor	1,784 sq. ft.
Garage	491 sq. ft.
Bedrooms	Three
Bathrooms	Two
Foundation	Slab
Total living area	**1,784 sq. ft.**

Price Code B

HIGH WIND LOAD ENGINEERING AVAILABLE
SEE PAGE 246 FOR DETAILS

Traditional Stucco

Design 94239

This traditional elevation features stucco and stone for a warm, elegant feel. Round columns grace the double door covered entryway. The living room features a warming fireplace, a two-story ceiling and bayed glass doors to the rear yard. The gallery leads past the formal dining room to the family areas. The open kitchen easily serves the dining room and family nook. The relaxing leisure room has a fireplace, a television niche, a coffered ceiling and French doors leading to a covered veranda in the rear. The master wing is privately located apart from the family areas and upstairs bedrooms. The bath has a walk-in shower, a large tub, and his and her vanities. Upstairs, three bedrooms provide privacy from the ground floor. One bedroom is a full suite with a private bath and deck. A gallery catwalk overlooks the two-story living room and foyer.

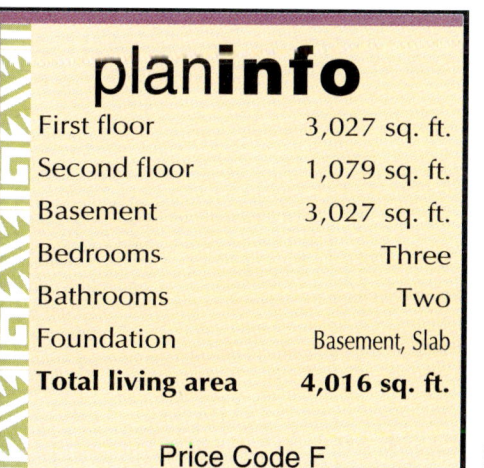

planinfo

First floor	3,027 sq. ft.
Second floor	1,079 sq. ft.
Basement	3,027 sq. ft.
Bedrooms	Three
Bathrooms	Two
Foundation	Basement, Slab
Total living area	**4,016 sq. ft.**

Price Code F

No materials list available for this plan

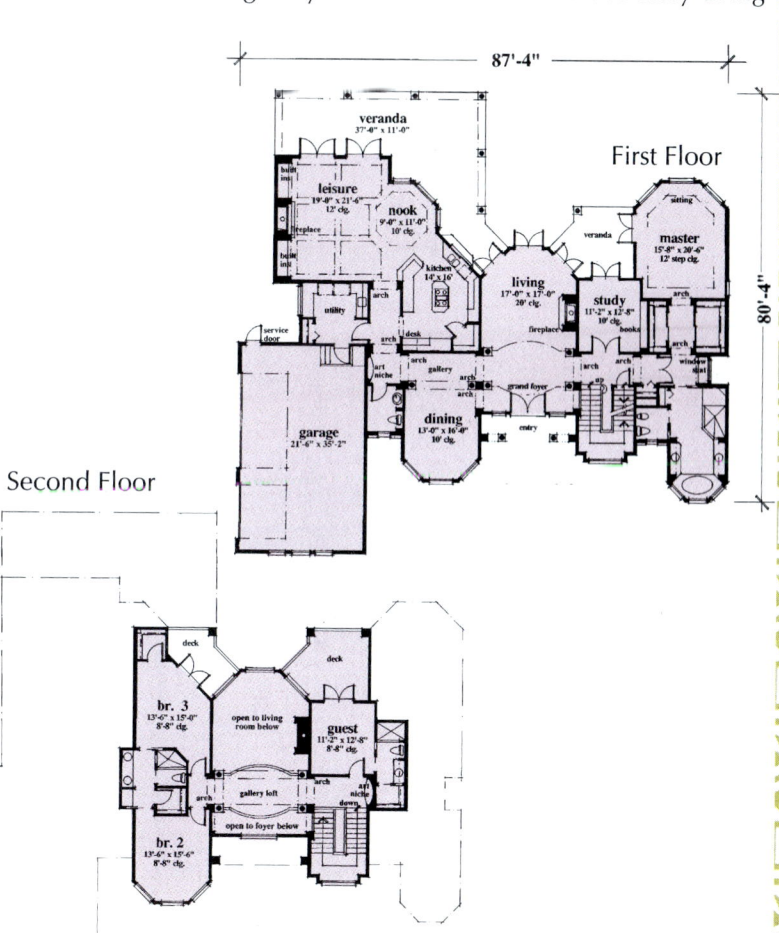

First Floor

Second Floor

Modern Livability

Design 94201

HIGH WIND LOAD ENGINEERING AVAILABLE
SEE PAGE 246 FOR DETAILS

A compact one-story home with a wealth of modern livability. A Great room topped by a vaulted ceiling opens to the lanai, offering wonderful options for either formal or informal entertaining. Look out onto the lanai and savor the outdoors from the delightful kitchen with its bay-windowed breakfast nook. The nook and the formal dining room include vaulted ceilings. Two secondary bedrooms, each with a walk-in closet, share a full bath. A pampering bath featuring a corner tub, a separate shower and a large walk-in closet are featured in the master suite.

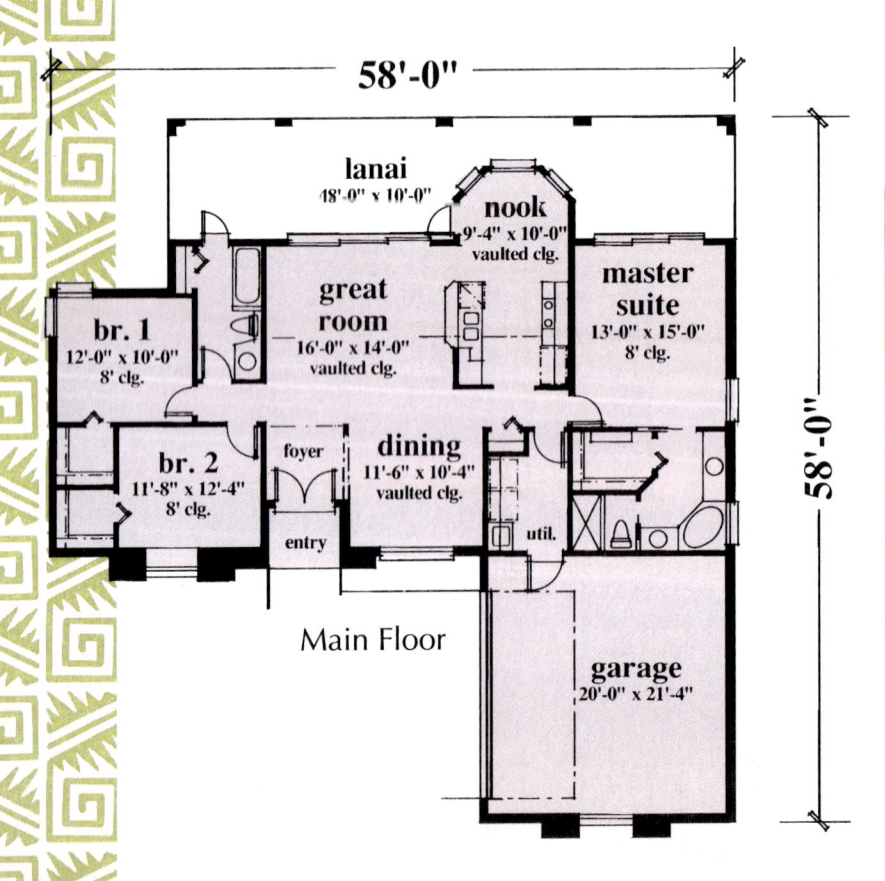

22

Main Floor

planinfo

Main floor	1,487 sq. ft.
Garage	427 sq. ft.
Bedrooms	Three
Bathrooms	Two
Foundation	Slab
Total living area	**1,487 sq. ft.**

Price Code A

Wrap-Around Porch
Design 93025

A roomy wrap-around porch accents this farmhouse-style elevation. Inside, ten foot ceilings in the Great room, kitchen, and dining room give this home a spacious look. The efficiently designed kitchen includes a large pantry and plenty of cabinet and counter space. The dining room is nearby, and perfect for either family gatherings or formal entertaining. The master bedroom is located at the back of the home and features a functional master bath with double vanities. Bedrooms two and three and a second full bath complete this compact plan.

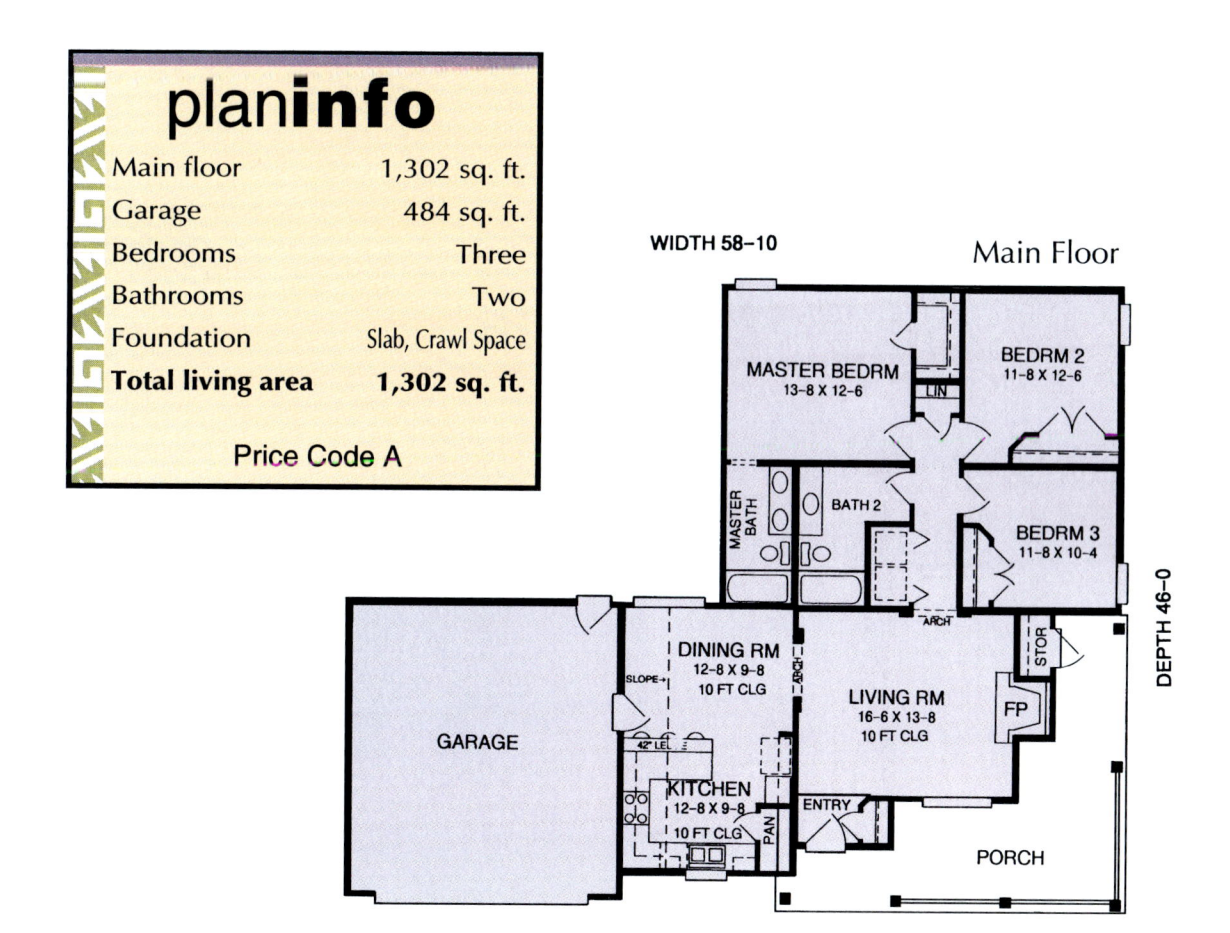

plan info

Main floor	1,302 sq. ft.
Garage	484 sq. ft.
Bedrooms	Three
Bathrooms	Two
Foundation	Slab, Crawl Space
Total living area	**1,302 sq. ft.**

Price Code A

WIDTH 58-10
DEPTH 46-0

Main Floor

MASTER BEDRM 13-8 X 12-6
BEDRM 2 11-8 X 12-6
MASTER BATH
BATH 2
BEDRM 3 11-8 X 10-4
GARAGE
DINING RM 12-8 X 9-8 10 FT CLG
LIVING RM 16-6 X 13-8 10 FT CLG
KITCHEN 12-8 X 9-8 10 FT CLG
ENTRY
PORCH

Impressive Foyer

Design 94622

HIGH WIND LOAD ENGINEERING AVAILABLE
SEE PAGE 246 FOR DETAILS

Creating a terrific first impression, the foyer of this home is open to the second floor. The formal areas are located to either side of the foyer. Casual, informal living is comforatably accommodated for in the large Great room. A fireplace enhances this spacious room. The kitchen will please the gourmet of the family. A cook top island, ample storage and work space have been provided. The breakfast room adjoins the kitchen. The expansive master suite includes a private sitting room and a master bath. Three additional bedrooms, each with private access to a full bath and a walk-in closet are on the second floor. This plan is available with a slab or crawl space foundation. Please specify when ordering.

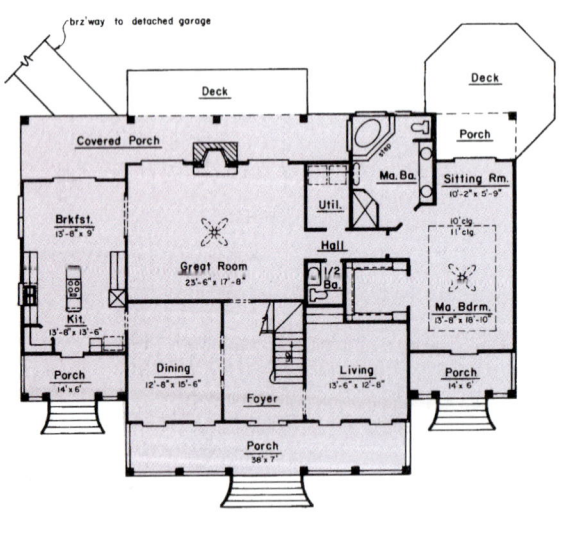

Width—66'-0"
Depth—56'-0"

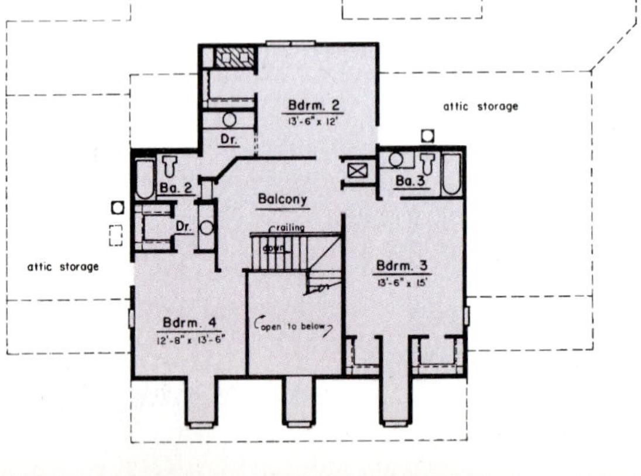

planinfo

First floor	2,033 sq. ft.
Second floor	1,116 sq. ft.
Bedrooms	Four
Bathrooms	3(Full), 1(Half)
Foundation	Slab or Crawl Space
Total living area	**3,149 sq. ft.**

Price Code E

No materials list available

HIGH WIND LOAD ENGINEERING AVAILABLE
SEE PAGE 246 FOR DETAILS

Elegant Country Home

Design 94211

A mixture of exterior elements, including brick, siding, and stucco, blended with a covered entry porch. An abundance of windows to the front of the plan allows bright, warming sunlight to flood the rooms. All rooms to the rear offer access to a full length veranda and a screened porch. An airy, open feeling is created by the combination of the formal dining room, the spacious Great room and the well-appointed kitchen. The kitchen is complete with a walk-in pantry and bayed breakfast nook. The nook has access to the veranda and views the rear yard. Split sleeping quarters contain the master wing to the left and two secondary bedrooms to the right. The secondary bedrooms have an ample bath that has outdoor access. The secluded master suite is highlighted by a double walk-in closet, a relaxing garden tub with a privacy wall, a separate shower and a double-bowl vanity.

planinfo

Main floor	2,200 sq. ft.
Garage	830 sq. ft.
Bedrooms	Three
Bathrooms	2(Full), 1(Half)
Foundation	Slab
Total living area	**2,200 sq. ft.**

Price Code C

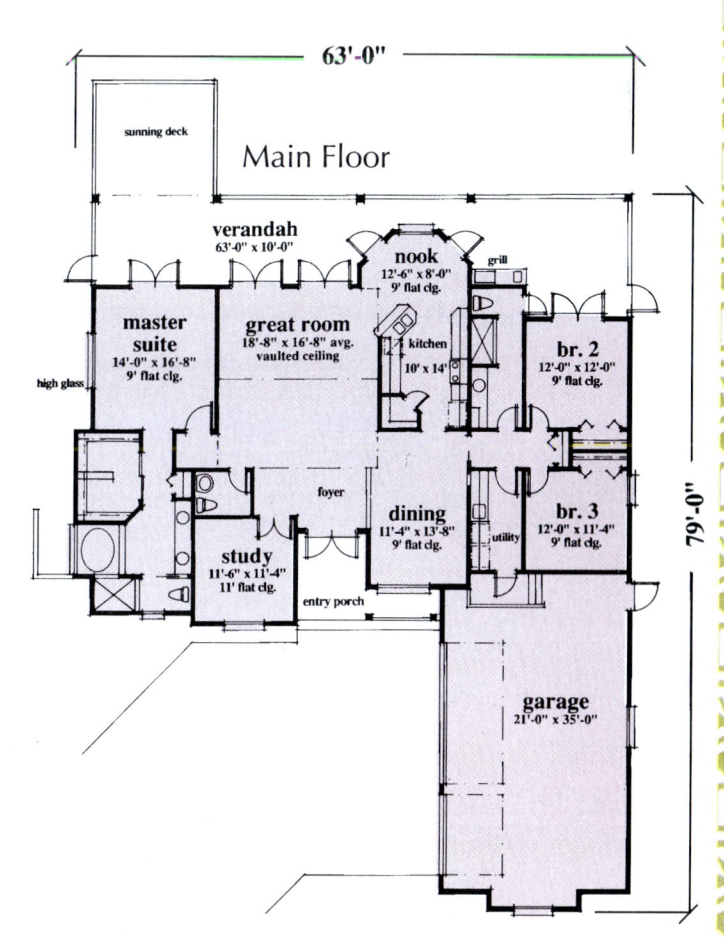

Main Floor

- sunning deck
- verandah 63'-0" x 10'-0"
- nook 12'-6" x 8'-0" 9' flat clg.
- grill
- master suite 14'-0" x 16'-8" 9' flat clg.
- great room 18'-8" x 16'-8" avg. vaulted ceiling
- kitchen 10' x 14'
- br. 2 12'-0" x 12'-0" 9' flat clg.
- high glass
- foyer
- dining 11'-4" x 13'-8" 9' flat clg.
- utility
- br. 3 12'-0" x 11'-4" 9' flat clg.
- study 11'-6" x 11'-4" 11' flat clg.
- entry porch
- garage 21'-0" x 35'-0"

63'-0" × 79'-0"

Elegant Entry

Design 93031

This traditional southern elevation features an entry flanked by large square columns and dominated by a gable finished with dentil molding and a graceful archway. Upon entering, an angled foyer opens the home to a large Great room with a fireplace. A formal dining room is defined with a series of columns that give the home an elegant, gracious feel. The master suite is entered through double doors and is privately located away from the other bedrooms. The master bath features all the luxuries with an angled whirlpool tub, separate shower and double vanities. An enormous walk-in closet completes the arrangement. The kitchen features a pantry and plenty of cabinet and counter space. A coffered ceiling treatment adds character to the breakfast room located on the rear of the home. Bedrooms two and three are arranged nearby with convenient access to the second bath. No materials list is available for this plan.

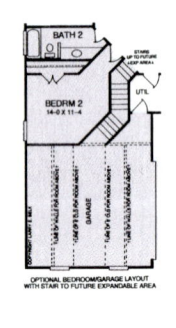

26

Main Floor

planinfo

Main floor	1,955 sq. ft.
Bedrooms	Three
Bathrooms	Two
Foundation	Slab, Crawl Space
Total living area	**1,955 sq. ft.**

Price Code C

Glass surrounds the entry doors of this appealing home. To the left of the foyer, the formal dining room faces the front garden area. An arched doorway leads from the formal living areas and dining room to the sleeping areas and the informal living spaces. Ideally suited for family entertaining, the gourmet kitchen shares space with a sunny breakfast nook and spacious leisure room. The leisure room offers an optional fireplace and entertainment center area with glass above facing the rear views. On this side of the plan, two bedrooms share a full bath. On the opposite side is the owner's area. The master suite has two closets, a walk-in and wardrobe closet. The bath has a private garden tub, a walk-in shower and garden access door. There is also a half bath off the master veranda that is an outdoor bath, but can option as another indoor bathroom.

No materials list available

Main Floor

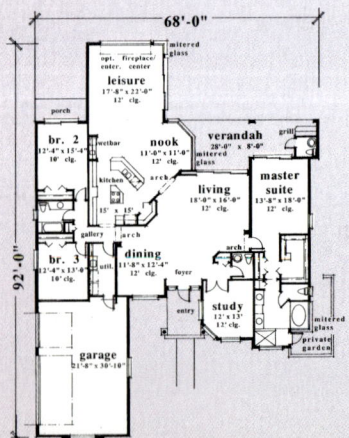

planinfo

First floor	2,894 sq. ft.
Garage	734 sq. ft.
Bedrooms	Three
Bathrooms	2(Full), 1(Half)
Foundation	Slab
Total living area	**2,894 sq. ft.**

Price Code E

Design 94225 — Casual Elegance

HIGH WIND LOAD ENGINEERING AVAILABLE — SEE PAGE 246 FOR DETAILS

This plan comes with two elevation styles, a contemporary stucco exterior and a more traditional style that features brick accents. This two-story home features a grand, open foyer, dining and formal living area that opens up off the entry way. Highlights of the formal living area are the corner fireplace and the graceful curved staircase. The informal family area includes a large leisure room with corner glass for expanded views, a covered deck and an optional entertainment center. The eat-in kitchen and nook comes complete with a message center desk and a large walk-in pantry. The owner's wing comprises an entire ground floor side. Upstairs, two full bedrooms share a bath and feature walk-in closets and large windows. The loft has an optional wet bar, lots of glass for extended rear yard views and an observation deck.

planinfo

First floor	2,551 sq. ft.
Second floor	1,037 sq. ft.
Garage	1,010 sq. ft.
Bedrooms	Three
Bathrooms	2(Full), 1(3/4)
Foundation	Slab
Total living area	**3,588 sq. ft.**
Price Code F	

No materials list available

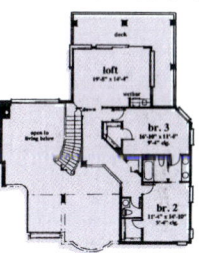

First Floor

Second Floor

Design 94210 — Custom Look

HIGH WIND LOAD ENGINEERING AVAILABLE — SEE PAGE 246 FOR DETAILS

Traditional Charm Design 94226

The soft stucco and brick exterior and the nice roof lines create a visually elegant exterior that would be perfect in any setting. The open foyer leads to the formal parlor and dining room spaces to the left. The owners' study is to the right and it can double as a music room or home theater room. The large, well appointed kitchen workspace opens up to the informal eating nook. It is easily accessible to the dining room and leisure areas. The leisure room is the center feature on the first floor. A built-in entertainment center wall and fireplace create a relaxing area. Three pairs of French doors open up to the veranda. The master suite has a sitting bay with French door access to the rear grounds. Upstairs, there are three suites of luxury living space for guest or children. Each has large walk-in closets and two feature connecting baths.

First Floor

Second Floor

No materials list available

planinfo

First floor	2,638 sq. ft.
Second floor	1,032 sq. ft.
Garage	708 sq. ft.
Bedrooms	Four
Bathrooms	3(Full), 2(Half)
Foundation	Slab
Total living area	**3,670 sq. ft.**
Price Code F	

The southern styled romantic front porch on this home is reminiscent of plantation houses of the past. Arched topped windows with shutters and two dormer windows add to the charm of this elevation. Entertaining in this home is both elegant and convenient. The dining room adjoins the kitchen and the expansive family room. A fireplace in the family room provides a warm atmosphere. Informal meals are provided for in the breakfast area or at the eating bar in the kitchen. A covered rear porch and patio extend living space to the outdoors. Luxuriant pampering and privacy are the theme in the master suite. A secondary bedroom on the first floor includes a walk-in closet and private access to a full bath. There are two additional bedrooms on the second floor, each with a walk-in closet, sharing use of a full bath in the hall. This plan is available with a slab or crawl space foundation. Please specify when ordering.

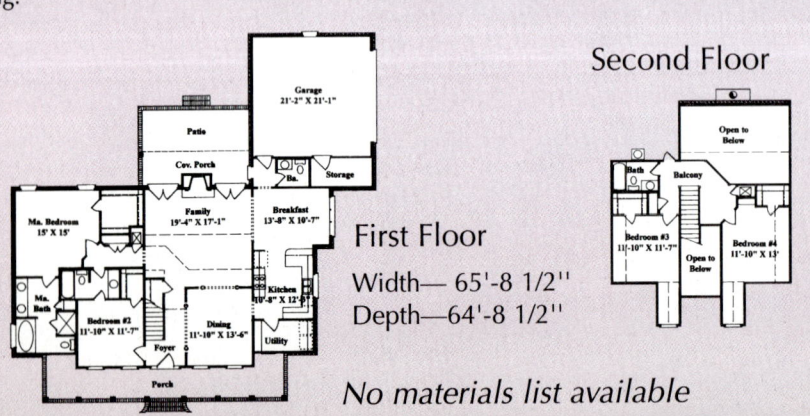

First Floor

Width— 65'-8 1/2"
Depth— 64'-8 1/2"

Second Floor

No materials list available

planinfo

First floor	1,796 sq. ft.
Second floor	610 sq. ft.
Garage	570 sq. ft.
Bedrooms	Four
Bathrooms	3(Full), 1(Half)
Foundation	Crawl, Slab
Total living area	**2,406 sq. ft.**
Price Code D	

Design 94610 — Convenient Living

Attention to detail dresses this home in style. Once inside, the style turns into elegance. An expansive living room flows from the foyer. A corner fireplace serves as a cozy focal point to the room. Formal dining takes place in the dining room, accented by columns at the entrance. The efficient kitchen includes an island, an abundance of counter and storage space, and a breakfast area. The master suite is privately located on one end of the home, while the three additional bedrooms are at the opposite end. The perfect retreat, master suite includes two walk-in closets and a lavish bath. The secondary bedrooms share the full bath in the hall and include ample storage space. A covered porch, accessed from the breakfast area, extends living space outdoors in the warmer weather. This plan is available with either a slab or crawlspace foundation. Please specify when ordering.

Width— 61'-10''
Depth— 65'-5''

Main Floor

plan**info**

First floor	2,246 sq. ft.
Garage	546 sq. ft.
Bedrooms	Four
Bathrooms	2(Full), 1(Half)
Foundation	Slab or Crawl Space
Total living area	**2,246 sq. ft.**
Price Code D	

No materials list available

Design 94611 — Southern Touch

Tasteful Exterior
Design 94809

A striking two-story foyer and Great room are overlooked by a balcony from the second floor. The luxurious first floor master suite is highlighted by a designer garden bath and his-n-her walk-in closets, providing a retreat from the hustle of the day. There is an abundance of family bedrooms and baths, with one other bedroom also being on the first floor. The unique angular kitchen counter design makes the kitchen perfect for entertaining. Bright windows abound bringing the outdoors in. The combination of exterior treatments provide a look of elegance and cheer. This plan is available with a basement or crawl space foundation. Please specify when ordering.

Width — 64'-0"
Depth — 52'-2"

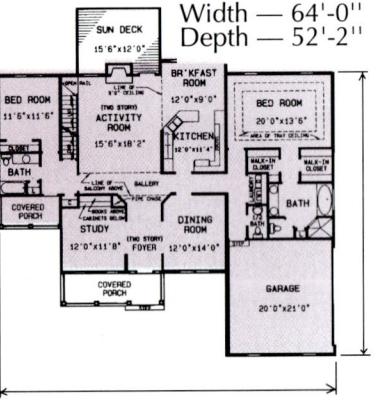

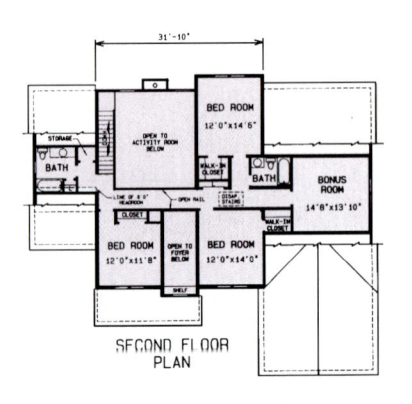

planinfo

First floor	2,090 sq. ft.
Second floor	943 sq. ft.
Basement	2,090 sq. ft.
Garage	439 sq. ft.
Bedrooms	Five
Bathrooms	4(Full), 1(Half)
Foundation	Basement, Crawl Space
Total living area	**3,033 sq. ft.**

Price Code E

Inside the foyer area, double arches lead into the formal living room and out to the rear through triple french doors. A two-sided fireplace is shared with the owners study. The expansive kitchen easily serves the dining room and informal nook area. The kitchen has plenty of work space, a walk-in pantry area, a cooktop island, an eating bar, and a pass-through that serves the veranda. The expansive kitchen easily serves the dining room and informal nook area. Double doors lead into the owners suite. Large his'n'her wardrobe closets framed with arches lead into the sleeping area. The bayed suite has doors to the veranda, a high stepped ceiling and a sitting area. The elegant bath is well appointed. Up the grand staircase are three secondary suites.

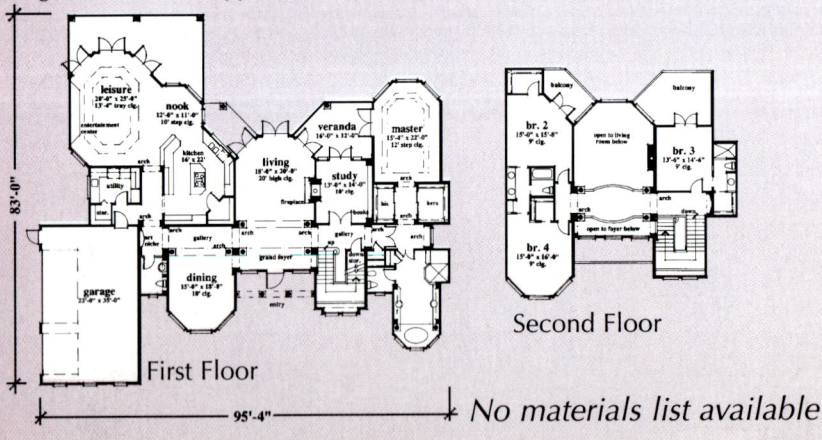

No materials list available

planinfo

First floor	3,546 sq. ft.
Second floor	1,213 sq. ft.
Garage	822 sq. ft.
Bedrooms	Four
Bathrooms	2(Full), 1(3/4)
Foundation	Basement, Slab
Total living area	**4,759 sq. ft.**

Price Code F

Design 94613

Modern Country

A columned porch shelters the entrance of this home. From the foyer direct access is gained to the dining room, master bedroom, or the living room. The spacious kitchen is made efficient by a work island and an abundance of work and storage space. A bayed breakfast area provides an informal eating area. A fireplace enhances the expansive living room, which is overlooked by the second floor balcony. Three additional bedrooms are located on the second floor. Each second floor bedroom includes a walk-in closet and easy access to a full bath. There is an unfinished area over the garage that may become a game room in the future.

No materials list available

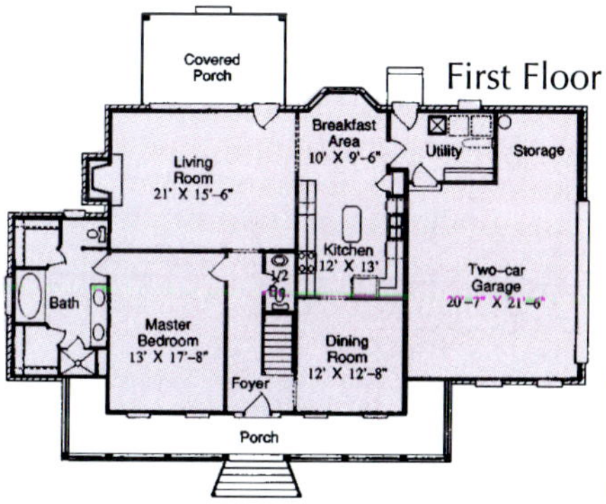

planinfo

Main floor	1,492 sq. ft.
Second floor	865 sq. ft.
Garage	574 sq. ft.
Bedrooms	Four
Bathrooms	2(Full), 1(3/4)
Foundation	Slab
Total living area	**2,357 sq. ft.**
Price Code D	

Width — 66'-10''
Depth — 49'-7''

First Floor
Second Floor

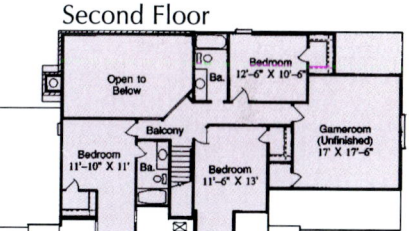

Design 94230

Grand Traditional

HIGH WIND LOAD ENGINEERING AVAILABLE
SEE PAGE 246 FOR DETAILS

Elegant Beauty

Design 94231

HIGH WIND LOAD ENGINEERING AVAILABLE
SEE PAGE 246 FOR DETAILS

An elegant blend of exterior materials make this home a visual beauty from the street. A raised study, barrel vault entryway and a two-story turret make this home look and feel larger. The foyer opens up to the grand room. Triple French doors lead to the veranda. The gourmet kitchen easily serves the nook and formal dining room. The nook has windows to the rear yard views and access to the covered veranda. A study can easily be a home office, a reading room, an exercise area or any useful bonus space one could need. The master suite has a step ceiling and a sitting space and dual his and her wardrobe closets. A step-up tub, a walk-in glass shower and a make-up space highlight the pampering bath. Upstairs, two bay window bedrooms have ample closet space and share a double vanity bath. No materials list is available.

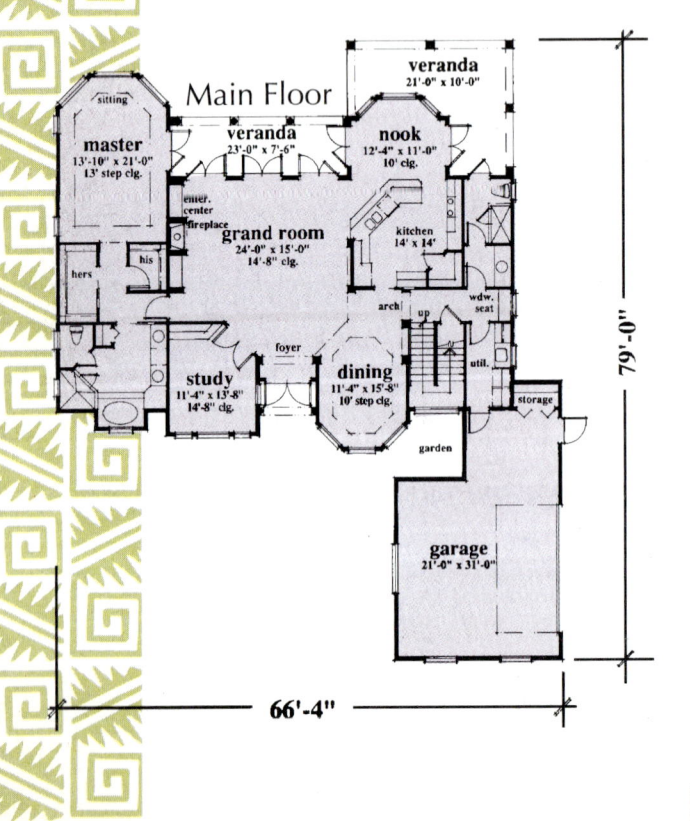

planinfo

First floor	2,181 sq. ft.
Second floor	710 sq. ft.
Garage	658 sq. ft.
Bedrooms	3(Full), 1(3/4)
Bathrooms	Three
Foundation	Basement, Slab
Total living area	**2,891 sq. ft.**

Price Code E

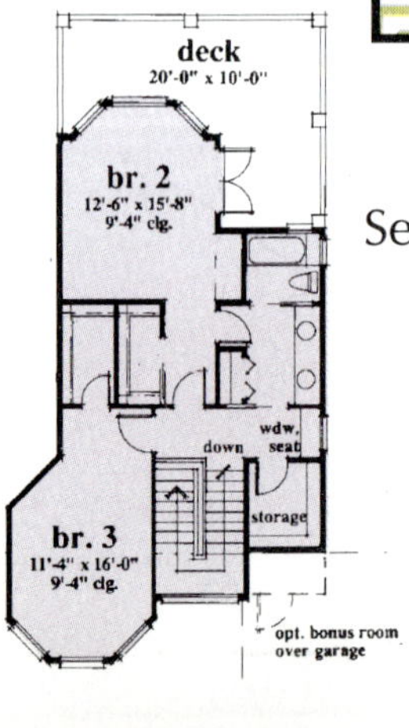

Main Floor

Second Floor

DESIGN NO. 10108

PRICE CODE D

Double doors give a Spanish welcome

No. 10108

- This plan features:
- — Three bedrooms
- — Two full and one half baths
- Massive double doors opening to the foyer
- A 27-foot Living Room to the right of the foyer
- A large Master Bedroom with a walk-in closet and a private full bath

FIRST FLOOR — 1,176 SQ. FT.
SECOND FLOOR — 1,176 SQ. FT.
BASEMENT — 1,176 SQ. FT.
GARAGE — 576 SQ. FT.

TOTAL LIVING AREA: 2,352 SQ. FT.

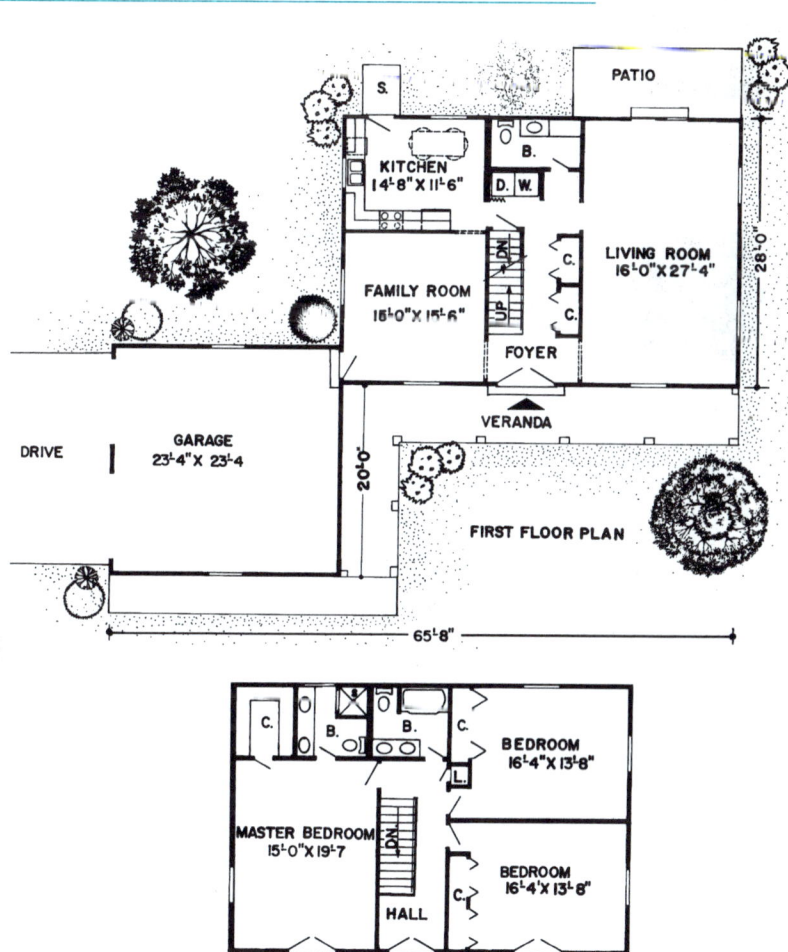

DESIGN NO. 93026

PRICE CODE A

A LOVELY SMALL HOME

No. 93026

- This plan features:
— Three bedrooms
— Two full baths
- A large Living Room with a ten foot ceiling
- A Dining Room with a distinctive bay window
- A Breakfast Room located off the Kitchen
- A Kitchen with an angled eating bar to open that opens the room to the Living Room
- A Master Suite with ten foot ceiling and his-n-her vanities, a combination whirlpool tub and shower, plus a huge walk-in closet
- Two additional bedrooms that share a full bath

Main area — 1,402 sq. ft.
Garage — 437 sq. ft.

Total living area: 1,402 sq. ft.

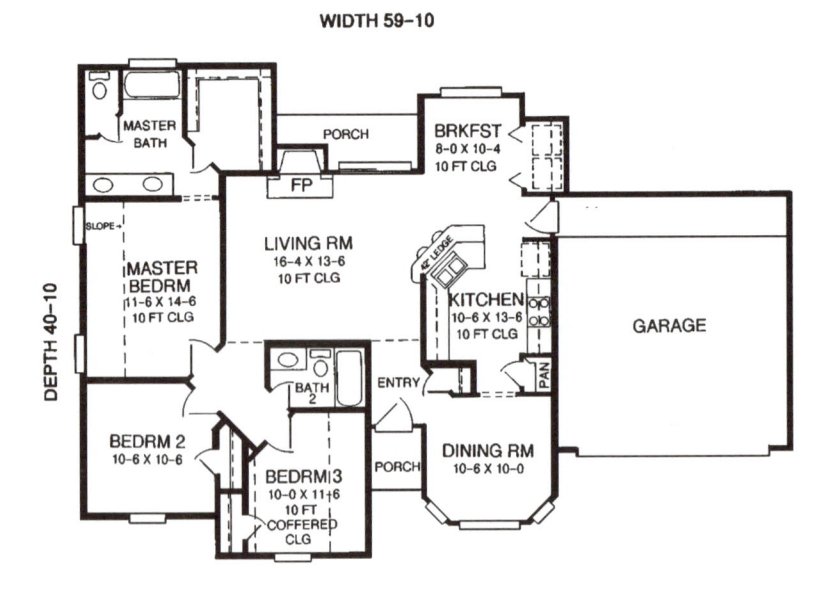

MAIN AREA

No materials list available

DESIGN NO. 92415

PRICE CODE D

Two-Story Family Room

TOTAL LIVING AREA: 2,270 SQ. FT.

No materials list available

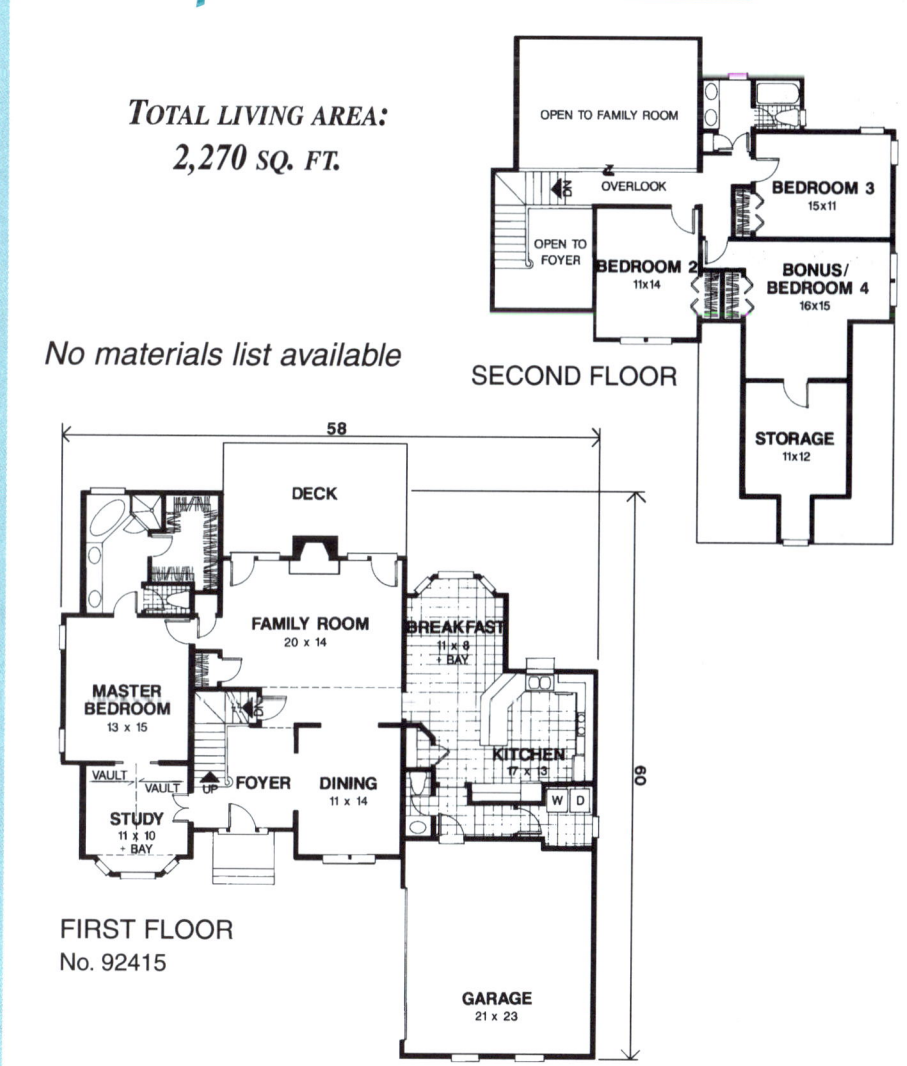

No. 92415

This plan features:

- Four bedrooms
- Two full and one half baths
- The formal Foyer is decorated by a graceful staircase
- A secluded Study is topped by a vaulted ceiling and accented by a bay window
- Pocket doors provide the entrance to the Study from the Master Suite
- A two-story Family room is enhanced by a fireplace and has direct access to the rear deck
- The breakfast bay flows into the Kitchen
- A peninsula counter and double sink are two highlights of the Kitchen
- Three additional bedrooms on the second floor share the use of a full bath
- An optional basement foundation is available, please specify when ordering

FIRST FLOOR — 1,728 SQ. FT.
SECOND FLOOR — 542 SQ. FT.
BONUS — 255 SQ. FT.

SECOND FLOOR

- OPEN TO FAMILY ROOM
- OVERLOOK
- OPEN TO FOYER
- BEDROOM 2 — 11x14
- BEDROOM 3 — 15x11
- BONUS/BEDROOM 4 — 16x15
- STORAGE — 11x12

FIRST FLOOR
No. 92415

- DECK
- FAMILY ROOM — 20 x 14
- BREAKFAST — 11 x 8 + BAY
- MASTER BEDROOM — 13 x 15
- KITCHEN — 17 x 13
- FOYER
- DINING — 11 x 14
- STUDY — 11 x 10 + BAY
- GARAGE — 21 x 23

Dimensions: 58 x 60

DESIGN NO. 9828

PRICE CODE E

SUPERIOR COMFORT AND PRIVACY

No. 9828
- This plan features:
— Four bedrooms
— Three full baths
- A natural stone exterior, Foyer with slate floors, leads into Living room and Dining Room
- A two-way fireplace between the Living Room and Family Room
- Open Family Room with Terrace access and Pool
- A Breakfast Nook with a large bow window facing the terrace and pool
- Four bedrooms grouped in one wing for privacy

MAIN AREA — 2,679 SQ. FT.
BASEMENT — 2,679 SQ. FT.
GARAGE — 541 SQ. FT.

TOTAL LIVING AREA: 2,679 SQ. FT.

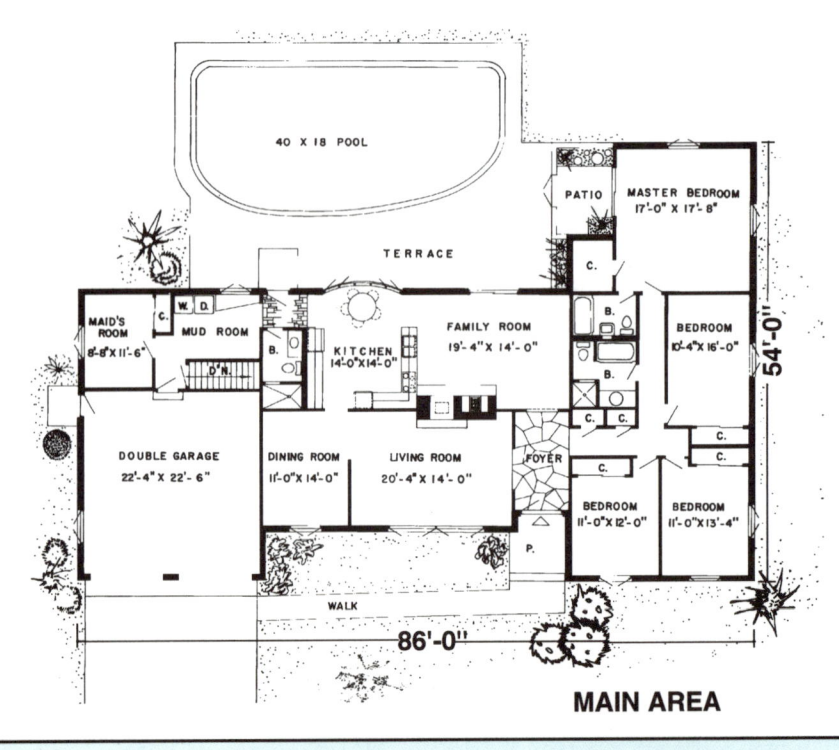

MAIN AREA

DESIGN NO. 92238

PRICE CODE B

PRIVATE MASTER SUITE

No. 92238

- This plan features:
— Three bedrooms
— Two full baths
- Segmented arches, sidelight and transom windows accent the front entrance
- Efficient Kitchen features a cooktop island, Utility area and walk-in Pantry
- A secluded Master Bedroom suite highlighted by an atrium door, a large walk-in closet and a double vanity bath

MAIN FLOOR — 1,664 SQ. FT.
BASEMENT — 1,600 SQ. FT.
GARAGE — 440 SQ. FT.

TOTAL LIVING AREA:
1,664 SQ. FT

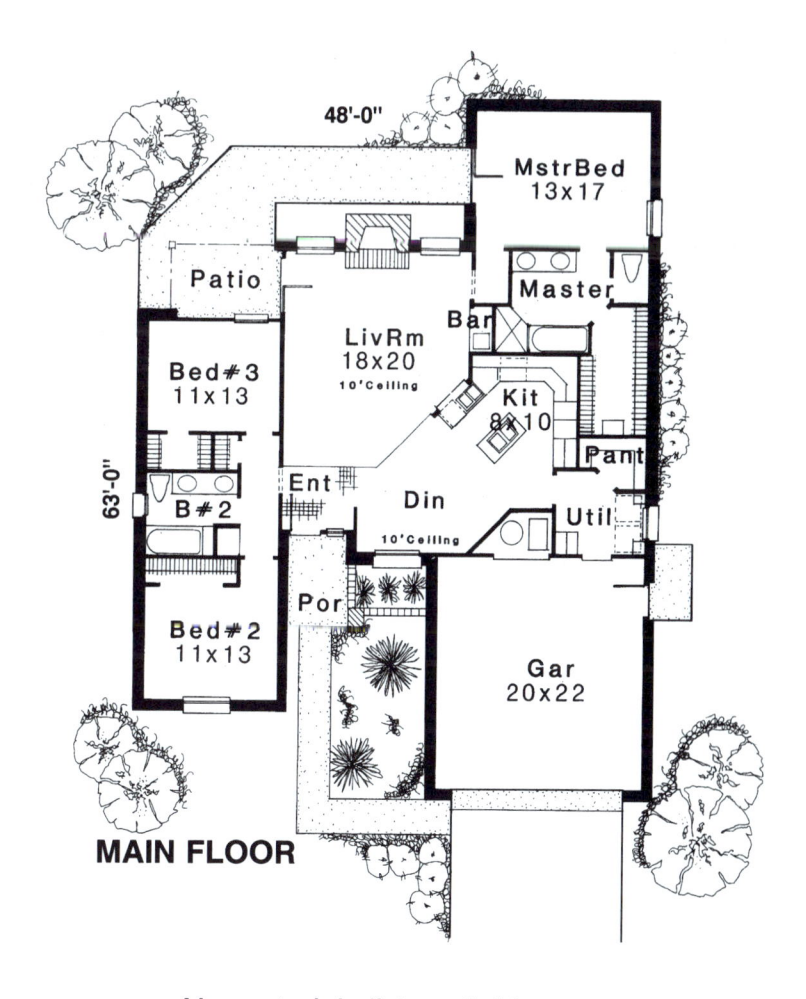

MAIN FLOOR

No materials list available

DESIGN NO. 92219

PRICE CODE F

GRAND COLUMNED ENTRANCE

No. 92219

- This plan features:
— Four bedrooms
— Two full, one three quarter and one half baths
- Covered Porch with grand columns enhances entrance
- Entry hall with a graceful landing staircase, flanked by formal Living and Dining rooms
- Fireplaces highlight both the Living Room/Parlor and formal Dining Room
- An efficient Kitchen with an island cooktop, built-in pantry and open Breakfast area
- Cathedral ceiling crowns expansive Family Room, accented by a fireplace and a built-in entertainment center
- An over-sized Garage with Workshop and rear entry to Kitchen and Utility area

MAIN FLOOR — 2,432 SQ. FT.
UPPER FLOOR — 903 SQ. FT.
BASEMENT — 2,432 SQ. FT.
GARAGE — 742 SQ. FT.

TOTAL LIVING AREA: 3,335 SQ. FT.

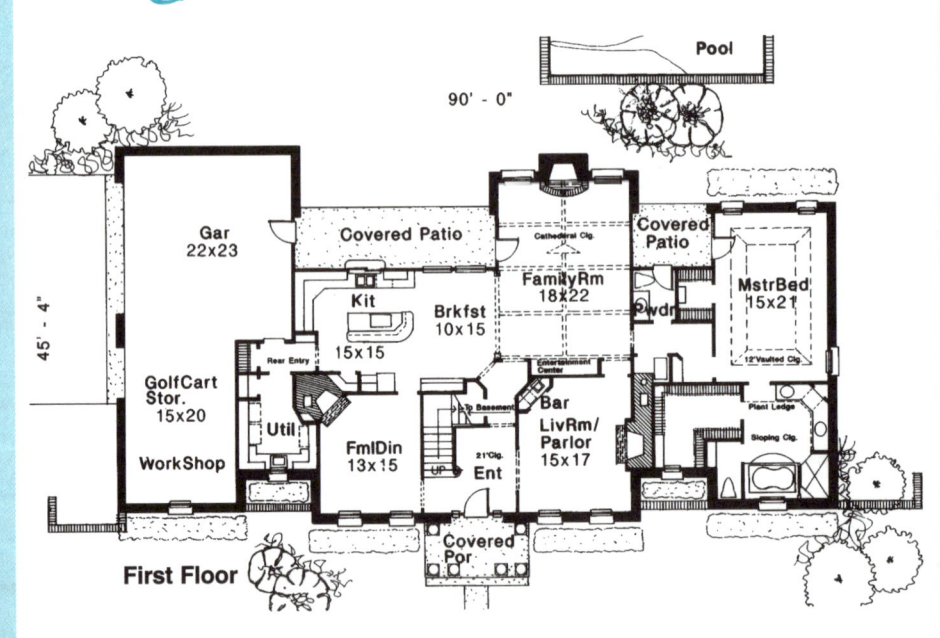

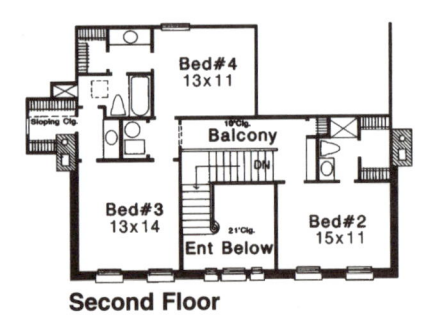

First Floor
- Gar 22x23
- Covered Patio
- Covered Patio
- MstrBed 15x21
- Kit
- Brkfst 10x15
- FamilyRm 18x22
- GolfCart Stor. 15x20
- Rear Entry
- Bar
- LivRm/Parlor 15x17
- WorkShop
- Util
- FmlDin 13x15
- Ent
- Covered Por
- 90' - 0"
- 45' - 4"
- Pool

Second Floor
- Bed #4 13x11
- Balcony
- Bed #3 13x14
- Ent Below
- Bed #2 15x11

No materials list available

DESIGN NO. 92609

PRICE CODE B

TRADITION WITH A HINT OF DRAMA

No. 92609

- This plan features:
  — Three bedrooms
  — Two full and one half baths
- A 12′ high Entry with transom and sidelights, multiple gables and a box window
- A sunken Great Room with a fireplace and access to a rear Porch
- A Breakfast Bay and Kitchen flowing into each other and accessing a rear Porch
- A Master Bedroom with a tray ceiling, walk-in closet and a private Master Bath

FIRST FLOOR — 960 SQ. FT.
SECOND FLOOR — 808 SQ. FT.

TOTAL LIVING AREA: 1,768 SQ. FT.

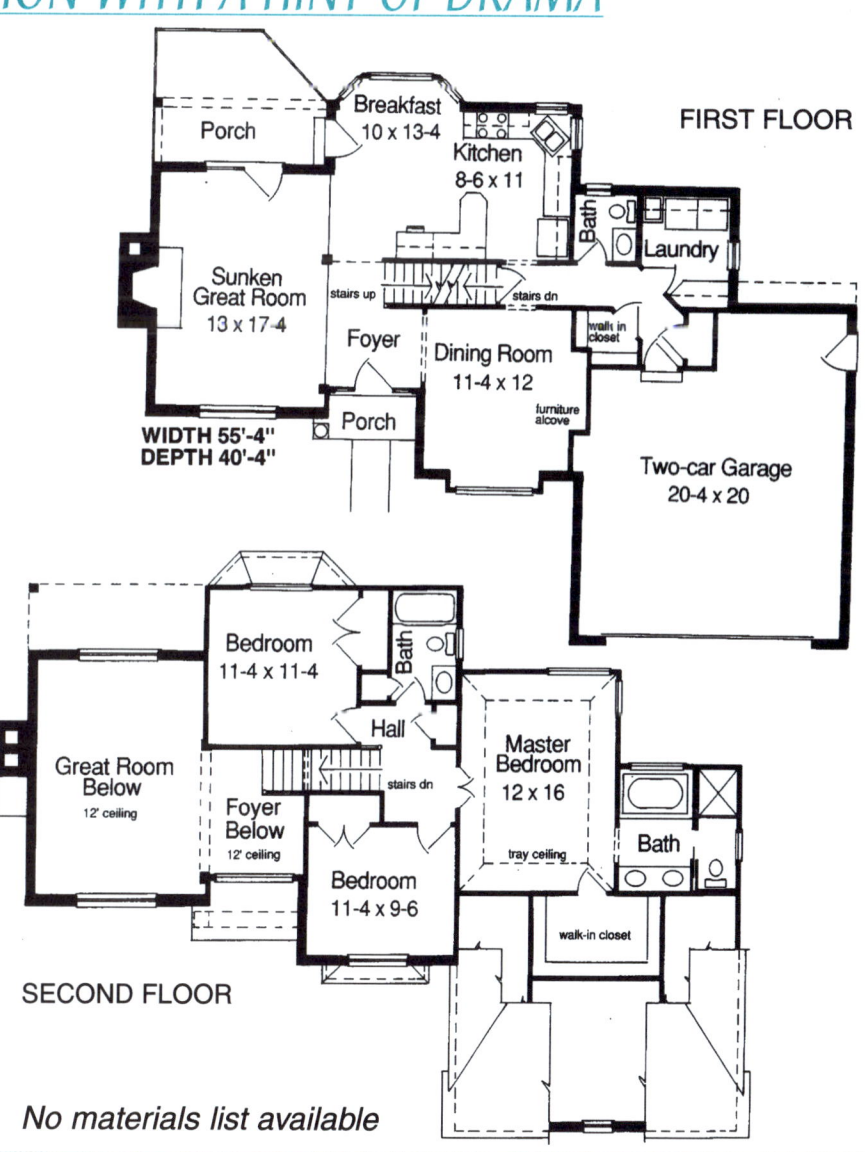

FIRST FLOOR

- Porch
- Breakfast 10 x 13-4
- Kitchen 8-6 x 11
- Bath
- Laundry
- Sunken Great Room 13 x 17-4
- Foyer
- Dining Room 11-4 x 12
- walk in closet
- furniture alcove
- Two-car Garage 20-4 x 20
- Porch
- WIDTH 55'-4"
- DEPTH 40'-4"

SECOND FLOOR

- Bedroom 11-4 x 11-4
- Bath
- Hall
- Great Room Below 12′ ceiling
- Foyer Below 12′ ceiling
- Master Bedroom 12 x 16
- tray ceiling
- Bath
- Bedroom 11-4 x 9-6
- walk-in closet

No materials list available

DESIGN NO. 92286

PRICE CODE A

Simple style with classic accents

No. 92286

■ This plan features:

— Three bedrooms

— Two full baths

■ Sheltered entry leads into busy living areas

■ Spacious Living Room with cozy fireplace and access to rear yard

■ An efficient Kitchen with a bright Dining area next to Utilities and Garage entry

■ Two walk-in closets and a plush private bath offered in Master Bedroom

■ Two additional bedrooms with ample closets share a double vanity sink

MAIN FLOOR — 1,415 SQ. FT.
GARAGE — 440 SQ. FT.

TOTAL LIVING AREA: 1,415 SQ. FT.

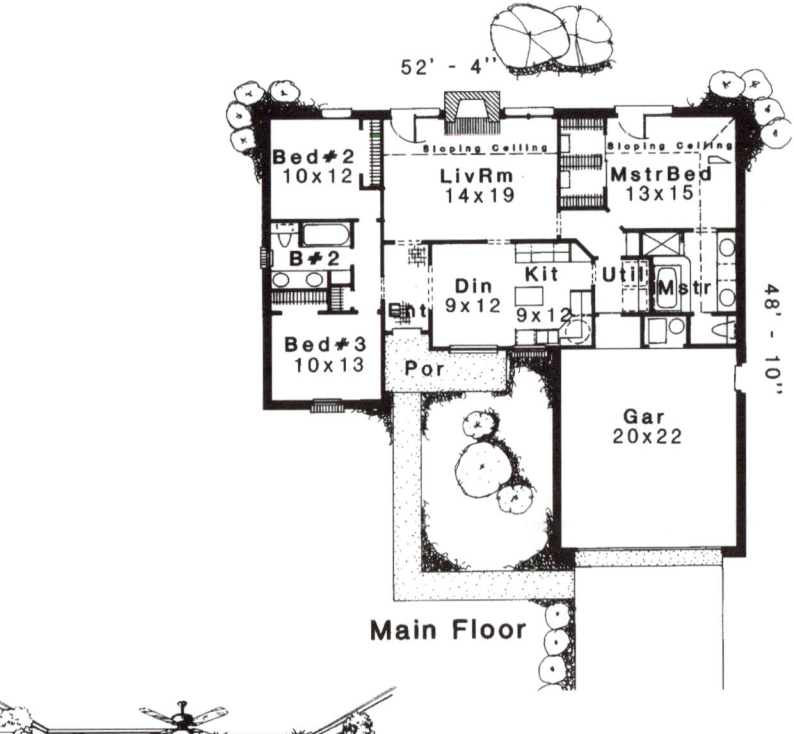

Main Floor

No materials list available

DESIGN NO. 94603

PRICE CODE B

Perfect Porch for a Swing

No. 94603

This plan features:

— Three bedrooms

— Two full and one half baths

- Country front Porch shelters entrance into central Foyer
- Living Room with a massive fireplace below a two-story sloped ceiling and access to Patio
- Convenient Kitchen with peninsula counter efficiently serves bright Breakfast area and formal Dining Room
- Bedroom featuring a dressing area with double vanity and a walk-in closet
- Two additional second floor bedrooms with dormers and large closets, share a full bath and a large attic storage
- An optional crawl space or slab foundation — please specify when ordering

FIRST FLOOR — 1,238 SQ. FT.
SECOND FLOOR — 499 SQ. FT.

TOTAL LIVING AREA: 1,737 SQ. FT.

WIDTH 38'-4"
DEPTH 49'-0"

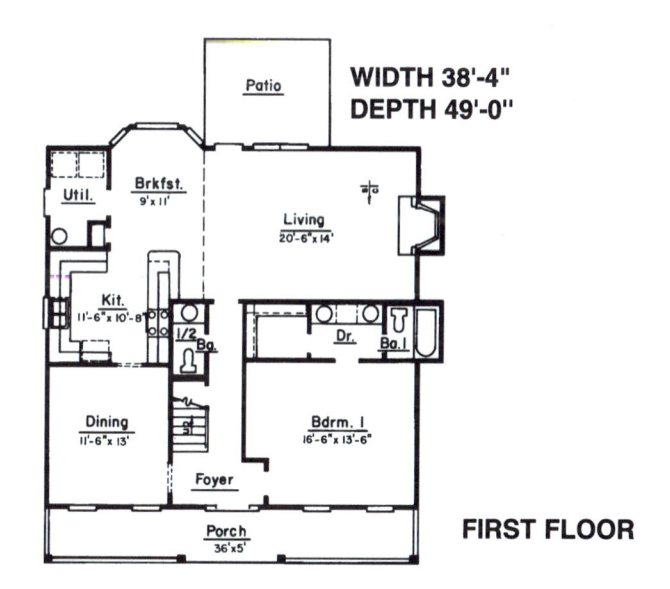

FIRST FLOOR

No materials list available

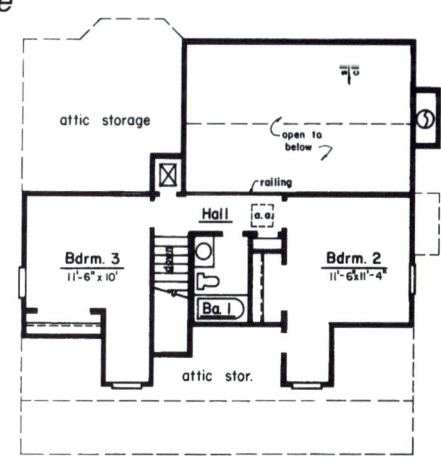

SECOND FLOOR

DESIGN NO. 93030

PRICE CODE C

ULTIMATE MASTER SUITE

No. 93030

■ This plan features:

— Three Bedrooms

— Two full baths

■ A covered porch leading into the tiled Foyer, a columned Dining Room and an expansive Great Room

■ A large hearth fireplace between sliding glass doors to a covered Porch and a Deck with hot tub

■ A spacious Kitchen with a built-in pantry, a peninsula sink and an octagon-shaped Breakfast area

■ A Master Bedroom wing with French doors, a vaulted ceiling, a plush Master Bath with a huge walk-in closet, a double vanity and a window tub

■ Two additional bedrooms with walk-in closets, sharing a full hall bath

MAIN AREA — 1,995 SQ. FT.
GARAGE — 561 SQ. FT.

TOTAL LIVING AREA: 1,995 SQ. FT.

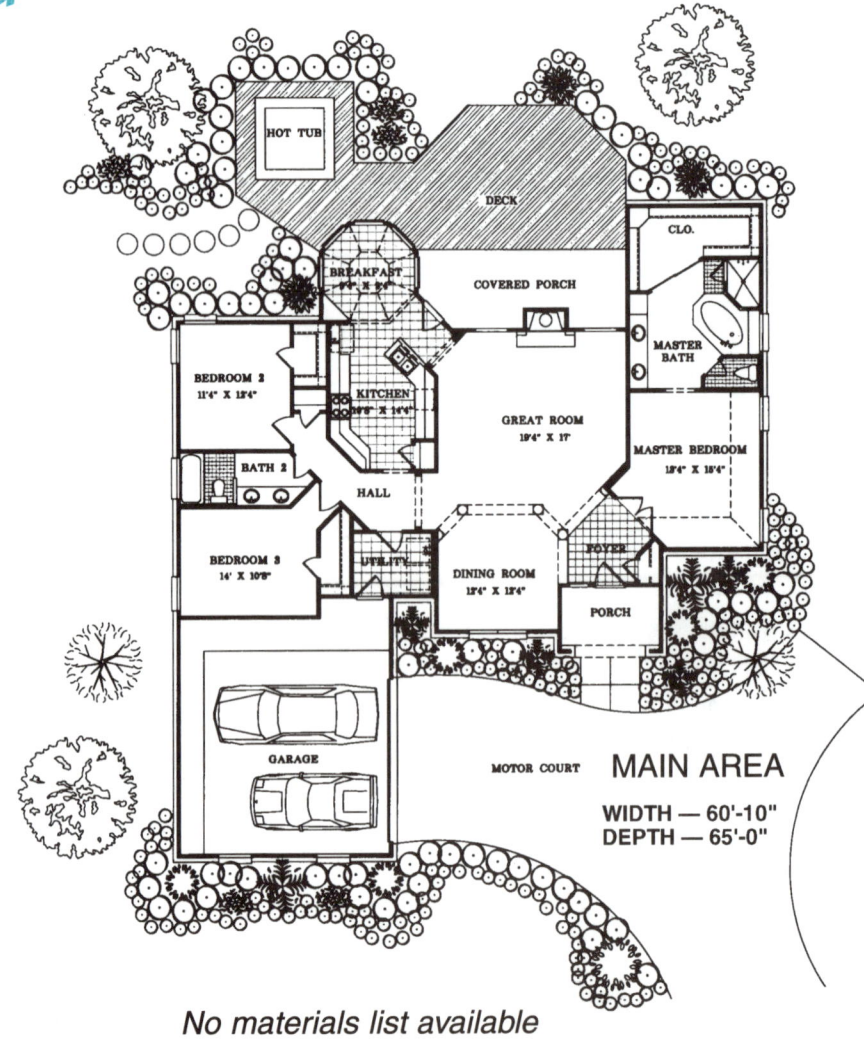

MAIN AREA
WIDTH — 60'-10"
DEPTH — 65'-0"

No materials list available

DESIGN NO. 92273

PRICE CODE F

Luxurious One Floor Living

No. 92273

- This plan features:
— Four bedrooms
— Three full baths
- Decorative windows enhance front entrance of elegant home
- Formal Living Room accented by fireplace between windows overlooking rear yard
- Formal Dining Room highlighted by decorative window
- Breakfast bar, work island, and an abundance of storage and counter space featured in Kitchen
- Spacious Master Bedroom with access to covered Patio, a lavish bath and huge walk-in closet
- Three additional bedrooms with large closets and private access to a full bath

MAIN FLOOR — 3,254 SQ. FT.
GARAGE — 588 SQ. FT.

TOTAL LIVING AREA: 3,254 SQ. FT.

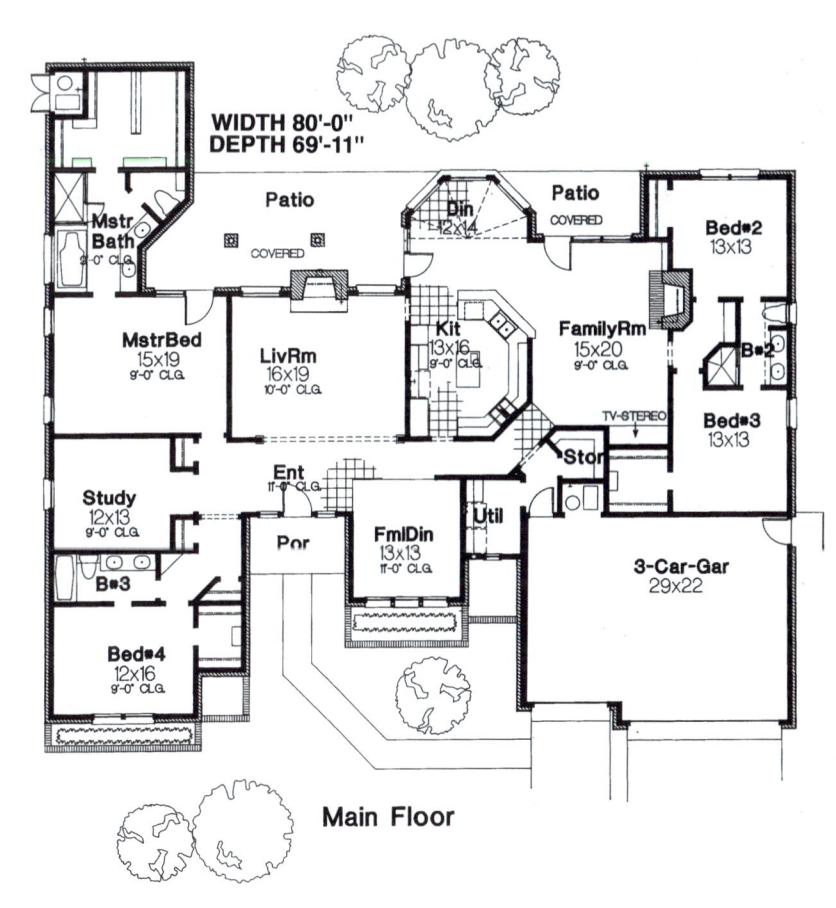

WIDTH 80'-0"
DEPTH 69'-11"

Main Floor

No materials list available

DESIGN NO. 92405

PRICE CODE B

*P*ERFECT FOR A FIRST HOME

No. 92405
■ This plan features:
— Three bedrooms
— Two full baths

■ A spacious Master Suite including a separate Master Bath with a garden tub and shower

■ A Dining Room and Family Room highlighted by vaulted ceilings

■ An oversized Patio accessible from the Master Suite, Family Room and Breakfast Room

■ A well planned Kitchen measuring 12′ x 11′

MAIN AREA — 1,564 SQ. FT.
GARAGE & STORAGE — 476 SQ. FT.

TOTAL LIVING AREA: 1,564 SQ. FT.

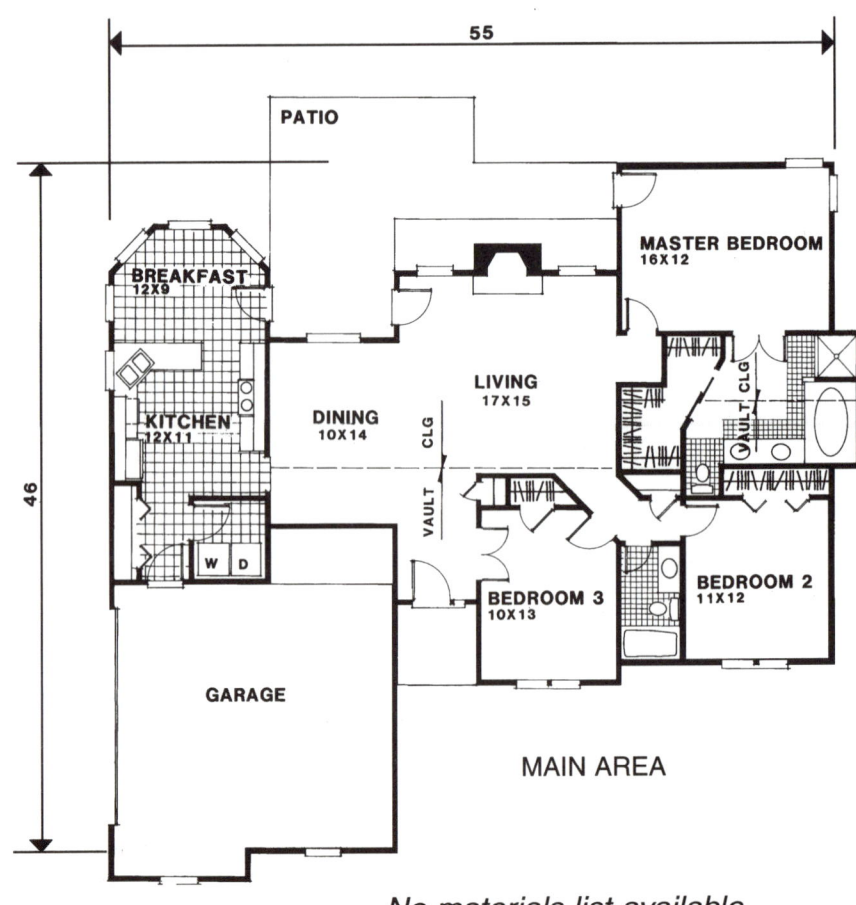

No materials list available

DESIGN NO. 90423

PRICE CODE B

Your classic hideaway

No. 90423

- This plan features:
— Three bedrooms
— Two full baths
- A lovely fireplace in the Living Room, which is both cozy and a source of heat for the core area
- An efficient country Kitchen connecting the large Dining and Living Rooms
- A lavish Master Suite enhanced by a step-up sunken tub, more than ample closet space, and separate shower
- A Screened Porch and Patio area for outdoor living
- An optional basement, slab or crawl space foundation — please specify when ordering

MAIN AREA — 1,773 SQ. FT.
SCREENED PORCH — 240 SQ. FT.

TOTAL LIVING AREA: 1,773 SQ. FT.

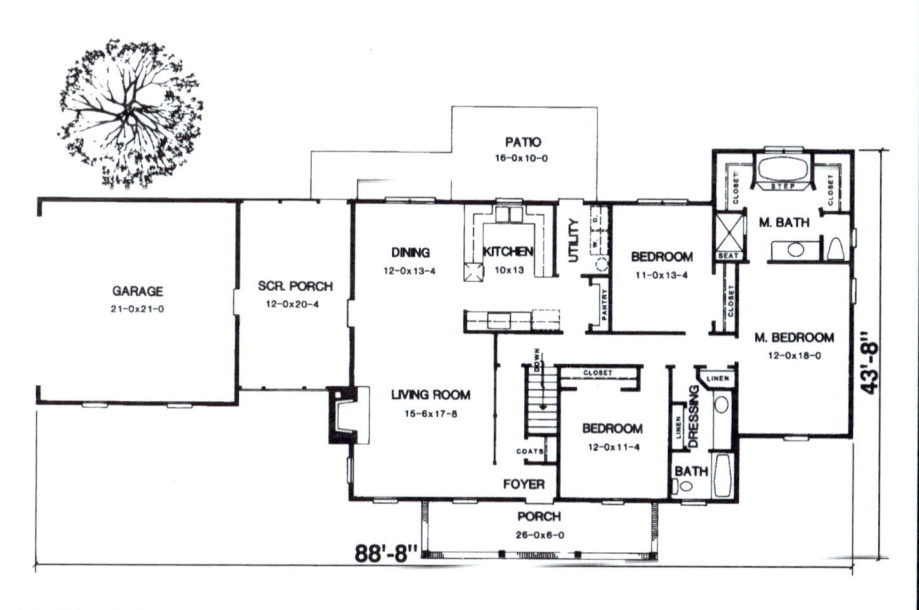

MAIN AREA

DESIGN NO. 94247

PRICE CODE E

DESIGNED FOR ENTERTAINING

No. 94247

- This plan features:
— Three bedrooms
— Three full and one half baths
- Large, open floor plan with an array of amenities for successful gatherings
- Grand Room and Dining area separated by 3-sided fireplace and wetbar both access Screened Verandah
- Spacious Kitchen with a cooktop island, eating Nook and ready access to Verandah and Dining Room
- Secluded Master Suite enhanced by a private Spa Deck, huge walk-in closet and whirlpool tub
- Study and two additional bedrooms have private access to full baths

FIRST FLOOR — 2,066 SQ. FT.
SECOND FLOOR — 809 SQ. FT.
GARAGE — 798 SQ. FT.
FOUNDATION — POST AND PIER

TOTAL LIVING AREA: 2,875 SQ. FT.

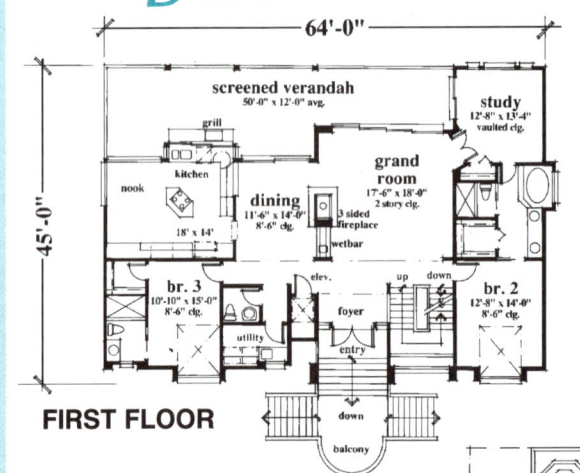

No materials list available

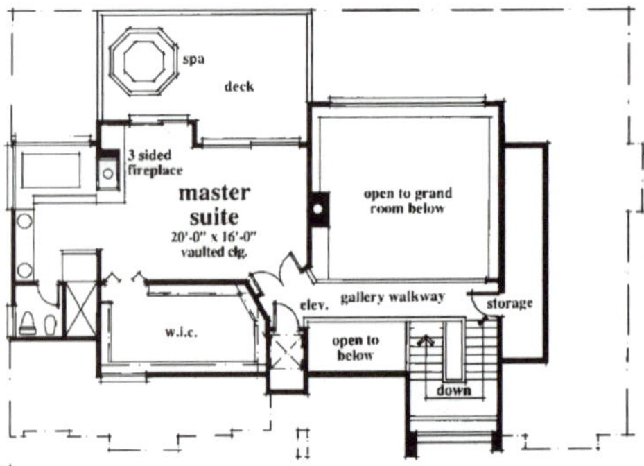

FIRST FLOOR

- screened verandah 50'-0" x 12'-0" avg.
- grill
- kitchen
- nook
- dining 11'-6" x 14'-0" 8'-6" clg.
- 18' x 14'
- 3 sided fireplace
- wetbar
- study 12'-8" x 13'-4" vaulted clg.
- grand room 17'-6" x 18'-0" 2 story clg.
- br. 3 10'-10" x 15'-0" 8'-6" clg.
- elev.
- up down
- br. 2 12'-8" x 14'-0" 8'-6" clg.
- foyer
- utility
- entry
- down balcony

64'-0"
45'-0"

SECOND FLOOR

- spa deck
- 3 sided fireplace
- master suite 20'-0" x 16'-0" vaulted clg.
- w.i.c.
- elev.
- gallery walkway
- open to grand room below
- open to below
- storage
- down

LOWER FLOOR

- deck 50'-0" x 12'-0"
- bonus
- bonus 36'-0" x 17'-0"
- garage 25'-0" x 27'-0"
- opt. elev.
- storage
- up
- bonus

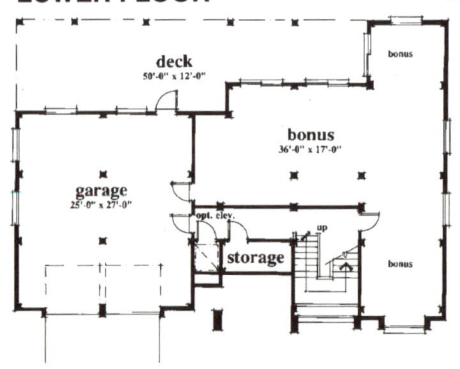

HIGH WIND LOAD ENGINEERING AVAILABLE
SEE PAGE 246 FOR DETAILS

DESIGN NO. 93027

PRICE CODE A

For today's sophisticated homeowner

No. 93027

■ This plan features:

— Three bedrooms

— Two full baths

■ A formal Dining Room that opens off the foyer and has a classic bay window

■ A Kitchen notable for it's angled eating bar that opens to the Living Room

■ A cozy fireplace in the Living Room that can be seen from the Kitchen

■ A Master Suite that includes a whirlpool tub/shower combination and a walk-in closet

■ Ten foot ceilings in the major living areas, including the Master Bedroom

MAIN AREA — 1,500 SQ. FT.
GARAGE — 437 SQ. FT.

TOTAL LIVING AREA: 1,500 SQ. FT.

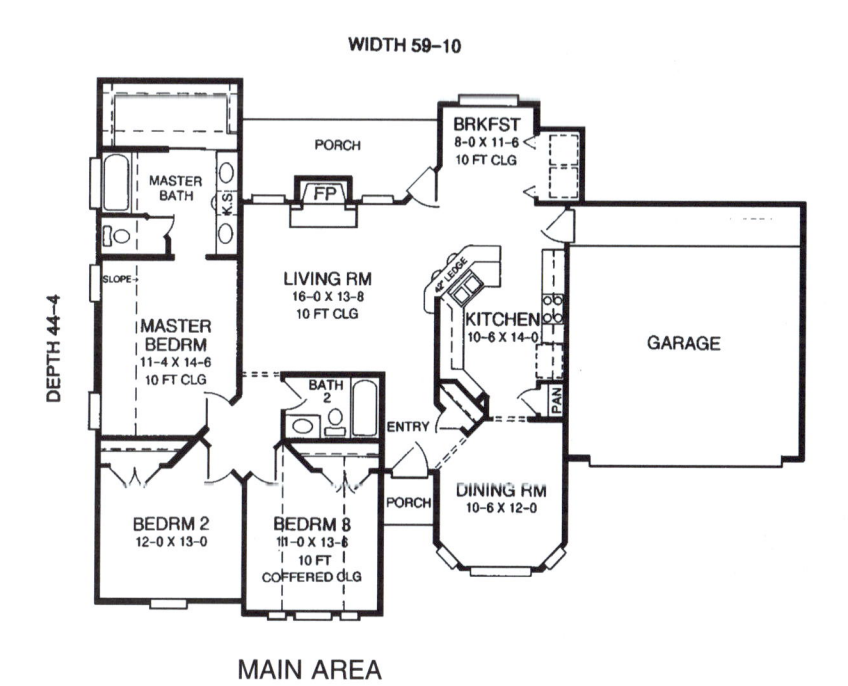

WIDTH 59-10
DEPTH 44-4

MAIN AREA

No materials list available

DESIGN NO. 94801

PRICE CODE B

A COMFORTABLE, INFORMAL DESIGN

No. 94801

■ This plan features:

— Three bedrooms

— Two full baths

■ Warm, country front Porch

■ Spacious Activity Room enhanced by a pre-fab fireplace

■ Open and efficient Kitchen/Dining area highlighted by bay window, adjacent to Laundry and Garage entry

■ Corner Master Bedroom offers a pampering bath with a garden tub and double vanity topped by a vaulted ceiling

■ Two additional bedrooms with ample closets, share a full bath

■ An optional crawl space or slab foundation — please specify when ordering

MAIN FLOOR — 1,300 SQ. FT.
GARAGE — 576 SQ. FT.

TOTAL LIVING AREA: 1,300 SQ. FT.

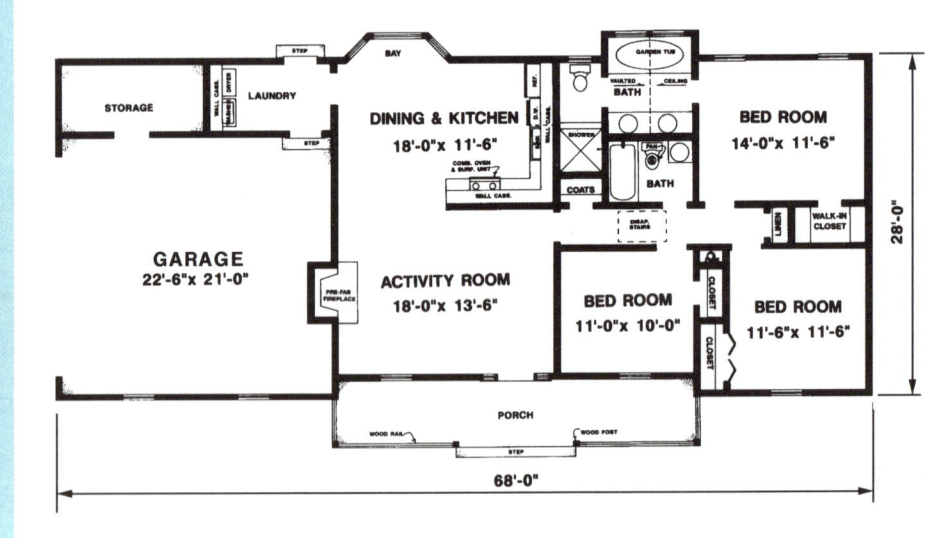

MAIN AREA

DESIGN NO. 92630

PRICE CODE B

CHARMING BRICK RANCH

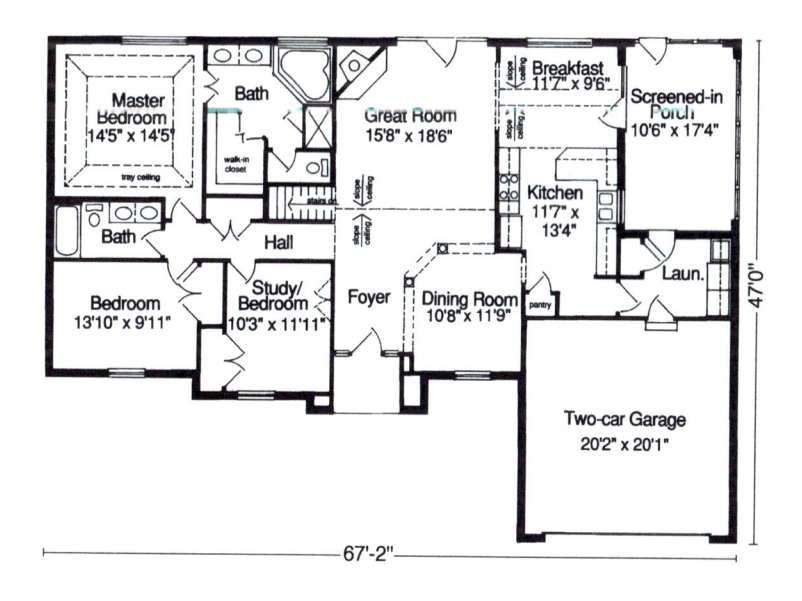

No. 92630

■ This plan features:

— Three bedrooms

— Two full baths

■ Sheltered entrance leads into open Foyer and Dining Room defined by columns

■ Vaulted ceiling spans Foyer, Dining Room, and Great Room with corner fireplace and Atrium door to rear year

■ Central Kitchen with separate Laundry and pantry easily serves Dining Room, Breakfast area and Screened Porch

■ Luxurious Master bedroom offers tray ceiling and French doors to double vanity, walk-in closet and whirlpool tub

■ Two additional bedrooms, one easily converted to a Study, share a full bath

MAIN FLOOR — 1,782 SQ. FT.
BASEMENT — 1,735 SQ. FT.
GARAGE — 407 SQ. FT.

TOTAL LIVING AREA: 1,782 SQ. FT.

MAIN FLOOR

No materials list available

DESIGN NO. 90448

PRICE CODE C

Classic Colonial

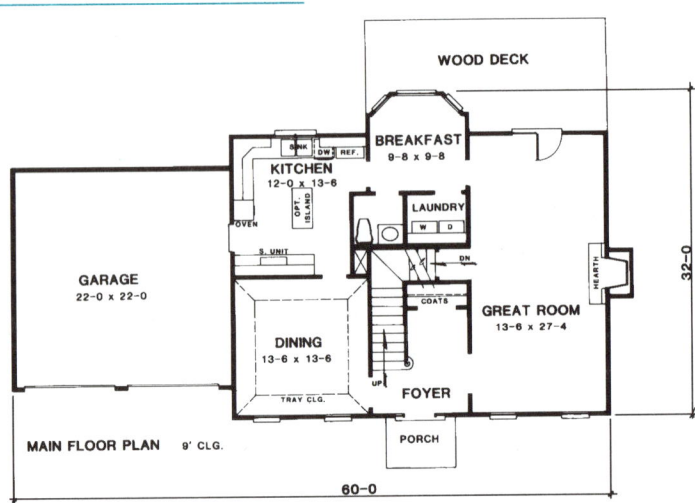

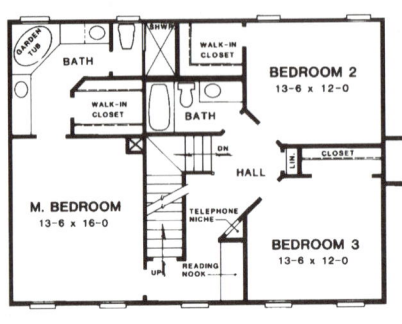

No. 90448

■ This plan features:

— Three or five bedrooms

— Two to three full and one half baths

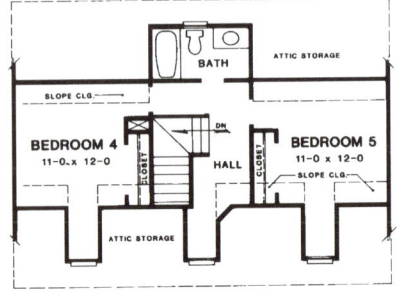

■ An optional third floor with two additional bedrooms and a third full bath

■ A Master Suite with a large walk-in closet, private bath with a corner tub, a full sized shower and double vanity

■ A formal Dining Room with a tray ceiling to add elegance

■ A sunny Breakfast bay for informal eating

■ An expansive Great Room with a fireplace

■ An optional basement or crawl space foundation — please specify when ordering

FIRST FLOOR — 1,098 SQ. FT.
SECOND FLOOR — 1,064 SQ. FT.
UNFINISHED THIRD FLOOR — 596 SQ. FT.

TOTAL LIVING AREA: 2,162 SQ. FT.

DESIGN NO. 94242

PRICE CODE E

A CUSTOM LOOK

No. 94242

- This plan features:
— Three bedrooms
— Two full, one three quarter and one half baths
- Wonderfully balanced exterior highlighted by triple arched glass in Entry Porch, leading into the Gallery Foyer
- Triple arches lead into Formal Living and Dining Room, Verandah and beyond
- Kitchen, Nook, and Leisure Room area easily flow together
- Owners' wing has a Master Suite with glass alcove to rear yard, a lavish bath and a Study offering many uses
- Two additional bedrooms with corner windows and over-sized closets access a full bath

MAIN AREA — 2,978 SQ. FT
GARAGE — 702 SQ. FT.

TOTAL LIVING AREA: 2,978 SQ. FT.

HIGH WIND LOAD ENGINEERING AVAILABLE
SEE PAGE 246 FOR DETAILS

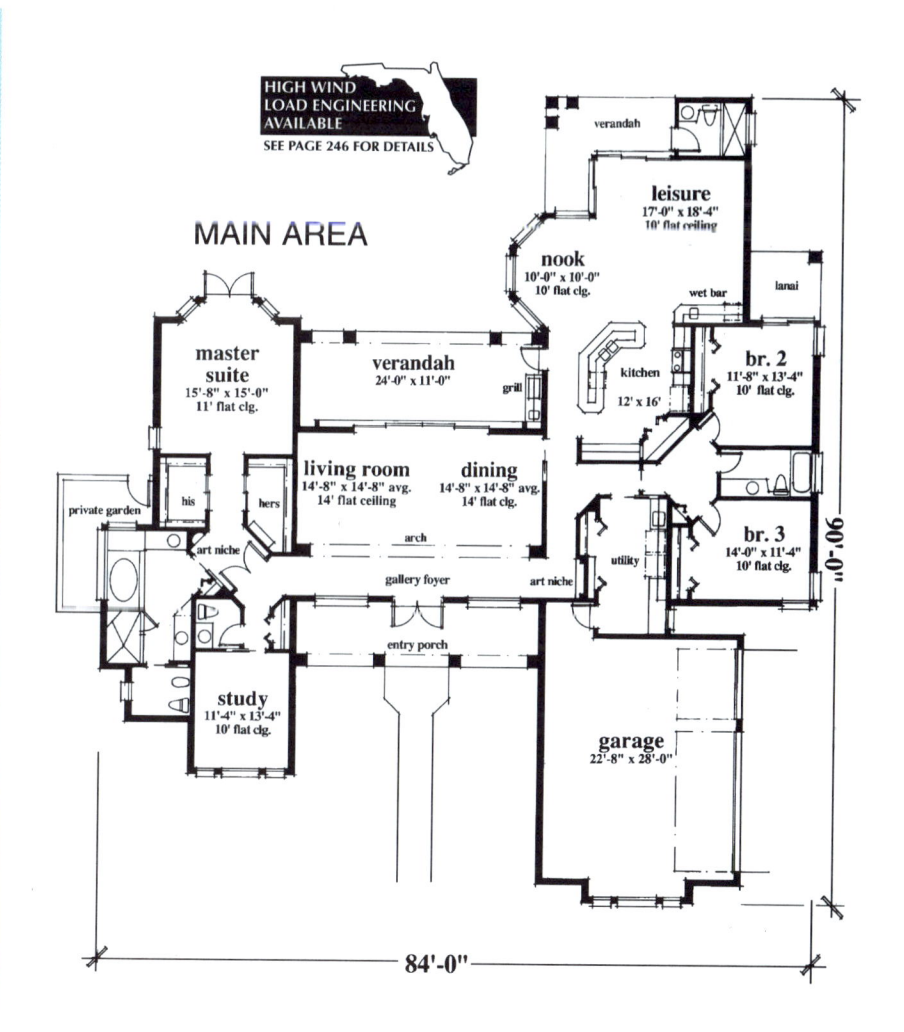

MAIN AREA

- verandah
- leisure 17'-0" x 18'-4" 10' flat ceiling
- nook 10'-0" x 10'-0" 10' flat clg.
- master suite 15'-8" x 15'-0" 11' flat clg.
- verandah 24'-0" x 11'-0"
- grill
- wet bar
- lanai
- kitchen 12' x 16'
- br. 2 11'-8" x 13'-4" 10' flat clg.
- private garden
- his
- hers
- art niche
- living room 14'-8" x 14'-8" avg. 14' flat ceiling
- dining 14'-8" x 14'-8" avg. 14' flat clg.
- arch
- gallery foyer
- art niche
- utility
- br. 3 14'-0" x 11'-4" 10' flat clg.
- entry porch
- study 11'-4" x 13'-4" 10' flat clg.
- garage 22'-8" x 28'-0"

84'-0" × 90'-0"

No materials list available

DESIGN NO. 92257

PRICE CODE D

EYE-APPEALING BALANCE

No. 92257

■ This plan features:

— Three bedrooms

— Two full and one half baths

■ Arched Portico enhances entry into Gallery and spacious Living Room, with focal point fireplace surrounded by glass

■ Cathedral ceilings top Family Room and formal Dining Room

■ An efficient Kitchen with breakfast area opens to Family Room, Utility Room with convenient Garage entry

■ Corner Master Bedroom suite with access to covered Patio and private bath with a double vanity and garden window tub

■ Two additional bedrooms with walk-in closets share a full bath

MAIN FLOOR — 2,470 SQ. FT.
GARAGE — 483 SQ. FT.

TOTAL LIVING AREA: 2,470 SQ. FT.

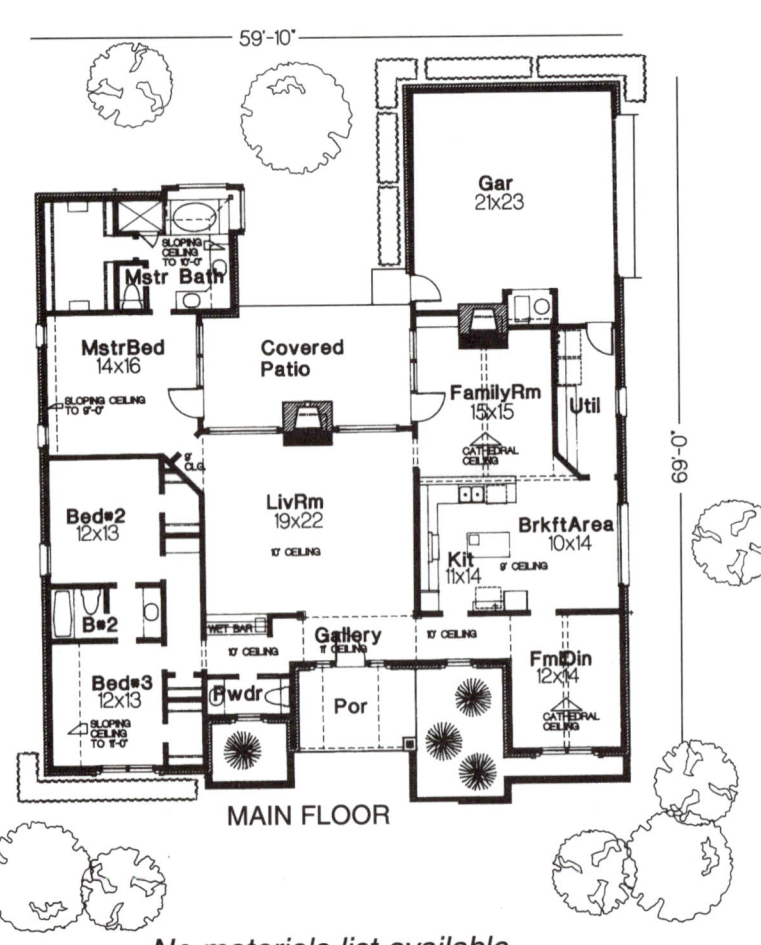

MAIN FLOOR

No materials list available

DESIGN NO. 92632

PRICE CODE B

GOOD TASTE AND FLEXIBILITY

No. 92632

- This plan features:
  — Three bedrooms
  — Two full and one half baths
- Sheltered entrance leads into large Foyer with landing staircase and Great Room
- Focal point fireplace and view to rear yard highlight Great Room
- Formal Dining Room enhanced by decorative window
- Efficient U-shaped Kitchen with peninsula serving counter easily serves glass Breakfast area and Dining Room
- Private Master Bedroom offers walk-in closet and double vanity bath
- Two additional bedrooms with over-sized closets
- Loft area with triple window can double as a Laundry

FIRST FLOOR — 934 SQ. FT.
SECOND FLOOR — 850 SQ. FT.
BASEMENT — 831 SQ. FT.
GARAGE — 229 SQ. FT.

TOTAL LIVING AREA: 1,784 SQ. FT.

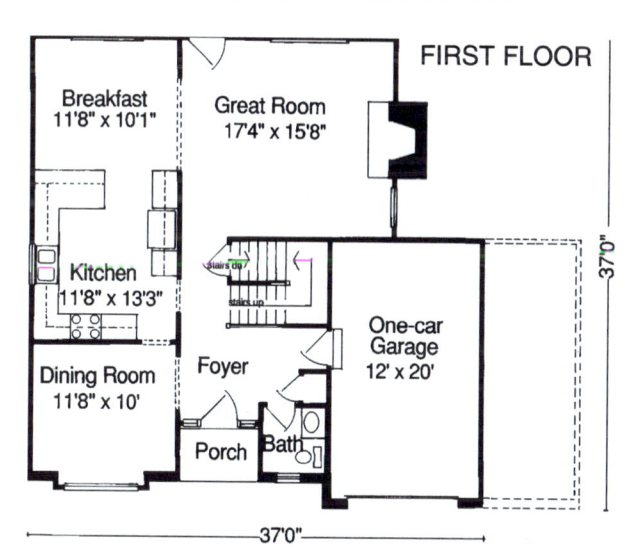

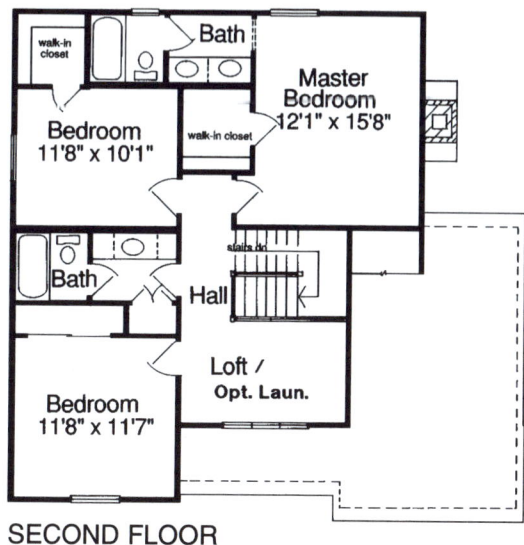

FIRST FLOOR

- Breakfast 11'8" x 10'1"
- Great Room 17'4" x 15'8"
- Kitchen 11'8" x 13'3"
- Dining Room 11'8" x 10'
- Foyer
- Porch
- Bath
- One-car Garage 12' x 20'

37'0" x 37'0"

SECOND FLOOR

- Bedroom 11'8" x 10'1"
- walk-in closet
- Bath
- Master Bedroom 12'1" x 15'8"
- walk-in closet
- Bath
- Hall
- Loft / Opt. Laun.
- Bedroom 11'8" x 11'7"

No materials list available

DESIGN NO. 92207

PRICE CODE E

UNCOMMON BRICKWORK ENHANCES FACADE

No. 92207

■ This plan features:

— Four bedrooms

— Three full and one half baths

■ Sheltered Porch leads into Entry and spacious Living Room with pool access

■ Quiet Study with focal point fireplace and open formal Dining Room

■ Expansive Kitchen with cooktop work island, efficiently serves Breakfast Nook, Patio and Dining Room

■ Master Bedroom wing offers a vaulted ceiling, two walk-in closets and a corner window tub

■ Three second floor bedrooms share two full baths

MAIN FLOOR — 2,304 SQ. FT.
UPPER FLOOR — 852 SQ. FT.
GARAGE — 690 SQ. FT.

TOTAL LIVING AREA: 3,156 SQ. FT.

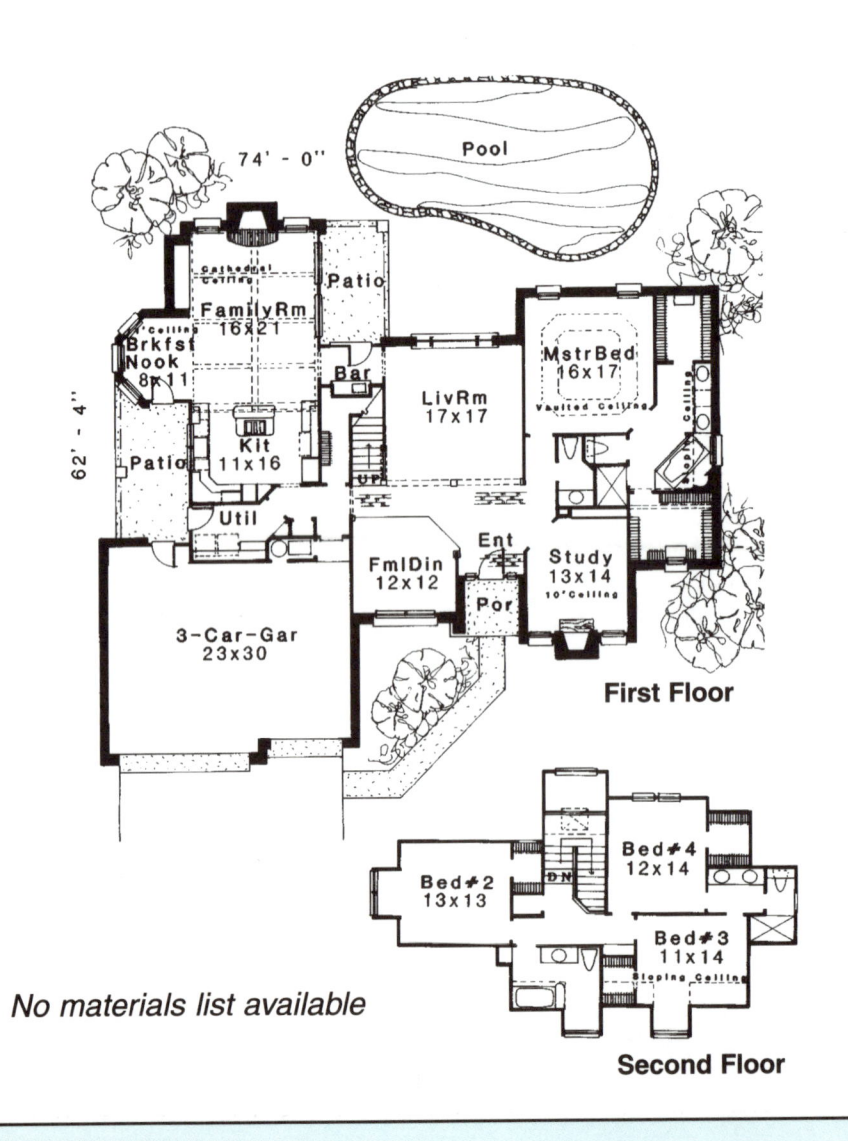

No materials list available

DESIGN NO. 93029

PRICE CODE C

Reminiscent of America's Farm House

No. 93029

- This plan features:
- — Three bedrooms
- — Two full baths
- A covered front Porch
- A matching pair of French doors in the Great Room that flank the fireplace
- A formal Dining Room with square columns connected by arched openings
- An angled bar design in the Kitchen, providing a convenient pass-through for entertaining and family gatherings
- A Master Suite with a coffered ceiling and an enormous walk-in closet
- A double vanity, corner whirlpool tub and a shower in the Master Bath

MAIN AREA — 1,834 SQ. FT.
GARAGE — 547 SQ. FT.

TOTAL LIVING AREA: 1,834 SQ. FT.

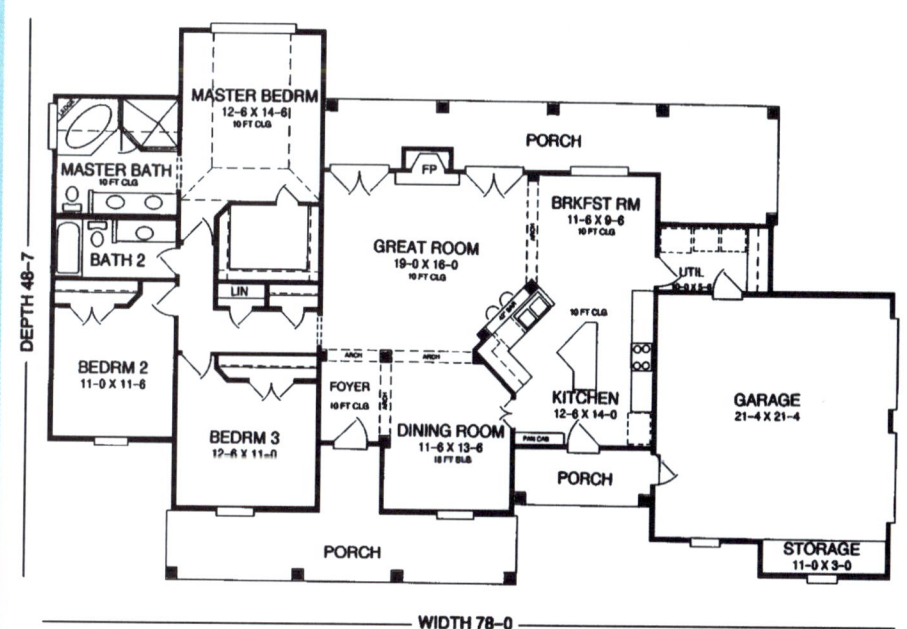

MAIN AREA

No materials list available

DESIGN NO. 92401

PRICE CODE C

Loads of closet space

No. 92401

- This plan features:
- — Three bedrooms
- — Two full baths
- Formal Living and Dining rooms enhanced by decorative windows and tray ceilings
- Spacious Family Room with a vaulted ceiling, fireplace and access to rear yard
- Efficient Kitchen/Breakfast area with built-in pantry and serving counter
- Private Master Bedroom suite enhanced by cathedral ceiling, two walk-in closets and luxurious bath
- Two additional bedrooms share a full bath and Laundry area

MAIN FLOOR — 2,022 SQ. FT.
BASEMENT — 1,970 SQ. FT.
GARAGE — 361 SQ. FT.

TOTAL LIVING AREA: 2,022 SQ. FT.

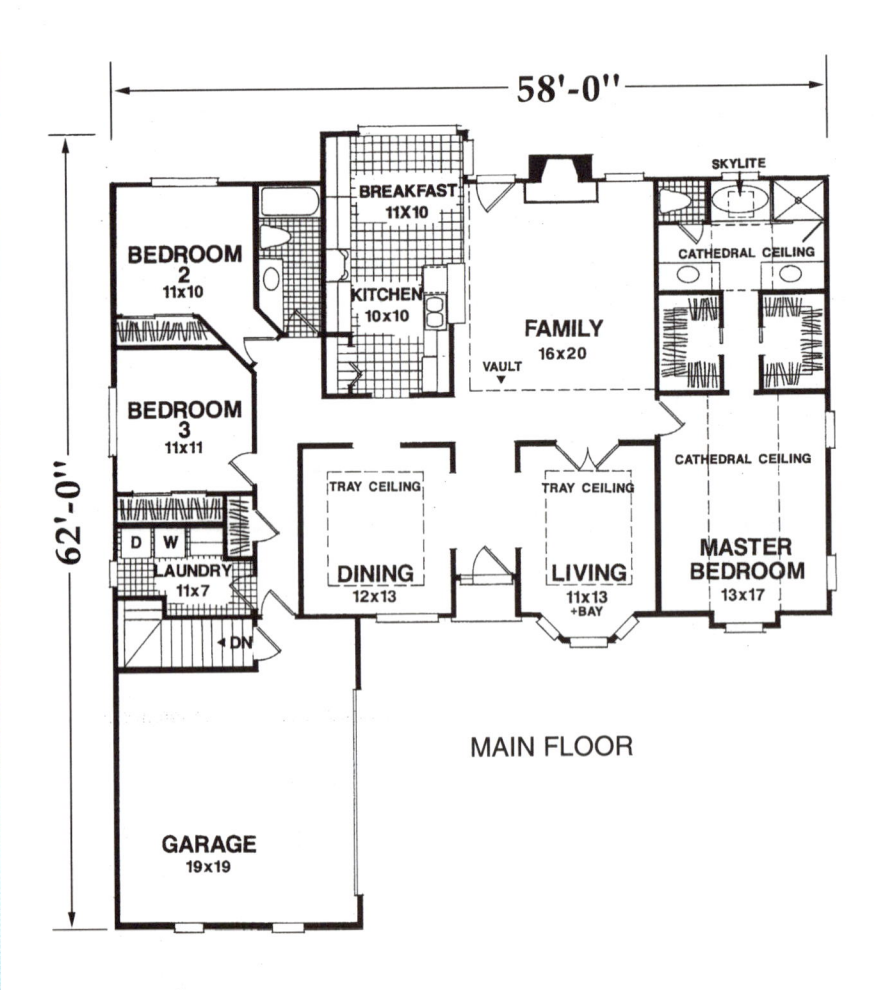

MAIN FLOOR

58'-0"
62'-0"

BREAKFAST 11X10
BEDROOM 2 11x10
KITCHEN 10x10
FAMILY 16x20
BEDROOM 3 11x11
LAUNDRY 11x7
DINING 12x13
LIVING 11x13 +BAY
MASTER BEDROOM 13x17
GARAGE 19x19

No materials list available

56

DESIGN NO. 92277

PRICE CODE E

IMPRESSIVE FIELDSTONE FACADE

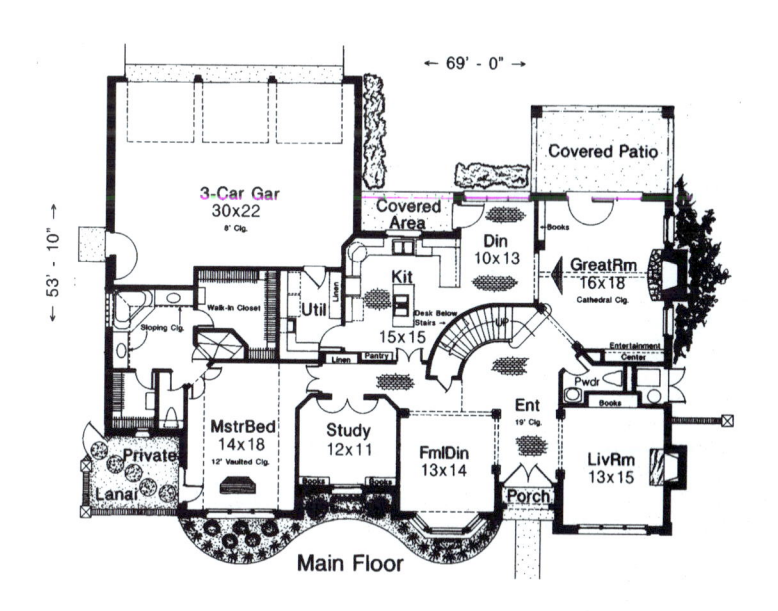

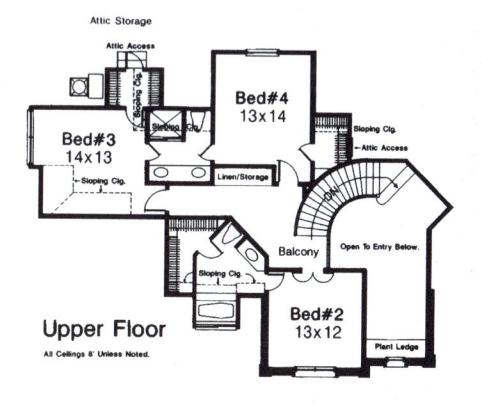

No. 92277

- This plan features:
- — Four bedrooms
- — Three full and one half baths
- Double door leads into two-story entry with an exquisite curved staircase
- Formal Living Room features a marble hearth fireplace, triple window and built-in book shelves
- Formal Dining Room defined by columns and a lovely bay window
- Efficient Kitchen offers cooktop/work island, Utility/Garage entry and serving counter for informal Dining area
- Expansive Great Room with entertainment center, fieldstone fireplace, cathedral ceiling and access to Covered Patio
- Vaulted ceiling crowns Master Bedroom suite offering a plush bath and two walk-in closets

FIRST FLOOR — 2,190 SQ. FT.
SECOND FLOOR — 920 SQ. FT.
GARAGE — 624 SQ. FT.

TOTAL LIVING AREA: 3,110 SQ. FT.

No materials list available

DESIGN NO. 94206

PRICE CODE D

TURRET ADDS APPEAL

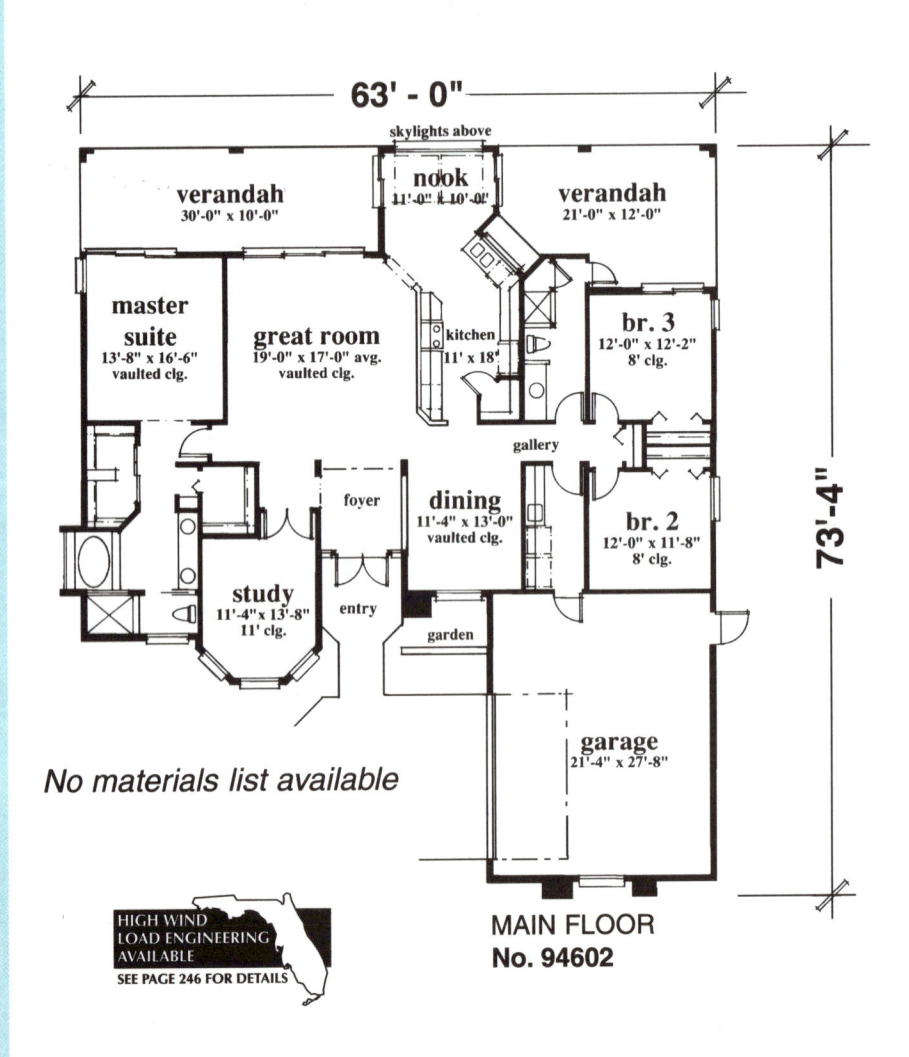

- **This plan features:**
- — Three bedrooms
- — Two full baths
- A garden Entry with double door leading into an open Foyer and Great Room
- Vaulted ceilings above a decorative window in the Dining area and sliding glass doors to the Veranda in the Great Room
- A private Study with double door and turret windows
- A large, efficient Kitchen featuring a walk-in pantry and glassed Nook, with skylights, near the laundry area and Garage
- A Master Suite with a vaulted ceiling, two huge, walk-in closets, a luxurious bath and sliding glass doors to the Veranda
- Two additional bedrooms with over-sized closets sharing a full bath

MAIN FLOOR — 2,214 SQ. FT.
GARAGE — 652 SQ. FT.

TOTAL LIVING AREA: 2,214 SQ. FT.

Floor Plan (63'-0" x 73'-4")

- verandah 30'-0" x 10'-0"
- nook 11'-0" x 10'-0" (skylights above)
- verandah 21'-0" x 12'-0"
- master suite 13'-8" x 16'-6" vaulted clg.
- great room 19'-0" x 17'-0" avg. vaulted clg.
- kitchen 11' x 18'
- br. 3 12'-0" x 12'-2" 8' clg.
- gallery
- foyer
- dining 11'-4" x 13'-0" vaulted clg.
- br. 2 12'-0" x 11'-8" 8' clg.
- study 11'-4" x 13'-8" 11' clg.
- entry
- garden
- garage 21'-4" x 27'-8"

No materials list available

HIGH WIND LOAD ENGINEERING AVAILABLE — SEE PAGE 246 FOR DETAILS

MAIN FLOOR No. 94602

DESIGN NO. 93032

PRICE CODE D

Entry Graced by Arches

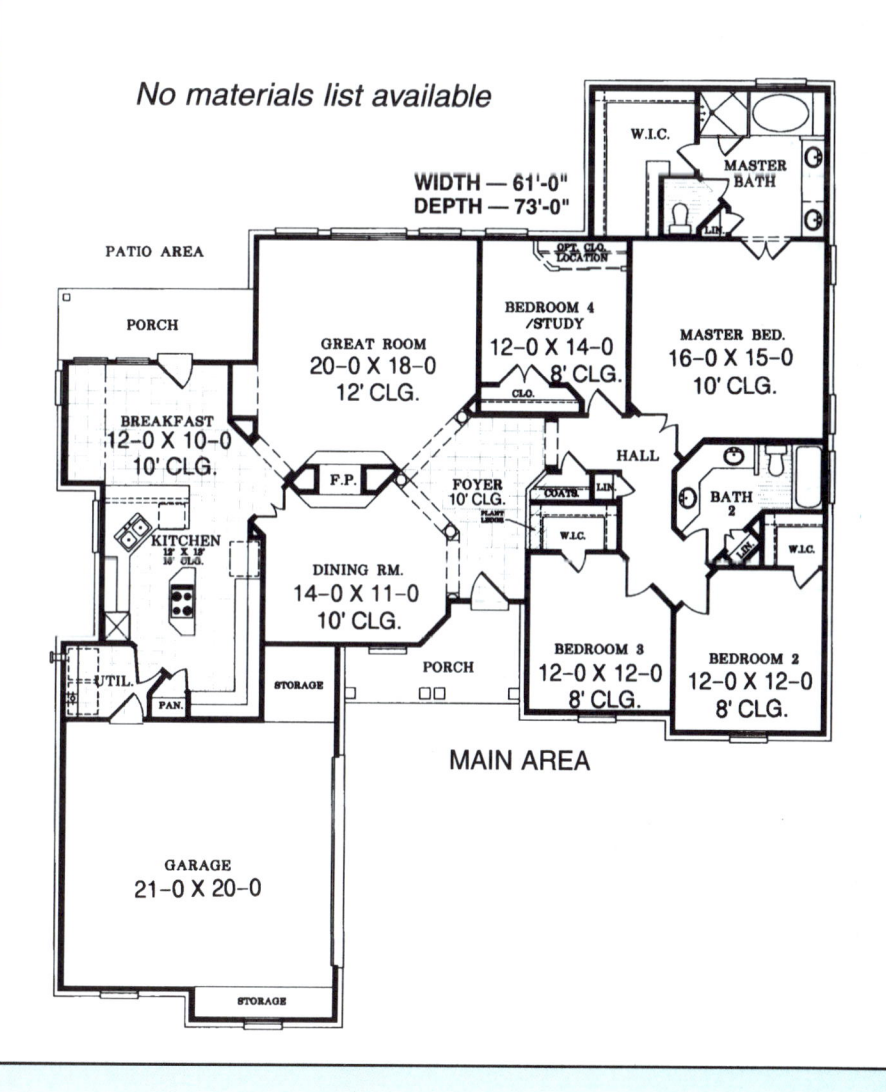

No. 93032

■ This plan features:

— Four bedrooms

— Two full baths

■ A combination of brick and wood siding finishes with a pair of graceful arches at the entry creating an all-time favorite curb elevation

■ An angled foyer design that provides views to the Great Room and the Dining Room

■ A see-through fireplace between the Great Room and the Dining Room as an elegant detail

■ A Kitchen that includes a cooktop work island and eating bar, plenty of cabinets and more than ample counter space

■ A Master Suite with a whirlpool tub, shower and double vanity with knee space, plus a walk-in closet

MAIN AREA — 2,250 SQ. FT.
GARAGE — 543 SQ. FT.

**TOTAL LIVING AREA:
2,250 SQ. FT.**

No materials list available

WIDTH — 61'-0"
DEPTH — 73'-0"

MAIN AREA

DESIGN NO. 92209

PRICE CODE F

Multiple roof lines add to charm

No. 92209

■ This plan features:

— Four bedrooms

— Three full baths

■ Entry opens to Gallery, formal Dining and Living rooms with decorative ceilings

■ Spacious Kitchen with a work island opens to Dining alcove, Family Room and Patio beyond

■ Comfortable Family Room offers vaulted ceiling above fireplace and a wetbar

■ Corner Master Bedroom suite enhanced by a vaulted ceiling, double vanity bath and huge walk-in closet

■ Three additional bedrooms with walk-in closets have access to full baths

MAIN FLOOR — 3,292 SQ. FT.
GARAGE — 670 SQ. FT.

TOTAL LIVING AREA:
3,292 SQ. FT.

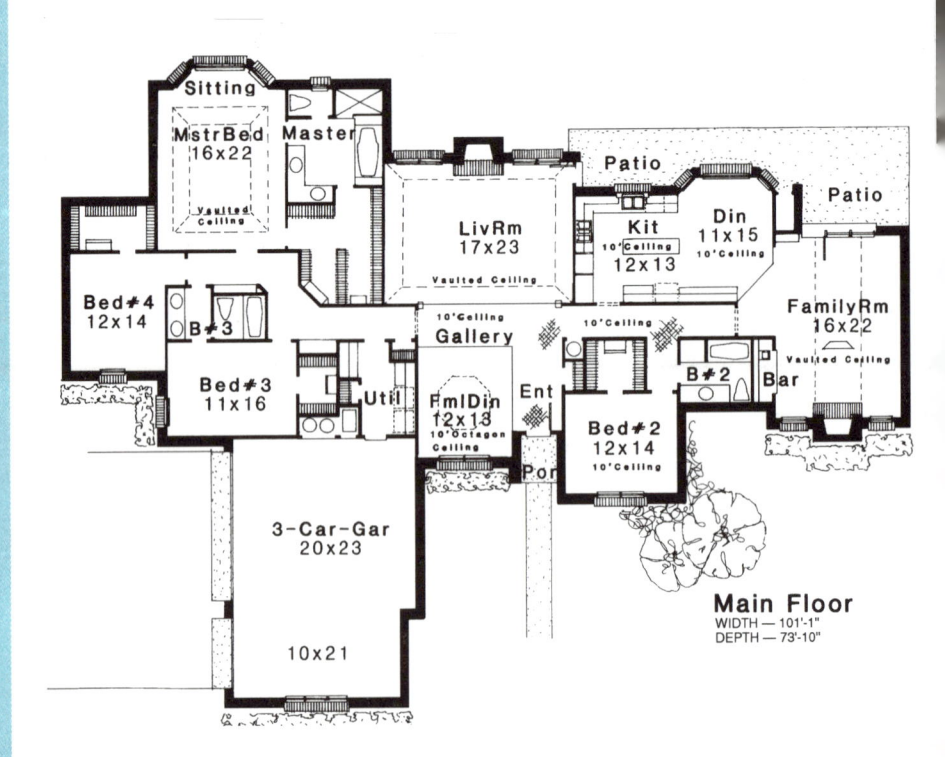

Main Floor
WIDTH — 101'-1"
DEPTH — 73'-10"

No materials list available

DESIGN NO. 93049

PRICE CODE D

DIGNIFIED TRADITIONAL

No. 93049

- This plan features:
— Four bedrooms
— Two full and one half baths
- Dramatic columns defining the elegant Dining Room and framing the entrance to the large, spacious Great Room
- A breakfast bar and work island in the gourmet Kitchen which also includes an abundance of counter and cabinet space
- A Master Suite with an enormous walk-in closet and a luxuriant Master Bath

MAIN FLOOR — 2,292 SQ. FT.
GARAGE — 526 SQ. FT.

TOTAL LIVING AREA: 2,292 SQ. FT.

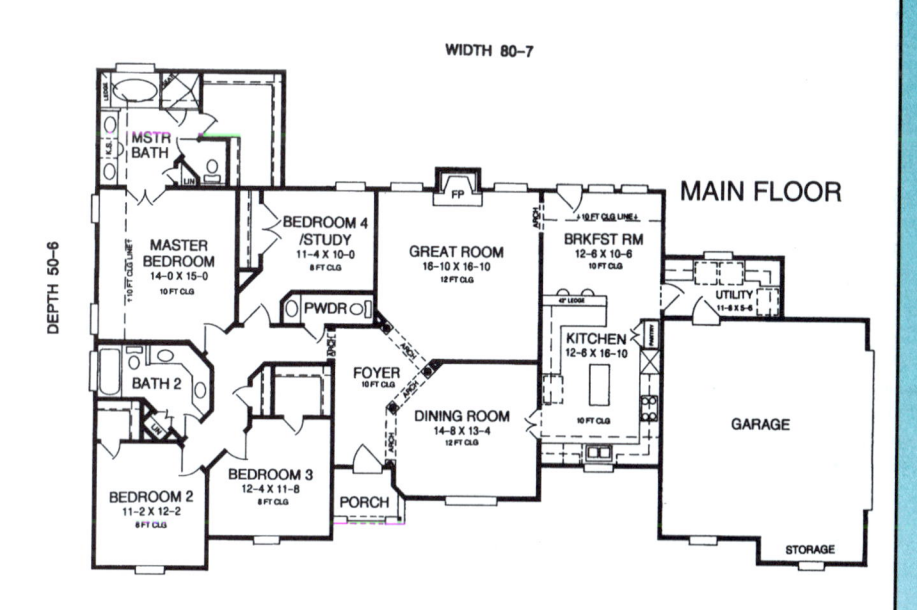

MAIN FLOOR

WIDTH 80-7
DEPTH 50-6

- MSTR BATH
- MASTER BEDROOM 14-0 X 15-0, 10 FT CLG
- BEDROOM 4 /STUDY 11-4 X 10-0, 8 FT CLG
- GREAT ROOM 16-10 X 16-10, 12 FT CLG
- BRKFST RM 12-6 X 10-6, 10 FT CLG
- UTILITY 11-6 X 5-6
- PWDR
- BATH 2
- FOYER 10 FT CLG
- KITCHEN 12-6 X 16-10
- BEDROOM 2 11-2 X 12-2, 8 FT CLG
- BEDROOM 3 12-4 X 11-8, 8 FT CLG
- PORCH
- DINING ROOM 14-8 X 13-4, 12 FT CLG
- GARAGE
- STORAGE

No materials list available

DESIGN NO. 92279

PRICE CODE E

Roomy and Rustic Fieldstone

No. 92279

■ This plan features:

— Four bedrooms

— Three full and one half baths

■ Cathedral Porch leads into easy-care Entry and formal Living Room with fieldstone fireplace

■ Hub Kitchen with curved peninsula serving counter convenient to Breakfast area, Covered Patio, Family Room, Utility/Garage entry and Dining Room

■ Corner Master Bedroom enhanced by vaulted ceiling, plush bath and a huge walk-in closet

■ Three additional bedrooms with walk-in closets and private access to a full bath

MAIN FLOOR — 3,079 SQ. FT.
GARAGE — 630 SQ. FT.

TOTAL LIVING AREA: 3,079 SQ. FT.

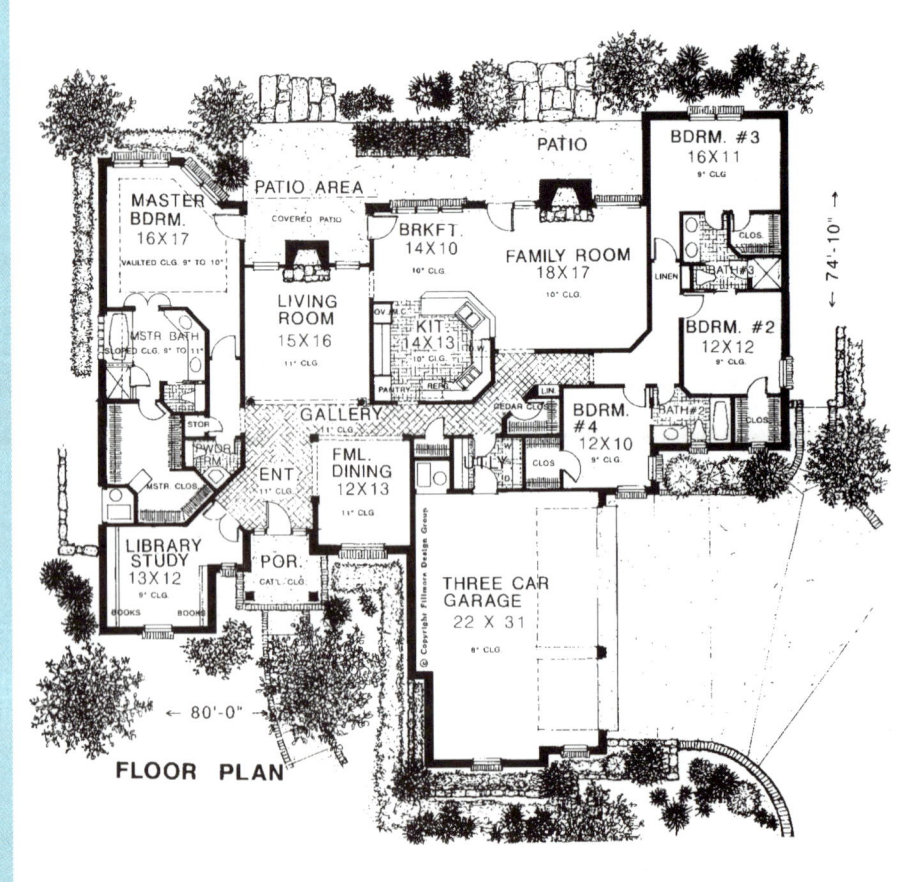

FLOOR PLAN

No materials list available

DESIGN NO. 92237

PRICE CODE F

OPULENT LUXURY

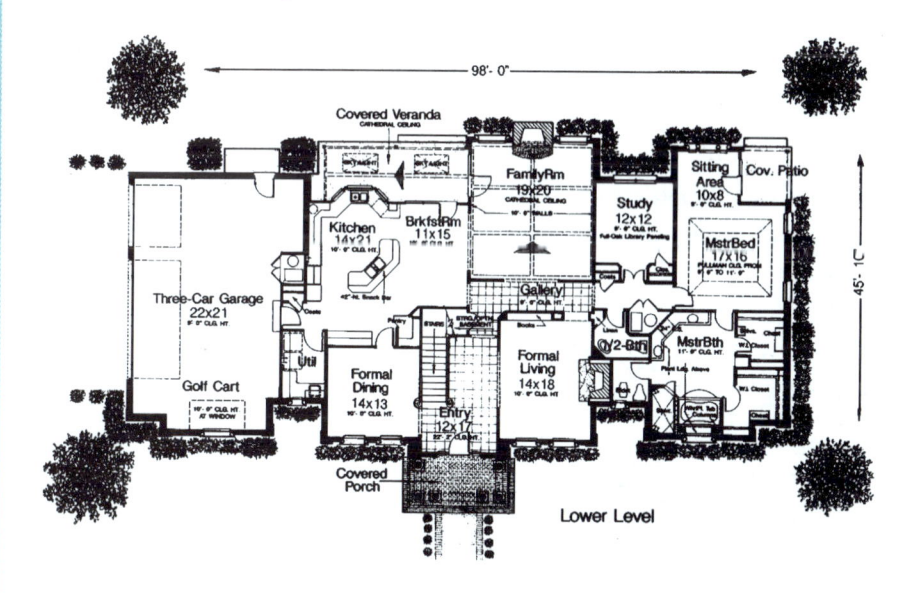

No. 92237

- This plan features:
— Four bedrooms
— Three full and one half baths
- Magnificent columns frame elegant two-story Entry with a graceful banister staircase
- A stone hearth fireplace and built-in book shelves enhance the Living Room
- Comfortable Family Room with a huge fireplace, cathedral ceiling and access to Covered Veranda
- Spacious Kitchen with cooktop island/snackbar, built-in pantry and Breakfast Room
- Lavish Master Bedroom wing with a pullman ceiling, sitting area, private Covered Patio and a huge bath with two walk-in closets and a whirlpool tub

LOWER LEVEL — 2,804 SQ. FT.
UPPER LEVEL — 979 SQ. FT.
BASEMENT — 2,804 SQ. FT.
GARAGE — 802 SQ. FT.

TOTAL LIVING AREA: 3,783 SQ. FT.

No materials list available

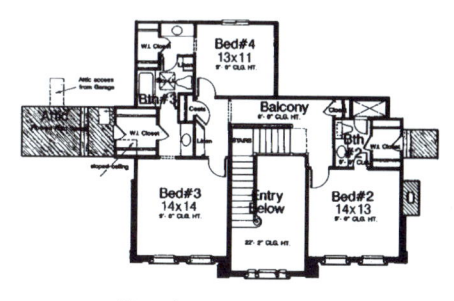

Lower Level

Upper Level

DESIGN NO. 92625

PRICE CODE B

FOR THE DISCRIMINATING BUYER

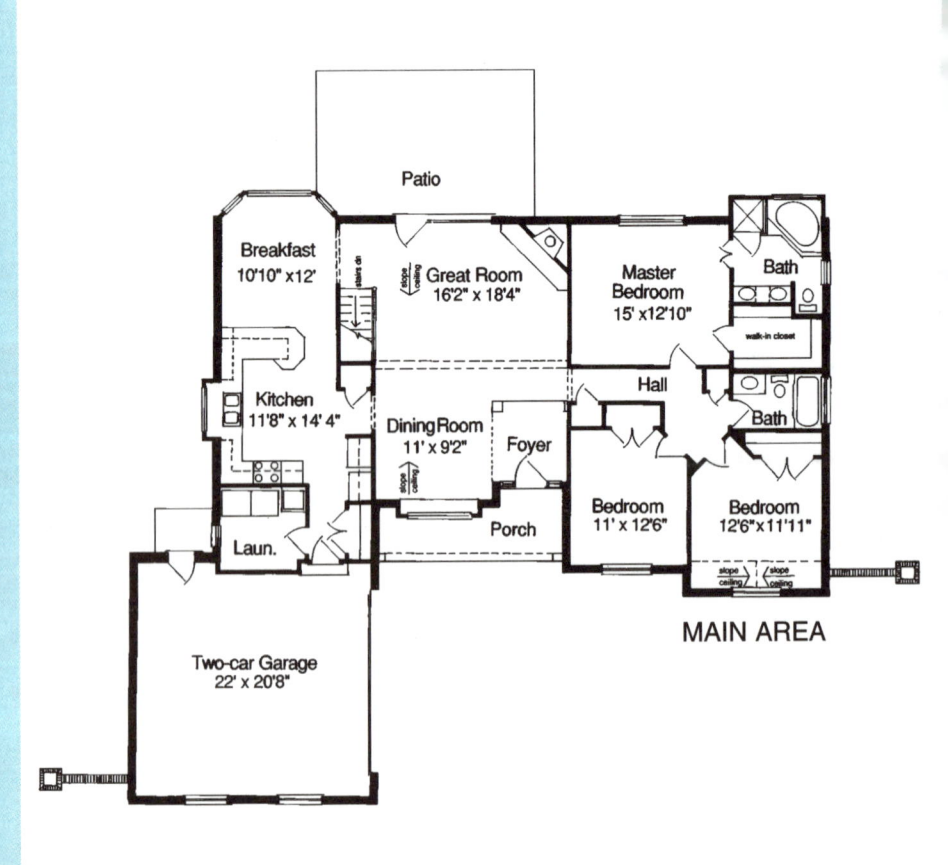

No. 92625

■ This plan features:

— Three bedrooms

— Two full baths

■ An attractive, classic brick design, with wood trim, multiple gables, and wing walls

■ A sheltered entrance into the Foyer

■ A sloped ceiling adding elegance to the formal Dining Room

■ A sloped ceiling and a corner fireplace enhancing the Great Room

■ A peninsula counter in the Kitchen and the Breakfast Room

■ A Master Suite equipped, with a large walk-in closet and a private bath with an oval corner tub, separate shower and double vanity

■ Two additional bedrooms

MAIN AREA — 1,710 SQ. FT.
BASEMENT — 1,560 SQ. FT.
GARAGE — 455 SQ. FT.
WIDTH — 65'-10"
DEPTH — 56'-0"

TOTAL LIVING AREA:
1,710 SQ. FT.

MAIN AREA

No materials list available

DESIGN NO. 92265

PRICE CODE F

LUXURIOUS MASTERPIECE

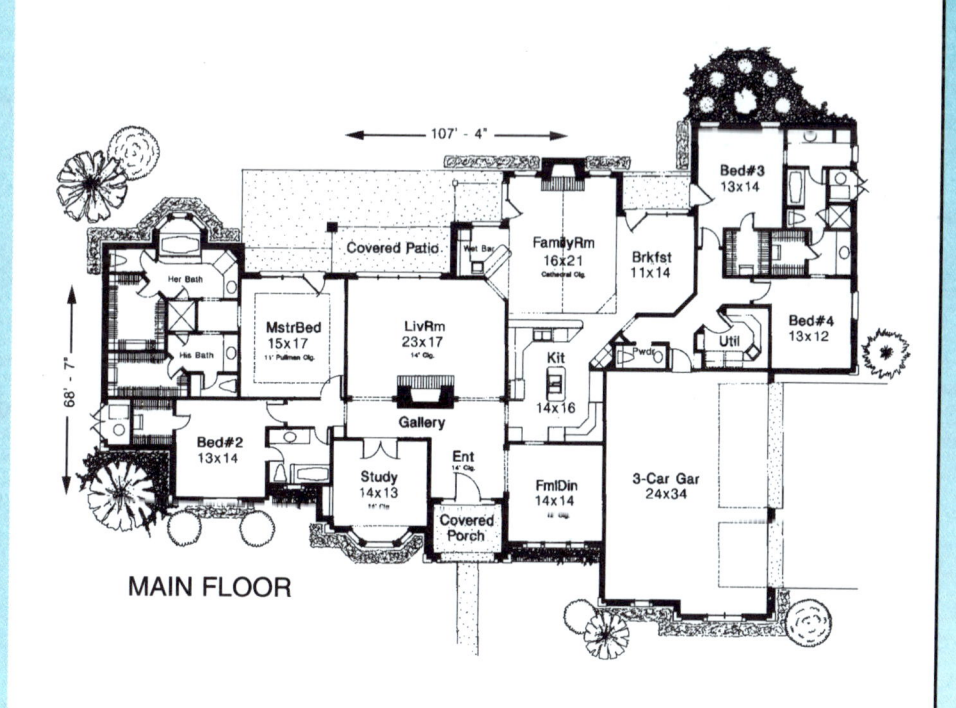

No. 92265

■ This plan features:

— Four bedrooms

— Three full, one three quarter and one half baths

■ An elegant and distinguished exterior

■ An expansive formal Living Room with a fourteen foot ceiling and a raised hearth fireplace

■ Informal Family Room offers another fireplace, wetbar, cathedral ceiling and access to the Covered Patio

■ A hub Kitchen with a cooktop island, peninsula counter/snack-bar, and a bright breakfast area

■ French doors lead into a quiet Study offering many uses

■ Private Master Bedroom enhanced by pullman ceiling and lavish his-n-her baths including walk-in closets and a garden window tub

MAIN FLOOR — 3,818 SQ. FT.
GARAGE — 816 SQ. FT.

TOTAL LIVING AREA: 3,818 SQ. FT.

MAIN FLOOR

No materials list available

DESIGN NO. 92536

PRICE CODE D

TRADITIONAL BRICK WITH DETAILING

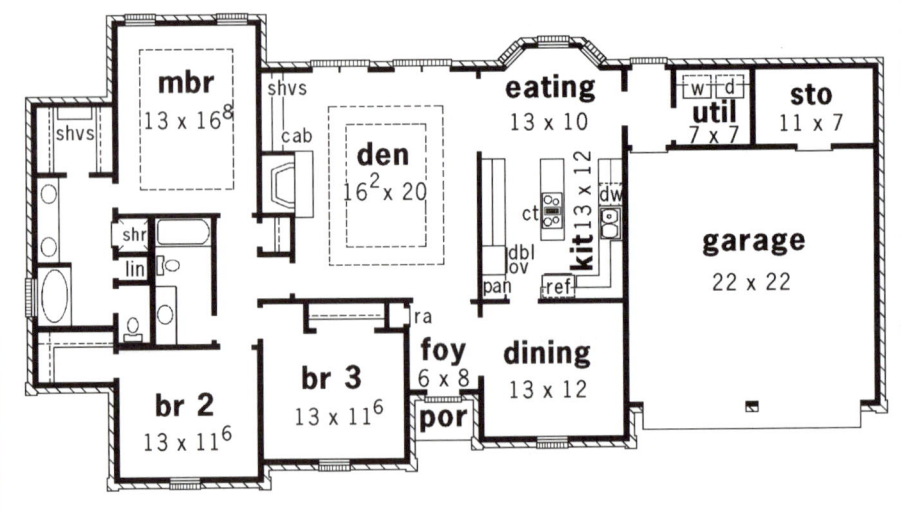

No. 92536

■ This plan features:

— Three bedrooms

— Two full baths

■ Covered entry leads into the Foyer, the formal Dining Room and the Den

■ Expansive Den with a decorative ceiling over a hearth fireplace and sliding glass doors to the rear yard

■ Country Kitchen with a built-in pantry, double ovens and a cooktop island easily serves the Breakfast area and Dining Room

■ Private Master Bedroom suite with a decorative ceiling, a walk-in closet, a double vanity and a whirlpool tub

■ This plan is available with a slab or crawl space foundation — please specify when ordering

MAIN AREA — 1,869 SQ. FT.
GARAGE — 561 SQ. FT.
WIDTH — 74' - 10"
DEPTH — 40' - 4"

TOTAL LIVING AREA:
1,869 SQ. FT.

MAIN AREA

DESIGN NO. 90450

PRICE CODE D

ELEGANT BRICK TWO-STORY

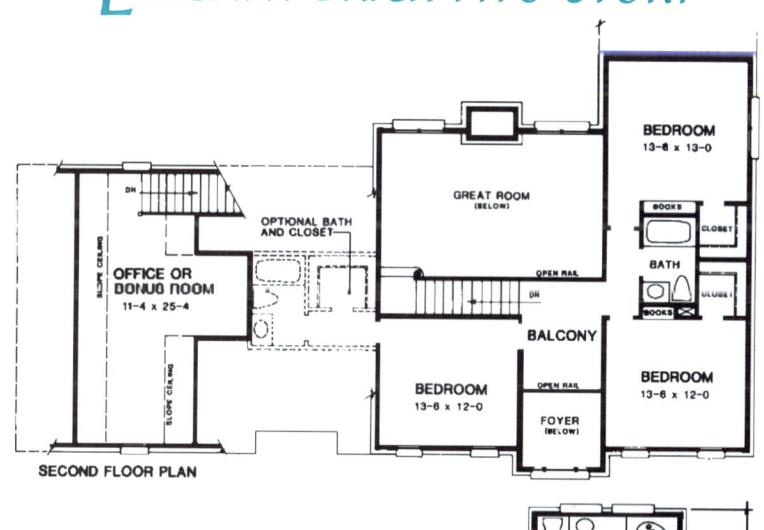

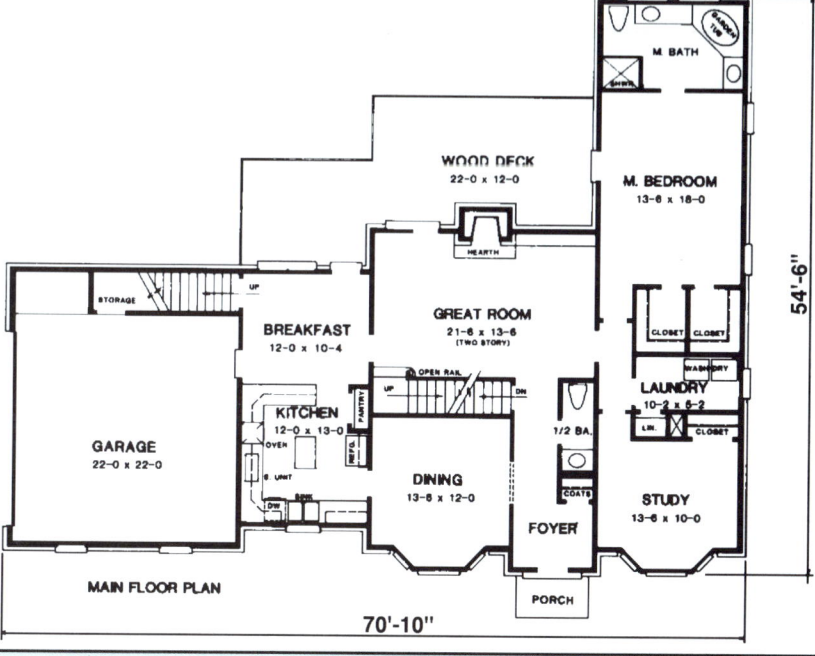

No. 90450

■ This plan features:

— Four bedrooms

— Two or three full and one half baths

■ A large two-story Great Room with a fireplace and access to a wood deck

■ A secluded Master Suite with two walk-in closets and a private, lavish, Master Bath

■ A large island Kitchen serving the formal Dining Room and the sunny Breakfast Nook with ease

■ Three additional bedrooms, two with walk-in closets, sharing a full hall bath

■ An optional Bonus Room with a private entrance from below

■ An optional basement or crawl space foundation — please specify when ordering

FIRST FLOOR — 1,637 SQ. FT.
SECOND FLOOR — 761 SQ. FT.
OPT. BATH & CLOSET — 106 SQ. FT.
OPT. BONUS — 347 SQ. FT.

TOTAL LIVING AREA: 2,398 SQ. FT.

DESIGN NO. 92702

PRICE CODE A

VICTORIAN ACCENTS ENHANCE APPEAL

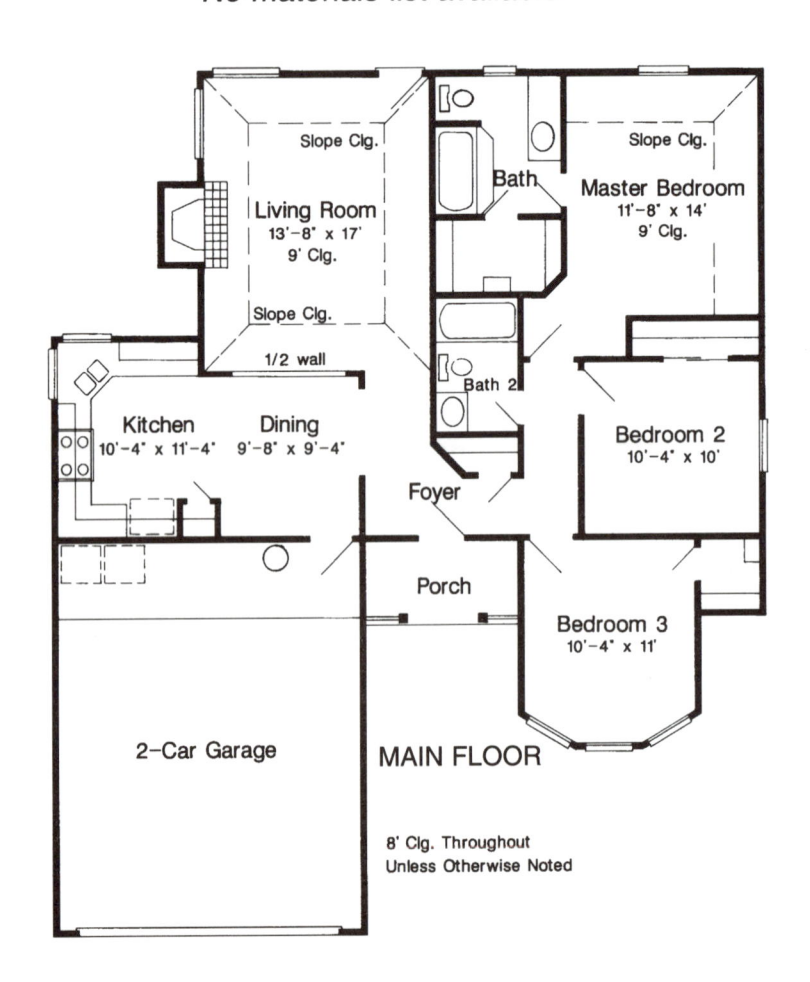

No materials list available

No. 92702

■ This plan features:

— Three bedrooms

— Two full baths

■ Entry Porch into the Foyer leads to the Dining area and the Living Room

■ A corner window and a hearth fireplace topped by a sloped ceiling highlight the Living Room with access to the rear yard

■ Efficient, U-shaped Kitchen with a wonderful corner window, a built-in pantry and a Dining area

■ Private Master Bedroom suite with a sloped ceiling, a walk-in closet and a private bath with a raised tub

■ This plan is available with a Slab foundation only

MAIN FLOOR — 1,198 SQ. FT.
GARAGE — 431 SQ. FT.
WIDTH — 43'-4"
DEPTH — 50'-0"

TOTAL LIVING AREA: 1,198 SQ. FT.

MAIN FLOOR

8' Clg. Throughout Unless Otherwise Noted

DESIGN NO. 92503

PRICE CODE B

CHARMING SOUTHERN TRADITIONAL

No. 92503

■ This plan features:

— Three bedrooms

— Two full baths

■ A covered front Porch with striking columns, brick quoins, and dental molding

■ A spacious Great Room with vaulted ceilings, a fireplace, and built-in cabinets

■ A Utility Room adjacent to the Kitchen, which leads to the two-car Garage and Storage Rooms

■ A Master Bedroom including a large walk-in closet and a compartmentalized bath

■ An optional crawl space or slab foundation — please specify when ordering

MAIN AREA — 1,271 SQ. FT.
GARAGE — 506 SQ. FT.

TOTAL LIVING AREA: 1,271 SQ. FT.

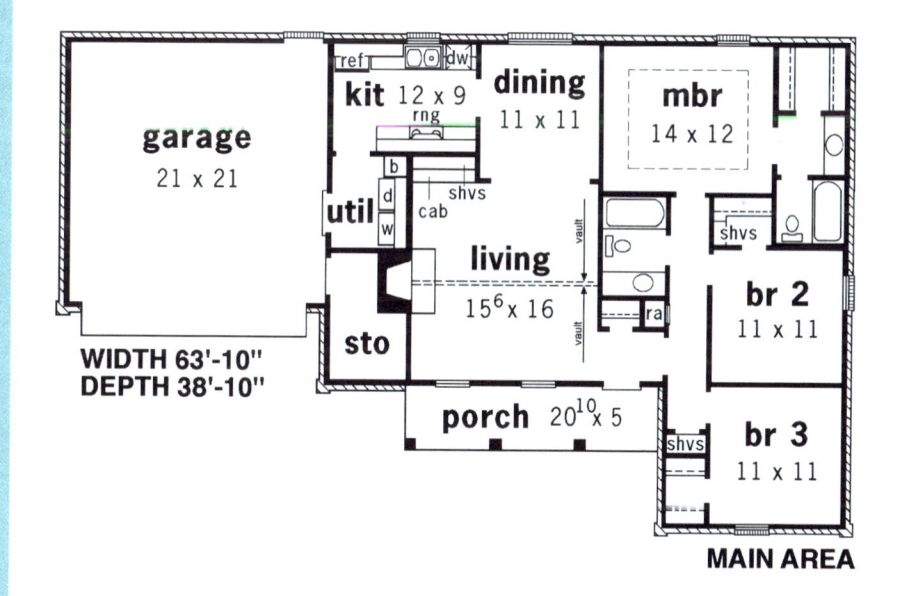

WIDTH 63'-10"
DEPTH 38'-10"

MAIN AREA

DESIGN NO. 90436

PRICE CODE C

Country living in any neighborhood

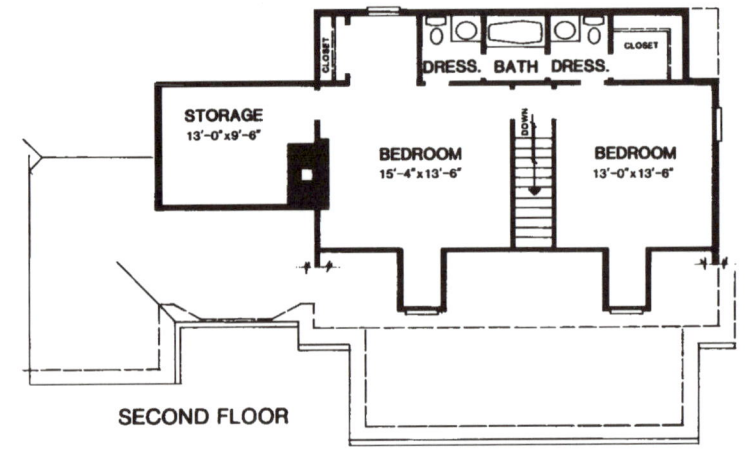

No. 90436

- This plan features:
— Three bedrooms
— Two full and two half baths
- An expansive Family Room with fireplace
- A Dining Room and Breakfast Nook lit by flowing natural light from bay windows
- A first floor Master Suite with a double vanity bath that wraps around his-n-her closets
- An optional basement, slab or crawl space foundation — please specify when ordering

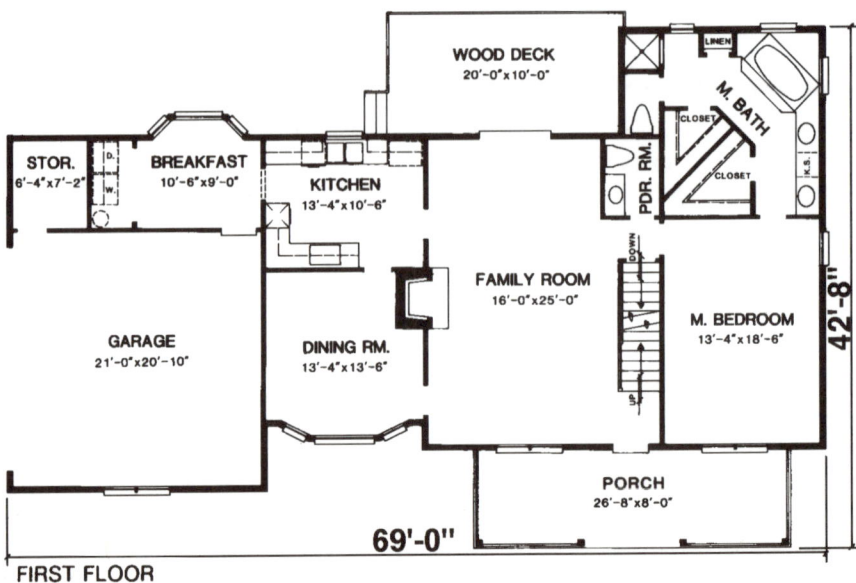

First floor — 1,477 sq. ft.
Second floor — 704 sq. ft.
Basement — 1,374 sq. ft.

Total living area: 2,181 sq. ft.

DESIGN NO. 90444

PRICE CODE D

TRADITONAL RANCH HAS MANY MODERN FEATURES

No. 90444
- This plan features:
— Three bedrooms
— Three full baths
- A vaulted-ceiling Great Room with skylights and a fireplace
- A double L-shaped Kitchen with an eating bar opening to a bayed Breakfast Room
- A Master Suite with a walk-in closet, corner garden tub, separate vanities and a linen closet
- Two additional bedrooms each with a walk-in closet and built-in desk, sharing a full hall bath
- A loft that overlooks the Great Room, which includes a vaulted ceiling and open rail balcony
- An optional basement or crawl space foundation — please specify when ordering

MAIN FLOOR — 1,996 SQ. FT.
LOFT — 305 SQ. FT.

TOTAL LIVING AREA: 2,301 SQ. FT.

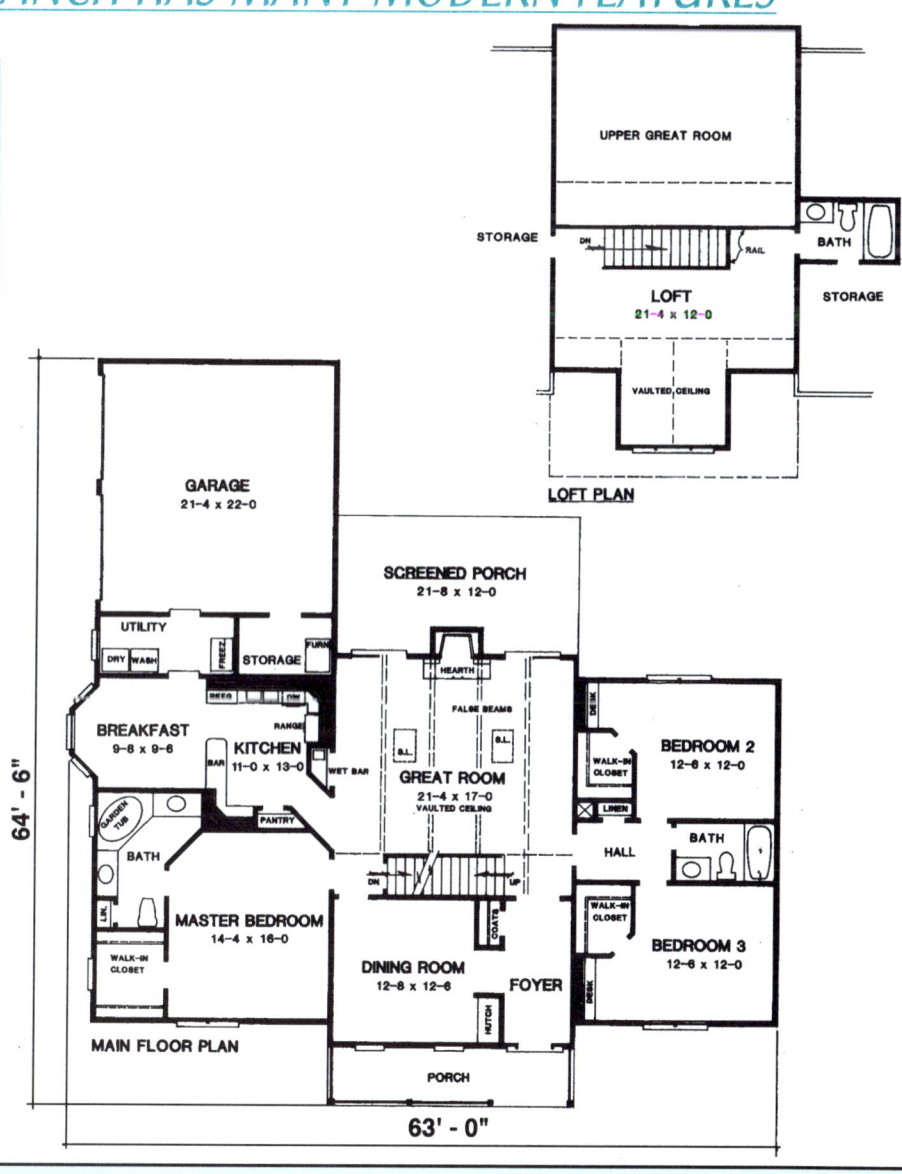

DESIGN NO. 94237

PRICE CODE F

ATTRACTIVE TURRETS AND GLASS

No. 94237

■ This plan features:

— Four or five bedrooms

— Five full and one half bath

■ Split Entry highlighted by a three-story glassed staircase

■ Two-story Grand Room separated from Dining Room by 3-sided fireplace and wet bar

■ Open Kitchen with cooktop island, eating Nook and access to Screened Verandah

■ Two first floor bedrooms and Study with bay window and private access to a full bath

■ Master Suite with a two sided fireplace, Deck access and his and hers baths and closets

■ Guest bedroom suite offers a private bath and deck access

■ Garage, Bonus/Storage space and Lanai below main living areas

MAIN FLOOR — 2,725 SQ. FT.
SECOND FLOOR — 1,418 SQ. FT.
GARAGE — 812 SQ. FT.

TOTAL LIVING AREA: 4,143 SQ. FT.

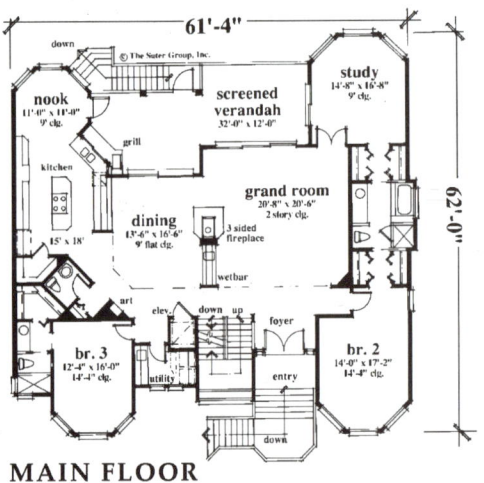

MAIN FLOOR

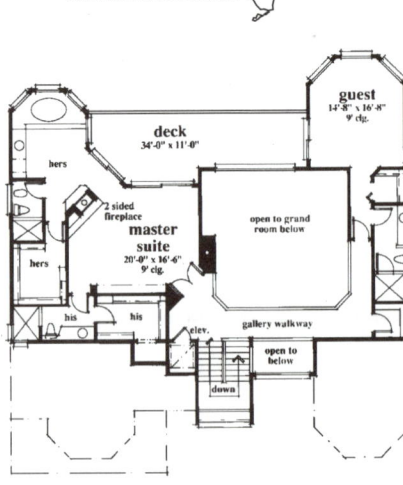

SECOND FLOOR

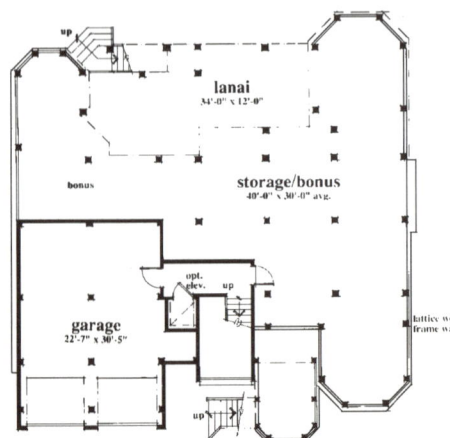

LOWER FLOOR

HIGH WIND LOAD ENGINEERING AVAILABLE
SEE PAGE 246 FOR DETAILS

DESIGN NO. 93311

PRICE CODE C

CONVENIENT AND EFFICIENT RANCH

No. 93311

- This plan features:
  — Three bedrooms
  — Two full and one half baths
- A barrel vault ceiling in the Foyer
- A stepped ceiling in both the Dinette and the formal Dining Room
- An expansive Gathering Room with a large focal point fireplace and access to the wood deck
- An efficient Kitchen that includes a work island and a built-in pantry
- A luxurious Master Suite with a private bath that includes a separate tub and step-in shower
- Two additional bedrooms that share a full hall bath

FIRST FLOOR — 1,810 SQ. FT.
GARAGE — 528 SQ. FT.

TOTAL LIVING AREA: 1,810 SQ. FT.

An EXCLUSIVE DESIGN
By Patrick Morabito, A.I.A. Architect

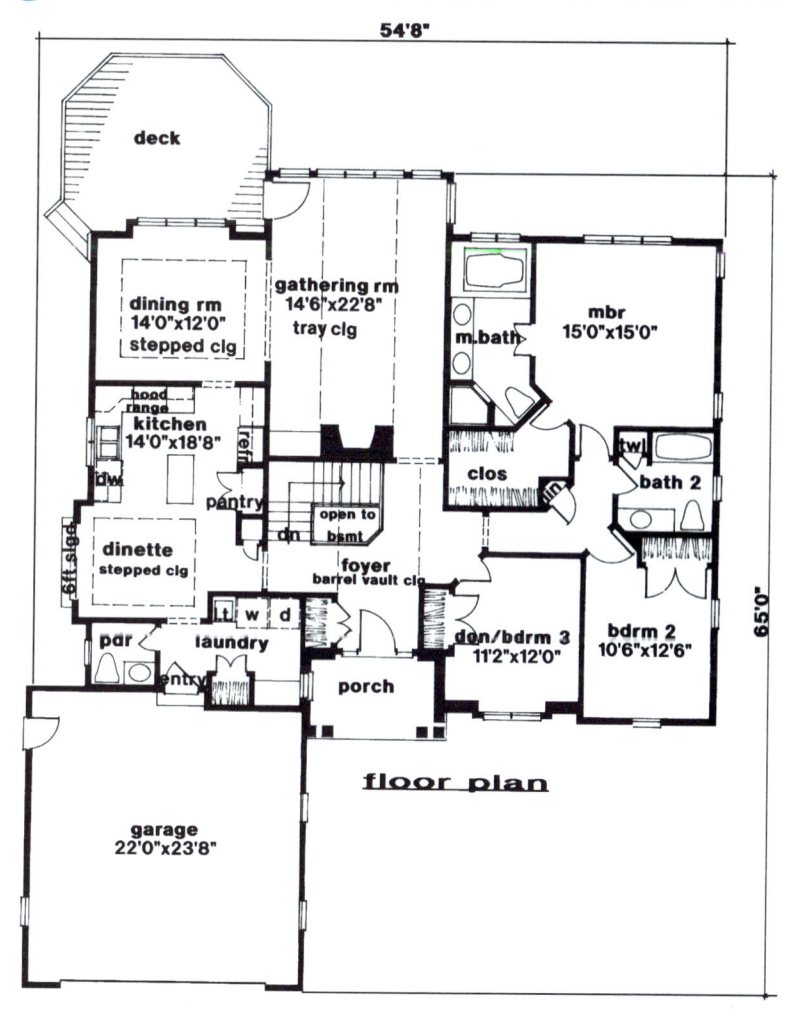

No materials list available

DESIGN NO. 93216

PRICE CODE C

TOUCH OF CLASS

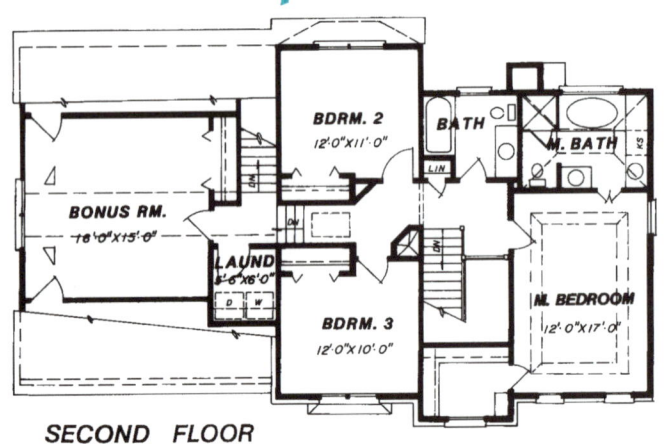

No. 93216

- This plan features:
- Three bedrooms
- Two full and one half baths
- Family Room with fireplace
- A bright Breakfast Room with direct access to the Sun Deck
- Kitchen equipped with a peninsula counter/eating bar and a built-in pantry
- A Master Suite with a decorative ceiling and a private Bath equipped with an oval tub, separate shower and two vanities
- Two roomy additional bedrooms that share a full hall bath
- A Bonus Room for future expansion
- An optional basement, crawl space or slab foundation — please specify when ordering

FIRST FLOOR — 986 SQ. FT.
SECOND FLOOR — 932 SQ. FT.
BONUS ROOM — 274 SQ. FT.
BASEMENT — 882 SQ. FT.
GARAGE — 532 SQ. FT.

TOTAL LIVING AREA: 1,918 SQ. FT.

An **EXCLUSIVE DESIGN** By *Jannis Vann & Associates, Inc.*

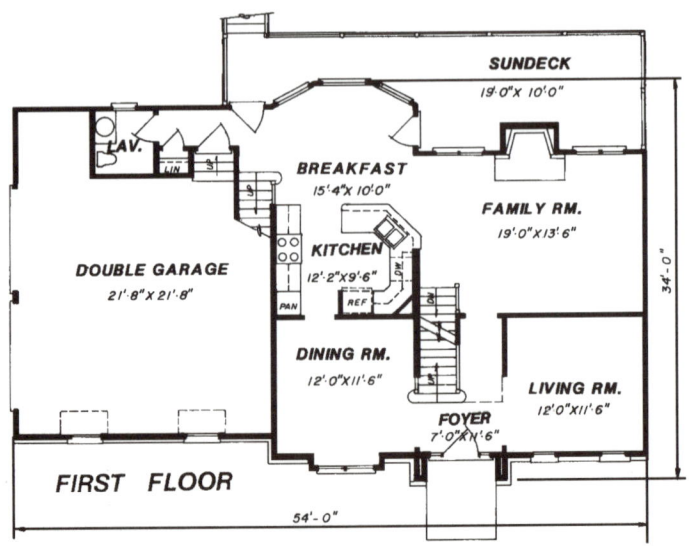

DESIGN NO. 94240

PRICE CODE B

Three bedroom stucco

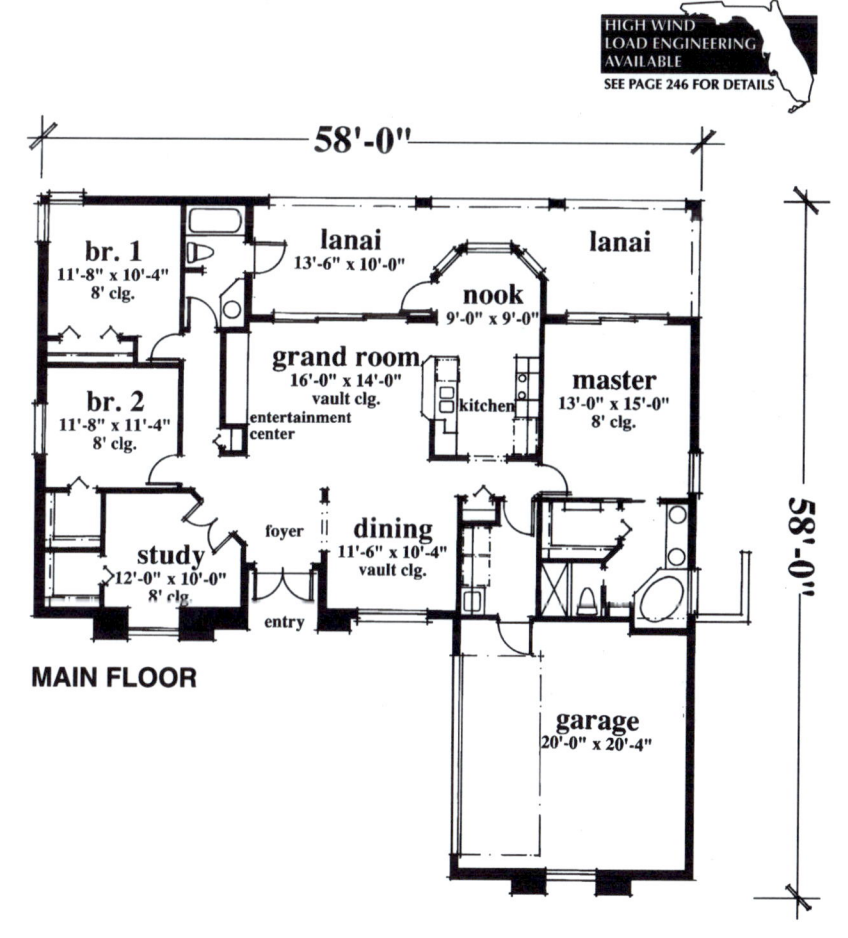

No. 94240

- This plan features:
- — Three bedrooms
- — Two full baths
- Fits easily on narrow depth lots
- Grand Room layout has vaulted ceiling that includes the Foyer and Dining Room
- Grand Room is highlighted by a built-in entertainment center and access to Lanai
- Compact Kitchen opens to glass Nook and formal Dining area
- Private Master suite has glass doors to the Lanai area and a plush bath
- Two bedrooms and a study or third bedroom located on the opposite side have ample closet space
- Guest bath has outdoor access for the pool area

Main floor — 1,647 sq. ft.
Garage — 427 sq. ft.

Total living area: 1,647 sq.ft.

HIGH WIND LOAD ENGINEERING AVAILABLE
SEE PAGE 246 FOR DETAILS

58'-0" x 58'-0"

br. 1 — 11'-8" x 10'-4" 8' clg.
lanai — 13'-6" x 10'-0"
lanai
nook — 9'-0" x 9'-0"
grand room — 16'-0" x 14'-0" vault clg.
master — 13'-0" x 15'-0" 8' clg.
br. 2 — 11'-8" x 11'-4" 8' clg.
entertainment center
kitchen
study — 12'-0" x 10'-0" 8' clg.
foyer
dining — 11'-6" x 10'-4" vault clg.
entry
garage — 20'-0" x 20'-4"

MAIN FLOOR

No materials list available

DESIGN NO. 93269

PRICE CODE B

Cozy Front Porch

No. 93269

- This plan features:
- — Three bedrooms
- — Two full and one half bath
- A Living Room enhanced by a large fireplace
- A formal Dining Room that is open to the Living Room
- An efficient Kitchen with ample counter and cabinet space, double sinks and a pass-thru window
- A Breakfast Area with vaulted ceiling and a door to the sun deck
- A first floor Master Suite with a separate tub and shower stall and walk-in closet
- A first floor powder room with a hide-away laundry center
- Two additional bedrooms that share a full hall bath

FIRST FLOOR — 1,045 SQ. FT.
SECOND FLOOR — 690 SQ. FT.
BASEMENT — 465 SQ. FT.
GARAGE — 580 SQ. FT.

TOTAL LIVING AREA: 1,735 SQ. FT.

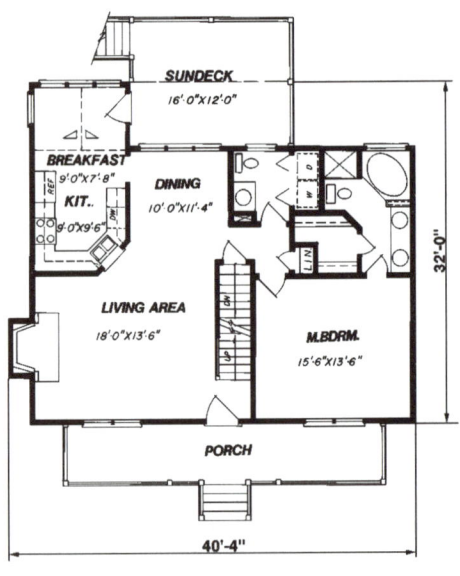

FIRST FLOOR

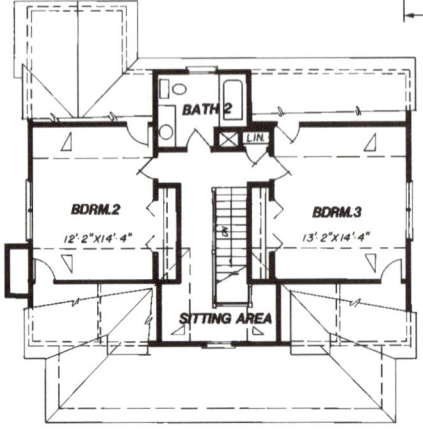

SECOND FLOOR

An EXCLUSIVE DESIGN
By Jannis Vann & Associates, Inc.

DESIGN NO. 92288

PRICE CODE F

DISTINCTIVE AND ELEGANT DETAILS

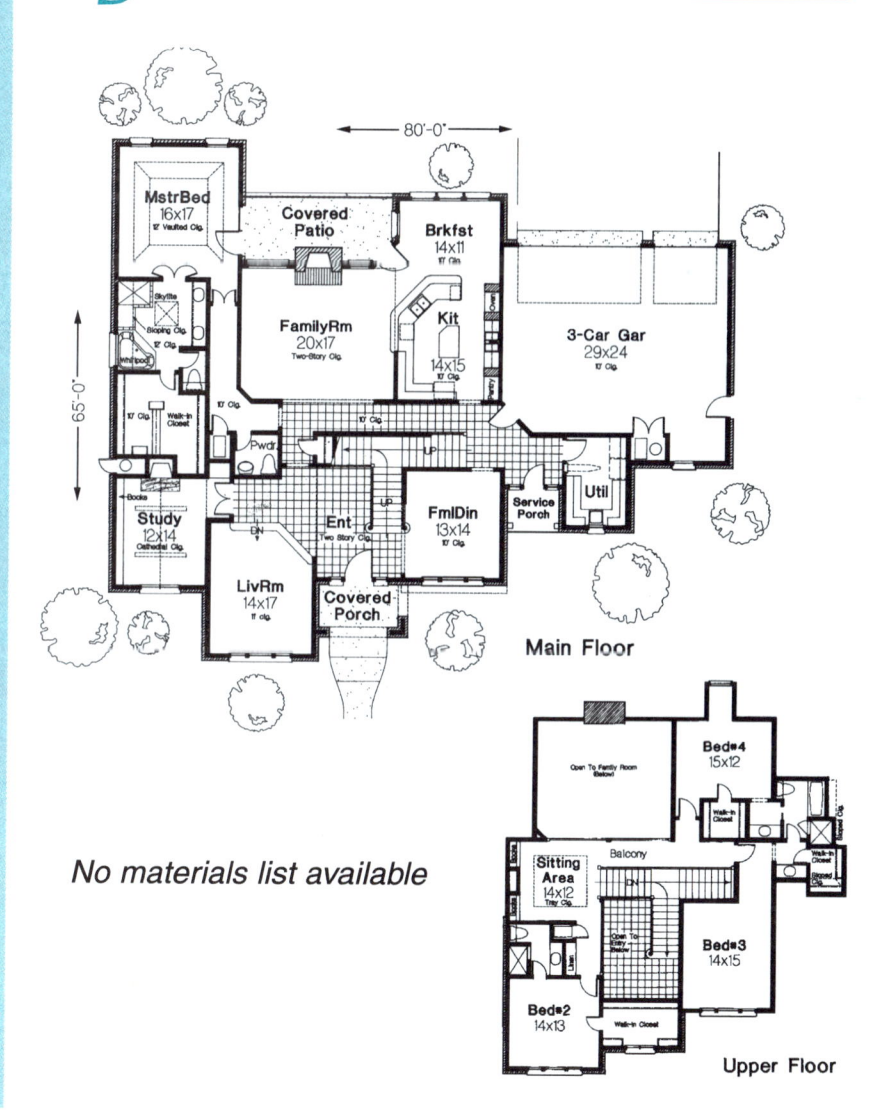

No. 92288

■ This plan features:

— Four bedrooms

— Two full, one three quarter and one half baths

■ Exterior accented by keystone arches, decorative windows and multiple roof lines

■ Two-story Entry dominated by a cascading staircase

■ Formal Living Room highlighted by decorative windows

■ Double door entry into Study with fireplace, built-in shelves and a cathedral ceiling

■ Expansive two-story Family Room with a focal point fireplace opens to Kitchen, Covered Patio and Breakfast area

■ French doors, vaulted ceiling, a huge walk-in closet and lavish bath enhance Master Bedroom suite

MAIN FLOOR — 2,736 SQ. FT.
UPPER FLOOR — 1,276 SQ. FT.
GARAGE — 696 SQ. FT.

TOTAL LIVING AREA: 4,012 SQ. FT.

No materials list available

Main Floor

Upper Floor

DESIGN NO. 94238

PRICE CODE D

SUITABLE FOR NARROW LOT

No. 94238

- This plan features:
— Three bedrooms
— Three full baths
- Portico with bench and gardens leads into Entry and open Foyer
- Spacious Great Room with twelve foot ceiling, adjoining circular Dining Room and Lanai
- Double door entry into Study with tray ceiling and built-ins
- Efficient Kitchen with cooktop island and serving counter
- Corner Master Suite with a stepped ceiling, large walk-in closet and luxurious bath
- Two additional bedrooms with private access to a double vanity bath

MAIN FLOOR — 2,387 SQ. FT.
GARAGE — 527 SQ. FT.

TOTAL LIVING AREA: 2,387 SQ. FT.

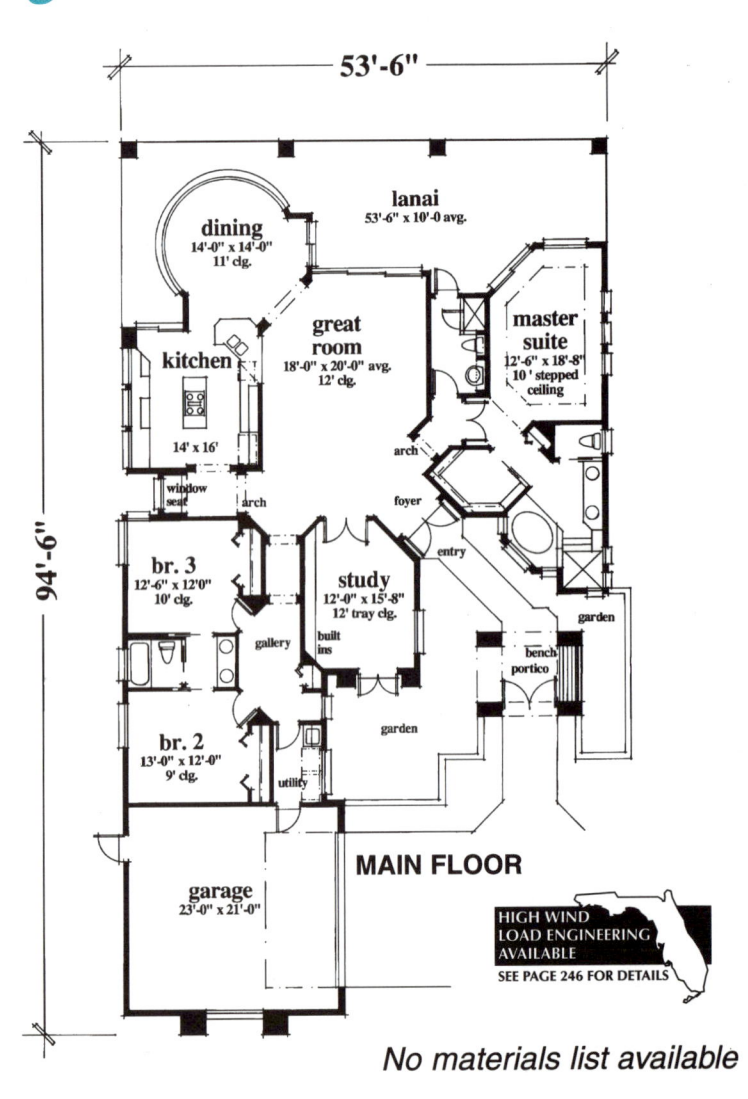

MAIN FLOOR

53'-6" x 94'-6"

- lanai 53'-6" x 10'-0 avg.
- dining 14'-0" x 14'-0" 11' clg.
- great room 18'-0" x 20'-0" avg. 12' clg.
- kitchen 14' x 16'
- master suite 12'-6" x 18'-8" 10' stepped ceiling
- br. 3 12'-6" x 12'-0" 10' clg.
- study 12'-0" x 15'-8" 12' tray clg.
- br. 2 13'-0" x 12'-0" 9' clg.
- garage 23'-0" x 21'-0"

HIGH WIND LOAD ENGINEERING AVAILABLE
SEE PAGE 246 FOR DETAILS

No materials list available

DESIGN NO. 93222

PRICE CODE A

FOR AN ESTABLISHED NEIGHBORHOOD

No. 93222

■ This plan features:

— Three bedrooms

— Two full baths

■ A covered entrance sheltering and welcoming visitors

■ An expansive Living Room enhanced by natural light streaming in from the large front window

■ A bayed formal Dining Room with direct access to the Sun Deck and the Living Room for entertainment ease

■ An efficient, galley Kitchen equipped with a double sink

■ An informal Breakfast Room

■ A large Master Suite equipped with a walk-in closet and a full private Bath

■ Two additional bedrooms that share a full hall bath

MAIN AREA — 1,276 SQ. FT.
FINISHED STAIRCASE — 16 SQ. FT.
BASEMENT — 392 SQ. FT.
GARAGE — 728 SQ. FT.

TOTAL LIVING AREA: 1,292 SQ. FT.

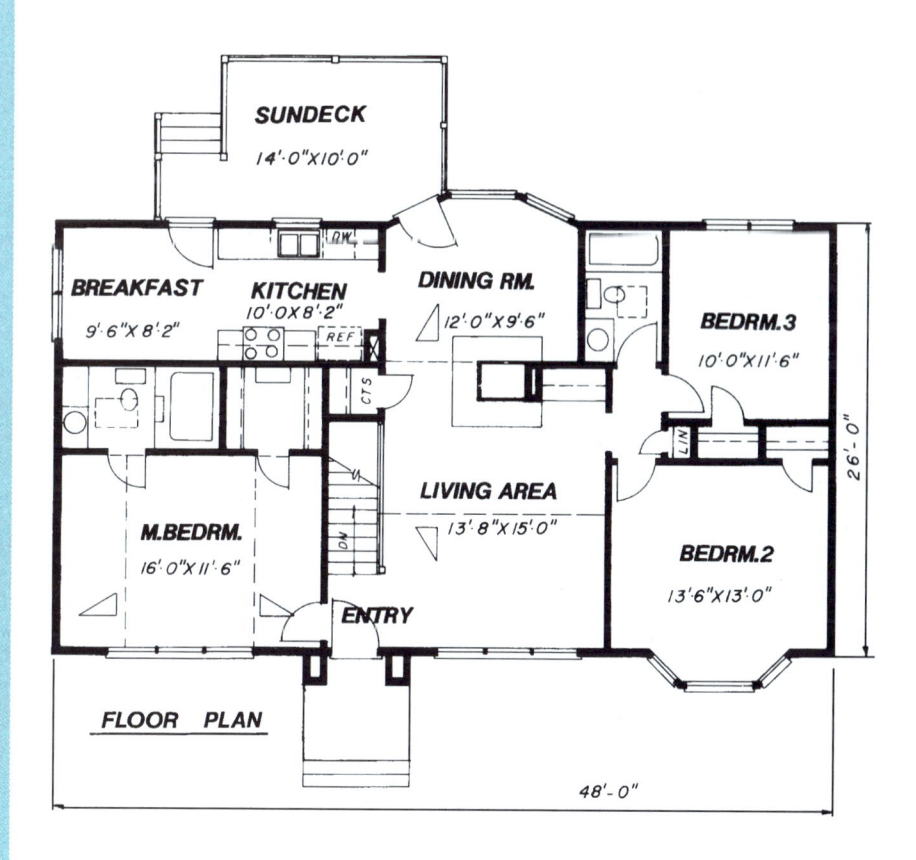

FLOOR PLAN

- SUNDECK 14'-0" X 10'-0"
- BREAKFAST 9'6" X 8'2"
- KITCHEN 10'0" X 8'2"
- DINING RM. 12'0" X 9'6"
- BEDRM. 3 10'0" X 11'6"
- M.BEDRM. 16'0" X 11'6"
- LIVING AREA 13'8" X 15'0"
- BEDRM. 2 13'6" X 13'0"
- ENTRY
- 48'-0"
- 26'-0"

An EXCLUSIVE DESIGN
By Jannis Vann & Associates, Inc.

DESIGN NO. 92404

PRICE CODE D

Traditional Ranch

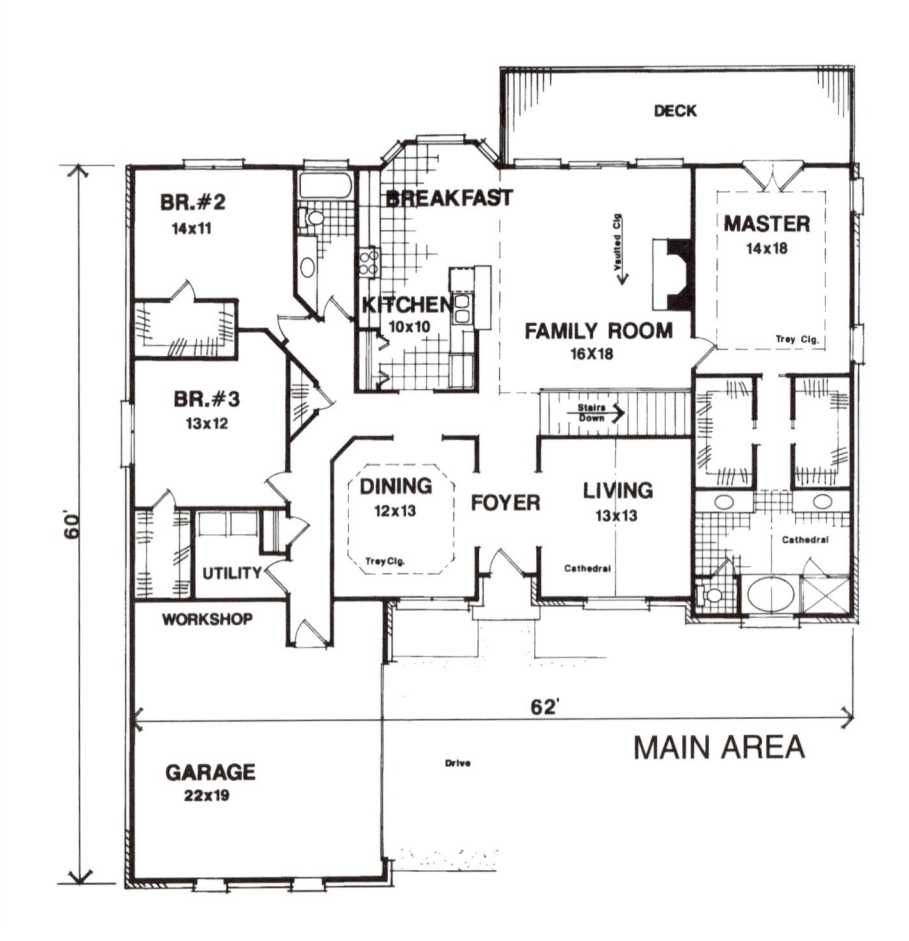

No. 92404

■ This plan features:

— Three bedrooms

— Two full baths

■ A tray ceiling in the Master Suite that is equipped with his-n-her walk-in closets and a private Master Bath with a cathedral ceiling

■ A formal Living Room with a cathedral ceiling

■ A decorative tray ceiling in the elegant formal Dining Room

■ A spacious Family Room with a vaulted ceiling and a fireplace

■ A modern, well-appointed Kitchen with snack bar and bayed Breakfast area

■ Two additional bedrooms that share a full hall bath each having a walk-in closet

Main area — 2,275 sq. ft.
Basement — 2,207 sq. ft.
Garage — 512 sq. ft.

Total living area: 2,275 sq. ft.

DESIGN NO. 94808

PRICE CODE F

COUNTRY VICTORIAN

No. 94808

- This plan features:
— Four bedrooms
— Three full baths
- Twin gable roofs over the wide porch embellished by Victorian details
- Central Foyer opens to Living and Dining rooms for ease in entertaining
- Country Kitchen/Breakfast Room opens to Sun Deck, Family Room, Laundry and Garage entry
- Tray ceilings crown Master Bedroom and Bath with a large walk-in closet and a whirlpool tub

FIRST FLOOR — 1,689 SQ. FT.
SECOND FLOOR — 1,120 SQ. FT.
BASEMENT — 1,130 SQ. FT.
GARAGE — 540 SQ. FT.

TOTAL LIVING AREA: 2,809 SQ. FT.

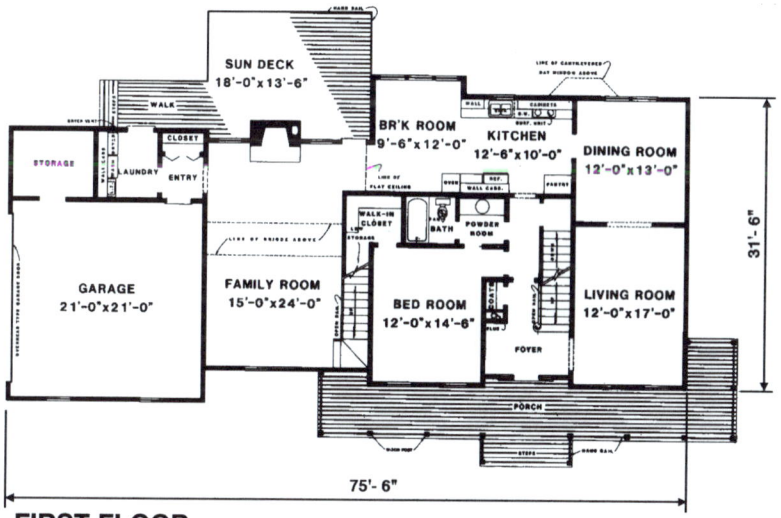

FIRST FLOOR

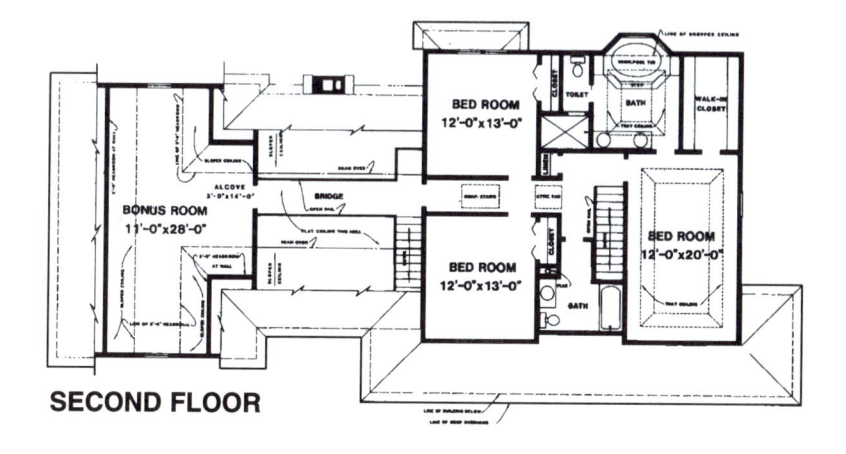

SECOND FLOOR

DESIGN NO. 94215

PRICE CODE D

MEDITERRANEAN EXTERIOR

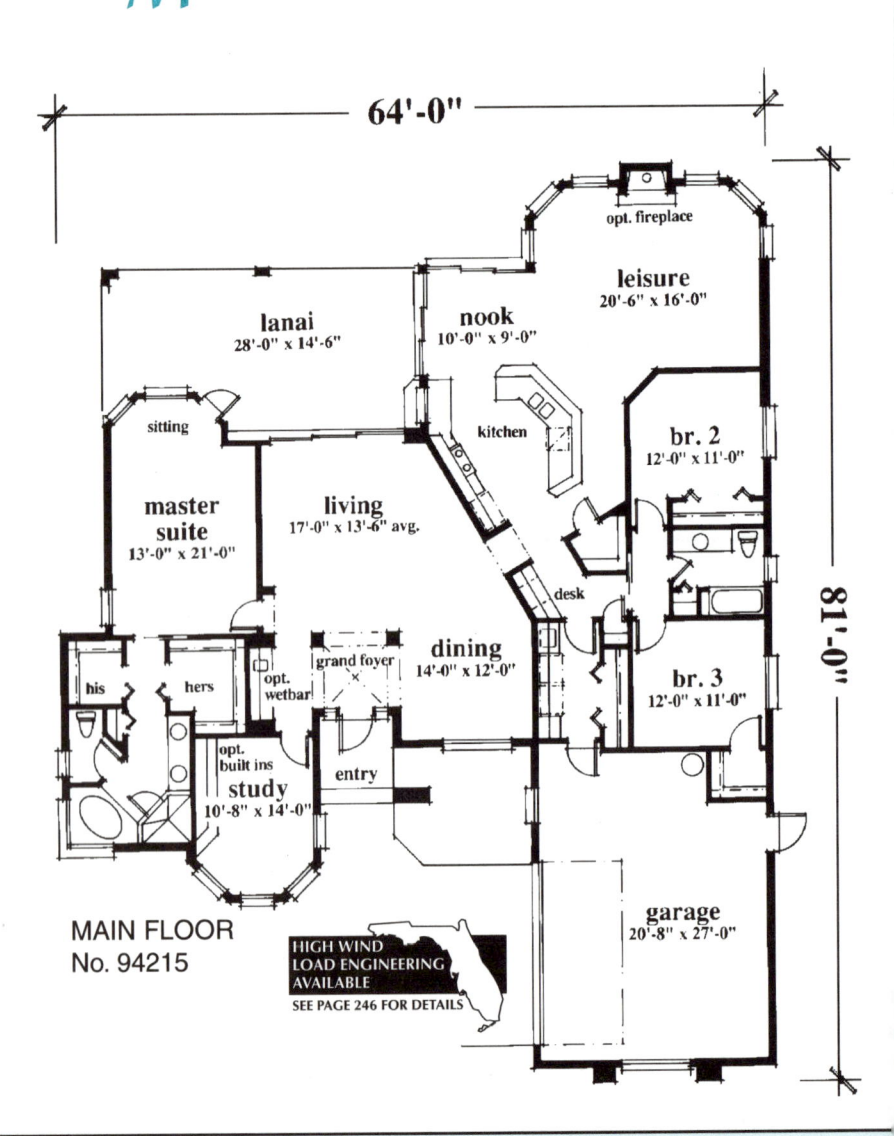

- **This plan features:**
- — Three bedrooms
- — Two full baths
- **A grand Foyer with columns greets you upon entering
- **The Living room and Dining room are open to each other
- **The Master suite has a bayed sitting area that opens out to the lanai
- **The efficient Kitchen is located next to the nook for informal meals
- **The large Leisure room has numerous windows and a fireplace
- **Two secondary bedrooms and a bath are secluded from the main living space
- **Past the wetbar is the study with built in cabinets
- **No materials list is available for this plan

MAIN FLOOR — 2589 SQ. FT.
GARAGE — 583 SQ. FT.

TOTAL LIVING AREA — 2,589 SQ. FT.

MAIN FLOOR
No. 94215

Overall: 64'-0" x 81'-0"

Rooms:
- lanai 28'-0" x 14'-6"
- nook 10'-0" x 9'-0"
- leisure 20'-6" x 16'-0" (opt. fireplace)
- master suite 13'-0" x 21'-0" (sitting)
- living 17'-0" x 13'-6" avg.
- kitchen
- br. 2 12'-0" x 11'-0"
- dining 14'-0" x 12'-0"
- br. 3 12'-0" x 11'-0"
- study 10'-8" x 14'-0"
- grand foyer / entry / opt. wetbar / opt. built ins / his / hers / desk
- garage 20'-8" x 27'-0"

HIGH WIND LOAD ENGINEERING AVAILABLE
SEE PAGE 246 FOR DETAILS

DESIGN NO. 93219

PRICE CODE B

OLD-FASHIONED COUNTRY PORCH

No. 93219

- This plan features:
— Three bedrooms
— Two full and one half baths
- A Traditional front Porch, with matching dormers above and a garage hidden below, leading into a open, contemporary layout
- A Living Area with a cozy fireplace visible from the Dining Room for warm entertaining
- A U-shaped, efficient Kitchen featuring a corner, double sink and pass-thru to the Dining Room
- A convenient half bath with a laundry center on the first floor
- A spacious, first floor Master Suite with a lavish Bath including a double vanity, walk-in closet and an oval, corner window tub
- Two large bedrooms with dormer windows

FIRST FLOOR — 1,057 SQ. FT.
SECOND FLOOR — 611 SQ. FT.
BASEMENT — 511 SQ. FT.
GARAGE — 546 SQ. FT.

TOTAL LIVING AREA: 1,668 SQ. FT.

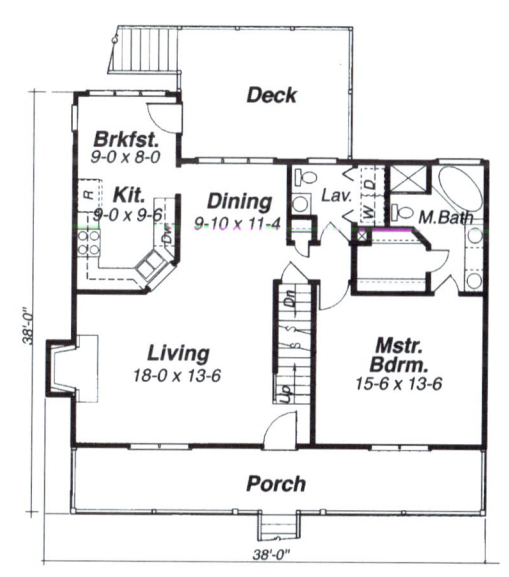

FIRST FLOOR

SECOND FLOOR

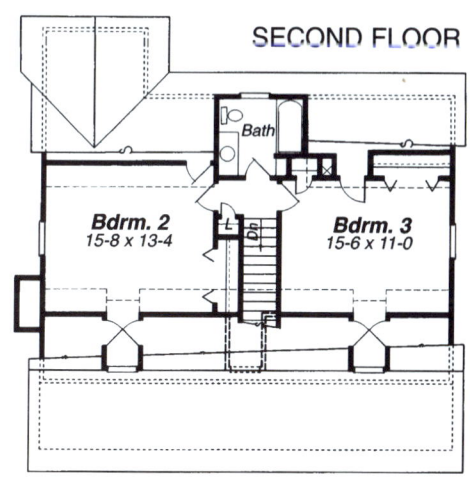

An *Exclusive Design* By *Jannis Vann & Associates, Inc.*

DESIGN NO. 92523

PRICE CODE B

PRIVATE MASTER SUITE

No. 92523

■ This plan features:

— Three bedrooms

— Two full baths

■ A spacious Great Room enhanced by a vaulted ceiling and fireplace

■ A well-equipped Kitchen with windowed double sink

■ A secluded Master Suite with decorative ceiling, private Master Bath, and walk-in closet

■ Two additional bedrooms sharing hall bath

■ An optional crawl space or slab foundation — please specify when ordering

MAIN AREA — 1,293 SQ. FT.
GARAGE — 400 SQ. FT.

TOTAL LIVING AREA: 1,293 SQ. FT.

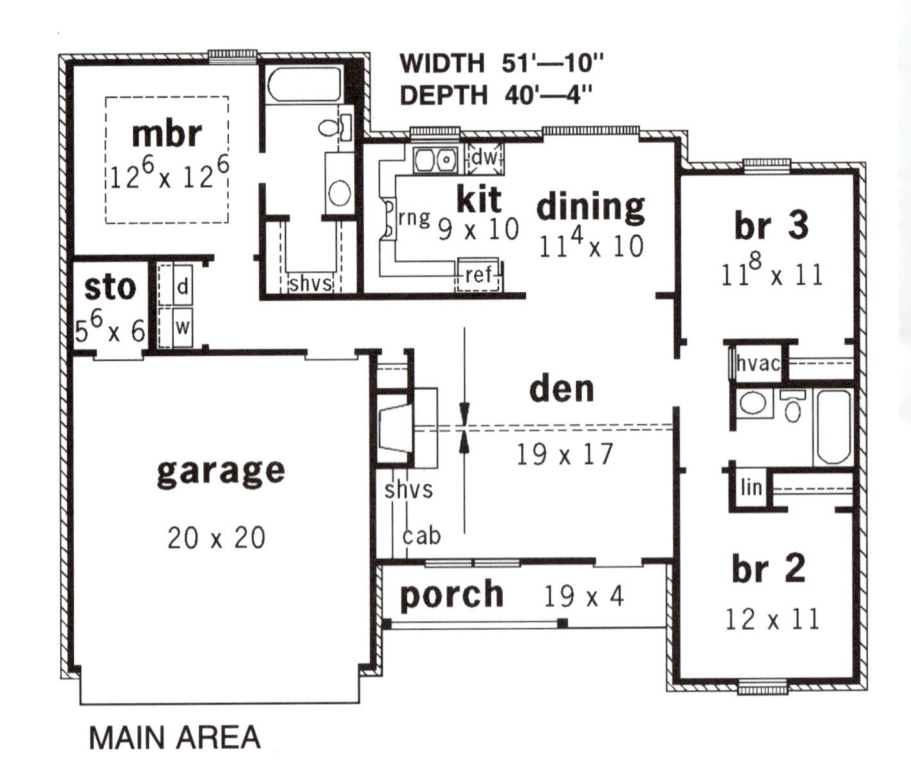

WIDTH 51'—10''
DEPTH 40'—4''

mbr 12^6 x 12^6

kit 9 x 10

dining 11^4 x 10

br 3 11^8 x 11

sto 5^6 x 6

den 19 x 17

garage 20 x 20

porch 19 x 4

br 2 12 x 11

MAIN AREA

DESIGN NO. 93205

PRICE CODE D

Home sweet home

No. 93205

- This plan features:
— Four bedrooms
— Two full and one half baths
- A wonderful wrap-around Porch
- Formal Living and Dining Rooms
- A U-shaped Kitchen equipped with a peninsula counter, a double sink, and a Pantry
- An expansive Family Room with a large focal point fireplace, and access to the rear Deck and Porch
- A second floor Master Suite with a decorative ceiling, a lavish bath and a huge walk-in closet
- A Bonus Room for future use
- An optional basement, slab or crawl space foundation is available — please specify when ordering

FIRST FLOOR — 1,320 SQ. FT.
SECOND FLOOR — 1,268 SQ. FT.
BONUS ROOM — 389 SQ. FT.
BASEMENT — 1,320 SQ. FT.
GARAGE — 482 SQ. FT.

TOTAL LIVING AREA: 2,588 SQ. FT.

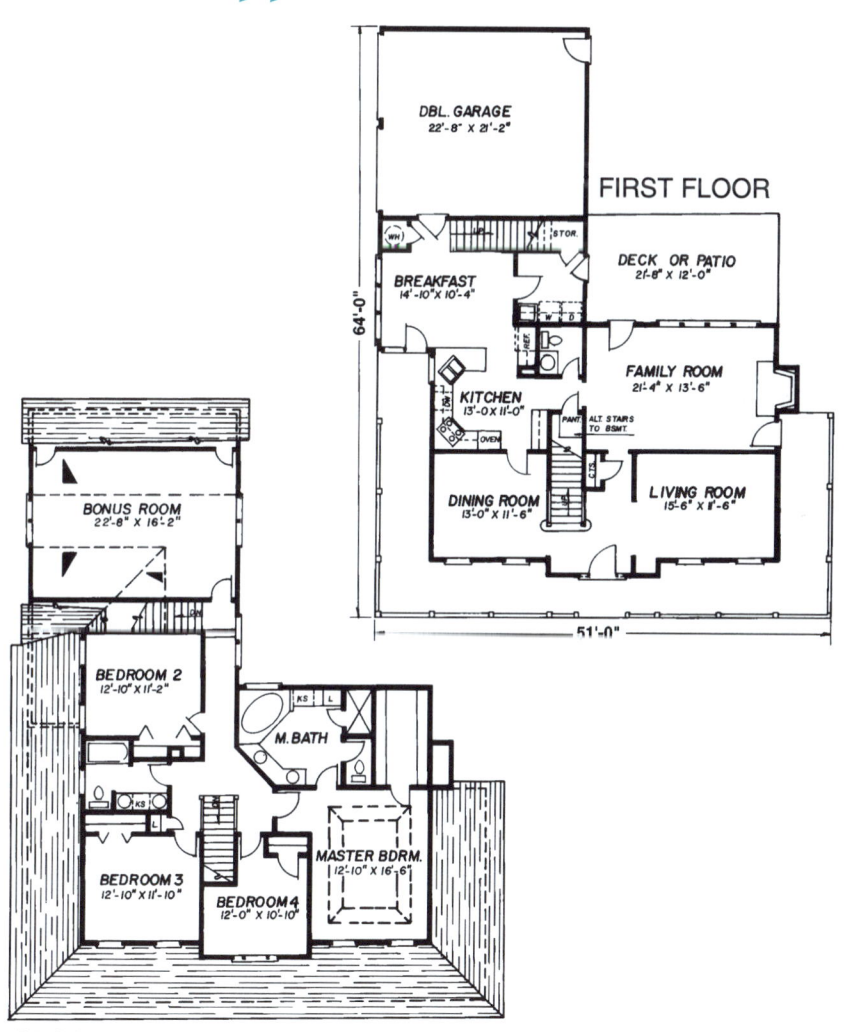

An **EXCLUSIVE DESIGN** *By Jannis Vann & Associates, Inc.*

DESIGN NO. 93212

PRICE CODE C

AN OLD-FASHIONED COUNTRY FEEL

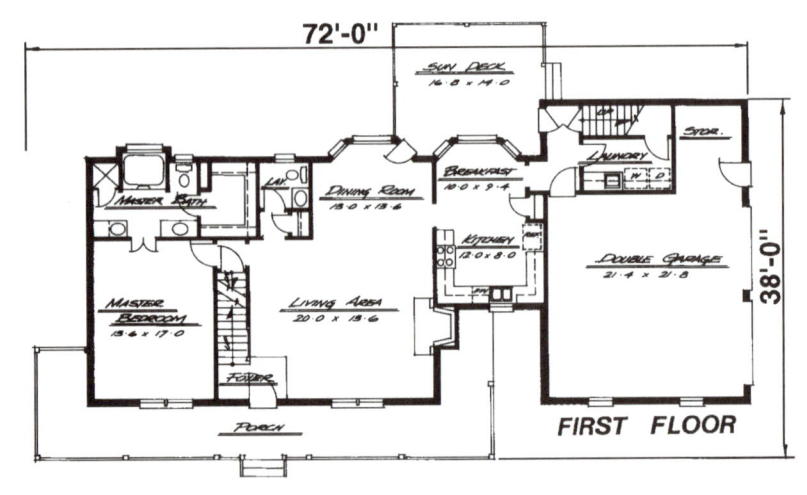

No. 93212

- This plan features:
— Three bedrooms
— Two full and one half baths
- A country-style porch and dormers lend charm
- A large Living Room with a cozy fireplace
- A formal Dining Room with a bay window and direct access to the Sun Deck
- A U-shaped Kitchen, efficiently arranged with ample work space
- A first floor Master Suite with an elegant private bath complete with jacuzzi and a step-in shower
- A second floor Study or Hobby Room overlooking the Deck
- A future Bonus Room
- An optional basement, slab or crawl space foundation — please specify when ordering

FIRST FLOOR — 1,362 SQ. FT.
SECOND FLOOR — 729 SQ. FT.
BONUS ROOM — 384 SQ. FT.
BASEMENT — 988 SQ. FT.
GARAGE — 559 SQ. FT.

TOTAL LIVING AREA: 2,091 SQ. FT.

No materials list available

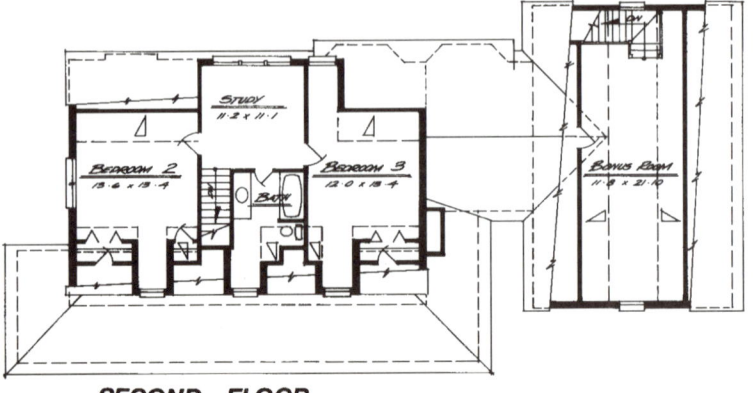

FIRST FLOOR

SECOND FLOOR

An **EXCLUSIVE DESIGN** *By Jannis Vann & Associates, Inc.*

DESIGN NO. 92531

PRICE CODE C

Enhanced by a Columned Porch

No. 92531

- This plan features:
   Three bedrooms
— Two full baths
- A Great room with a fireplace and decorative ceiling
- A large efficient Kitchen with Breakfast area
- A Master Bedroom with a private Master Bath and walk-in closet
- A formal Dining Room conveniently located near the Kitchen
- Two additional bedrooms with walk-in closets and use of full hall bath
- An optional crawl space or slab foundation available, please specify when ordering this plan

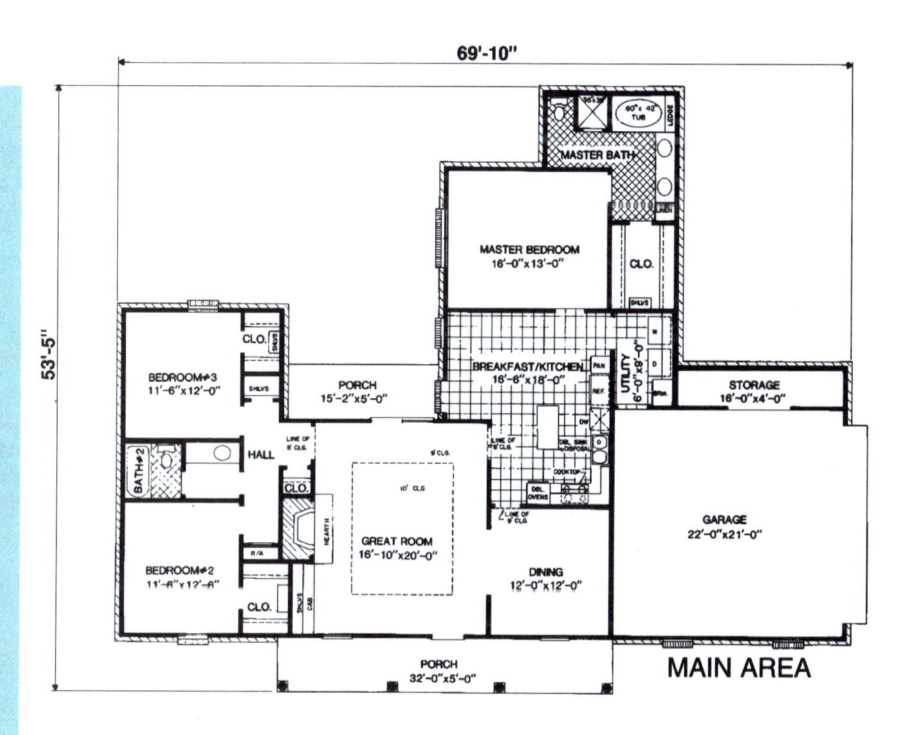

First floor — 1,754 sq. ft.
Garage — 552 sq. ft.

Total living area: 1,754 sq. ft.

DESIGN NO. 93266

PRICE CODE C

Neat and tidy floor plan

No. 93266

- This plan features:
— Three bedrooms
— Two full and one half baths
- A large Family Room includes a huge fireplace and double doors opening to the front porch
- A Breakfast area with direct access to the Sun Deck, expanding your living space in the warmer weather
- A formal Living Room
- An efficiently located Kitchen
- A large Master Suite with a decorative ceiling, a walk-in closet and a private Master Bath
- Two additional bedrooms that share a full hall bath
- A second floor laundry center

FIRST FLOOR — 990 SQ. FT.
SECOND FLOOR — 976 SQ. FT.
BASEMENT — 431 SQ. FT.
GARAGE — 559 SQ. FT.

TOTAL LIVING AREA: 1,966 SQ. FT.

No materials list available

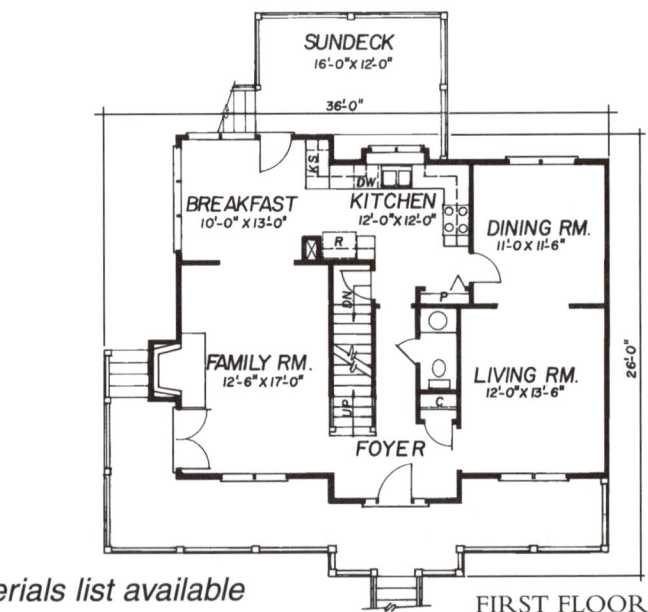

FIRST FLOOR

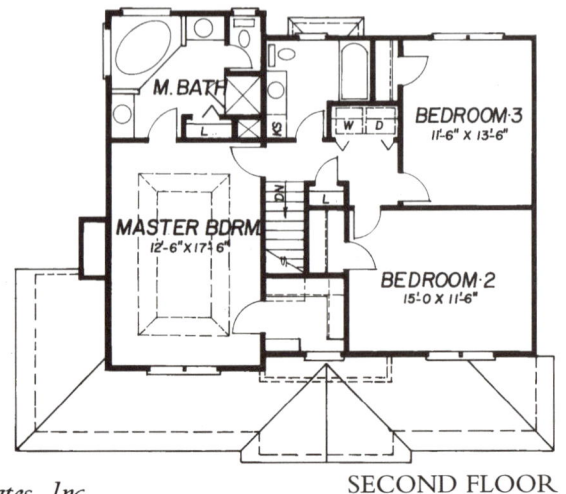

SECOND FLOOR

An EXCLUSIVE DESIGN *By Jannis Vann & Associates, Inc.*

DESIGN NO. 93220

PRICE CODE B

No. 93220

■ This plan features:

— Three bedrooms

— Two full and one half baths

■ Two-story Foyer with landing staircase leads to formal Living and Dining Rooms

■ Open layout for Kitchen/Breakfast area and Family Room offers a spacious feeling and easy interaction

■ Efficient Kitchen with cooktop peninsula, built-in pantry and a glassed Breakfast area

■ Comfortable Family Room with a focal point fireplace and a wall of windows with access to Sundeck

■ Master Bedroom enhanced by decorative ceiling and French doors

■ Two additional bedrooms, full bath, laundry closet and Bonus Room complete second floor

■ An optional basement, crawl space or slab foundation available, please specify when ordering

Spacious Family Areas

An EXCLUSIVE DESIGN *By Jannis Vann & Associates, Inc.*

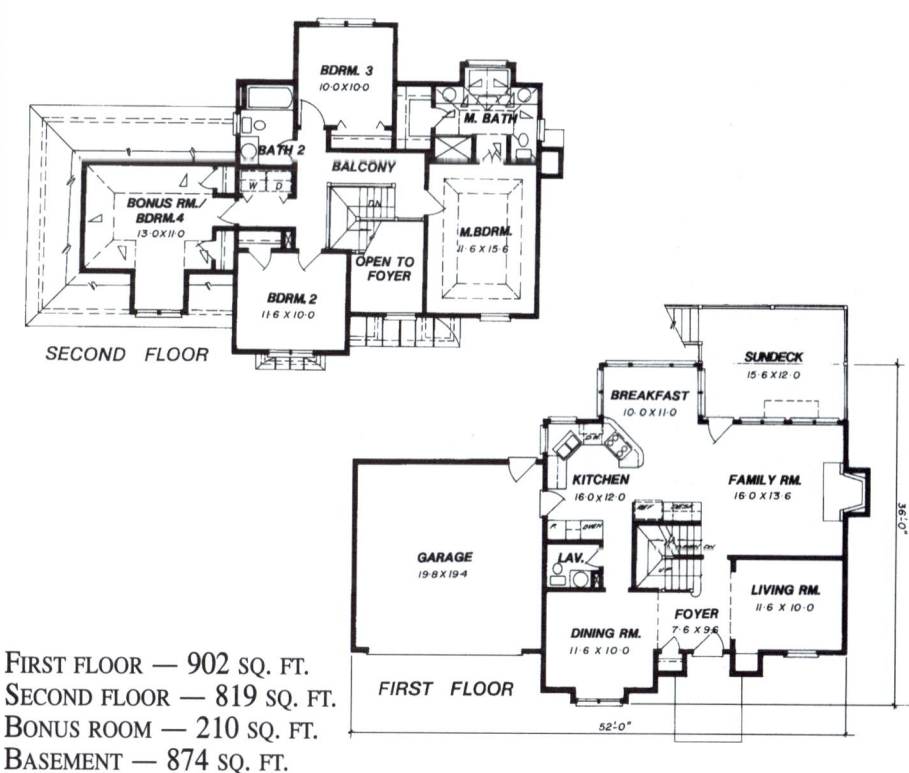

FIRST FLOOR — 902 SQ. FT.
SECOND FLOOR — 819 SQ. FT.
BONUS ROOM — 210 SQ. FT.
BASEMENT — 874 SQ. FT.
GARAGE — 400 SQ. FT.
FINISHED STAIRCASE — 28 SQ. FT.

TOTAL LIVING AREA:
1,721 SQ. FT.

DESIGN NO. 93206

PRICE CODE E

DISTINCTIVE EXPANDABLE BRICK

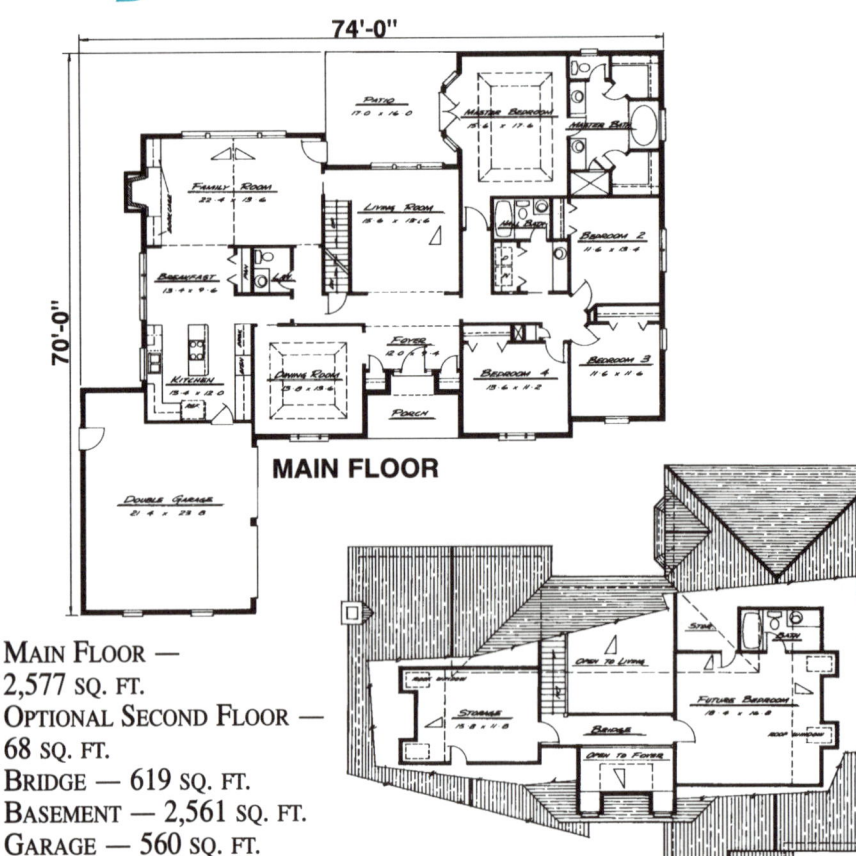

No. 93206

- This plan features:
- — Four bedrooms
- — Two full and one half baths
- Arched entrance with decorative glass leads into two-story Foyer
- Formal Dining Room with tray ceiling above decorative window
- Kitchen with island, cooktop, built-in desk and Pantry
- Master Bedroom wing has tray ceiling, French door to Patio, huge Private Bath with garden tub, and two walk-in closets
- Three additional bedrooms share Laundry and full bath
- Second Floor optional space for Storage and huge Future Bedroom with full bath
- An optional basement, slab, or crawl space foundation — please specify when ordering

MAIN FLOOR

OPTIONAL SECOND FLOOR

MAIN FLOOR — 2,577 SQ. FT.
OPTIONAL SECOND FLOOR — 68 SQ. FT.
BRIDGE — 619 SQ. FT.
BASEMENT — 2,561 SQ. FT.
GARAGE — 560 SQ. FT.

TOTAL LIVING AREA: 2,645 SQ. FT.

An EXCLUSIVE DESIGN
By Jannis Vann & Associates, Inc.

DESIGN NO. 92275

PRICE CODE E

FOUR-BEDROOM WITH ONE FLOOR CONVENIENCE

No. 92275

- This plan features:
- — Four bedrooms
- — Three full baths
- A distinguished brick exterior adds curb appeal
- Formal Entry/Gallery opens to large Living Room with hearth fireplace set between windows overlooking Patio and rear yard
- Efficient Kitchen with angled counters and serving bar easily serves Breakfast Room, Patio and formal Dining Room
- Corner Master Bedroom enhanced by a vaulted ceiling and pampering bath with a large walk-in closet
- Three additional bedrooms with walk-in closets have access to full baths

MAIN FLOOR — 2,675 SQ. FT.
GARAGE — 638 SQ. FT.

TOTAL LIVING AREA: 2,675 SQ. FT.

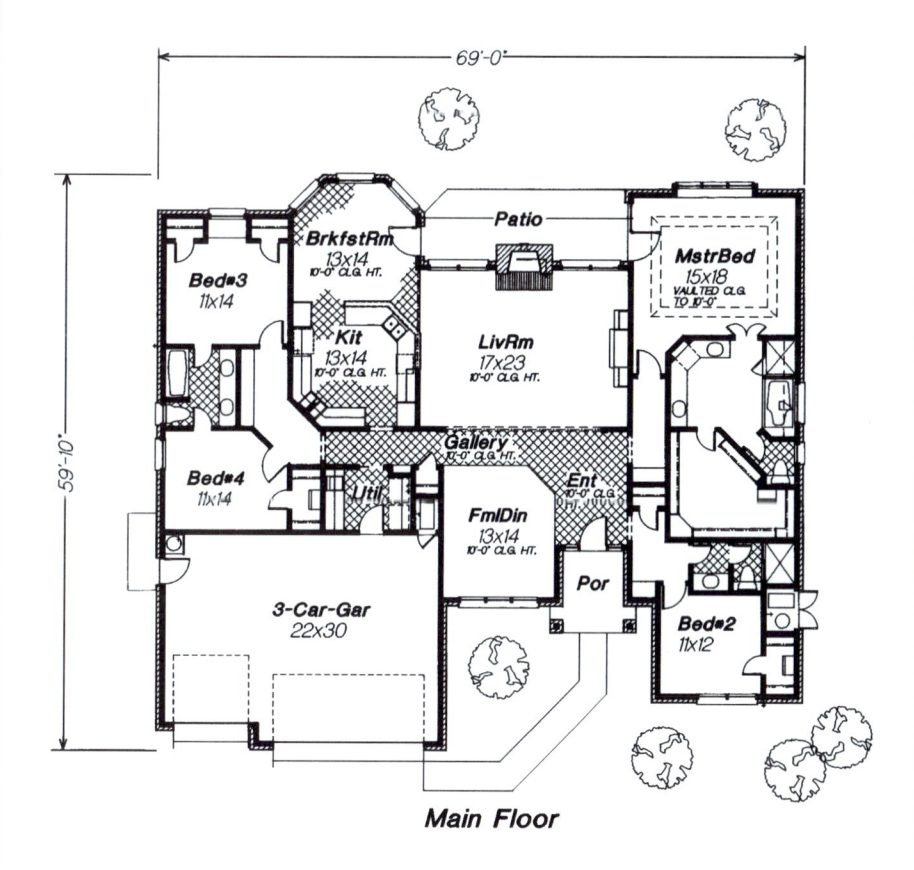

No materials list available

DESIGN NO. 90443

PRICE CODE E

Traditional that has it all

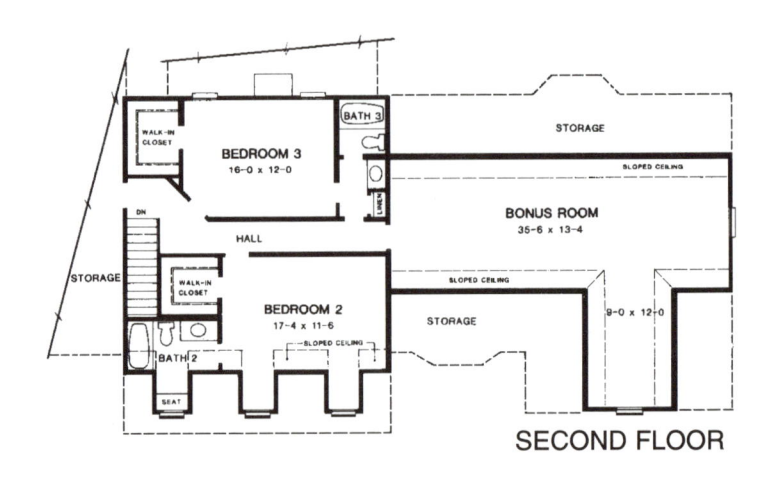

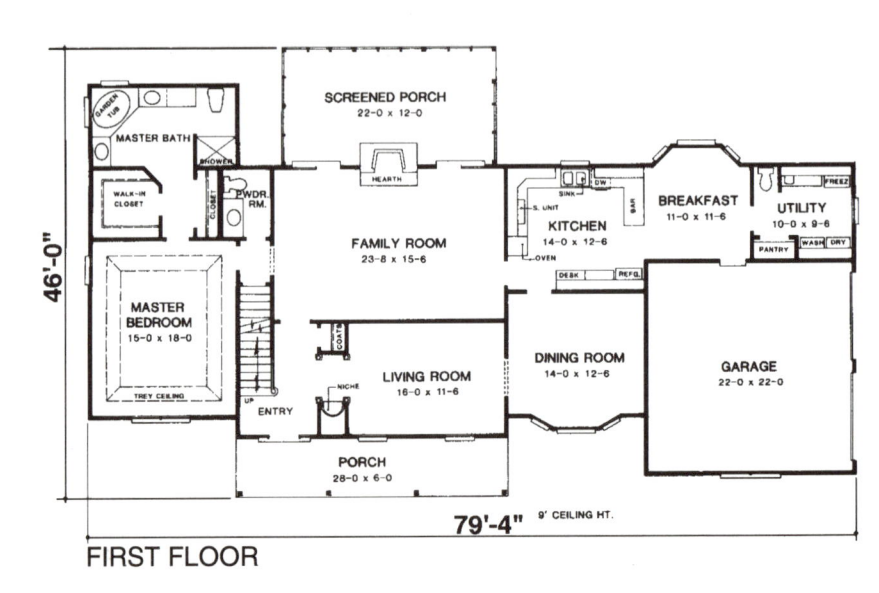

No. 90443

■ This plan features:

— Three bedrooms

— Three full and one half baths

■ A Master Suite with two closets and a private bath with separate shower, corner tub and dual vanity

■ A large Dining Room with a bay window, adjacent to the Kitchen

■ A formal Living Room for entertaining and a cozy Family Room with fireplace for informal relaxation

■ Two upstairs bedrooms with walk-in closets sharing a full hall bath

■ A Bonus Room to allow the house to grow with your needs

■ An optional basement or crawl space foundation — please specify when ordering

First floor — 1,927 sq. ft.
Second floor — 832 sq. ft.
Bonus room — 624 sq. ft.
Basement — 1,674 sq. ft.

Total living area: 2,759 sq. ft.

DESIGN NO. 93035

PRICE CODE D

COMPACT SOUTHERN TRADITIONAL

No. 93035

■ This plan features:

— Four bedrooms

— Two full and one half baths

■ An entrance flanked by columns and imposing gables, accented with dentil molding

■ An angled Foyer, drawing the eye to an arched passage in the Living Room

■ A large Kitchen/Family Room combination with an octagonal shaped breakfast area

■ A Master Bedroom that is entered through angled double doors and has a cathedral ceiling

■ A Master Bath with his-n-her vanities and walk-in closets

MAIN FLOOR — 2,545 SQ. FT.
GARAGE — 436 SQ. FT.

TOTAL LIVING AREA: 2,545 SQ. FT.

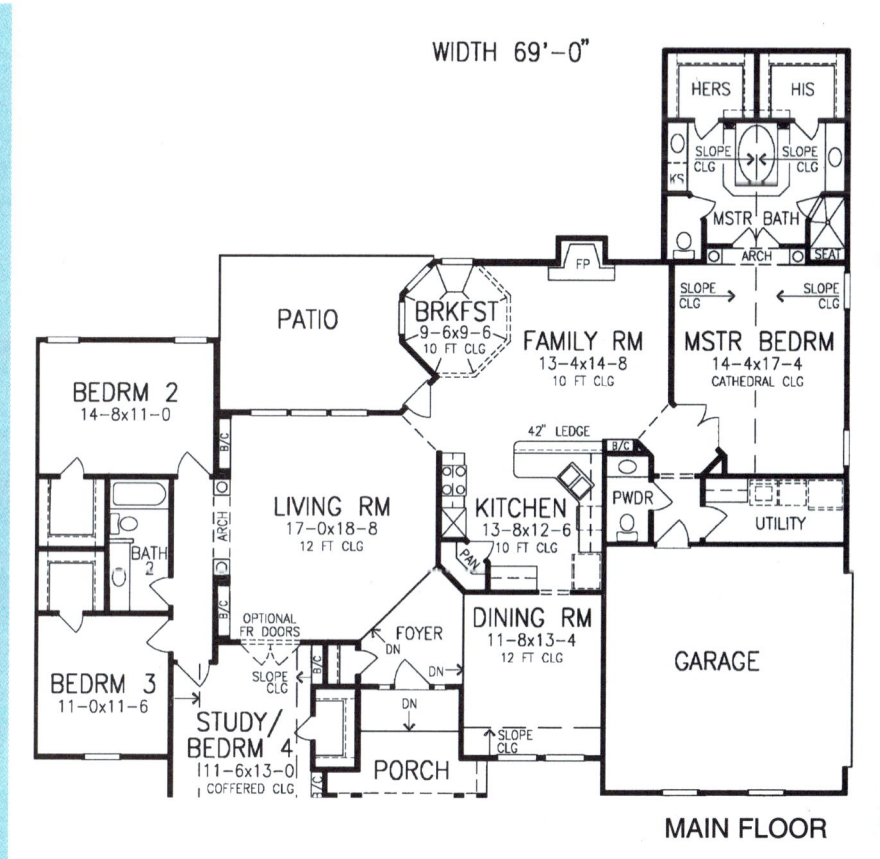

WIDTH 69'-0"
DEPTH 63'-6"

MAIN FLOOR

No materials list available

DESIGN NO. 92626

PRICE CODE C

Elegant Detail Inside and Out

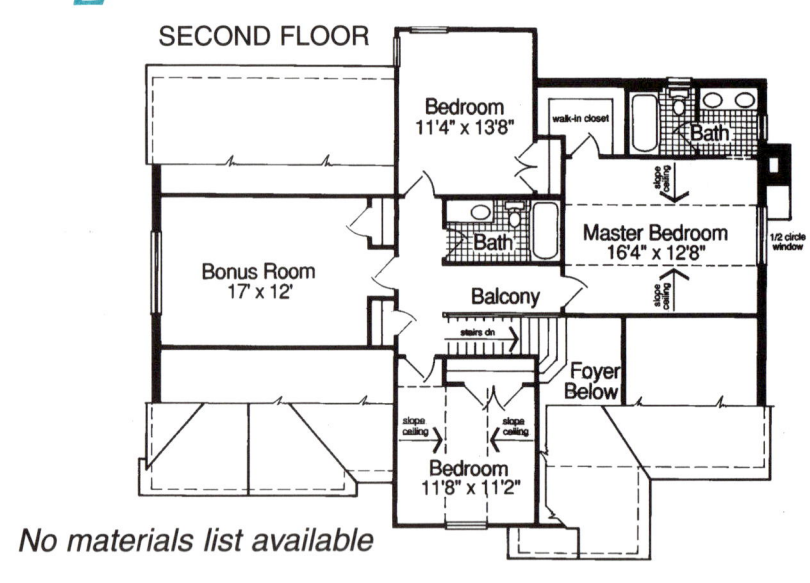

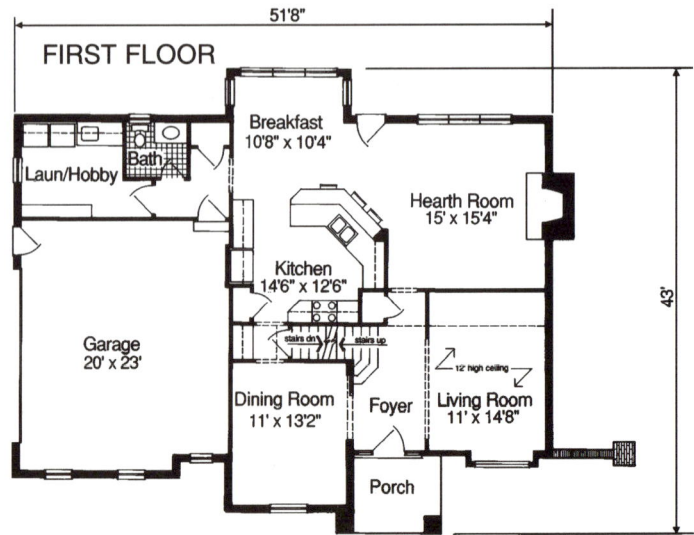

No. 92626

- This plan features:
— Three bedrooms
— Two full and one half baths
- Bold, arched entry with two-story Foyer and angled staircase
- Twelve foot ceiling in Living Room crowns decorative window
- Hearth Room with cozy fireplace and a wall of windows with access to rear yard opens to Kitchen/Breakfast area
- Kitchen efficiently serves formal Dining Room via butler's pantry, peninsula snackbar and bright Breakfast alcove
- Convenient Laundry/Hobby Room, half bath and Garage entrance off Kitchen
- Master Bedroom features half circle window topped by a sloped ceiling, a walk-in closet and private bath with a double vanity

FIRST FLOOR — 1,251 SQ. FT.
SECOND FLOOR — 835 SQ. FT.
BONUS ROOM — 249 SQ. FT.
BASEMENT — 1,197 SQ. FT.

TOTAL LIVING AREA: 2,086 SQ. FT.

No materials list available

DESIGN NO. 92269

PRICE CODE E

QUALITY INSIDE AND OUT

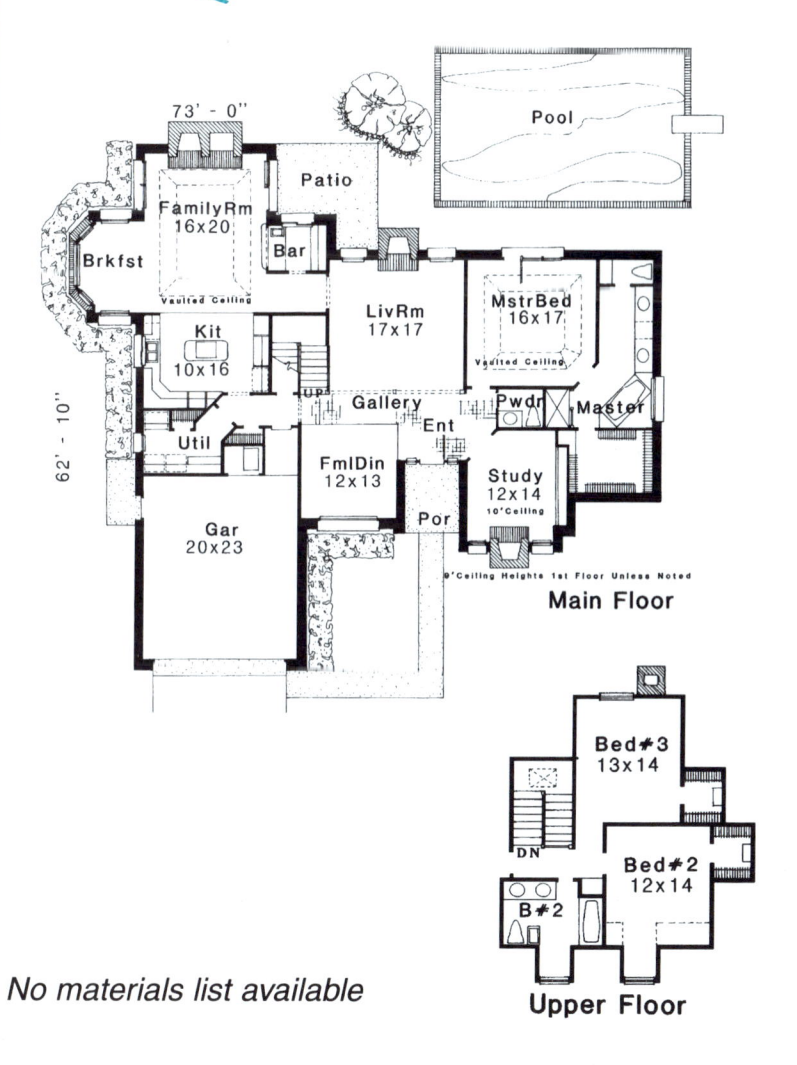

No. 92269

- This plan features:
- — Three bedrooms
- — Two full and one half baths
- Decorative brick treatment adds to attractive facade and appeal
- A spacious Entry/Gallery opens to Living Room with focal point fireplace
- Convenient Study offers built-ins and another fireplace
- Country Kitchen with work island opens to Breakfast bay, Family Room, Dining Room, Utility and Garage entry
- Expansive Family Room offers a vaulted ceiling, third fireplace and access to Patio
- Private Master Bedroom suite with a vaulted ceiling, lavish bath and walk-in closet

FIRST FLOOR — 2,273 SQ. FT.
SECOND FLOOR — 562 SQ. FT.
GARAGE — 460 SQ. FT.

TOTAL LIVING AREA: 2,835 SQ. FT.

Main Floor

Upper Floor

No materials list available

DESIGN NO. 94612

PRICE CODE D

Stylish Detailing

No materials list available

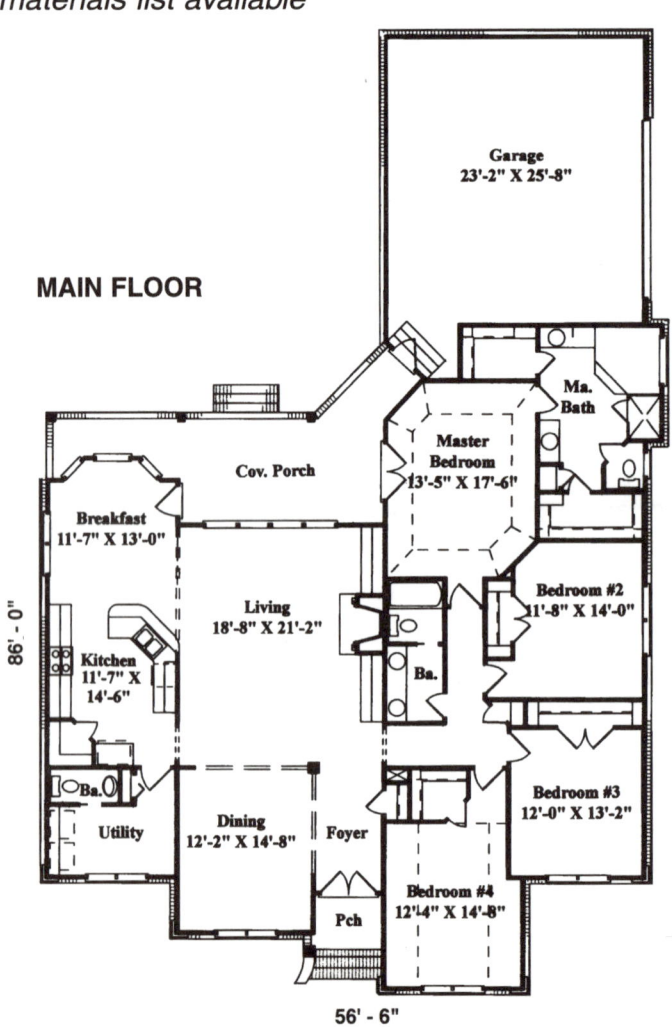

No. 94612

- This plan features:
- — Four bedrooms
- — Two full and one half baths
- Impressive double door entry leading into an open Foyer
- Expansive Living Room with a large fireplace between built-in shelves and a wall of windows
- Formal Dining Room opens to Living Room and Kitchen
- Well-appointed Kitchen with built-in pantry and peninsula counter/snackbar serving Breakfast area and Covered Porch
- Master Bedroom topped by decorative ceiling offers access to Covered Porch and a plush bath with a corner tub and two walk-in closets
- An optional crawl space or slab foundation — please specify when ordering

Main floor — 2,434 sq. ft.
Garage — 651 sq. ft.

Total living area: 2,434 sq. ft.

MAIN FLOOR

- Garage 23'-2" X 25'-8"
- Ma. Bath
- Master Bedroom 13'-5" X 17'-6"
- Cov. Porch
- Breakfast 11'-7" X 13'-0"
- Bedroom #2 11'-8" X 14'-0"
- Living 18'-8" X 21'-2"
- Kitchen 11'-7" X 14'-6"
- Ba.
- Bedroom #3 12'-0" X 13'-2"
- Ba.
- Utility
- Dining 12'-2" X 14'-8"
- Foyer
- Bedroom #4 12'-4" X 14'-8"
- Pch

86'-0"

56'-6"

DESIGN NO. 94710

PRICE CODE B

CLASSIC STYLE WITH CONTEMPORARY FLAIR

No. 94710

- This plan features:
— Three bedrooms
— Two full baths
- Inviting front Porch leads into open Dining and Great rooms for easy entertaining
- Efficient Kitchen with peninsula serving counter/snackbar serves Keeping room, Deck and Dining area
- Corner Master Suite offers Deck access, a walk-in closet and a plush bath with whirlpool window tub and a double vanity
- An optional 1/2 basement, 1/2 crawl space or full basement foundation — please specify when ordering

MAIN FLOOR — 1,779 SQ. FT.
BASEMENT/GARAGE — 545 SQ. FT.

TOTAL LIVING AREA: 1,779 SQ. FT.

MAIN AREA

HIGH WIND LOAD ENGINEERING AVAILABLE
SEE PAGE 246 FOR DETAILS

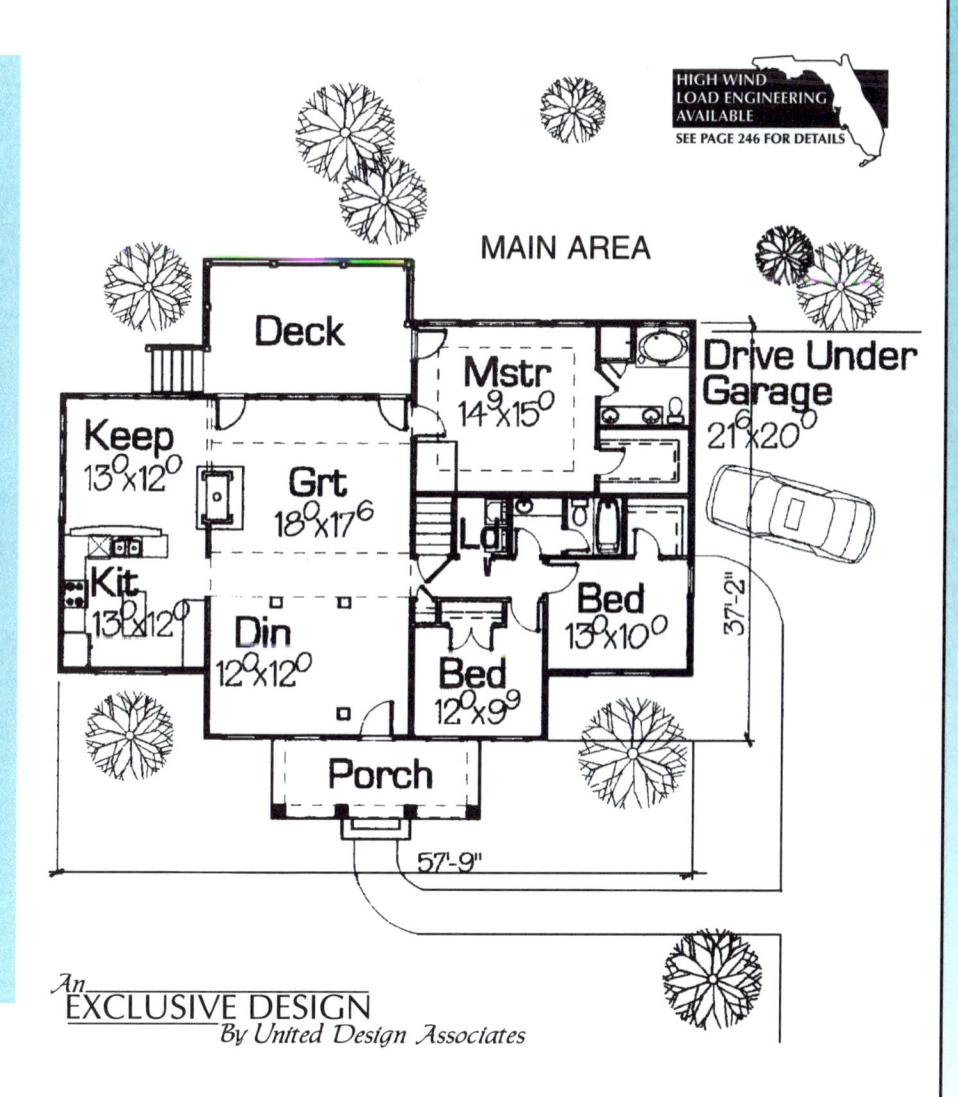

Deck
Mstr 14'9" x 15'0"
Drive Under Garage 21'6" x 20'0"
Keep 13'0" x 12'0"
Grt 18'0" x 17'6"
Ld
Kit 13'0" x 12'0"
Bed 13'0" x 10'0"
Din 12'0" x 12'0"
Bed 12'0" x 9'0"
Porch

37'-2"
57'-9"

An EXCLUSIVE DESIGN
By United Design Associates

DESIGN NO. 94218

PRICE CODE D

Narrow lot design

No materials list available

No. 94218

■ This plan features:

— Three bedrooms

— Two full baths

■ Sheltered Entry leads into open Foyer and Living/Dining Room with glass doors to Verandah

■ Efficient Kitchen with walk-in pantry, serving counter/snackbar and a bright, eating Nook

■ Leisure Room offers a corner fireplace, entertainment center and Verandah access

■ Corner Master Suite enhanced by sitting area, a large walk-in closet and a pampering bath

■ Quiet Study with alcove of windows offers many uses

■ Two additional bedrooms with large closets, share a full bath

MAIN FLOOR — 2,562 SQ. FT.
GARAGE — 489 SQ. FT.

TOTAL LIVING AREA: 2,562 SQ. FT.

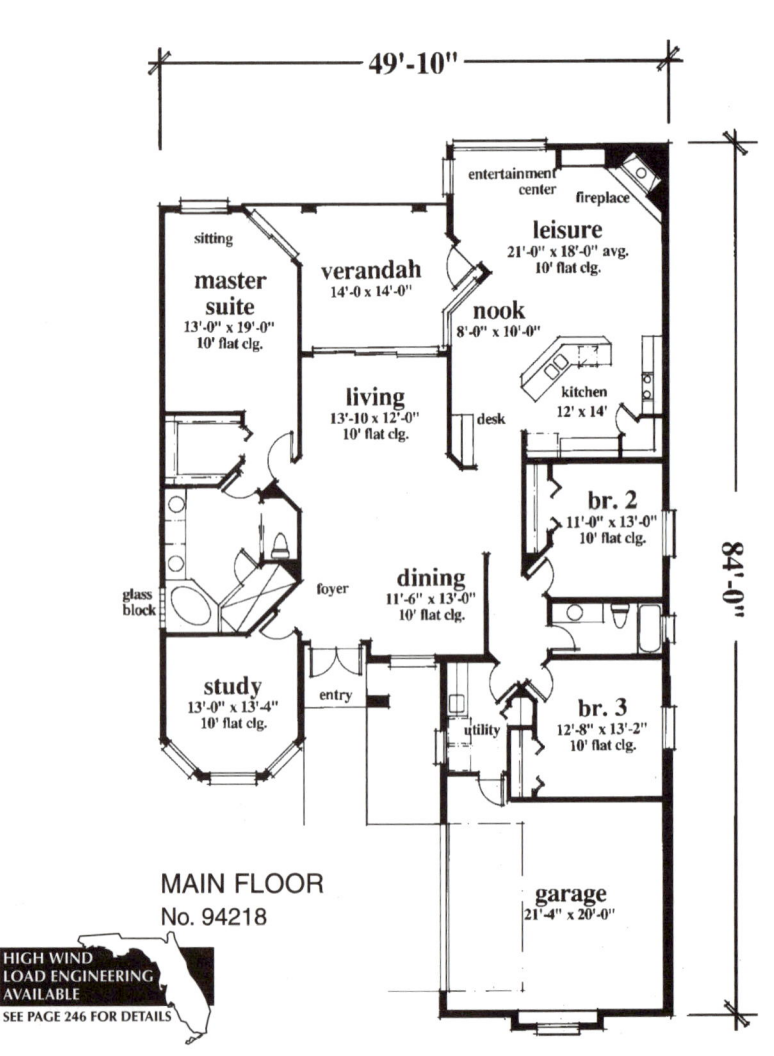

MAIN FLOOR
No. 94218

- Overall: 49'-10" x 84'-0"
- master suite: 13'-0" x 19'-0", 10' flat clg.
- verandah: 14'-0 x 14'-0"
- leisure: 21'-0" x 18'-0" avg., 10' flat clg., entertainment center, fireplace
- nook: 8'-0" x 10'-0"
- kitchen: 12' x 14'
- living: 13'-10 x 12'-0", 10' flat clg.
- dining: 11'-6" x 13'-0", 10' flat clg.
- br. 2: 11'-0" x 13'-0", 10' flat clg.
- study: 13'-0" x 13'-4", 10' flat clg.
- br. 3: 12'-8" x 13'-2", 10' flat clg.
- garage: 21'-4" x 20'-0"

HIGH WIND LOAD ENGINEERING AVAILABLE
SEE PAGE 246 FOR DETAILS

DESIGN NO. 93228

PRICE CODE C

SMART STUCCO

SECOND FLOOR

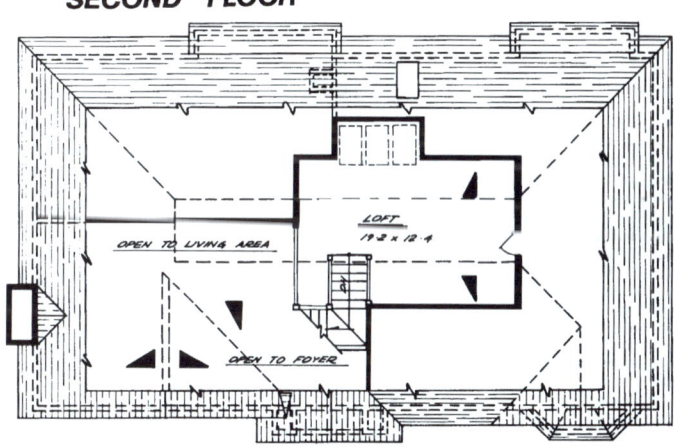

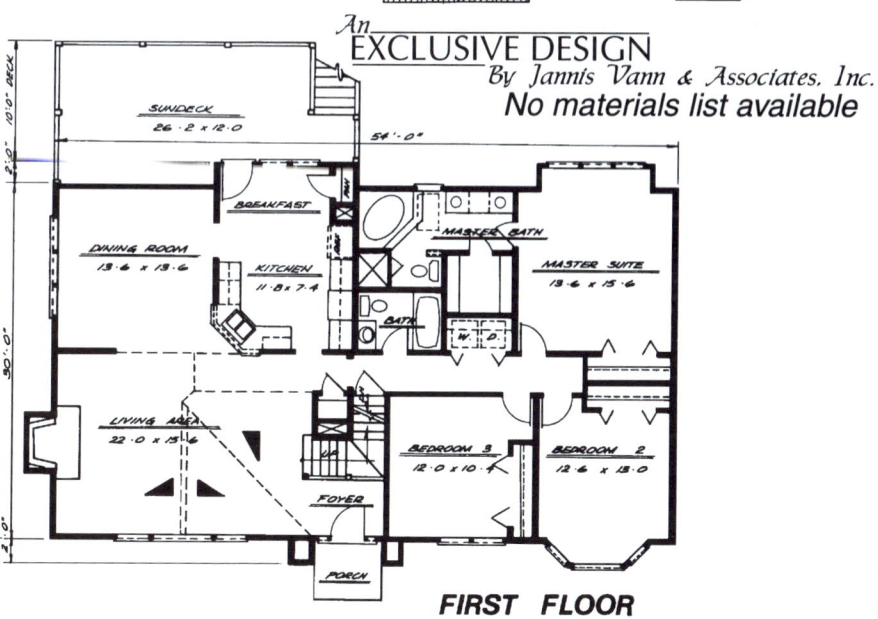

An **EXCLUSIVE DESIGN**
By Jannis Vann & Associates, Inc.
No materials list available

FIRST FLOOR

No. 93228

■ This plan features:

— Three bedrooms

— Two full baths

■ A large Living Area with a warm fireplace

■ A formal Dining Room conveniently located off the kitchen for entertaining ease

■ A double sink, ample cabinet and counter area, a built-in pantry and direct access to a sun deck in the Kitchen/Breakfast Room

■ A wonderful Master Suite with private five piece Bath and a walk-in closet

■ Two additional bedrooms that share a full hall bath

■ A Loft Area with three skylights that will become a special area, customized for the family's needs

FIRST FLOOR — 1,678 SQ. FT.
LOFT — 282 SQ. FT.
BASEMENT — 836 SQ. FT.
GARAGE — 784 SQ. FT.
DECK — 288 SQ. FT.

TOTAL LIVING AREA: 1,960 SQ. FT.

DESIGN NO. 92629

PRICE CODE C

QUALITY AND DIVERSITY

No materials list available

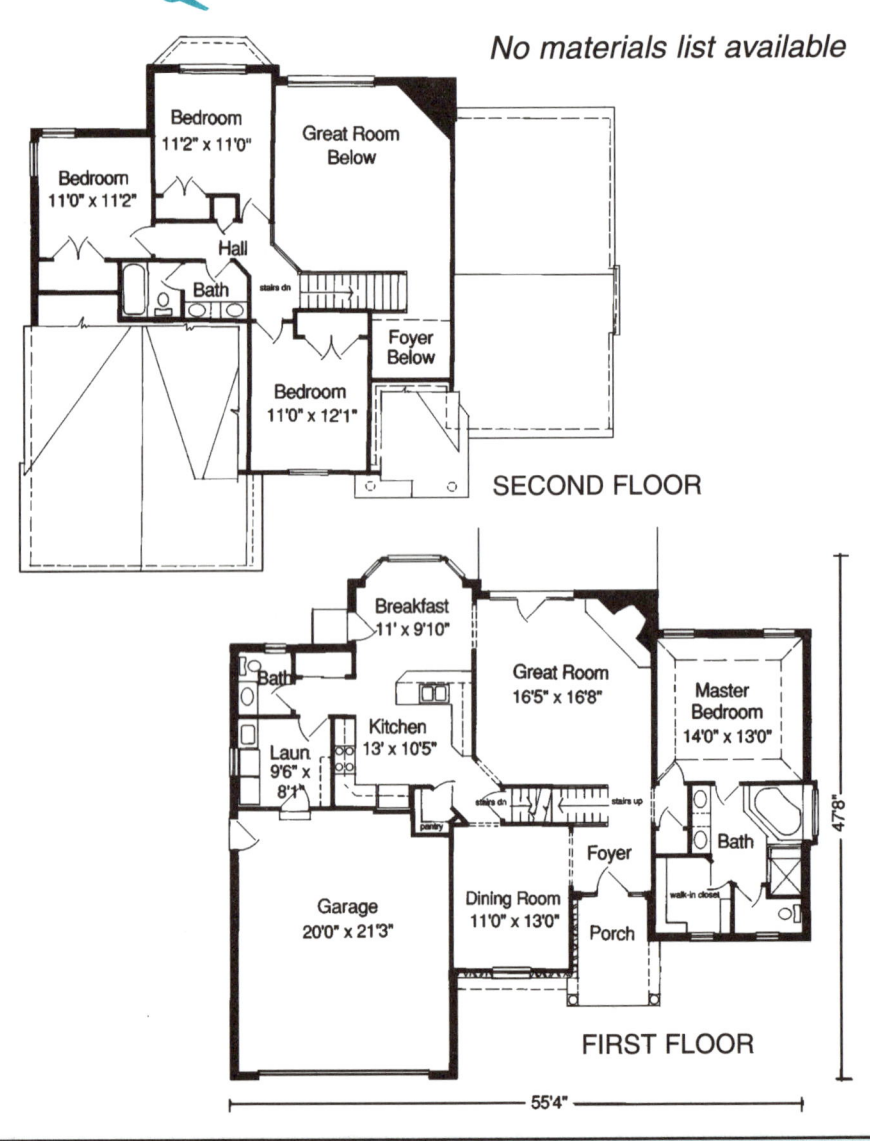

No. 92629

- This plan features:
— Four bedrooms
— Two full and one half bath
- Elegant arched entrance from Porch into Foyer and Great Room beyond
- Formal Dining Room for quiet entertaining
- Corner fireplace and atrium door highlight Great Room
- Hub Kitchen with walk-in pantry and peninsula counter easily accesses glass Breakfast bay, backyard, Great Room, Dining Room Laundry and Garage
- Master Bedroom wing crowned by tray ceiling offers plush bath and walk-in closet
- Three additional bedrooms with decorative windows and large closets, share a full bath

FIRST FLOOR — 1,401 SQ. FT.
SECOND FLOOR — 621 SQ. FT.
BASEMENT — 1,269 SQ. FT.
GARAGE — 478 SQ. FT.

TOTAL LIVING AREA: 2,022 SQ. FT.

SECOND FLOOR

- Bedroom 11'2" x 11'0"
- Bedroom 11'0" x 11'2"
- Great Room Below
- Hall
- Bath
- stairs dn
- Foyer Below
- Bedroom 11'0" x 12'1"

FIRST FLOOR

- Breakfast 11' x 9'10"
- Bath
- Kitchen 13' x 10'5"
- Laun. 9'6" x 8'1"
- pantry
- Great Room 16'5" x 16'8"
- Master Bedroom 14'0" x 13'0"
- stairs dn stairs up
- Foyer
- Dining Room 11'0" x 13'0"
- Porch
- Bath
- walk-in closet
- Garage 20'0" x 21'3"

47'8"
55'4"

DESIGN NO. 92283

PRICE CODE B

THREE BEDROOMS AND MORE

No. 92283

- This plan features:
  — Three bedrooms
  — Two full baths
- A sheltered Porch leads into an easy-care tile Entry
- Spacious Living Room offers a cozy fireplace, triple window and access to Patio
- An efficient Kitchen with a skylight, work island, Dining area, walk-in pantry and Utility/Garage entry
- Secluded Master Bedroom highlighted by a vaulted ceiling, access to Patio and a lavish bath
- Two additional bedrooms, one with a cathedral ceiling, share a full bath

MAIN FLOOR — 1,653 SQ. FT.
GARAGE — 420 SQ. FT.

TOTAL LIVING AREA: 1,653 SQ. FT.

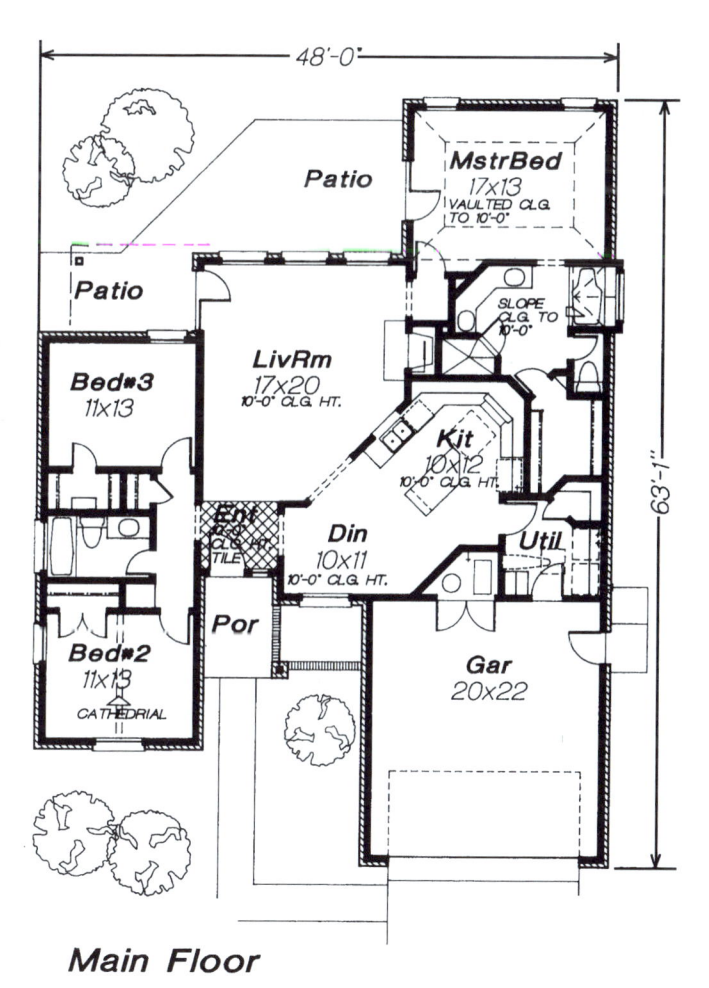

Main Floor

No materials list available

DESIGN NO. 93227

PRICE CODE B

Impressive Stucco and Stone

An EXCLUSIVE DESIGN
By Jannis Vann & Associates, Inc.

TOTAL LIVING AREA: 1,641 SQ. FT.

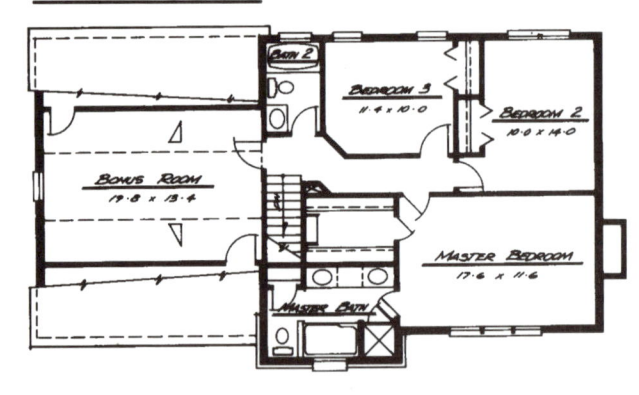

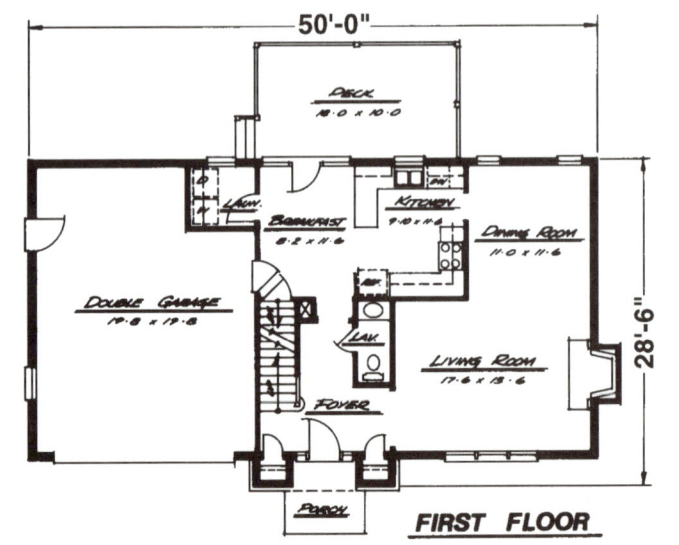

No. 93227

- This plan features:
— Three bedrooms
— Two full and one half baths
- Keystone entrance into central Foyer with gracefully curved staircase
- Living Room with decorative window and hearth fireplace opens to Dining Room for easy entertaining
- Hub Kitchen convenient to formal Dining Room, Breakfast area and Deck through atrium door, Laundry and Garage
- Spacious Master Bedroom with walk-in closet and double vanity Master Bath
- Two additional bedrooms with ample closets share a full bath
- Bonus Room offers many options
- An optional basement, crawl space or slab foundation available, please specify when ordering

FIRST FLOOR — 831 SQ. FT.
SECOND FLOOR — 810 SQ. FT.
BASEMENT — 816 SQ. FT.
GARAGE — 484 SQ. FT

DESIGN NO. 93702

PRICE CODE B

No. 93702

- This plan features:
- — Three bedrooms
- — Two full baths
- An open floor plan giving the appearance of spaciousness even though the home is small in square footage
- A sheltered entrance that leads to a short Foyer with a coat closet
- A large front window adding to the elegance of the Dining Room
- A tray ceiling in the Living Room which is also enhanced by a fireplace
- An octagonal Kitchen including a dining bar and open to the Breakfast Room
- A large and private Master Bedroom with an oversized walk-in closet
- A secondary bedroom located at the front of the house with a vaulted ceiling and a circle-topped window

MAIN FLOOR — 1,605 SQ. FT.
GARAGE — 436 SQ. FT.

TOTAL LIVING AREA: 1,605 SQ. FT.

AN OPEN PLAN

No materials list available

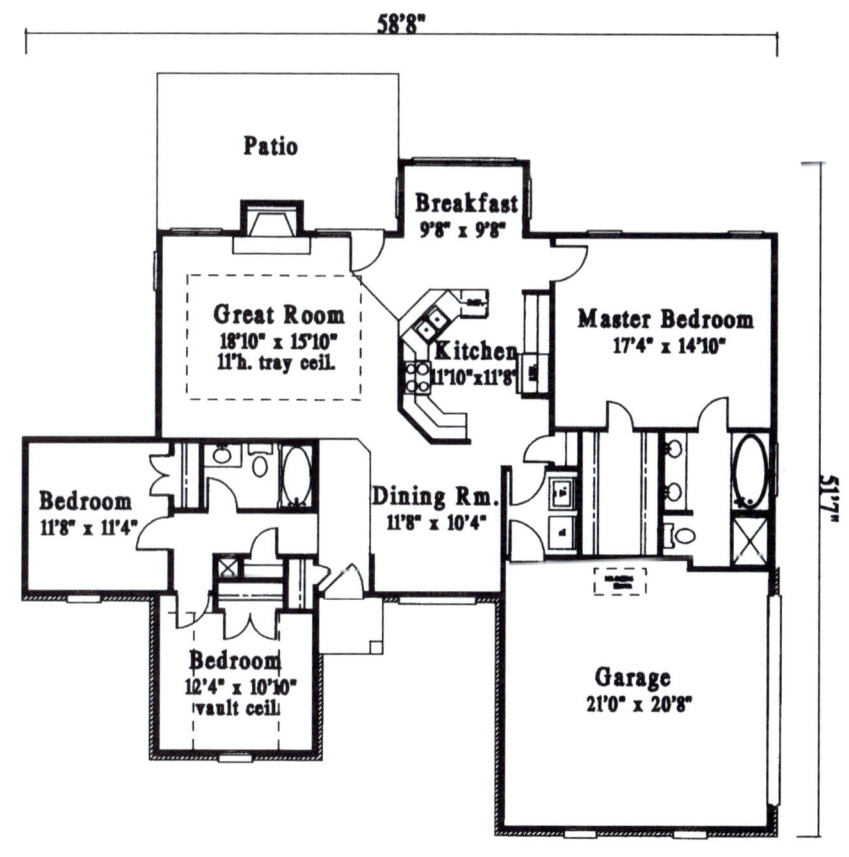

58'8"

Patio

Breakfast 9'8" x 9'8"

Great Room 18'10" x 15'10" 11'h. tray ceil.

Kitchen 11'10" x 11'8"

Master Bedroom 17'4" x 14'10"

Bedroom 11'8" x 11'4"

Dining Rm. 11'8" x 10'4"

Bedroom 12'4" x 10'10" vault ceil.

Garage 21'0" x 20'8"

51'7"

Main Level Floor Plan
8' Ceilings

An EXCLUSIVE DESIGN
By Building Science Associates

DESIGN NO. 94212

PRICE CODE E

Impressive Roof Lines

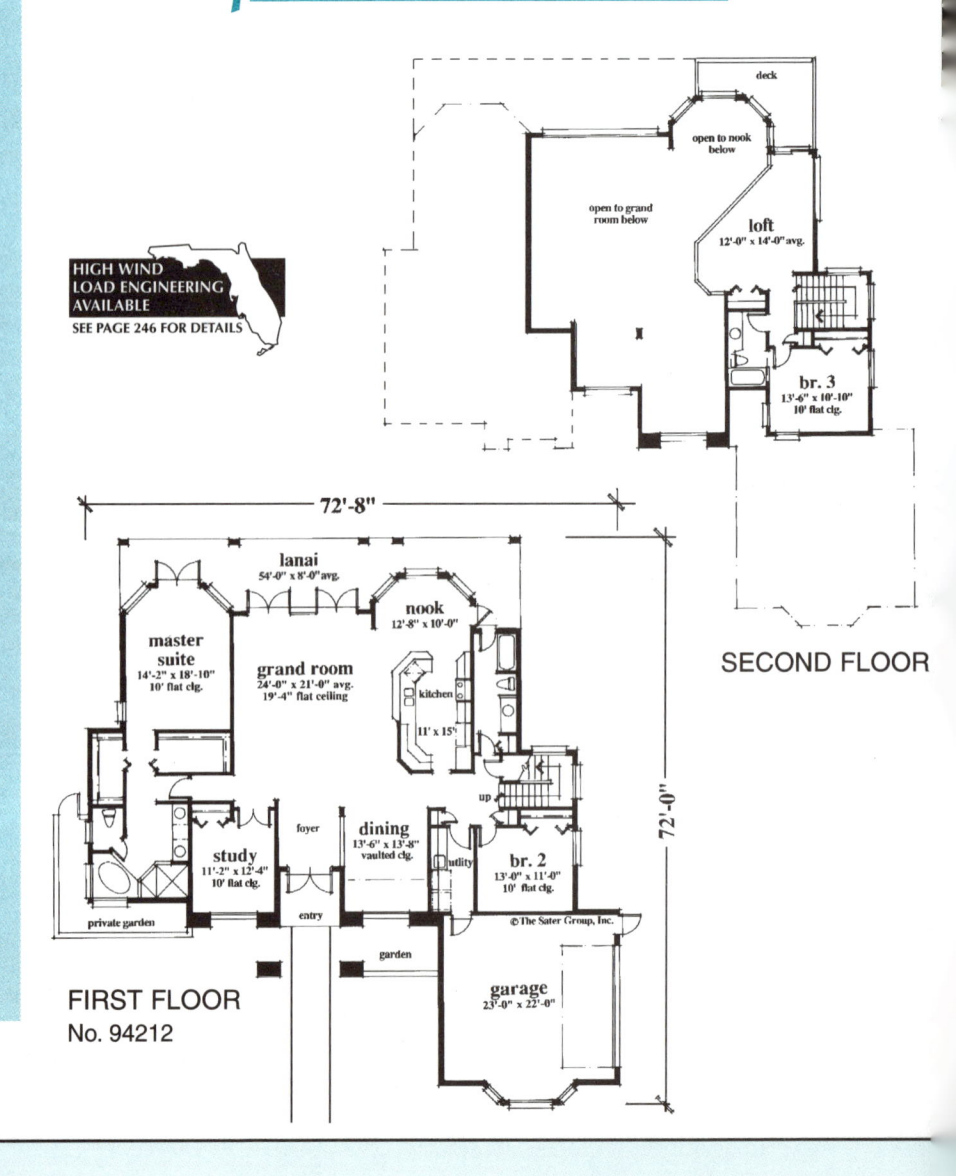

No. 94212

- This plan features:
— Three bedrooms
— Three full baths
- Grand two-story entry with double doors below an arched, head window
- Expansive Grand Room with two sets of French doors opening to the Lanai beyond
- Family Kitchen with island work counter and bright eating Nook and Utility/Garage entry
- Luxurious Master Suite with two walk-in closets, plush bath and french doors to Lanai
- Additional first floor bedroom with access to a full bath
- Second floor bedroom with full bath, Loft area and private Deck

FIRST FLOOR — 2,368 SQ. FT.
SECOND FLOOR — 428 SQ. FT.
GARAGE — 566 SQ. FT.

TOTAL LIVING AREA: 2,796 SQ. FT.

HIGH WIND LOAD ENGINEERING AVAILABLE
SEE PAGE 246 FOR DETAILS

SECOND FLOOR

FIRST FLOOR
No. 94212

DESIGN NO. 92274

PRICE CODE F

ELEGANT RESIDENCE

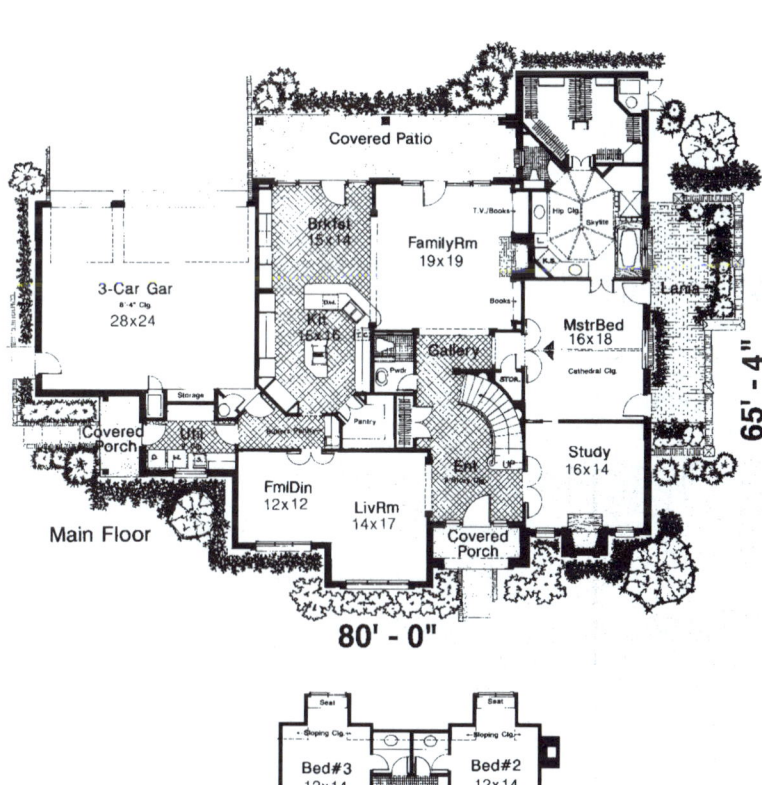

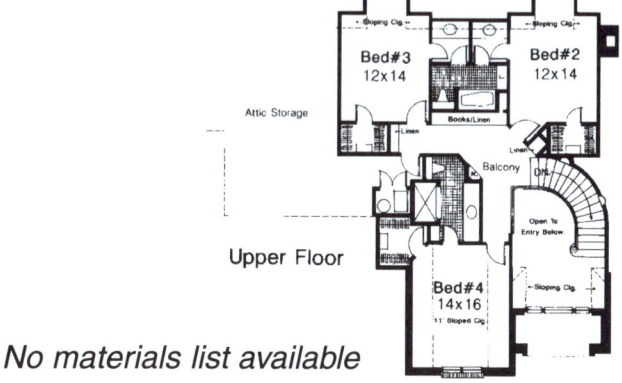

No. 92274

■ This plan features:

— Four bedrooms

— Three full and one half baths

■ Two-story glass Entry enhanced by a curved staircase

■ Open Living/Dining Room with decorative windows makes entertaining easy

■ Large, efficient Kitchen with cooktop/work island, huge walk-in pantry, Breakfast room, butler's Pantry and Utility/Garage entry

■ Comfortable Family Room with hearth fireplace, built-ins and access to Covered Patio

■ Cathedral ceiling tops luxurious Master Bedroom offering a private Lanai, skylit bath, double walk-in closet, and adjoining Study

MAIN FLOOR — 2,807 SQ. FT.
UPPER FLOOR — 1,063 SQ. FT.
GARAGE — 633 SQ. FT.

TOTAL LIVING AREA: 3,870 SQ. FT.

No materials list available

DESIGN NO. 94707

PRICE CODE D

Classic and Compact Country Manor

No. 94707

- This plan features:
— Four bedrooms
— Two full and one half baths
- Two story Foyer and Living Room highlighted by decorative windows
- Spacious Kitchen offers a work island/eating bar, curved Breakfast area with Deck access, Laundry and Garage entry
- Both formal Dining Room and Family Room conveniently adjoin Kitchen/Breakfast Room
- Corner Master Bedroom with a vaulted ceiling and a luxurious bath
- Three additional bedrooms with ample closets share a full bath

First floor — 1,282 sq. ft.
Second floor — 1,219 sq. ft.
Garage — 417 sq. ft.

Total living area: 2,501 sq. ft.

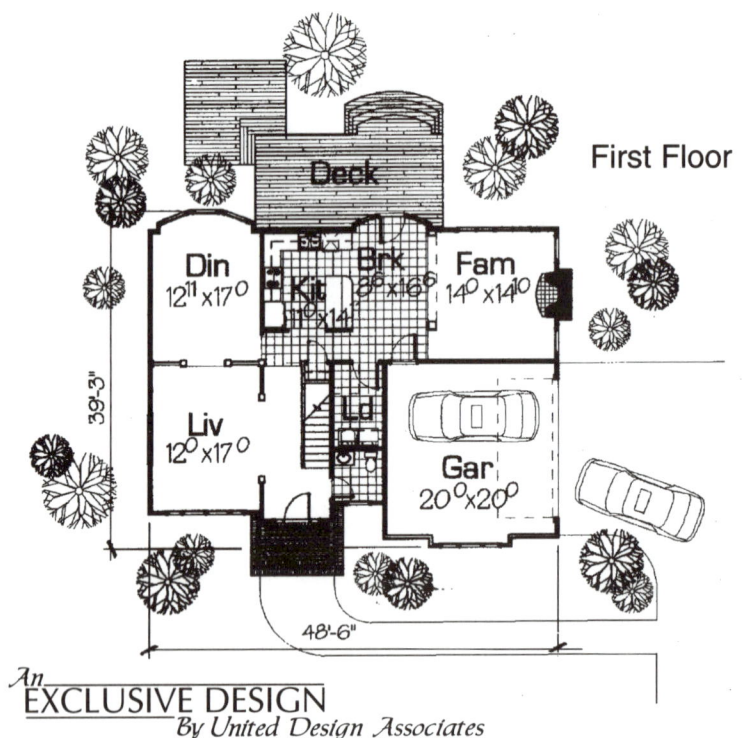

First Floor

An EXCLUSIVE DESIGN By United Design Associates

HIGH WIND LOAD ENGINEERING AVAILABLE
SEE PAGE 246 FOR DETAILS

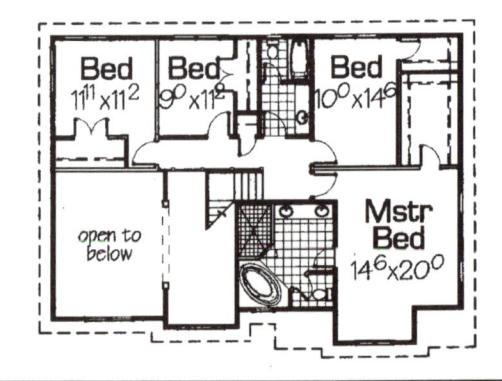

Second Floor

DESIGN NO. 93253

PRICE CODE D

Suitable for today's lifestyle

No. 93253

■ This plan features:

— Four bedrooms

— Two full and one half baths

■ A large Family Room with a fireplace and access to the patio

■ A Breakfast Area that flows directly into the Family Room

■ A well-appointed Kitchen equipped with an eating bar, double sinks, built-in pantry and an abundance of counter and cabinet space

■ A Master Suite with a decorative ceiling and a private Bath

■ Three additional bedrooms that share a full bath

MAIN AREA — 2,542 SQ. FT.
GARAGE — 510 SQ. FT.

TOTAL LIVING AREA: 2,542 SQ. FT.

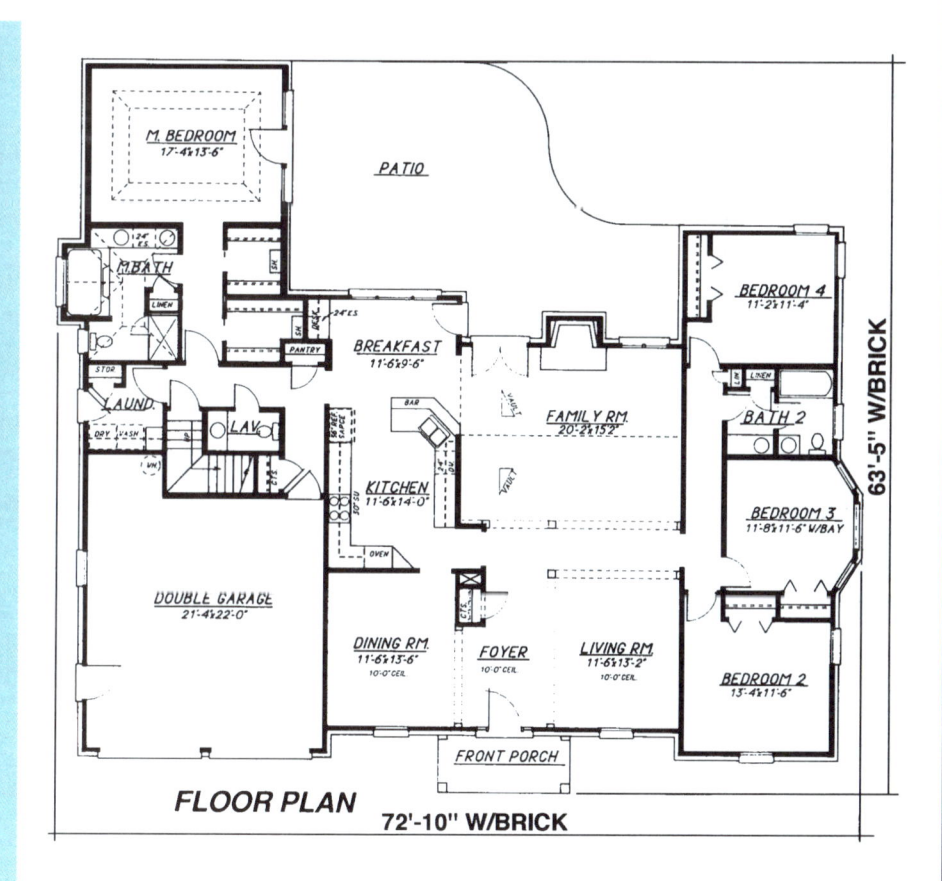

FLOOR PLAN 72'-10" W/BRICK 63'-5" W/BRICK

An **EXCLUSIVE DESIGN** By Jannis Vann & Associates, Inc.

DESIGN NO. 92202

PRICE CODE F

Arched Windows Add Light and Luxury

No. 92202

■ This plan features:

— Four bedrooms

— Three full and one half baths

■ Two-story entrance with barrel vaulted ceiling and a graceful, curving staircase

■ Formal Living Room enhanced by a hearth fireplace

■ Formal Dining Room and Study highlighted by decorative windows

■ Country-size Kitchen with walk-in pantry, Breakfast Room and access to Covered Patio

■ Private Master Bedroom suite with vaulted ceiling, huge walk-in closet and plush bath

■ Three second floor bedrooms with ample closets and private access to two full baths

MAIN FLOOR — 2,635 SQ. FT.
UPPER FLOOR — 1,005 SQ. FT.
GARAGE — 660 SQ. FT.

TOTAL LIVING AREA: 3,640 SQ. FT.

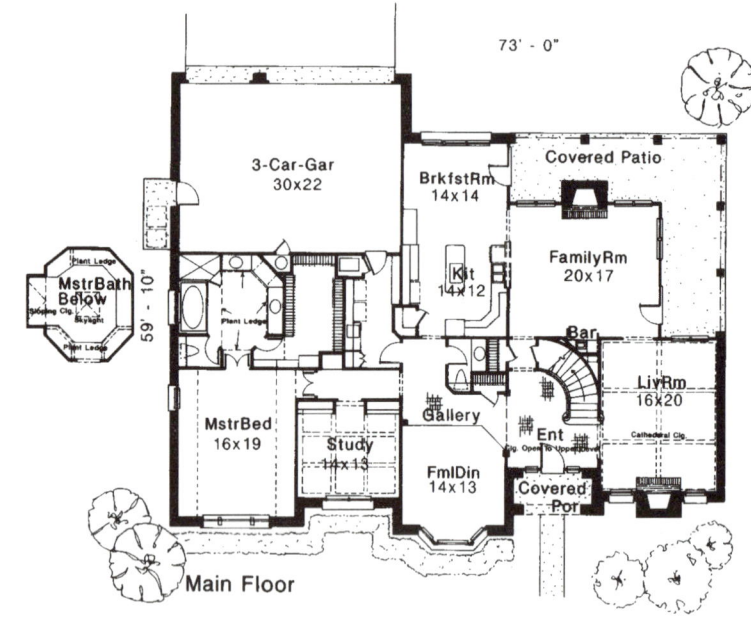

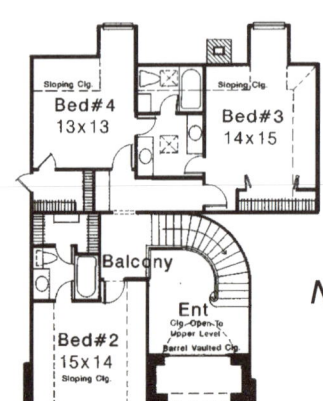

No materials list available

108

DESIGN NO. 94806

PRICE CODE C

Warm country house

No. 94806

■ This plan features:

— Three bedrooms

— Two full and one half baths

■ A wrap-around Porch expands living outdoors

■ Expansive Activity Room with a huge fireplace separated from Dining Room by a lovely banister staircase

■ Efficient Kitchen with work island/serving counter for Breakfast Room, Laundry and Garage entry

■ First floor Master Bedroom with a tray ceiling and a pampering bath

■ Two second floor bedrooms with dormer windows, share a full bath

FIRST FLOOR — 1,531 SQ. FT.
SECOND FLOOR — 640 SQ. FT.
BASEMENT — 1,531 SQ. FT.

TOTAL LIVING AREA: 2,171 SQ. FT.

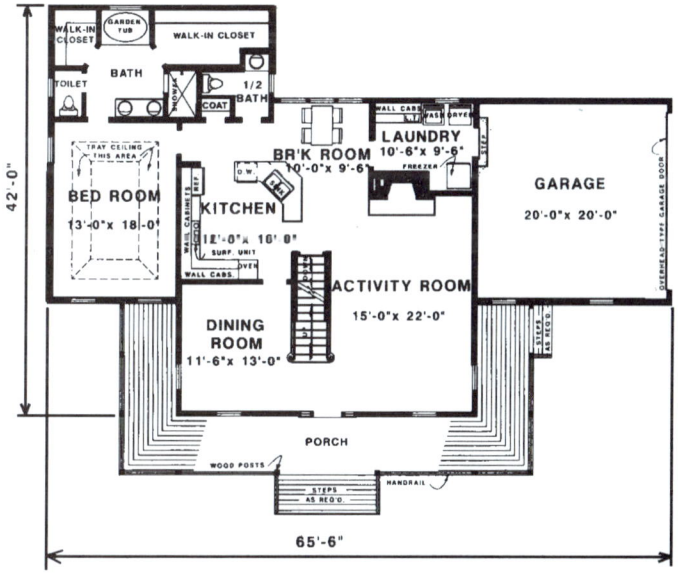

FIRST FLOOR PLAN

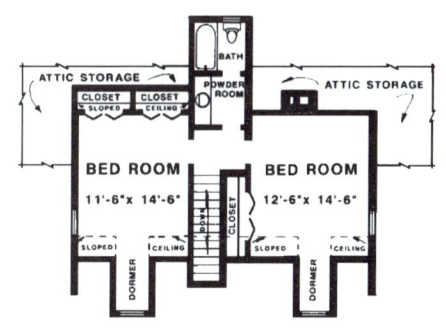

SECOND FLOOR PLAN

DESIGN NO. 94615

PRICE CODE E

GRAND COUNTRY PORCH

No. 94615

■ This plan features:

— Four bedrooms

— Three full baths

■ Large front Porch provides shade and Southern hospitality

■ Spacious Living Room with access to Covered Porch and Patio, and a cozy fireplace between built-in shelves

■ Country Kitchen with a cooktop island, bright Breakfast bay, Utility Room, Garage entry, and adjoining Dining Room

■ Corner Master Bedroom with a walk-in closet and private bath

■ Two additional second floor bedrooms with dormers, walk-in closets and vanities share a full bath

■ An optional crawl space or slab foundation — please specify when ordering

FIRST FLOOR — 1,916 SQ. FT.
SECOND FLOOR — 746 SQ. FT.
GARAGE — 478 SQ. FT.

TOTAL LIVING AREA: 2,665 SQ. FT.

WIDTH 62'-0"
DEPTH 63'-8 1/2"

FIRST FLOOR

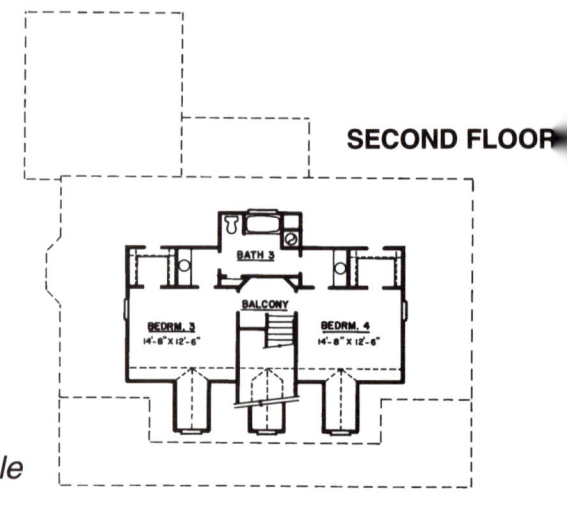

SECOND FLOOR

No materials list available

110

DESIGN NO. 99286

PRICE CODE C

Southern Country Farmhouse

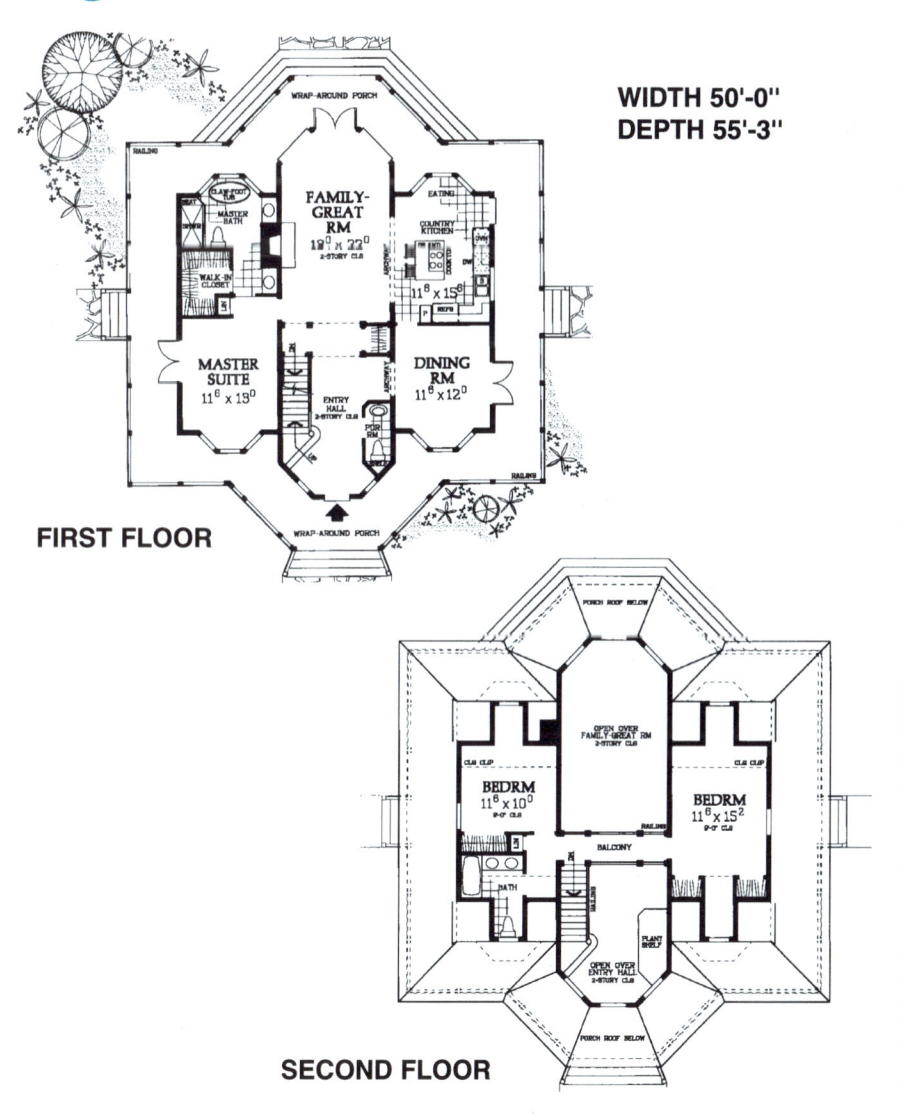

WIDTH 50'-0"
DEPTH 55'-3"

FIRST FLOOR

SECOND FLOOR

No. 99286

■ This plan features:

— Three bedrooms

— Two full and one half baths

■ Wrap-around Porch leads into two-story octagon Entry Hall highlighted by graceful staircase and a bay of windows

■ Two-story Family/Great Room enhanced by a huge fireplace and French doors opening onto wrap-around porch

■ L-shaped country Kitchen with a cooktop island/snackbar, Eating bay and access to formal Dining Room, Porch and Family Room

■ Spacious first floor Master Suite complemented by Porch access and a plush bath

■ Two large, second floor bedrooms share a balcony and double vanity bath

FIRST FLOOR — 1,295 SQ. FT.
SECOND FLOOR — 600 SQ. FT.

TOTAL LIVING AREA: 1,895 SQ. FT.

DESIGN NO. 94705

PRICE CODE D

BACK YARD VIEWS

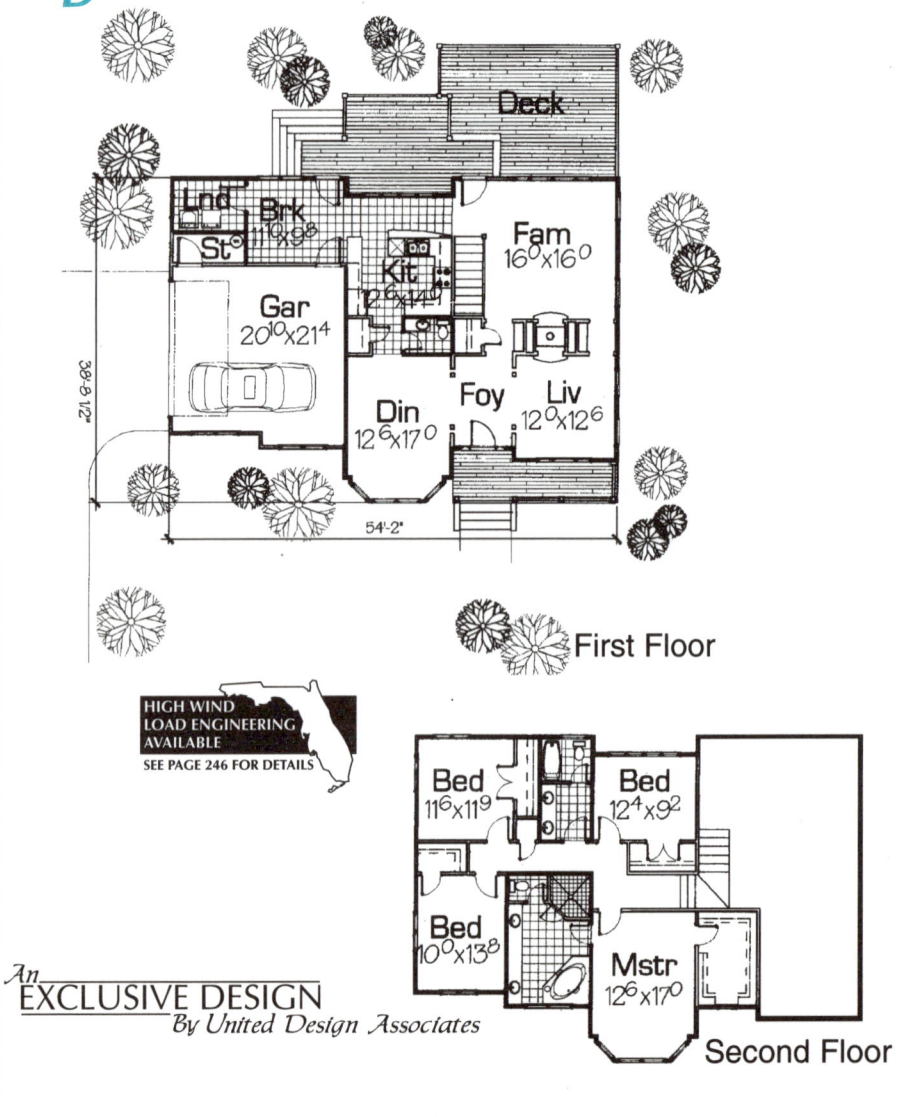

No. 94705
■ This home features:

— Four bedrooms

— Two full and one half baths

■ Lovely Porch leads into a spacious Foyer

■ Open Living and Family areas with vaulted ceilings, share a two-sided brick fireplace

■ Efficient Kitchen with a serving counter, Breakfast area, Laundry, Garage entry, and adjoining Deck and Dining room

■ Master Suite highlighted by a bay window, large walk-in closet and a spacious bath with a whirlpool tub

■ Three additional bedrooms with over-sized closets, share a double vanity bath

FIRST FLOOR — 1,320 SQ. FT.
SECOND FLOOR — 1,215 SQ. FT.
GARAGE — 477 SQ. FT.

TOTAL LIVING AREA: 2,535 SQ. FT.

HIGH WIND LOAD ENGINEERING AVAILABLE
SEE PAGE 246 FOR DETAILS

An EXCLUSIVE DESIGN *By United Design Associates*

First Floor

Second Floor

112

DESIGN NO. 99285

PRICE CODE B

Southern Hospitality

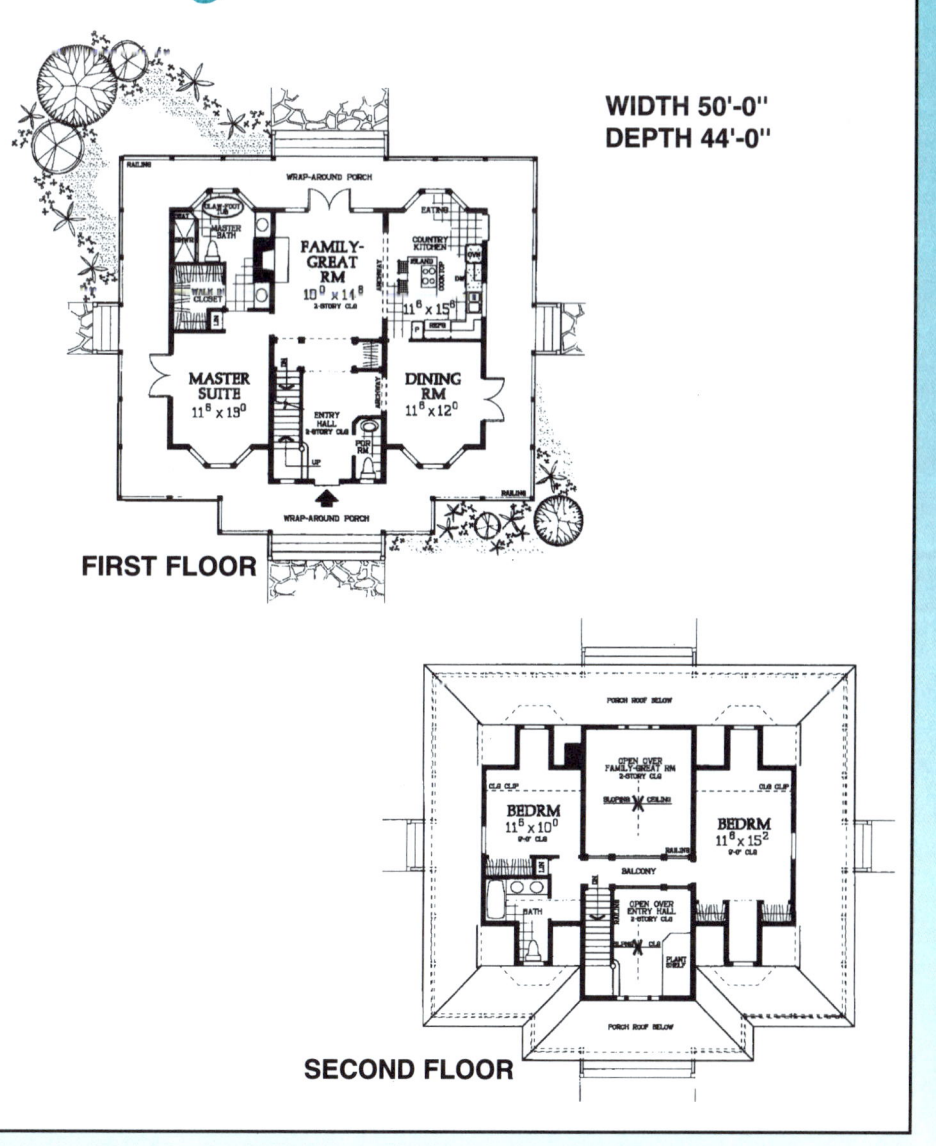

No. 99285

■ This plan features:

— Three bedrooms

— Two full and one half baths

■ Inviting atmosphere enhanced by Porch surrounding and shading home

■ Two-story Entry Hall graced by a landing staircase and arched window

■ Double doors access Porch from Family Great Room, Dining Room and Master Suite

■ Country Kitchen with cooktop island/snackbar, eating alcove and archway to Family Room with cozy fireplace

■ First floor Master Suite with bay window, walk-in closet and pampering bath

■ Two double dormer bedrooms on second floor catch breezes and share a full bath

FIRST FLOOR — 1171 SQ. FT.
SECOND FLOOR — 600 SQ. FT.

TOTAL LIVING AREA: 1,771 SQ. FT.

WIDTH 50'-0"
DEPTH 44'-0"

FIRST FLOOR

SECOND FLOOR

DESIGN NO. 94601

PRICE CODE B

Unique Design with Grand Front Porch

No. 94601

■ This plan features:

— Three bedrooms

— Two full bathrooms

■ Full front Porch invites relaxation and entry into open Foyer

■ Central Living Room with tray ceiling topping cozy fireplace, and access to Porch and Carport

■ Spacious Kitchen with glassed Breakfast area, built-in pantry and Utility Room

■ Largest bedroom has decorative ceiling and features double walk-in closets and a double vanity bath

■ Two additional bedrooms with large closets share a full bath

■ An optional crawl space or slab foundation — please specify when ordering

MAIN FLOOR —1,704 SQ. FT.
CARPORT WITH STORAGE — 500 SQ. FT.

TOTAL LIVING AREA: 1,704 SQ. FT.

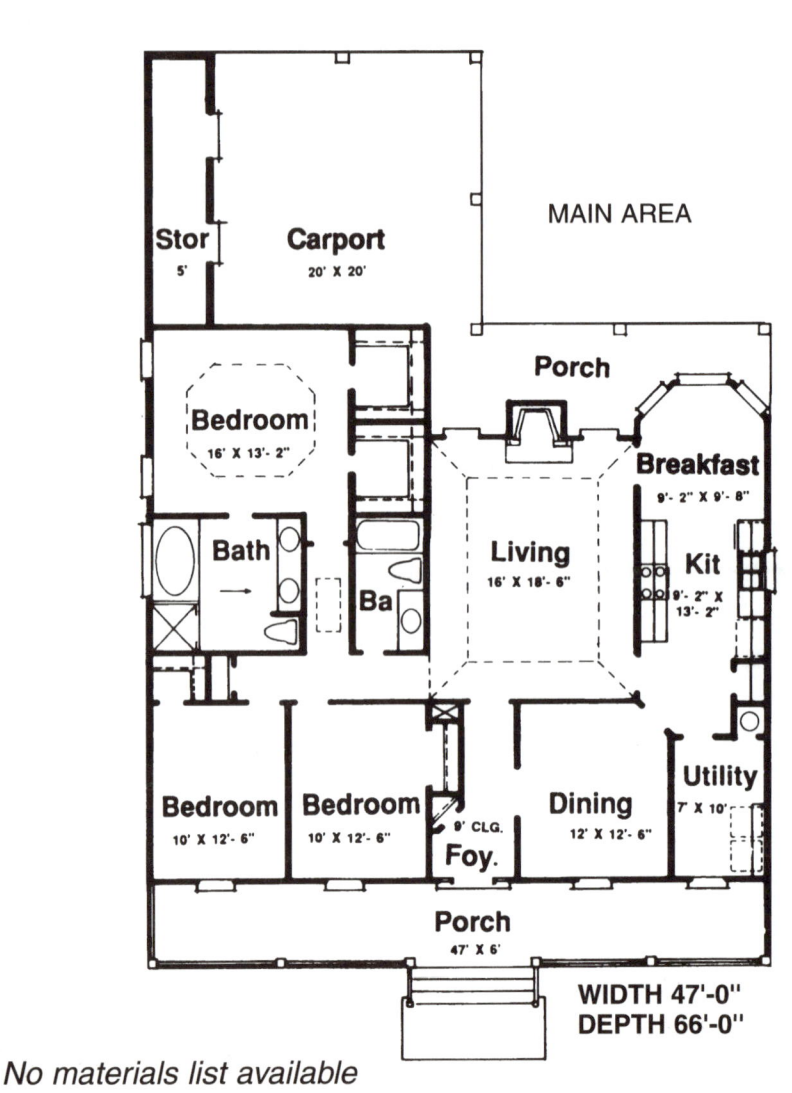

Stor 5'
Carport 20' X 20'
MAIN AREA
Porch
Bedroom 16' X 13'-2"
Breakfast 9'-2" X 9'-8"
Bath
Ba
Living 16' X 18'-6"
Kit 9'-2" X 13'-2"
Bedroom 10' X 12'-6"
Bedroom 10' X 12'-6"
9' CLG.
Foy.
Dining 12' X 12'-6"
Utility 7' X 10'
Porch 47' X 6'

WIDTH 47'-0"
DEPTH 66'-0"

No materials list available

DESIGN NO. 94714

PRICE CODE B

*C*LASSIC AMERICAN STYLE

No. 94714

■ This plan features:

— Three bedrooms

— Two full and one half baths

■ Sheltered entry into Foyer with pillars defining Dining area and Great Room with hearth fireplace and a wall of windows with Patio access

■ Efficient Kitchen with serving counter bright Breakfast area

■ Corner Master suite offers a tray ceiling, Patio access, a walk-in closet and double vanity bath

■ Two second floor bedrooms with large closets, share a full bath

■ An optional crawl space or slab foundation — please specify when ordering

FIRST FLOOR — 1,432 SQ. FT.
SECOND FLOOR — 470 SQ. FT.
GARAGE — 441 SQ. FT.

TOTAL LIVING AREA: 1,902 SQ. FT.

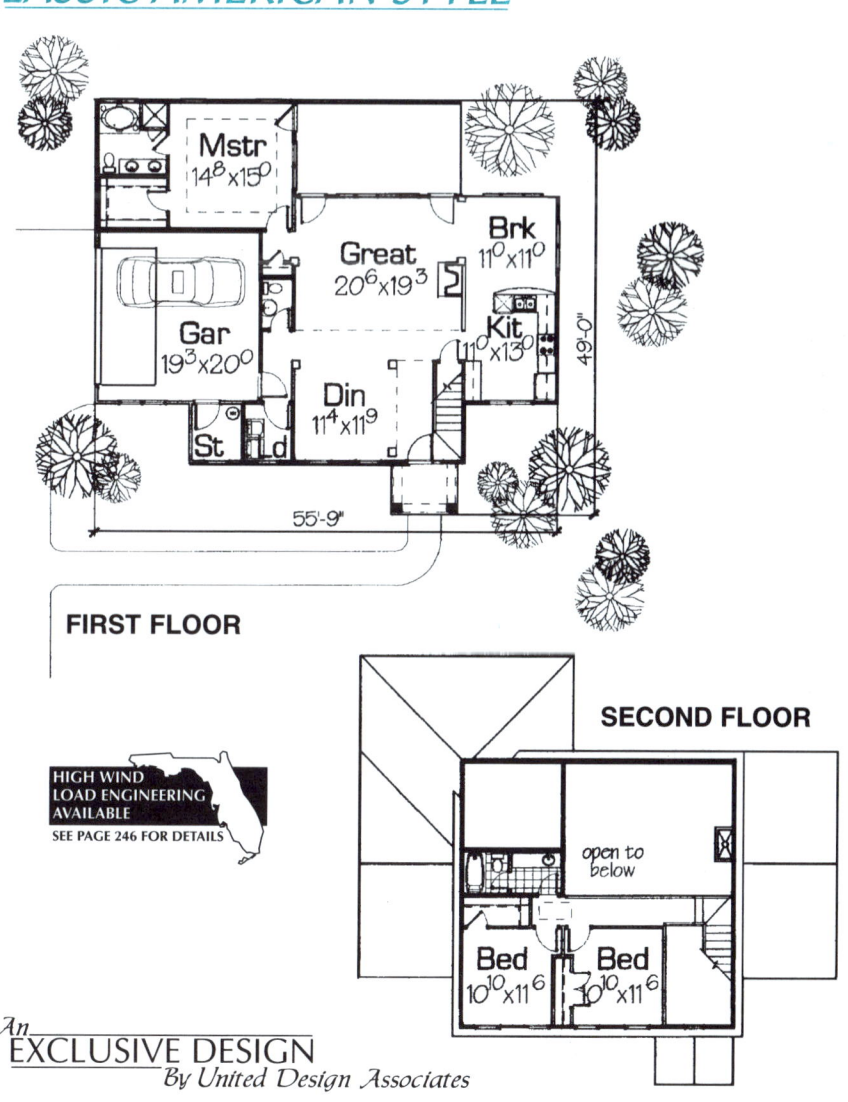

FIRST FLOOR

Mstr 14⁸ x 15⁰
Brk 11⁰ x 11⁰
Great 20⁶ x 19³
Gar 19³ x 20⁰
Kit 11⁰ x 13⁰
Din 11⁴ x 11⁹
St
55'-9"
49'-0"

HIGH WIND LOAD ENGINEERING AVAILABLE
SEE PAGE 246 FOR DETAILS

SECOND FLOOR

open to below
Bed 10¹⁰ x 11⁶
Bed 10¹⁰ x 11⁶

An EXCLUSIVE DESIGN By United Design Associates

DESIGN NO. 92403

PRICE CODE F

Elegant European Flavor

No. 92403

- This plan features:
— Four bedrooms
— Three full and two half baths
- A see-through fireplace highlighting the Master Suite
- A Master Bath with a spacious dressing area, a roomy walk-in closet, separate vanities, a separate garden tub and shower
- An island Kitchen with a corner double sink and ample counter and storage space
- A formal Dining Room with a bay window
- A spacious Great Room with a built-in bookcase and a fireplace
- Three additional bedrooms, one with vaulted ceilings, all with private access to a full bath

FIRST FLOOR — 2,082 SQ. FT.
SECOND FLOOR — 1,182 SQ. FT.
BASEMENT — 1,126 SQ. FT.
GARAGE — 625 SQ. FT.

TOTAL LIVING AREA: 3,264 SQ. FT.

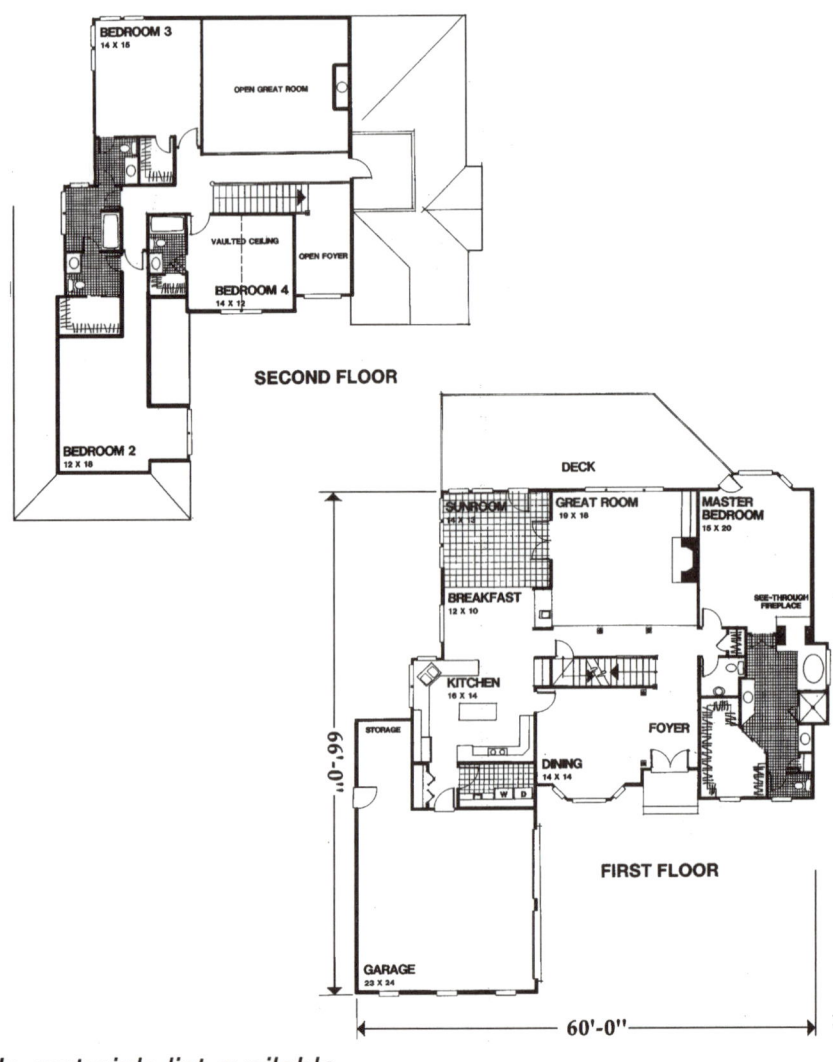

No materials list available

DESIGN NO. 92513

PRICE CODE D

Elegant European Style

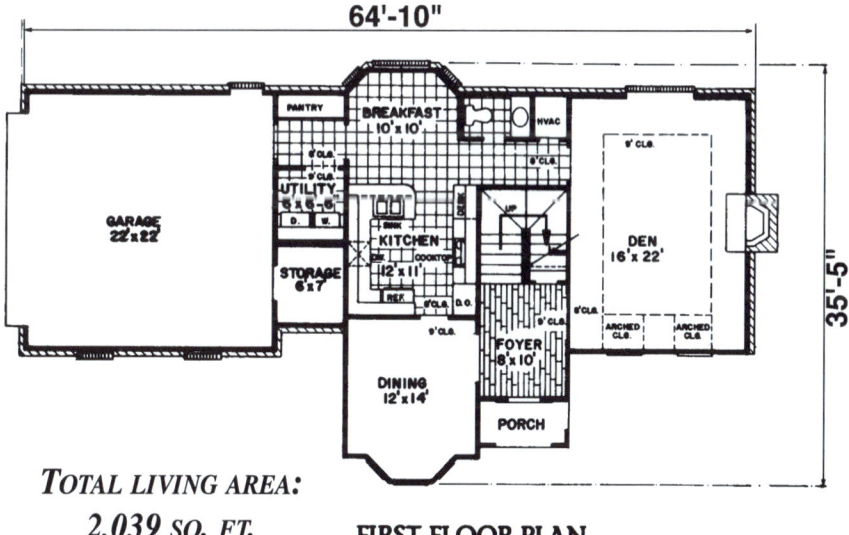

No. 92513

■ This plan features:

— Three bedrooms

— Two full and one half baths

■ Copper hood over double bay windows enhances facade of stucco, brick and arches

■ Balcony overlooks two-story Foyer highlighted by transom window above front door

■ Floor to ceiling bay window enhances formal Dining Room

■ Gourmet Kitchen with built-in desk, Breakfast bay, walk-in pantry and Utility area

■ Secluded Master Bedroom suite with decorative ceiling, oversized corner tub and vanity area

■ Two additional bedrooms share a double vanity bath

■ An optional crawl space or slab foundation available, please specify when ordering

FIRST FLOOR — 1,065 SQ. FT.
SECOND FLOOR — 974 SQ. FT.
GARAGE — 626 SQ. FT.

TOTAL LIVING AREA: 2,039 SQ. FT.

FIRST FLOOR PLAN

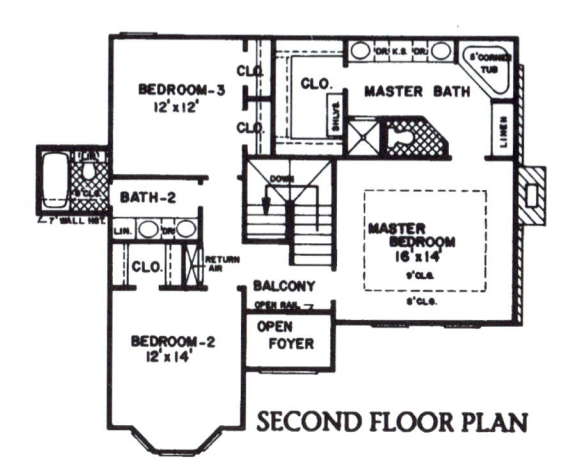

SECOND FLOOR PLAN

DESIGN NO. 93036

PRICE CODE F

Southwest styling

No. 93036

■ This plan features:
- Five bedrooms
- Four full and two half baths

■ A two-story Foyer with a cascading staircase

■ A large two-story Family Room, opening off the Gallery area that includes a video/audio area

■ A coffered ceiling in the elegant Dining Room

■ A magnificent Master Suite with a private Study that is separated from the bedroom by a see-through fireplace

■ A Master Bath with a centerpiece whirlpool tub, accented with a glass block

■ An in-law wing with a bath and Kitchenette

■ Three additional bedrooms and two full baths on the second floor

FIRST FLOOR — 3,300 SQ. FT.
SECOND FLOOR — 2,005 SQ. FT.

TOTAL LIVING AREA: 5,305 SQ. FT.

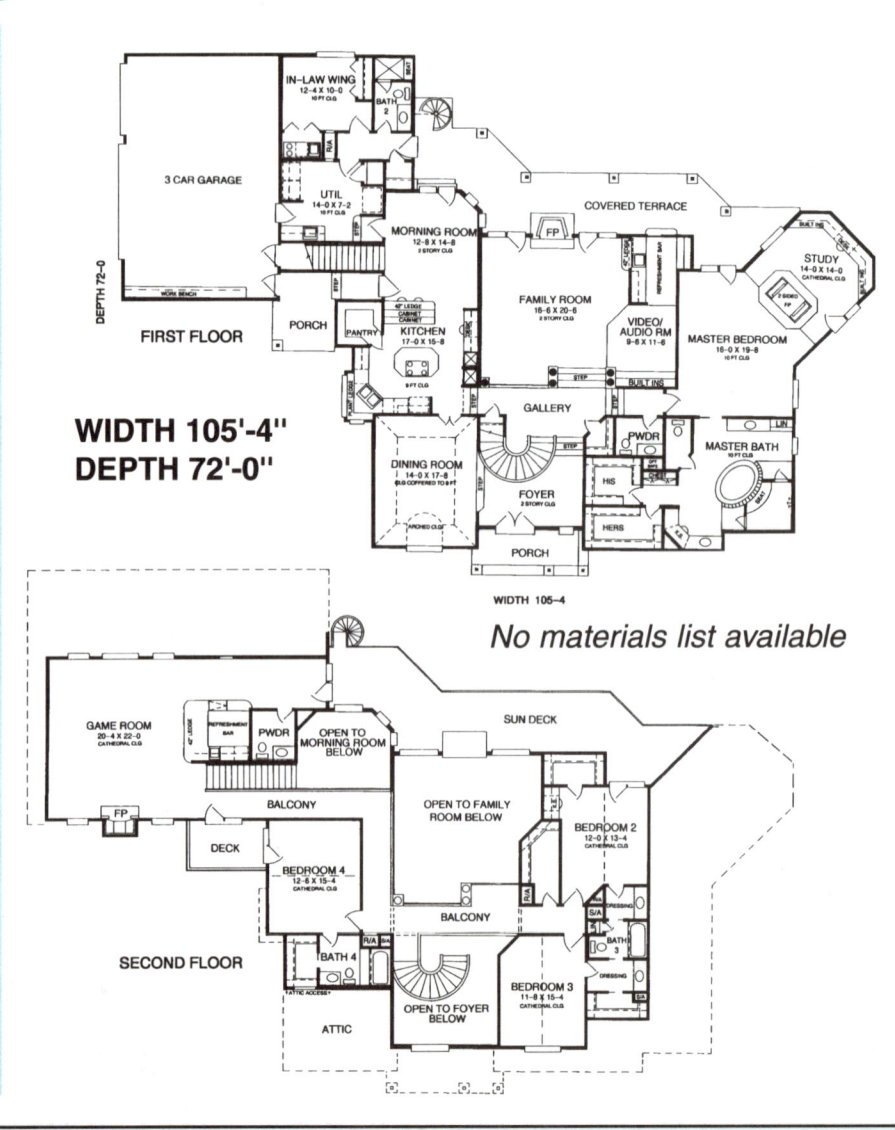

WIDTH 105'-4"
DEPTH 72'-0"

No materials list available

DESIGN NO. 94618

PRICE CODE E

Elegant Design Enhanced by Porch

No. 94618

■ This plan features:

— Four bedrooms

— Three full and one half baths

■ Floor to ceiling windows and stately pillars

■ Great Room with built-in shelving, focal point fireplace and access to Porch and Patio

■ Spacious Kitchen with built-in pantry, cooktop island, Breakfast bay, Utility and Garage entry

■ Corner Master Suite with large walk-in closet and double vanity bath

■ Guest bedroom with private access to a full bath

■ An optional crawl space or slab foundation — please specify when ordering

FIRST FLOOR — 2,120 SQ. FT.
SECOND FLOOR — 704 SQ. FT.
GARAGE — 516 SQ. FT.

TOTAL LIVING AREA: 2,824 SQ. FT.

No materials list available

WIDTH 66'-11.5"
DEPTH 64'-11.5"

SECOND FLOOR

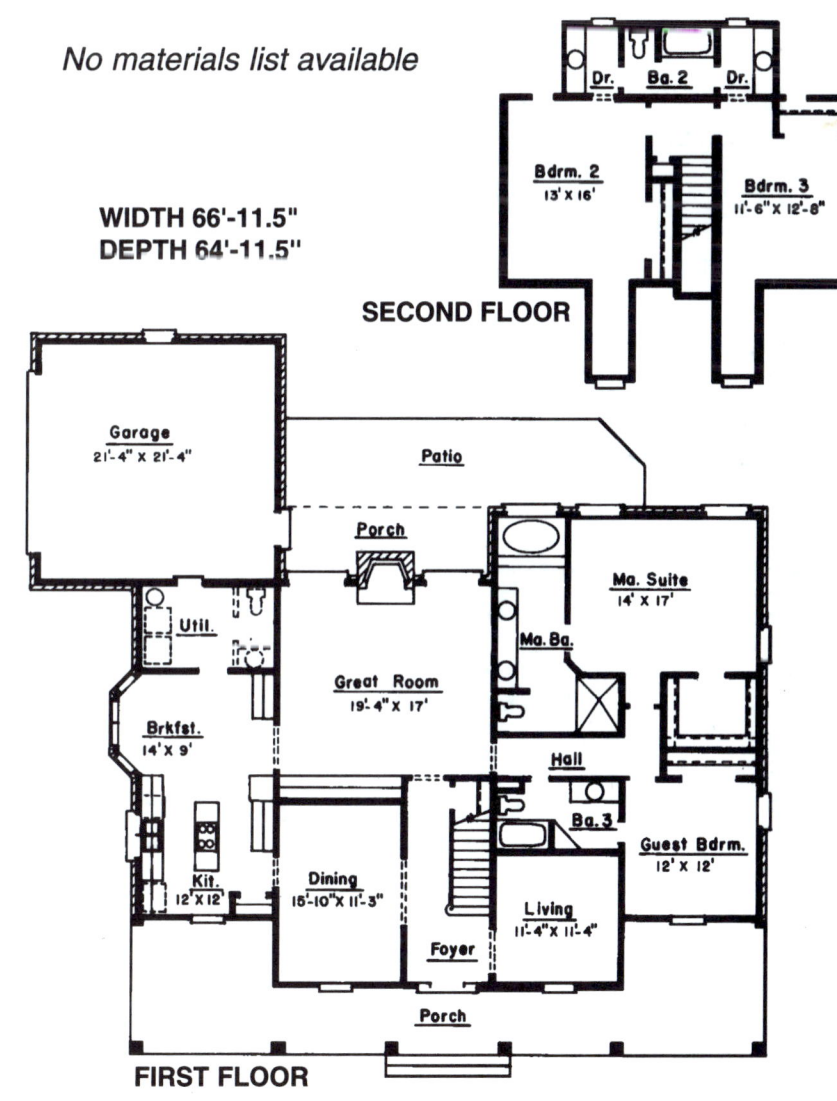

FIRST FLOOR

DESIGN NO. 94701

PRICE CODE E

SIMPLY ELEGANT

No. 94701

- This plan features:
— Four bedrooms
— Two full and one half baths
- The entry Portico leads into the main Foyer
- The combination of high ceilings, polished hardwood floors and elegant columns subtly define the spaces of the primary living areas
- An expansive Great room has a fireplace and French doors that lead to the rear patio
- The magnificent Kitchen has a cooking island and wrap around bar
- An adjoining Breakfast Room is punctuated by bright windows
- The Master suite boasts a five piece bath and a walk-in closet
- Three additional bedrooms, one with private access to the full bath

MAIN FLOOR — 2,688 SQ. FT.
GARAGE — 438 SQ. FT.

TOTAL LIVING AREA: 2,688 SQ. FT

No materials list available

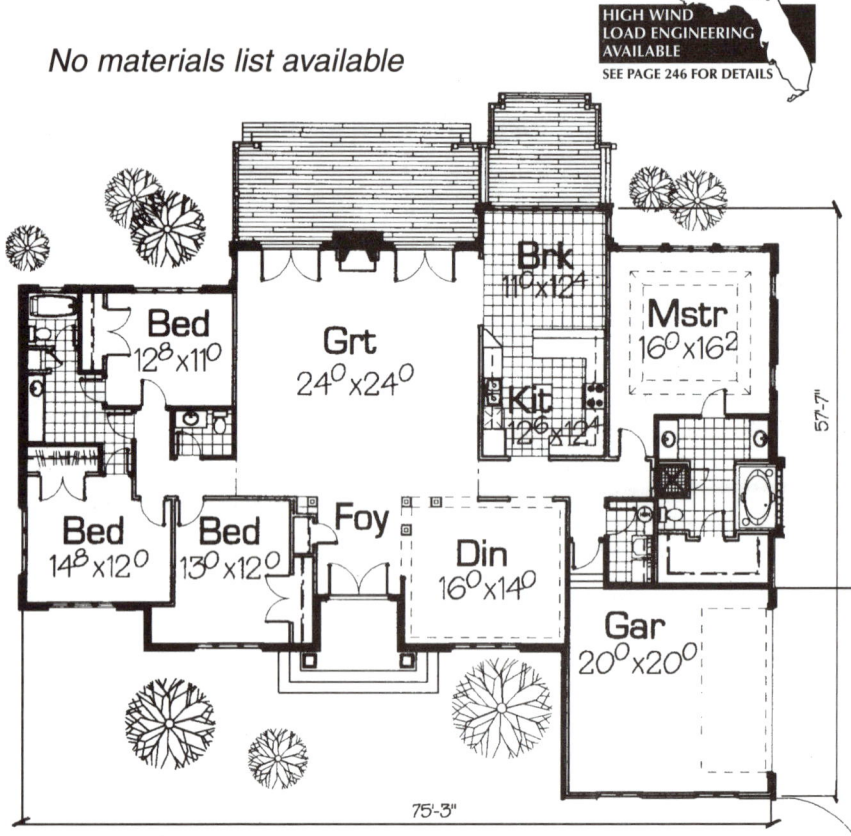

HIGH WIND LOAD ENGINEERING AVAILABLE
SEE PAGE 246 FOR DETAILS

MAIN FLOOR
No. 94701

An EXCLUSIVE DESIGN *By United Design Associates*

DESIGN NO. 99287

PRICE CODE D

Magnificent Mediterranean Style

No. 99287

■ This plan features:

— Three bedrooms

— Two full and one half baths

■ Covered Porch provides shady access to a bright Entry/Art Gallery enhanced by arches

■ Open Family/Great Room with raised, hearth fireplace, arches and Open Courtyard access

■ Country Kitchen efficiently serves island snackbar, Dining Room and Family Room

■ Master Bedroom corner offers a walk-in closet and a plush bath with a corner whirlpool tub

■ Two additional bedrooms with plant shelves share a double vanity bath

■ Corner Office-Den with access to Covered Porch and Powder Room

Main Floor — 2,539 sq. ft.
Garage — 586 sq. ft.

Total living area: 2,539 sq. ft.

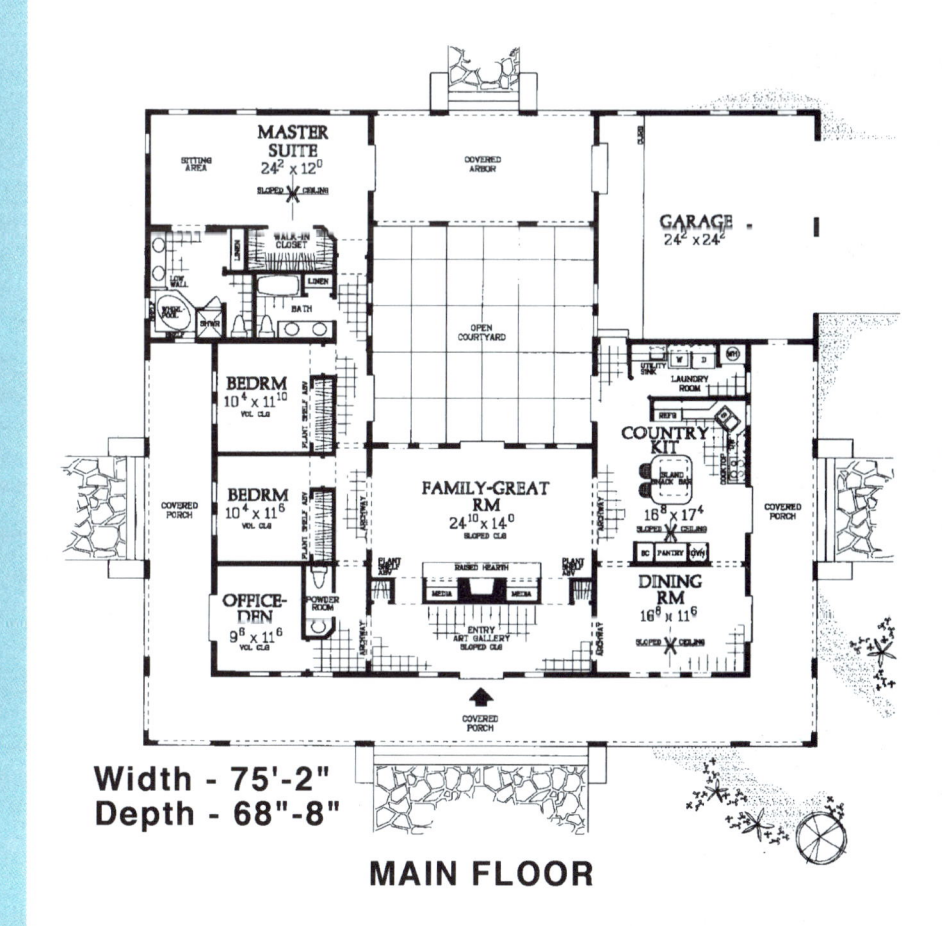

Width - 75'-2"
Depth - 68"-8"

MAIN FLOOR

DESIGN NO. 92509

PRICE CODE E

Arched Windows Accent Sophisticated Design

No. 92509

■ This plan features:

— Four bedrooms

— Two full and one half baths

■ Graceful columns and full-length windows highlight front Porch leading into central Foyer flanked by Living and Dining rooms

■ Spacious Great room with decorative ceiling over hearth fireplace between built-in cabinets and sliding glass door to covered back Porch

■ Secluded Master Bedroom suite offers access to back Porch, decorative ceiling and plush bath with walk-in closet, double vanity and spa tub

■ Three additional bedrooms with loads of closets space share double vanity bath

■ An optional crawl space or slab foundation available, please specify when ordering

MAIN FLOOR — 2,551 SQ. FT.
GARAGE — 532 SQ. FT.

TOTAL LIVING AREA:

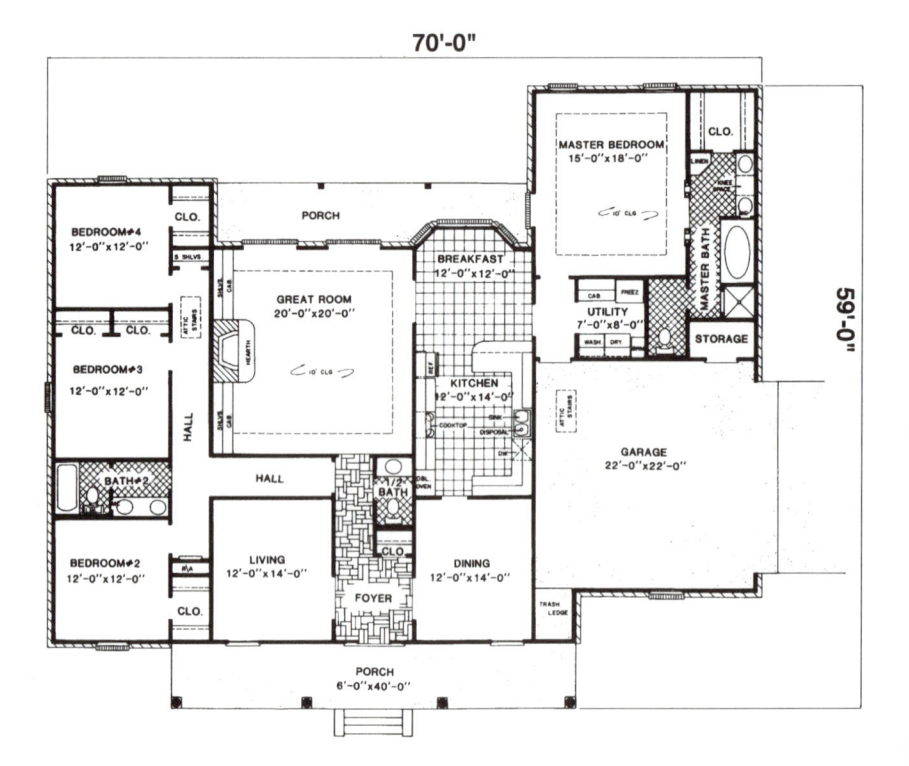

MAIN AREA

DESIGN NO. 94713

PRICE CODE C

Reminiscent of the Deep South

No. 94713

- This plan features:
- — Three bedrooms
- — Two full and one half baths
- Victorian Porch leads into Foyer and two-story Great Room with a focal point fireplace
- Efficient, U-shaped Kitchen opens to Great Room and Dining Room
- Private Master Suite with triple windows, walk-in closet and luxurious bath with a double vanity and garden window tub
- Two second floor bedrooms with large closets, share a full bath and Loft

FIRST FLOOR — 1,350 SQ. FT.
SECOND FLOOR — 589 SQ. FT.

TOTAL LIVING AREA: 1,939 SQ. FT.

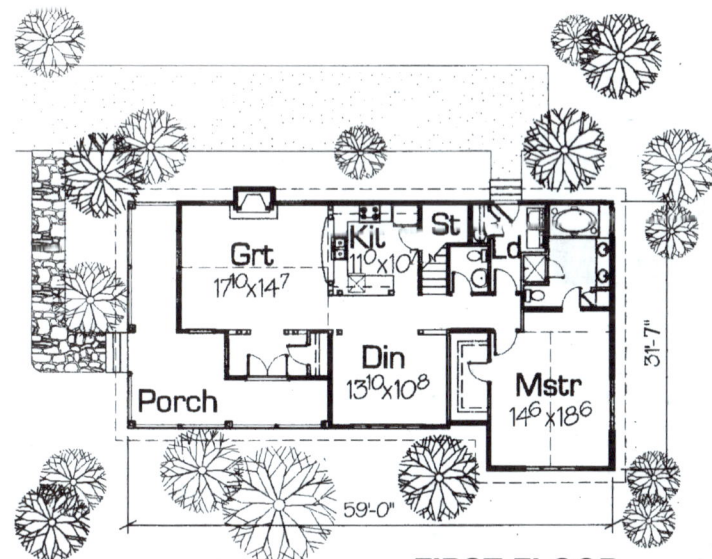

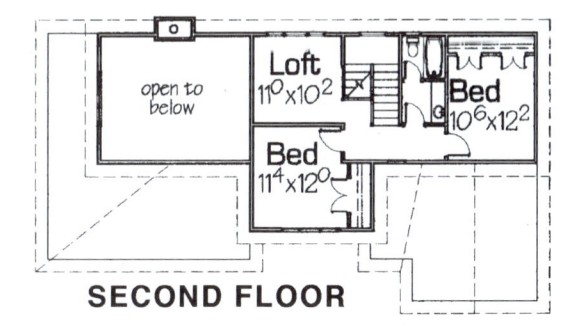

FIRST FLOOR

SECOND FLOOR

HIGH WIND LOAD ENGINEERING AVAILABLE
SEE PAGE 246 FOR DETAILS

An EXCLUSIVE DESIGN
By United Design Associates

DESIGN NO. 94709

PRICE CODE D

Country charm in stucco

No. 94709

- This plan features:
— Four bedrooms
— Two full and one half baths
- Front Porch with access to two-story Foyer, Dining and Great rooms
- Great Room with three-sided fireplace and French doors to Deck
- Country-size Kitchen with work island/snackbar, Breakfast corner, Deck and Garage access
- Private Master wing enhanced by two walk-in closets and vanities, whirlpool window tub and vaulted ceilings
- Three second floor bedrooms with ample closets, share a full bath, Laundry and Bonus Room

First floor — 1,518 sq. ft.
Second floor — 811 sq. ft.
Garage — 427 sq. ft.

Total living area: 2,329 sq. ft.

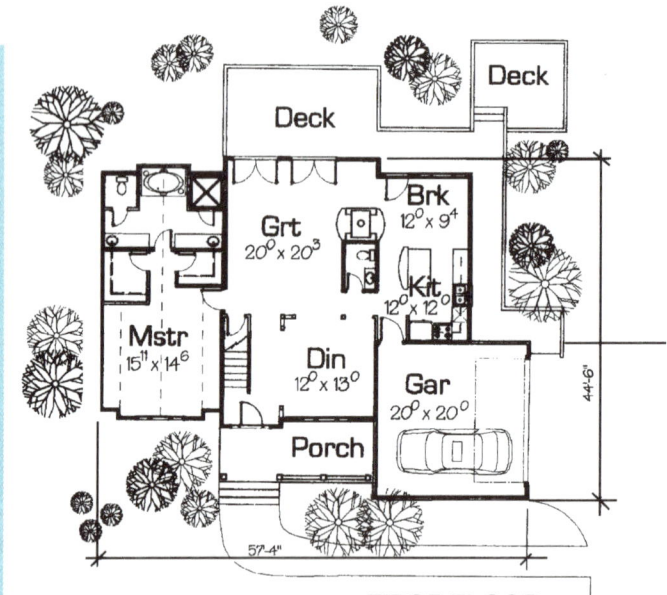

FIRST FLOOR

HIGH WIND LOAD ENGINEERING AVAILABLE
SEE PAGE 246 FOR DETAILS

SECOND FLOOR

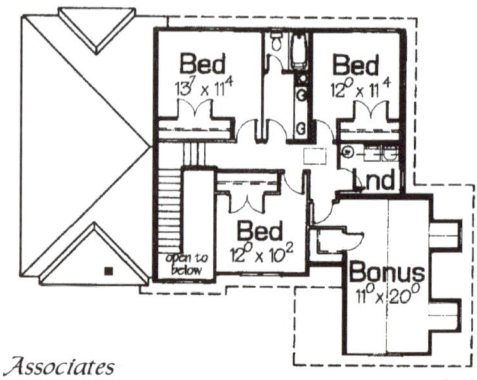

An EXCLUSIVE DESIGN
By United Design Associates

DESIGN NO. 94803

PRICE CODE B

Charming, Compact and Convenient

No. 94803

- This plan features:
— Three bedrooms
— Two full and one half bath
- Double dormer, arched window and Covered Porch add light
- Open Foyer graced by banister staircase and balcony
- Spacious Activity Room with a pre-fab fireplace opens to formal Dining Room
- Country-size Kitchen/ Breakfast area with island counter and access to Sun Deck and Laundry/Garage entry
- First floor bedroom highlighted by lovely arched window below a tray ceiling and a pampering bath
- An optional basement or crawl space foundation — please specify when ordering

FIRST FLOOR — 1,165 SQ. FT.
SECOND FLOOR — 587 SQ. FT.
GARAGE — 455 SQ. FT.

TOTAL LIVING AREA: 1,752 SQ. FT.

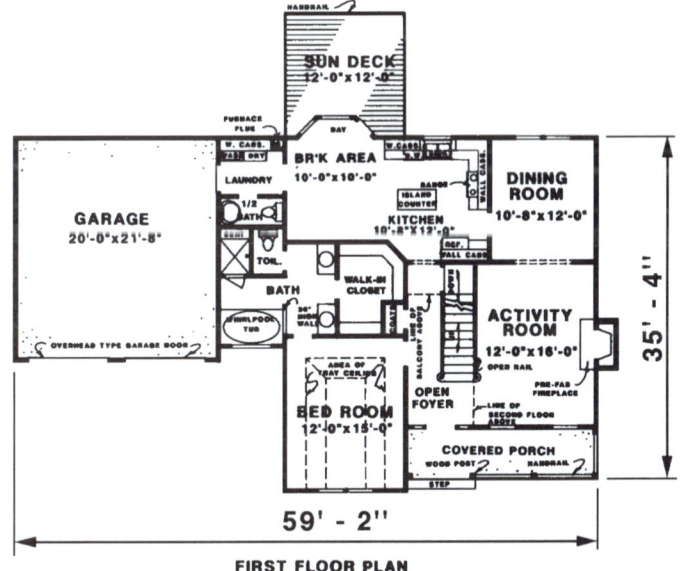

FIRST FLOOR PLAN

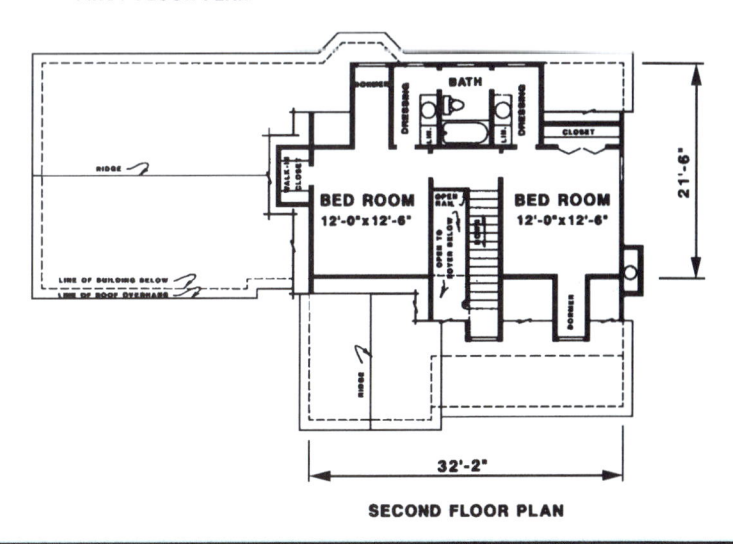

SECOND FLOOR PLAN

DESIGN NO. 99373

PRICE CODE F

HIGH IMPACT TWO-STORY DESIGN

No. 99373

■ This plan features:

— Four bedrooms

— Three full and one half baths

■ A high impact two-story, double door transom Entry

■ A two-story Family Room with a wall consisting of a fireplace and windows

■ A spacious Master Suite with unique curved glass block behind the tub in the Master Bath and a semi-circular window wall with see-through fireplace in sitting area

■ A gourmet Kitchen and Breakfast area opening to a Lanai

■ A Guest Suite with private deck and walk-in closet

FIRST FLOOR — 3,158 SQ. FT.
SECOND FLOOR — 1,374 SQ. FT.

TOTAL LIVING AREA: 4,532 SQ. FT.

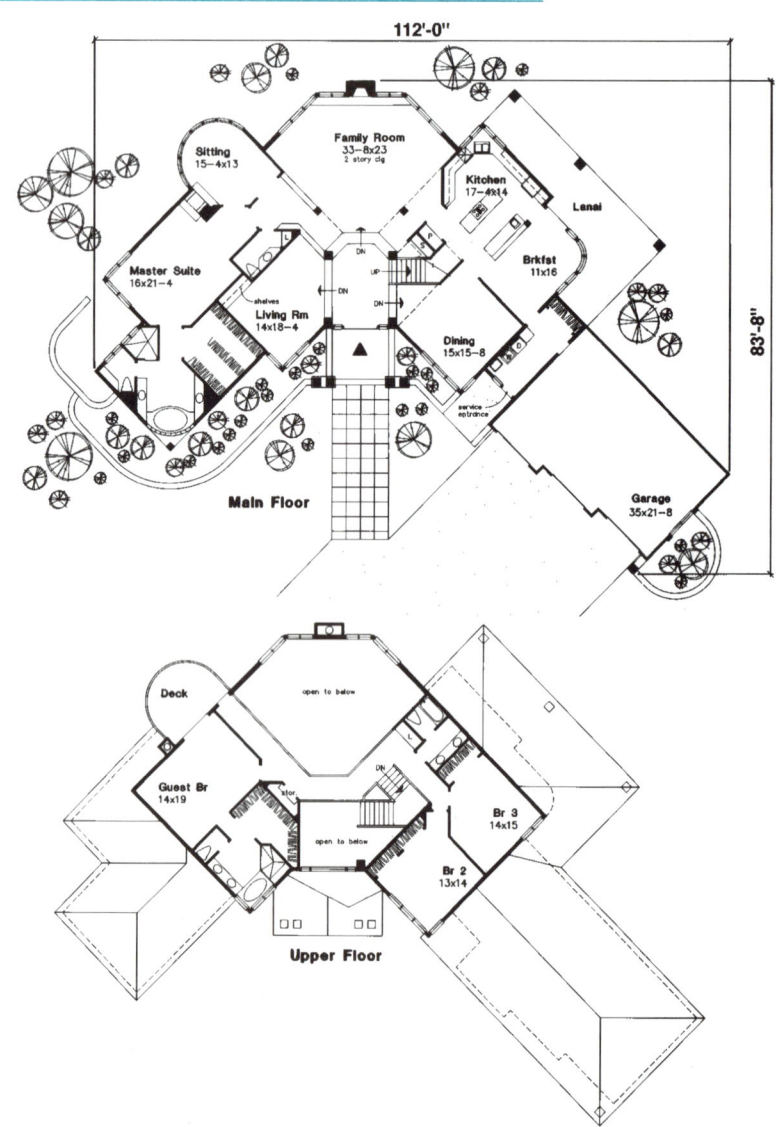

DESIGN NO. 94804

PRICE CODE C

European flair in tune with today

No. 94804

■ This plan features:

— Three bedrooms

— Two full baths

■ European flavor with decorative windows, gable roof lines and a stucco finish

■ Formal Dining Room with floor to ceiling window treatment

■ Expansive Activity Room with decorative ceiling, hearth fireplace and Deck access

■ Open, efficient Kitchen with snackbar, Laundry, Breakfast area and Screened Porch beyond

■ Private Master Bedroom suite with a decorative ceiling, large walk-in closet and luxurious bath

■ Two additional bedroom, one with a bay window, share a full bath

MAIN FLOOR — 1,855 SQ. FT.
BASEMENT — 1,855 SQ. FT.
GARAGE — 439 SQ. FT.

TOTAL LIVING AREA:
1,855 SQ. FT.

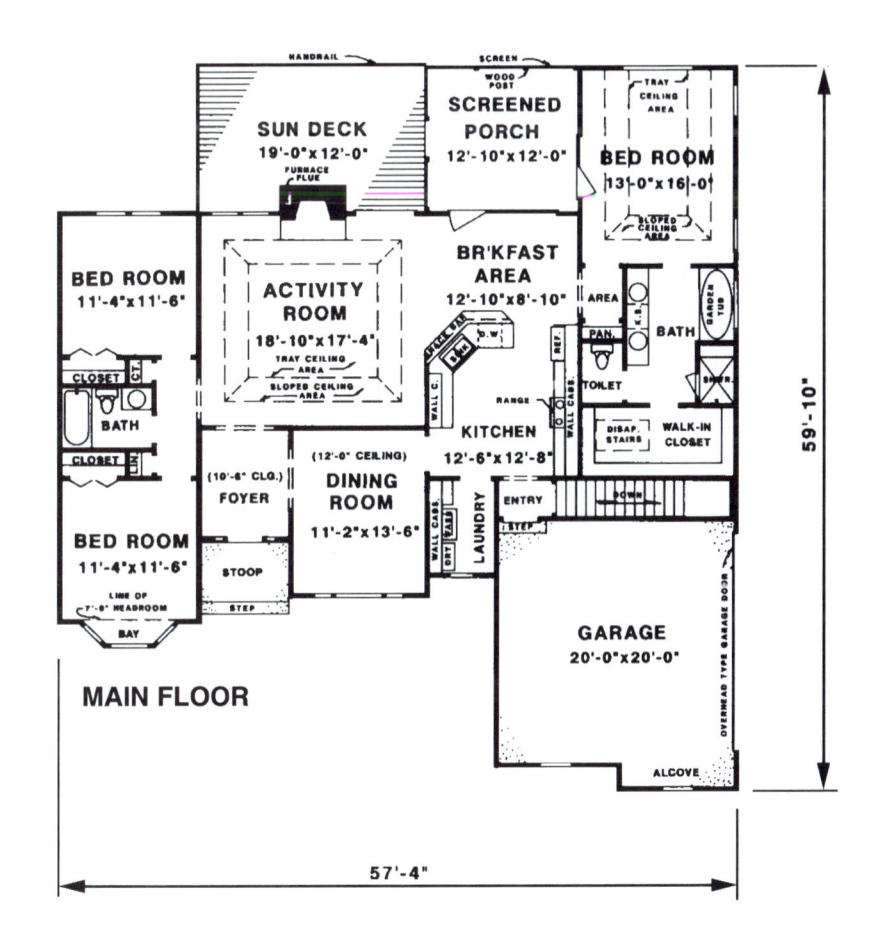

DESIGN NO. 92703

PRICE CODE B

Casual Living Inside and Out

No. 92703

■ This plan features:

— Three bedrooms

— Two full baths

■ A Living Room with a ten foot ceiling and a cozy corner fireplace

■ An enormous Dining Area that is able to handle even the largest family dinners

■ A large rear Porch that is perfect for outdoor dining

■ A conveniently placed Laundry Room

■ His-n-her walk-in closets and a double vanity in the Master Bath

■ Secondary bedrooms that share a full hall bath with a double vanity

MAIN AREA — 1,772 SQ. FT.

TOTAL LIVING AREA:
1,772 SQ. FT.

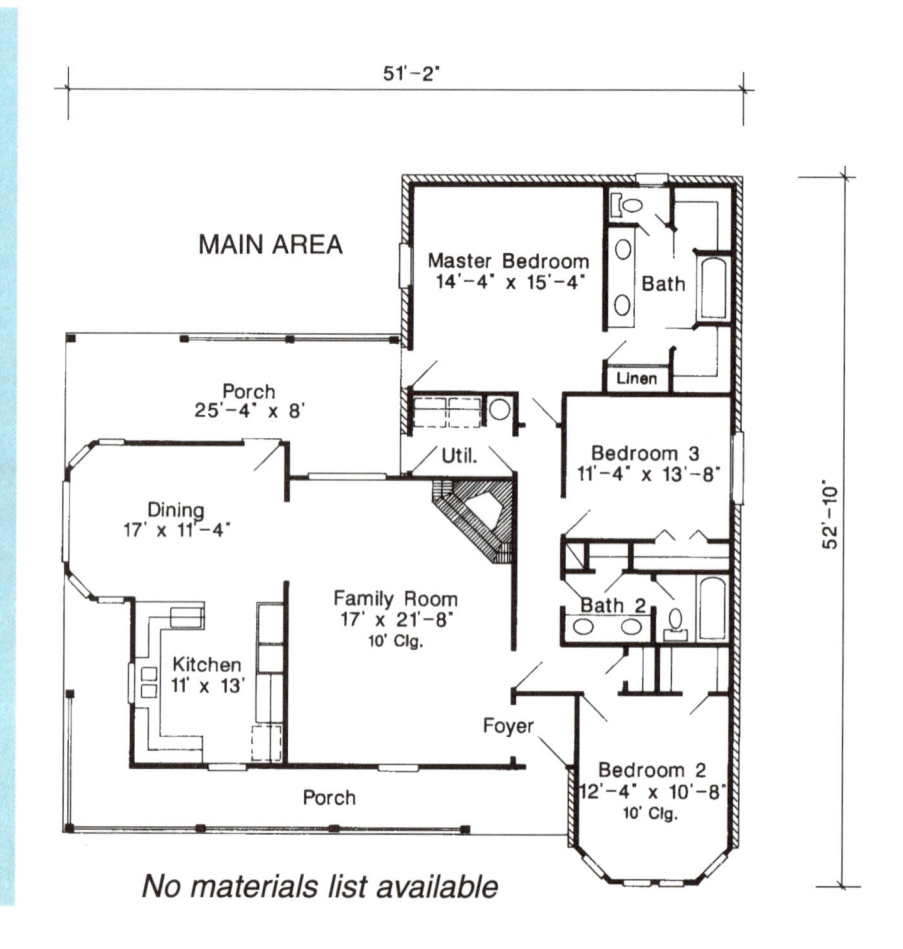

MAIN AREA

Master Bedroom 14'-4" x 15'-4"
Bath
Porch 25'-4" x 8'
Util.
Linen
Bedroom 3 11'-4" x 13'-8"
Dining 17' x 11'-4"
Family Room 17' x 21'-8" 10' Clg.
Bath 2
Kitchen 11' x 13'
Foyer
Porch
Bedroom 2 12'-4" x 10'-8" 10' Clg.

51'-2"
52'-10"

No materials list available

128

DESIGN NO. 92705

PRICE CODE C

PLUSH MASTER BEDROOM WING

No. 92705

- This plan features:
— Three bedrooms
— Two full baths

- A raised, tile Foyer with a decorative window leading into an expansive Living Room, accented by a tiled fireplace and framed by French doors

- An efficient Kitchen with a walk-in pantry and serving bar adjoining the Breakfast and Utility areas

- A private Master Bedroom, crowned by a stepped ceiling, offering an atrium door to outside, a huge, walk-in closet and a luxurious bath

MAIN AREA — 1,849 SQ. FT.
GARAGE — 437 SQ. FT.

TOTAL LIVING AREA: 1,849 SQ. FT.

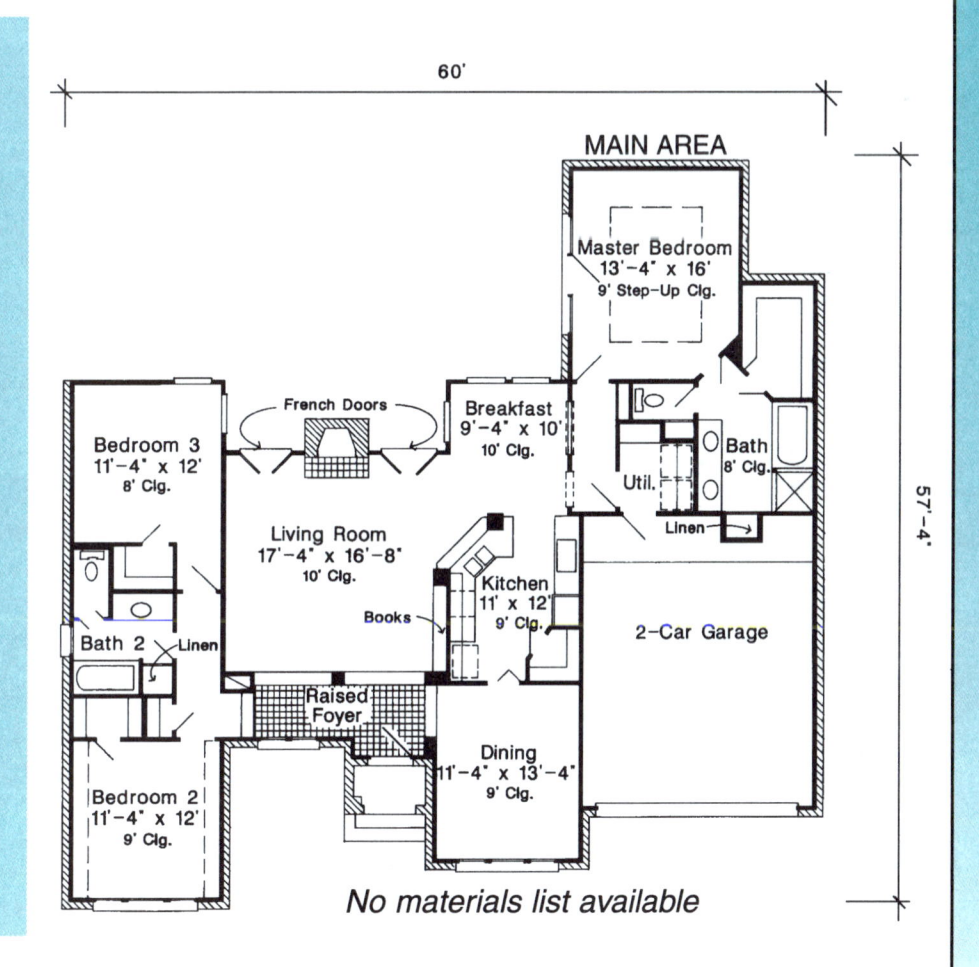

MAIN AREA

Master Bedroom 13'-4" x 16'
9' Step-Up Clg.

Bath 8' Clg.

Util.

Linen

Breakfast 9'-4" x 10'
10' Clg.

French Doors

Bedroom 3 11'-4" x 12'
8' Clg.

Living Room 17'-4" x 16'-8"
10' Clg.

Books

Kitchen 11' x 12'
9' Clg.

2-Car Garage

Bath 2   Linen

Raised Foyer

Dining 11'-4" x 13'-4"
9' Clg.

Bedroom 2 11'-4" x 12'
9' Clg.

60'

57'-4"

No materials list available

DESIGN NO. 99276

PRICE CODE D

Mexican Design Flair

No. 99276

- This plan features:
- Four bedrooms
- Two full and one half baths
- Entry Courtyard leads into skylight Foyer and open, airy Living/Dining area with triple fireplace and Covered Porch access
- An efficient Kitchen with a cooktop serving island, Breakfast area, Porch access, Laundry and Garage entry
- Corner Master Bedroom suite offers a private Porch, walk-in closet and plush bath
- Three additional bedrooms, two with private access to a full bath, have access to covered porches

MAIN FLOOR — 2,350 SQ. FT.
GARAGE — 644 SQ. FT.

TOTAL LIVING AREA: 2,350 SQ. FT.

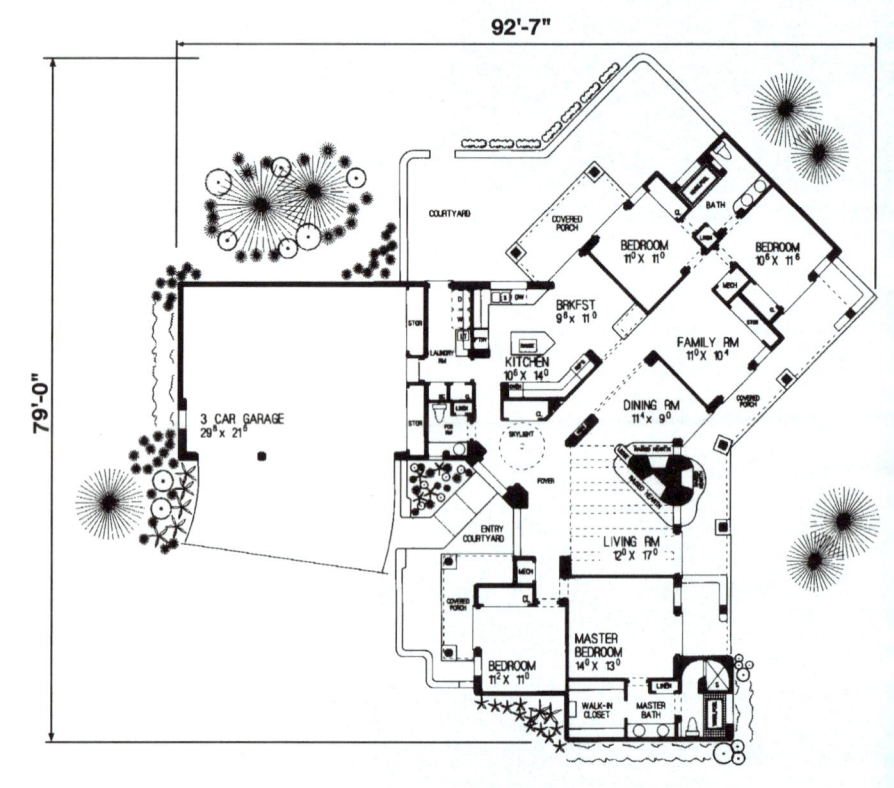

MAIN FLOOR

DESIGN NO. 99280

PRICE CODE C

FOCUS ON COUNTRY LIVING

No. 99280

- This plan features:
— Two or three bedrooms
— Two full baths
- Cozy, Covered Porch provides entry into easy-care Foyer
- Open Gathering and Dining rooms with cozy fireplace, afford easy entertaining and Terrace access
- Efficient Kitchen with a walk-in pantry, snack-bar/serving counter, Breakfast Room and Laundry/Garage entry
- Pampering Master Bedroom with Terrace access, two closets and whirlpool window tub
- Two additional bedrooms, one an optional Study, share a full bath

MAIN FLOOR — 1,835 SQ. FT.
GARAGE — 473 SQ. FT.

TOTAL LIVING AREA:
1,835 SQ. FT.

WIDTH 71'-0"
DEPTH 43'-5"

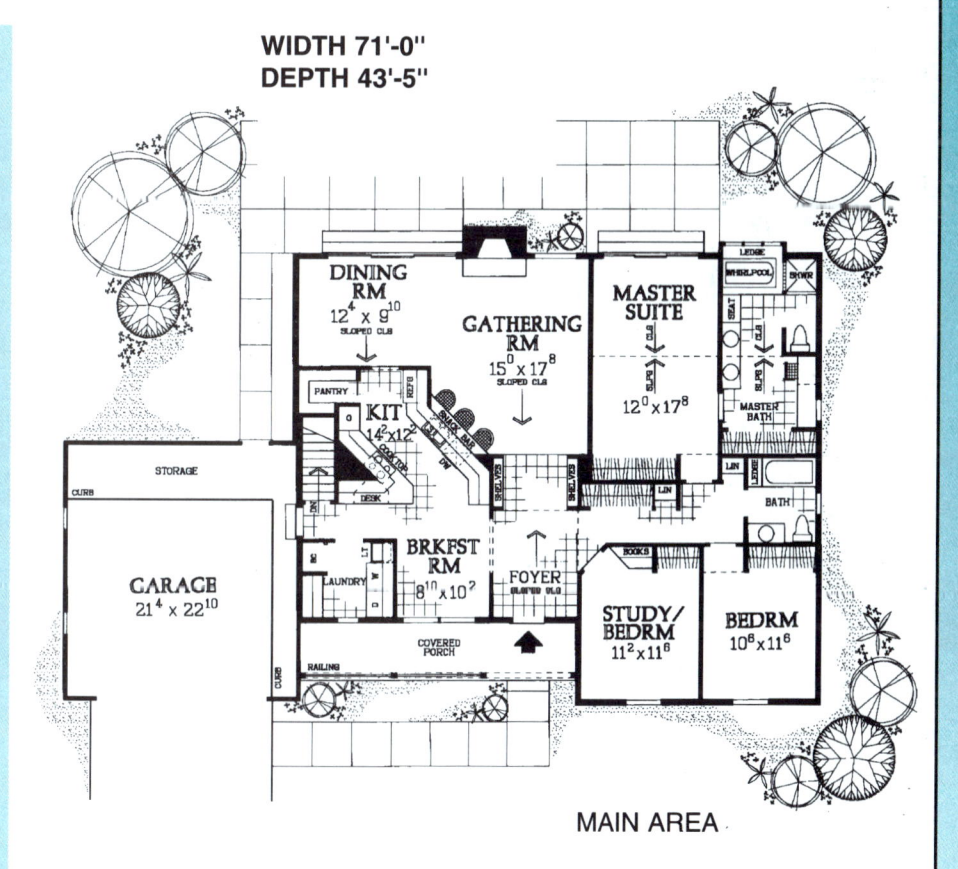

MAIN AREA

DESIGN NO. 99208

PRICE CODE C

Cozy traditional with style

No. 99208

■ This plan features:

— Three bedrooms

— Two full baths

■ A convenient one-level design

■ A galley-style Kitchen that shares a snackbar with the spacious Gathering Room

■ A focal point fireplace making the Gathering Room warm and inviting

■ An ample Master Suite with a luxurious bath which includes a whirlpool tub and separate Dressing Room

■ Two additional bedrooms, one that could double as a Study, located at the front of the house

First floor — 1,830 sq. ft.
Basement — 1,830 sq. ft.

Total living area: 1,830 sq. ft.

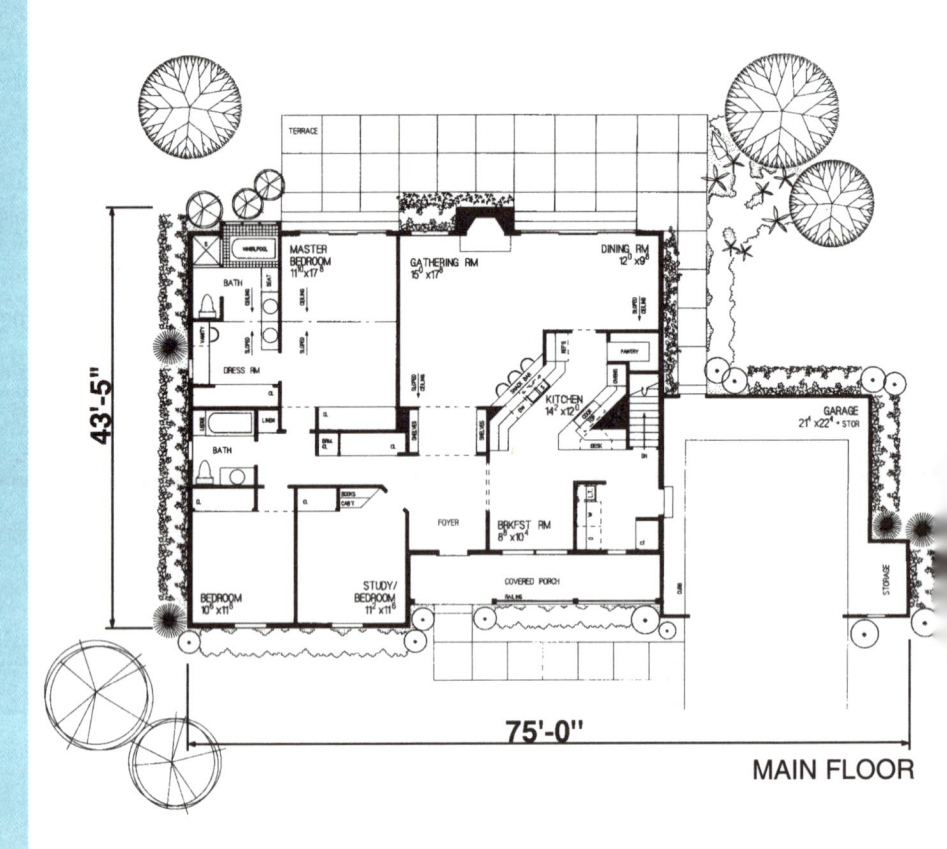

MAIN FLOOR

DESIGN NO. 92704

PRICE CODE A

Perfect first home

No. 92704

- This plan features:
- — Three bedrooms
- — Two full baths
- A front porch with turned posts and railing, and a corner box window
- A large Living Room with an 11 foot ceiling, sloping towards the sliding glass doors to the rear yard
- A cathedral ceiling in the Dining Area, with a view of the porch through an elegant window
- A corner double sink below the corner box window in the efficient Kitchen
- A secluded Master Bedroom that includes a private bath and a walk-in closet
- Two additional bedrooms that share a full hall bath

MAIN AREA — 1,078 SQ. FT.
GARAGE — 431 SQ. FT.

TOTAL LIVING AREA:
1,078 SQ. FT.

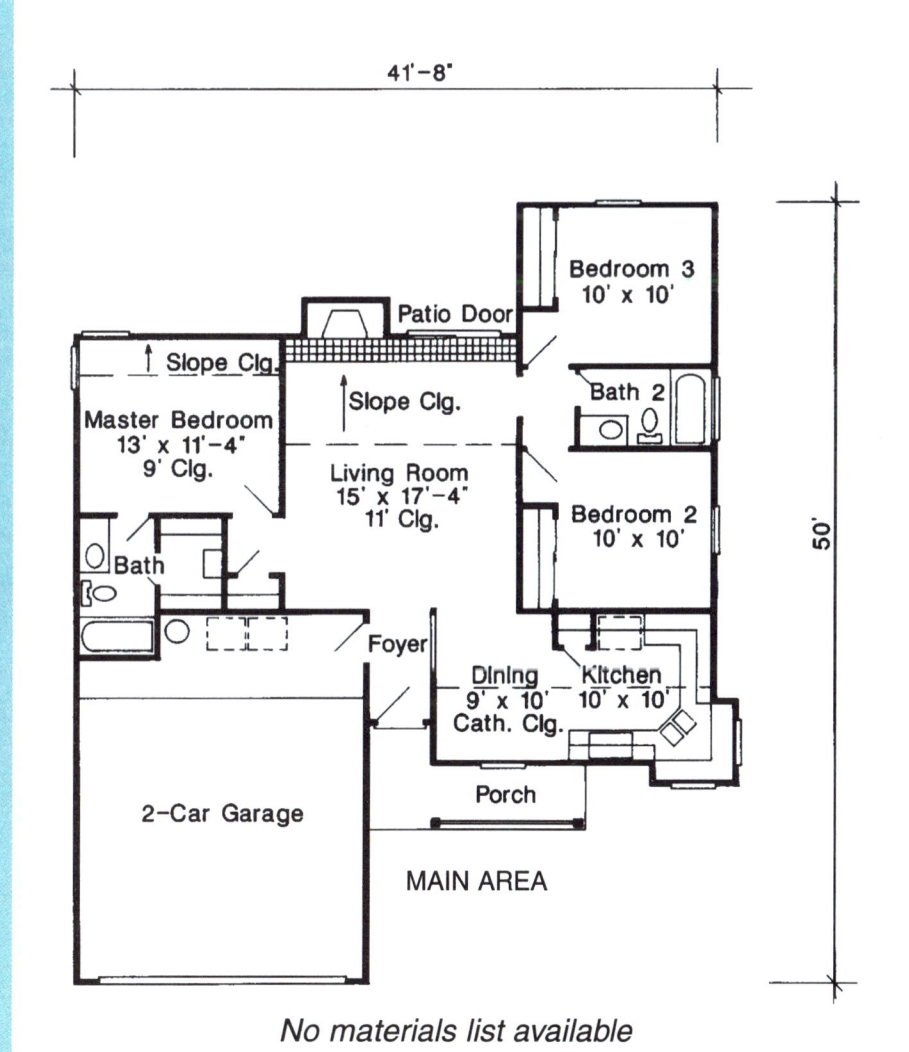

41'-8"

Bedroom 3
10' x 10'

Patio Door

Slope Clg.

Master Bedroom
13' x 11'-4"
9' Clg.

Slope Clg.

Bath 2

Living Room
15' x 17'-4"
11' Clg.

Bedroom 2
10' x 10'

50'

Bath

Foyer

Dining
9' x 10'
Cath. Clg.

Kitchen
10' x 10'

2-Car Garage

Porch

MAIN AREA

No materials list available

DESIGN NO. 90441

PRICE CODE C

Moderate ranch with exciting features

No. 90441

■ This plan features:

— Three bedrooms

— Two full baths

■ A large Great Room with a vaulted ceiling and a stone fireplace with bookshelves on either side

■ A spacious Kitchen with ample cabinet space, conveniently located next to the large Dining Room

■ A Master Suite having a large bath with a garden tub, double vanity and a walk-in closet

■ Two other large bedrooms, each with a walk-in closet and access to the full bath

■ An optional basement, slab or crawl space foundation — please specify when ordering

MAIN FLOOR — 1,811 SQ. FT.

TOTAL LIVING AREA:
1,811 SQ. FT.

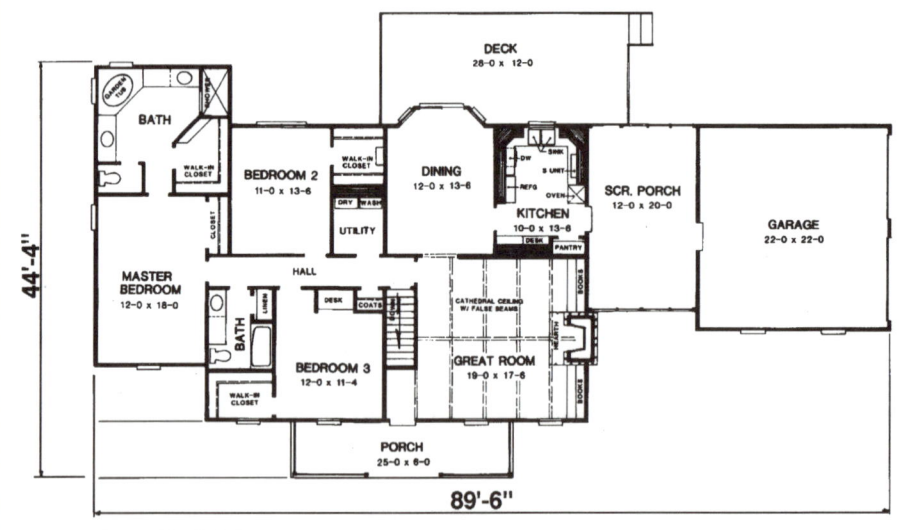

MAIN FLOOR

DESIGN NO. 99281

PRICE CODE C

TUDOR-TYPE RANCH

No. 99281

- This plan features:
— Two or three bedrooms
— Two full baths
- Covered Porch leads into tiled Foyer and Gathering and Dining rooms with a hearth fireplace and access to Entertainment Terrace
- Large, efficient Kitchen with walk-in Pantry, pass-thru snackbar, built-in desk, Laundry and Garage entry
- Master Suite pampered by sliding glass doors to Terrace, two closets and a lavish bath with double vanity and whirlpool garden tub
- Two additional bedrooms share a full bath

MAIN FLOOR — 1,944 SQ. FT.
GARAGE — 515 SQ. FT.

TOTAL LIVING AREA: 1,944 SQ. FT.

WIDTH 72'-8"
DEPTH 47'-4"

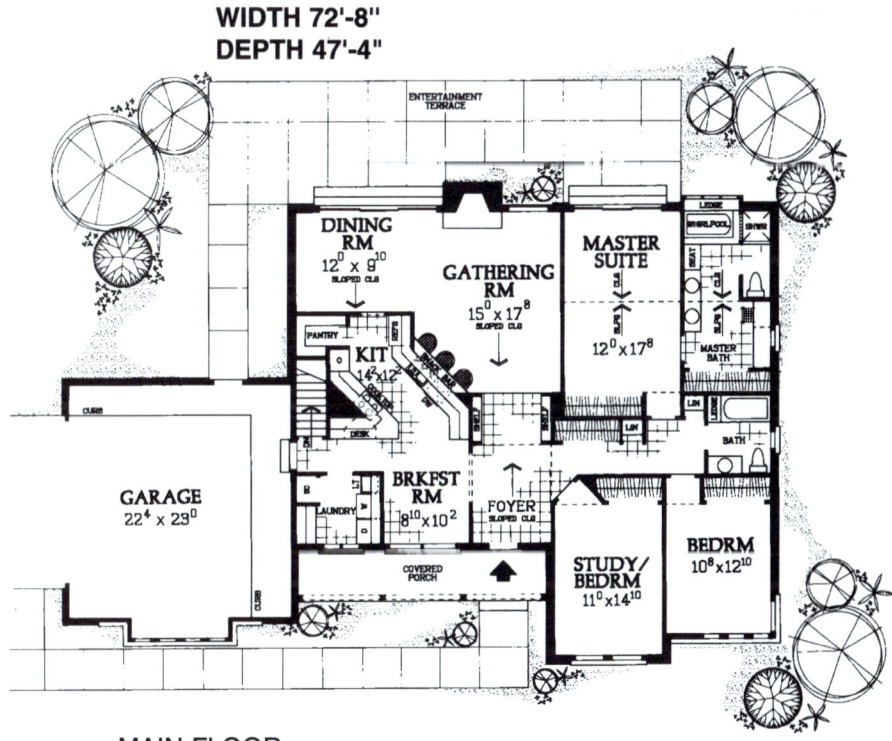

MAIN FLOOR

DESIGN NO. 99270

PRICE CODE E

IN-HOME OFFICE SPACE

No. 99270

■ This plan features:

— Three or four bedrooms

— Three full and one half baths

■ Friendly front Porch adds country charm to practical design

■ Open Foyer with lovely landing staircase, flanked by Study and Living Room

■ Hub Kitchen with built-in pantry, peninsula eating bar, eating Nook and adjoining Dining Room

■ Comfortable Family Room with beamed ceiling, large fireplace and access to rear yard, Laundry and Office/Guest space

■ Corner Master Bedroom with Dressing area and his-n-her walk-in closets

FIRST FLOOR — 1,762 SQ. FT.
SECOND FLOOR — 1,311 SQ. FT.
GARAGE — 561 SQ. FT.

TOTAL LIVING AREA: 3,073 SQ. FT.

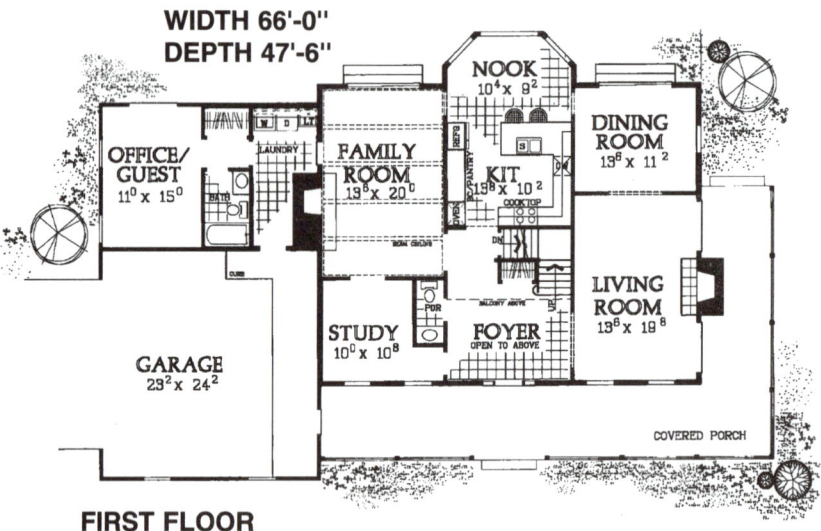

WIDTH 66'-0"
DEPTH 47'-6"

FIRST FLOOR

SECOND FLOOR

DESIGN NO. 92517

PRICE CODE D

DIGNIFIED FRENCH COUNTRY STYLE

No. 92517

- This plan features:
- — Three bedrooms
- — Two full baths
- Sheltered Porch leads into an open Foyer and Great Room enhanced by raised hearth fireplace between book shelves, access to Patio and a vaulted ceiling
- Hub Kitchen with a peninsula counter and Utility Garage entry easily serves Breakfast area and formal Dining Room
- Spacious Master Bedroom offers a Sitting area and a plush Master Bath
- Two additional roomy bedrooms with over-sized closets share a double vanity bath
- An optional crawl space or slab foundation available, please specify when ordering

MAIN FLOOR — 1,805 SQ. FT.
GARAGE & STORAGE — 524 SQ. FT.

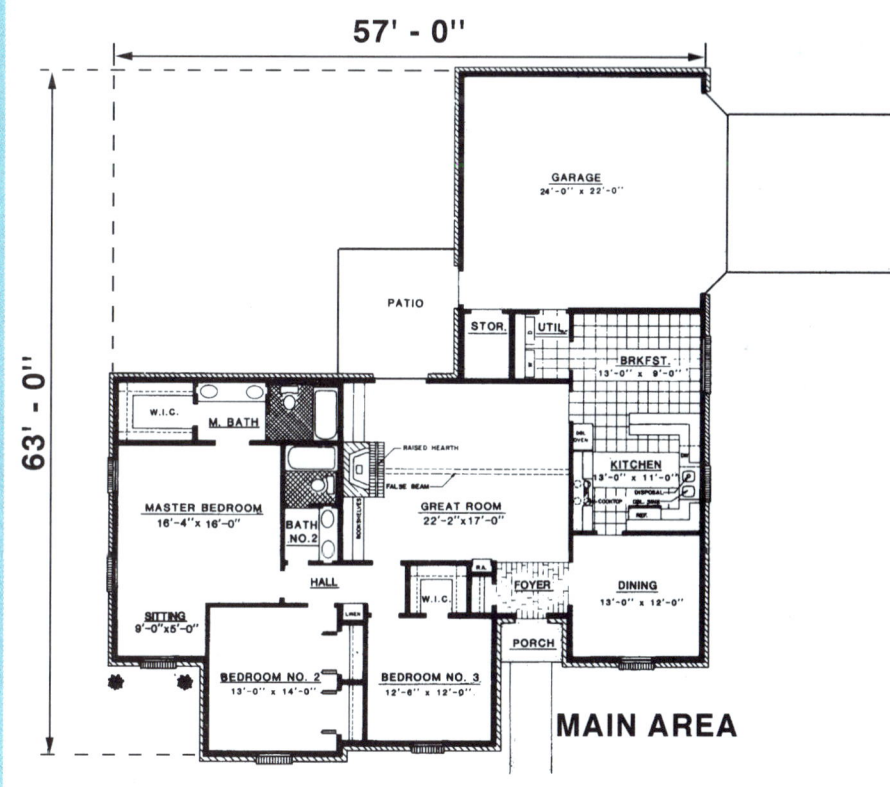

MAIN AREA

TOTAL LIVING AREA: 1,805 SQ. FT.

DESIGN NO. 92642

PRICE CODE C

ELEGANT AND STYLISH

No materials list available

No. 92642

- This plan features:
— Three bedrooms
— Two full and one half baths
- Brick trim, sidelights and a transom window at the front door
- A high ceiling through the Foyer and Great Room showcasing the deluxe staircase
- A cozy fireplace and a built-in entertainment center in the Great Room
- A convenient, modern Kitchen serving the formal Dining Room and the Breakfast area
- A whirlpool tub, shower stall, his-n-her vanities and a spacious walk-in closet in the Master Suite
- Spacious Study Loft with computer area and bookshelves
- Two bedrooms with walk-in closets share a full hall bath

FIRST FLOOR — 1,524 SQ. FT.
SECOND FLOOR — 558 SQ. FT.
BONUS — 267 SQ. FT.
BASEMENT — 1,460 SQ. FT.

TOTAL LIVING AREA: 2,082 SQ. FT.

SECOND FLOOR

- Bedroom 11'1" x 13'3"
- Bedroom 11'5" x 12'0"
- Bath
- Balcony
- Foyer Below
- Bonus Room 11'0" x 22'0"

FIRST FLOOR

- Master Bedroom 13'6" x 15'1"
- Great Room 17'4" x 21'2" (12' high ceiling)
- Dining Room 10'10" x 14'0"
- Bath
- Kitchen 12'4" x 11'6"
- Foyer
- Breakfast 11' x 9'4"
- Two-car Garage 22'9" x 22'0"

50'4" x 60'

DESIGN NO. 94715

PRICE CODE E

BRICK TRADITIONAL

No. 94715

- This plan features:
— Four bedrooms
— Three full and one half baths
- Old southern architecture incorporates today's open floor plan
- Gracious two-story Foyer between formal Living and Dining rooms
- Comfortable Great Room with a fireplace is nestled between French doors to the rear Decks
- Hub Kitchen offers a cooktop island, an eating bar and a Breakfast area
- Master Bedroom suite is enhanced by a fireplace and a plush bath

FIRST FLOOR — 2,094 SQ. FT.
SECOND FLOOR — 918 SQ. FT.
GARAGE — 537 SQ. FT.

TOTAL LIVING AREA: 3,012 SQ. FT.

An EXCLUSIVE DESIGN *By United Design Associates*

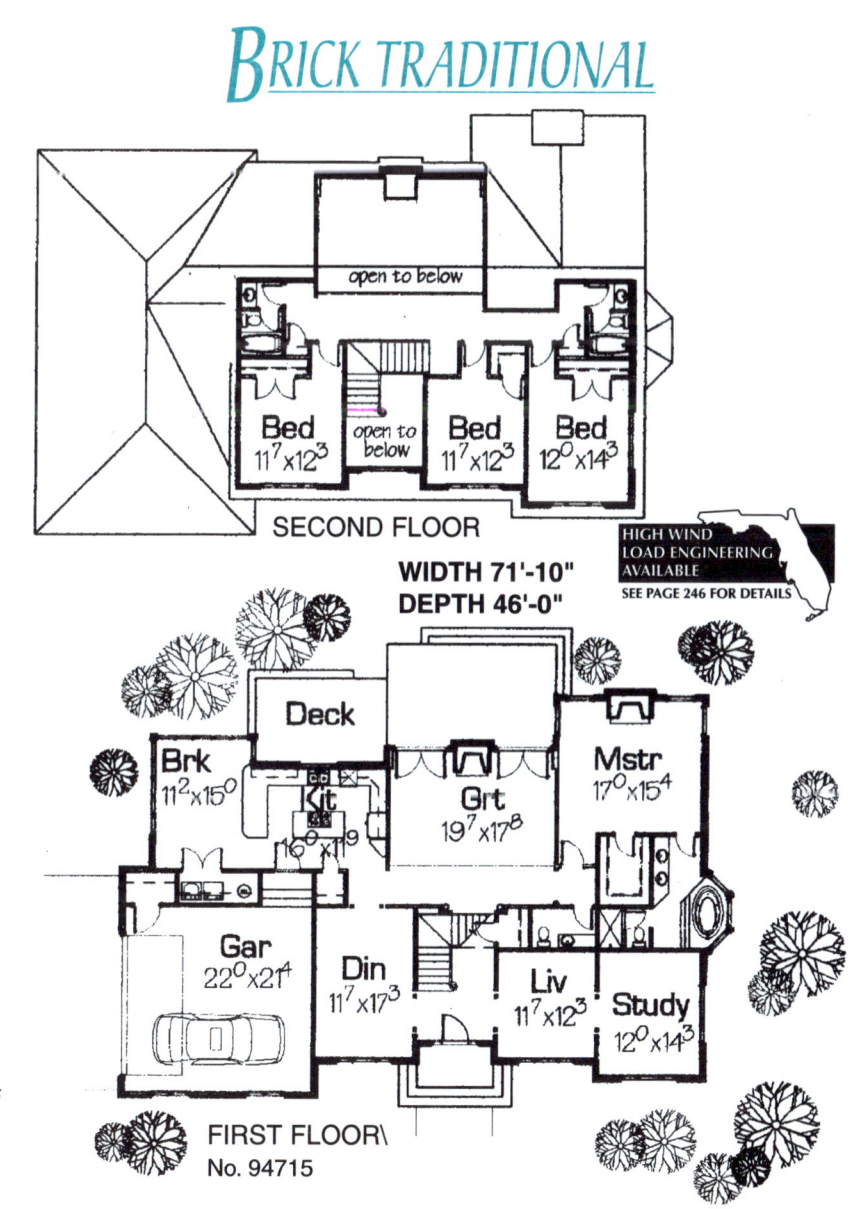

WIDTH 71'-10"
DEPTH 46'-0"

HIGH WIND LOAD ENGINEERING AVAILABLE
SEE PAGE 246 FOR DETAILS

SECOND FLOOR

Bed 11⁷x12³ | Bed 11⁷x12³ | Bed 12⁰x14³

FIRST FLOOR
No. 94715

Brk 11²x15⁰ | Kit 16⁹x11⁹ | Deck | Grt 19⁷x17⁸ | Mstr 17⁰x15⁴
Gar 22⁰x21⁴ | Din 11⁷x17³ | Liv 11⁷x12³ | Study 12⁰x14³

DESIGN NO. 99283

PRICE CODE C

Open Living Area

No. 99283

- This plan features:
— Three bedrooms
— Two full baths
- Inviting covered Porch leads into easy-care Foyer and Gathering Room beyond
- Large Gathering Room, with central fireplace below sloping ceiling opens to Dining Room with Patio access and built-in china cabinet
- U-shaped Kitchen with built-in pantry and desk, eating Nook and adjoining Laundry/Garage entry
- Master Bedroom with Patio Retreat, dressing area and plush bath with garden tub
- Two additional bedrooms share a double vanity bath

Main floor — 1,970 sq. ft.
Garage — 615 sq. ft.

Total living area: 1,970 sq. ft.

MAIN AREA

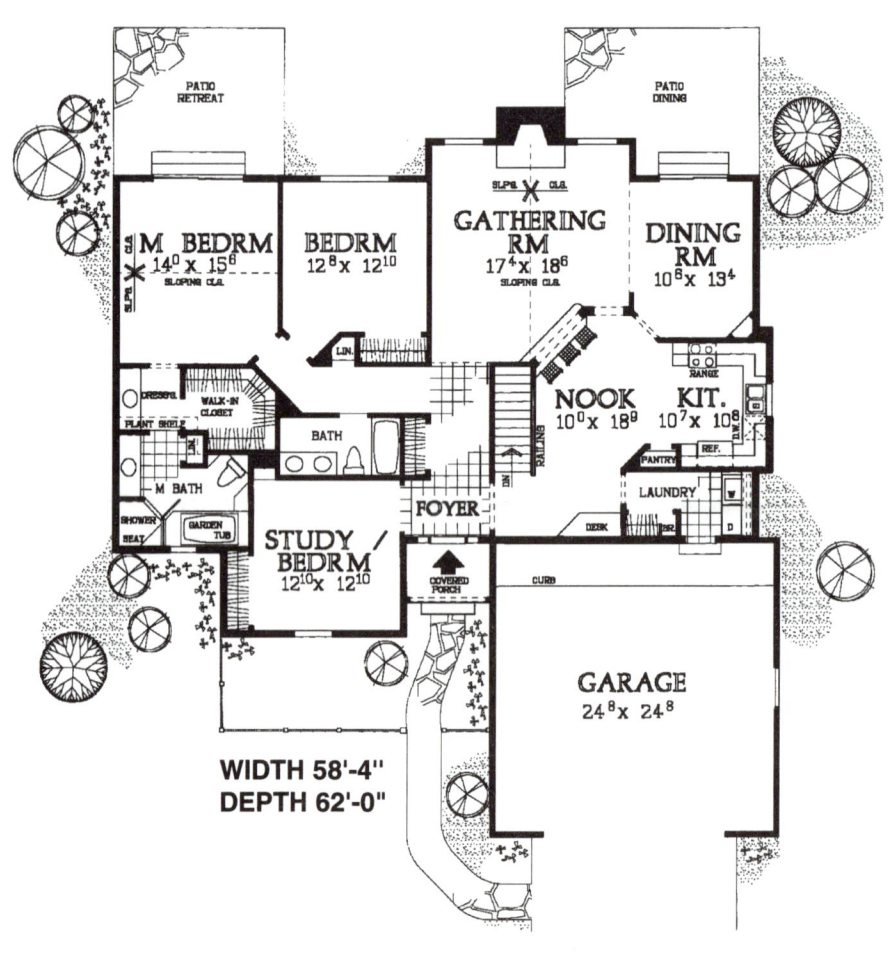

WIDTH 58'-4"
DEPTH 62'-0"

DESIGN NO. 99278

PRICE CODE F

Western Homestead with Expansive Porches

No. 99278

- This plan features:
- — Six bedrooms
- — Five full baths
- Central entrance enhanced by circular stairway and curved wall Parlor
- Formal Dining Room offers a built-in china alcove, service counter and fireplace
- Country Kitchen with a large cooktop island overlooks expansive Gathering Room with a wall of windows
- Master Bedroom highlighted by a raised hearth fireplace, porch access and a plush bath
- Separate Guest accommodations include Living/Dining area, bedroom and pool bath

First floor — 3,166 sq. ft.
Second floor — 950 sq. ft.
Guest House/Carport — 680 sq. ft.

Total living area:
4,116 sq. ft.

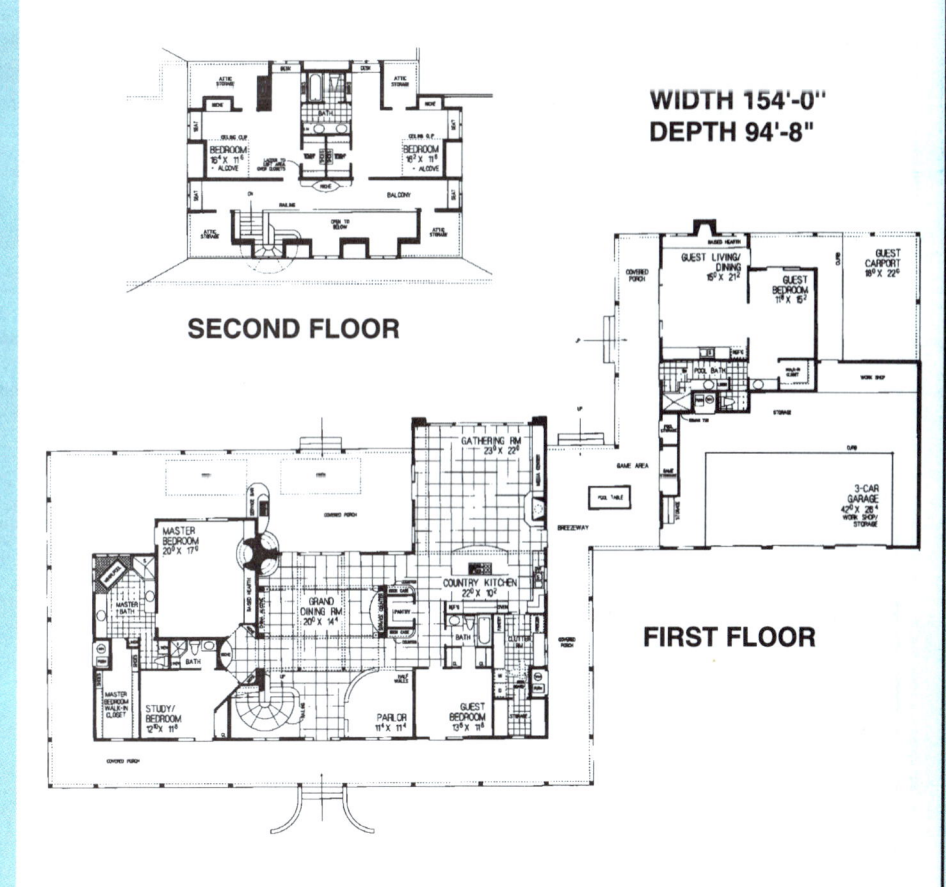

SECOND FLOOR

WIDTH 154'-0"
DEPTH 94'-8"

FIRST FLOOR

DESIGN NO. 99271

PRICE CODE E

SOUTHWESTERN CHARMER

No. 99271

■ This plan features:

— Four bedrooms

— Two full and one half baths

■ Shaded Porch wraps around full length windows in Living Room and accesses Foyer and Dining Room with a bay window

■ Spacious Kitchen with a work island, built-in pantry and pass-thru snackbar to Breakfast area

■ Open Family Room offers a hearth fireplace and Entertainment Patio access

■ Corner Master Suite offers two closets and a plush bath with a garden tub

■ Three additional bedrooms share a double vanity bath

FIRST FLOOR — 1,595 SQ. FT.
SECOND FLOOR — 1,112 SQ. FT.
GARAGE — 504 SQ. FT.

TOTAL LIVING AREA: 2,707 SQ. FT.

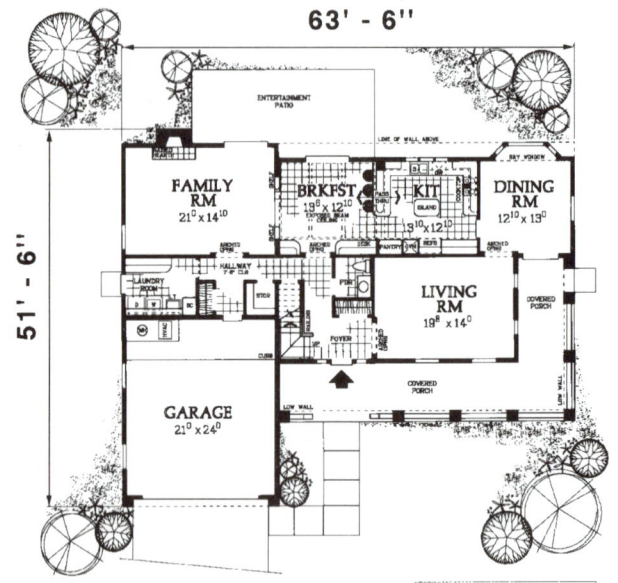

FIRST FLOOR

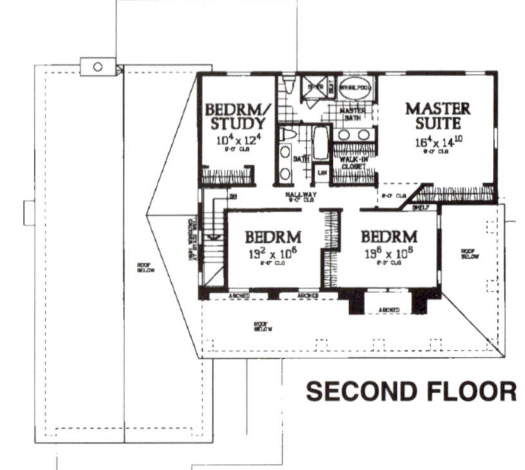

SECOND FLOOR

142

DESIGN NO. 99275

PRICE CODE E

COURTYARD ENHANCES ENTRANCE

90' - 0''

51' - 8''

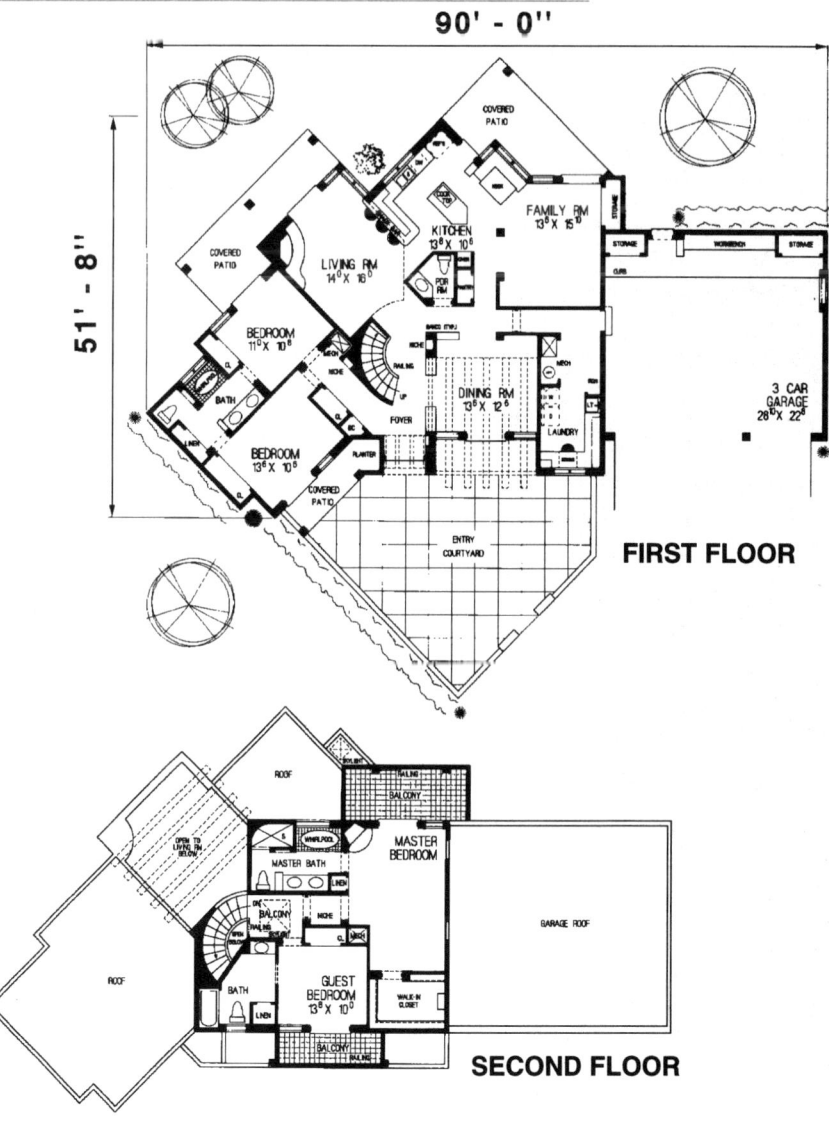

FIRST FLOOR

SECOND FLOOR

No. 99275

- This plan features:
— Four bedrooms
— Three full and one half baths
- Large Entry Courtyard provides gracious entrance into Foyer with a curved staircase
- Living Room enhanced by a corner fireplace and access to Covered Patio
- Dining Room topped with beamed ceiling opens to Courtyard
- L-shaped Kitchen with work island/cooktop easily serves eating Nook, snackbar and Covered Patio
- Secluded Master Bedroom offers private balcony, a large walk-in closet and deluxe bath

FIRST FLOOR — 1,966 SQ. FT.
SECOND FLOOR — 831 SQ. FT.
GARAGE — 595 SQ. FT.

TOTAL LIVING AREA: 2,797 SQ. FT.

DESIGN NO. 99288

PRICE CODE E

SYMMETRICAL, SIMPLE AND STUNNING

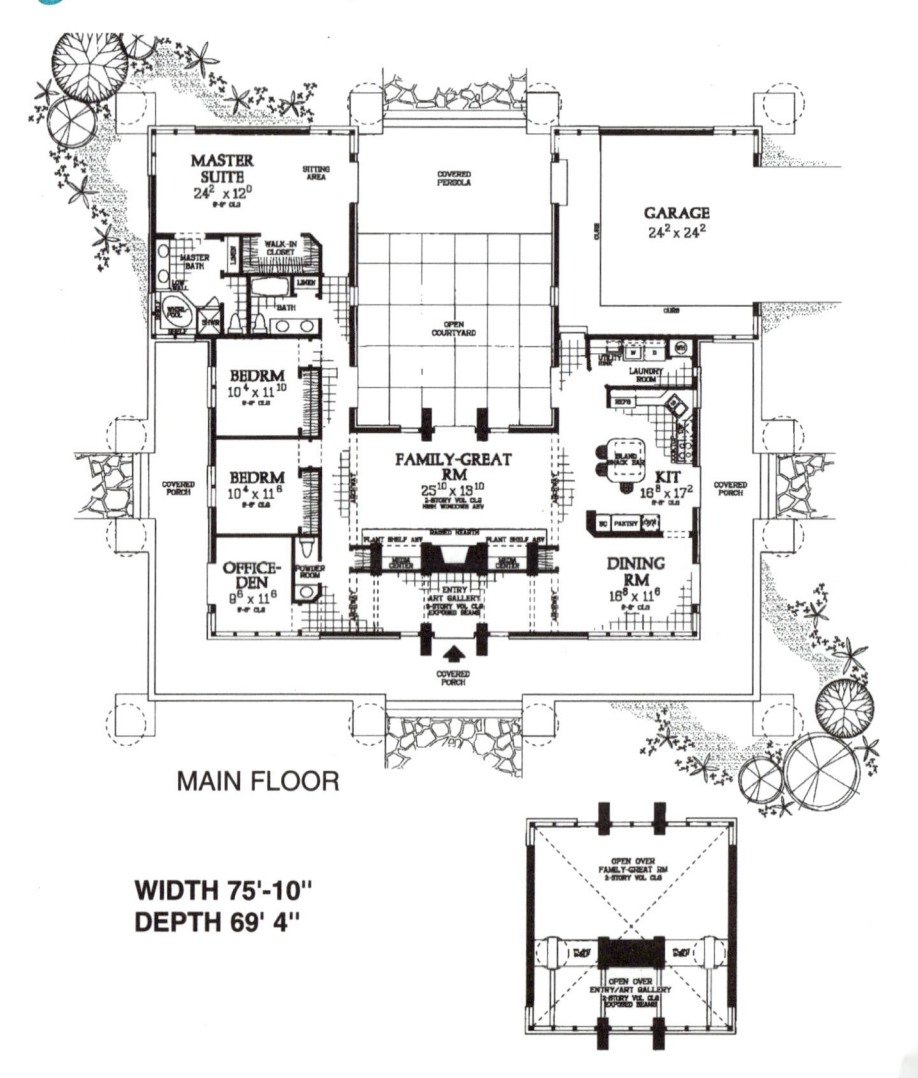

No. 99288

- This plan features:
— Three bedrooms
— Two full and one half baths
- Deep eaves create Covered Porch on three sides
- Entry/Art Gallery highlighted by second story windows and plant shelves
- Central, two-story Family/Great Room with a raised, hearth fireplace framed by media center and plant shelves, opens to Courtyard and Covered Pergola
- Spacious Kitchen with an island snackbar, built-in pantry accesses Laundry/Garage entry, formal Dining Room, Courtyard and Family Room
- Private Master Suite pampered by sitting area, walk-in closet and lavish Master Bath
- Corner Office/Den offers multiple uses

MAIN FLOOR — 2,626 SQ. FT.
GARAGE — 586 SQ. FT.

**TOTAL LIVING AREA:
2,626 SQ. FT.**

MAIN FLOOR

WIDTH 75'-10"
DEPTH 69' 4"

DESIGN NO. 93018

PRICE CODE A

A COMPACT HOME

No. 93018

- This plan features:
— Three bedrooms
— Two full baths
- Siding with brick wainscoting distinguishing the elevation
- A large Family Room with a corner fireplace and direct access to the outside
- An arched opening leading to the Breakfast Area
- A bay window illuminating the Breakfast Area with natural light
- An efficiently designed, U-shaped Kitchen with ample cabinet and counter space
- A Master Suite with a private Master Bath
- Two additional bedrooms that share a full hall bath

MAIN AREA — 1,142 SQ. FT.
GARAGE — 428 SQ. FT.

TOTAL LIVING AREA:
1,142 SQ. FT.

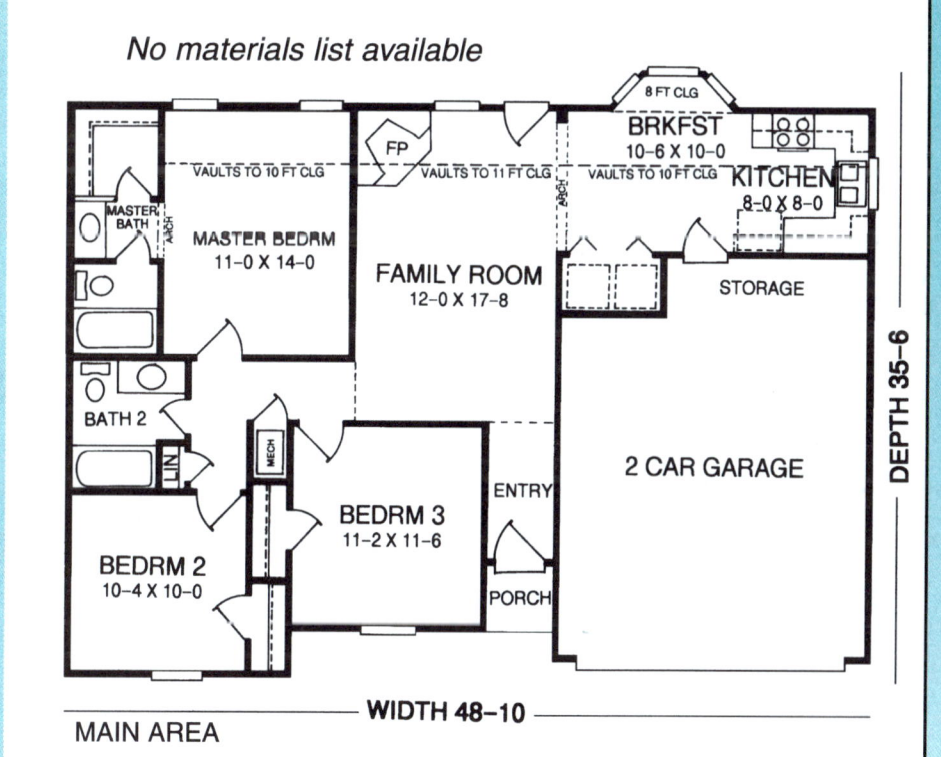

No materials list available

MAIN AREA — WIDTH 48-10 — DEPTH 35-6

DESIGN NO. 99272

PRICE CODE E

Santa Fe Flavor

MAIN AREA

WIDTH 120'-0"
DEPTH 76'-0"

No. 99272

- This plan features:
— Four bedrooms
— Three full and one half baths
- Projecting wood beams and Courtyard add distinctive details to facade
- Foyer opens to beamed Living Room with a corner fireplace and music alcove
- Three-way fireplace accents Kitchen, Deck and Family Room
- U-shaped Kitchen easily serves snackbar, Morning Room and Dining Room
- Master Bedroom wing offers a lavish bath, walk-in closet, and Office and Laundry nearby
- Three additional bedrooms, two full baths and a Study complete opposite wing

MAIN AREA — 2,968 SQ. FT.
GARAGE — 638 SQ. FT.

TOTAL LIVING AREA:
2,968 SQ. FT.

DESIGN NO. 99239

PRICE CODE F

COUNTRY HOME OOZES CHARM

No. 99239

■ This plan features:

— Three bedrooms

— Two full and two half baths

■ An elegant Living Room with a stone fireplace including an unusual Music Alcove, complete with custom built-ins for audio equipment

■ An adjoining Library having floor-to-ceiling, built-in bookcases and a second cozy fireplace

■ A formal Dining Room with a wall of windows and access to the back Porch

■ A wonderful Country Kitchen with its own fireplace, sitting/dining area, cooktop, snackbar and double sink

■ An incredible Master Suite with a large, luxurious Dressing/Bath equipped with a whirlpool tub, two vanities, an oversized shower and two closets

FIRST FLOOR — 2,026 SQ. FT.
SECOND FLOOR — 1,386 SQ. FT.
GARAGE — 576 SQ. FT.

TOTAL LIVING AREA: 3,412 SQ. FT.

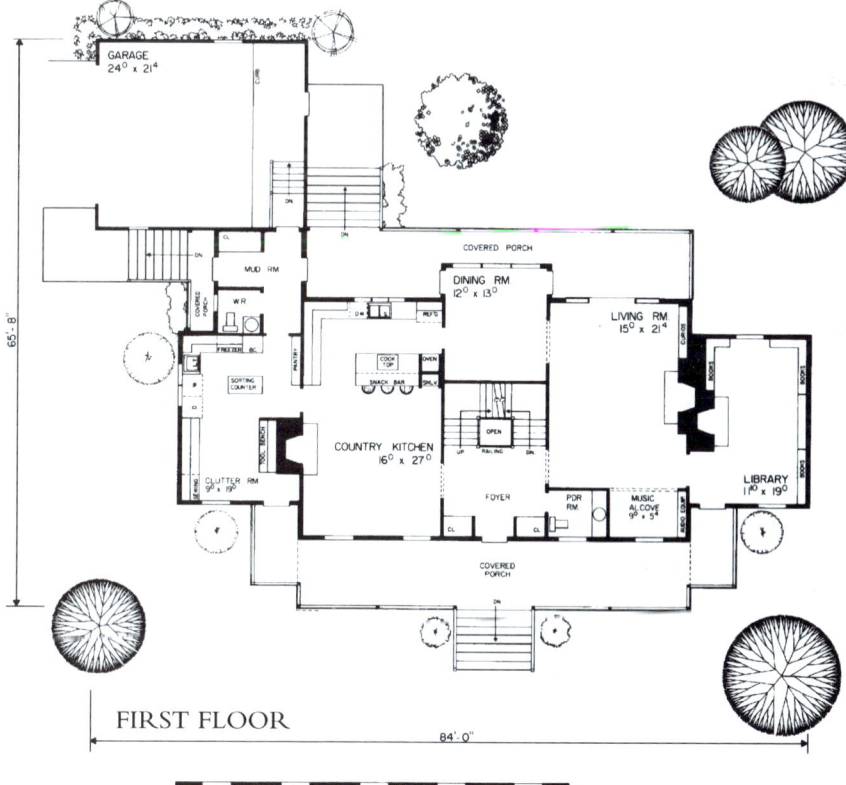

FIRST FLOOR

SECOND FLOOR

DESIGN NO. 99250

PRICE CODE C

Santa Fe-Styled Home

No. 99250

- This plan features:
  — Three bedrooms
  — Two full and one half baths
- A sunken Gathering Room with a beamed ceiling and a raised hearth fireplace
- A U-shaped Kitchen with a large pantry, and ample cabinet and counter space
- A Master Suite that is equipped with a walk-in closet and private bath that includes a whirlpool tub and a double vanity
- Two additional bedrooms that share an adjacent full bath with two vanities

Main floor — 1,907 sq. ft.

Total living area: 1,907 sq. ft.

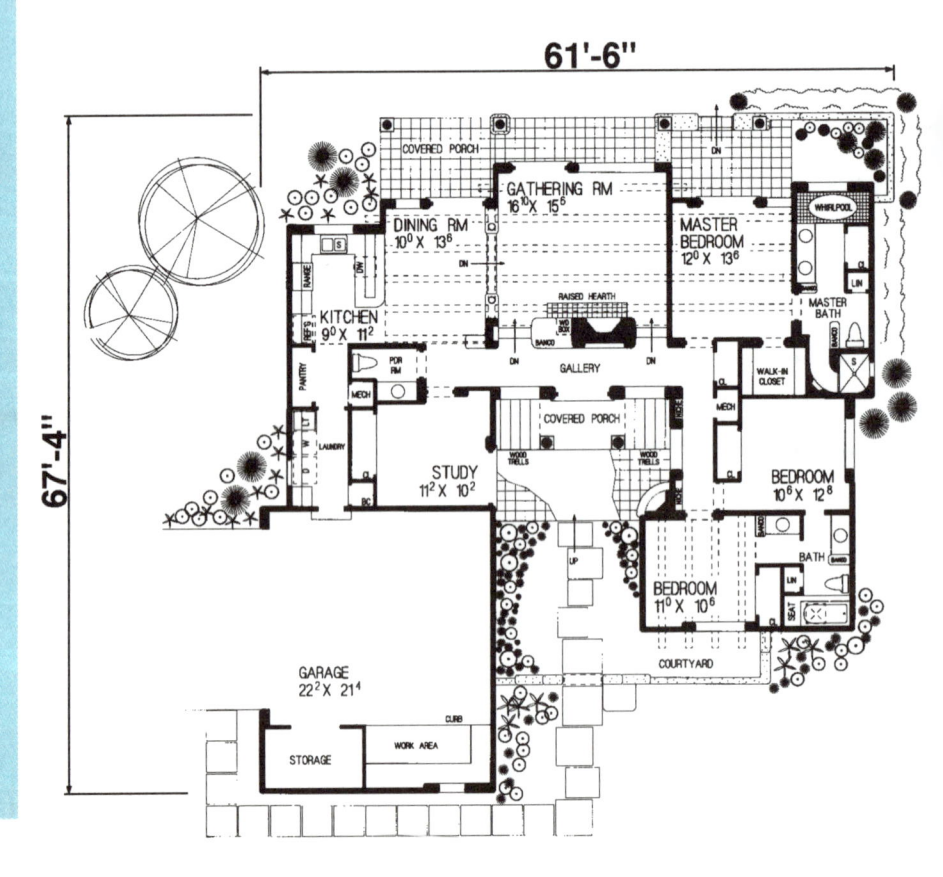

MAIN AREA

DESIGN NO. 93015

PRICE CODE A

GREAT ROOM IS HUB OF THE HOME

No materials list available

No. 93015

■ This plan features:
— Three bedrooms
— Two full baths

■ Sheltered porch leads into the Entry with arches and a Great Room

■ Spacious Great Room with a ten foot ceiling above a wall of windows and rear yard access

■ Efficient Kitchen with a built-in pantry, a laundry closet and a Breakfast area accented by a decorative window

■ Bay of windows enhances the Master Bedroom suite with a double vanity bath and a walk-in closet

■ Two additional bedrooms with ample closets, share a full bath

■ This plan is available with a Slab foundation only

MAIN AREA — 1,087 SQ. FT.

TOTAL LIVING AREA: 1,087 SQ. FT.

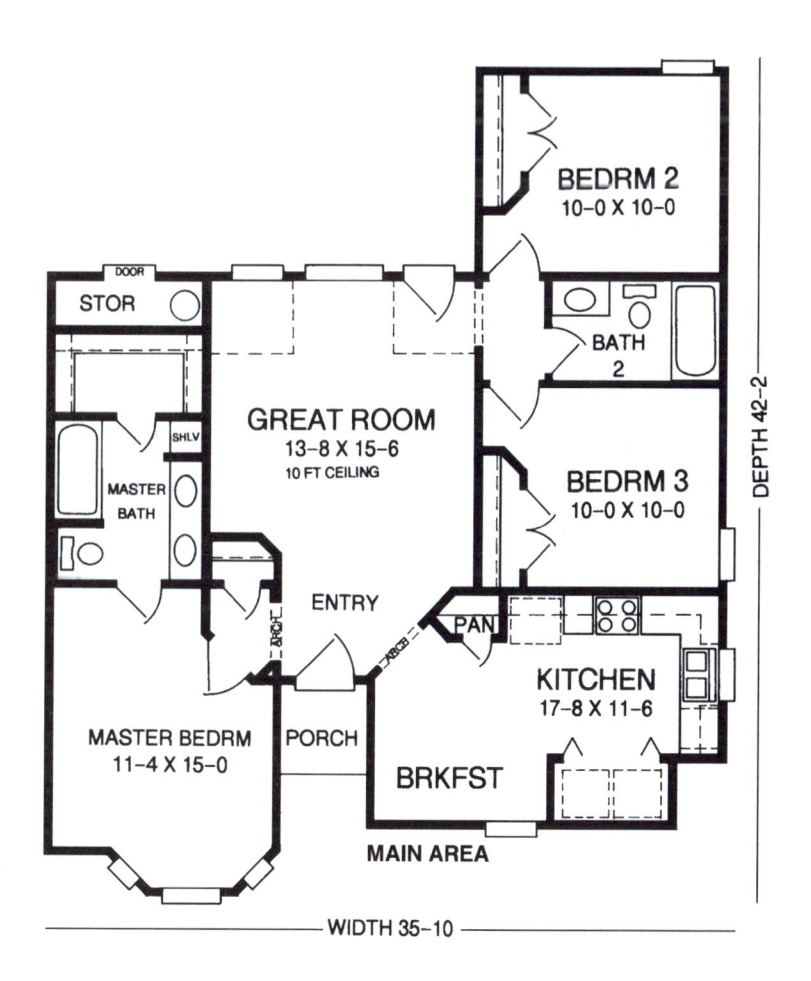

DESIGN NO. 93261

PRICE CODE B

Bay windows and a terriffic front porch

No. 93261

- This plan features:
— Three bedrooms
— Two full baths
- A country front porch
- An expansive Living Area that includes a fireplace
- A Master Suite with a private Master Bath and a walk-in closet, as well as a bay window view of the front yard
- An efficient Kitchen that serves the sunny Breakfast Area and the Dining Room with equal ease
- A built-in pantry and a desk add to the conveniences in the Breakfast Area
- Two additional bedrooms that share the full hall bath
- A convenient main floor Laundry Room

MAIN AREA — 1,778 SQ. FT.
BASEMENT — 1,008 SQ. FT.
GARAGE — 728 SQ. FT.

TOTAL LIVING AREA: 1,778 SQ. FT.

MAIN FLOOR

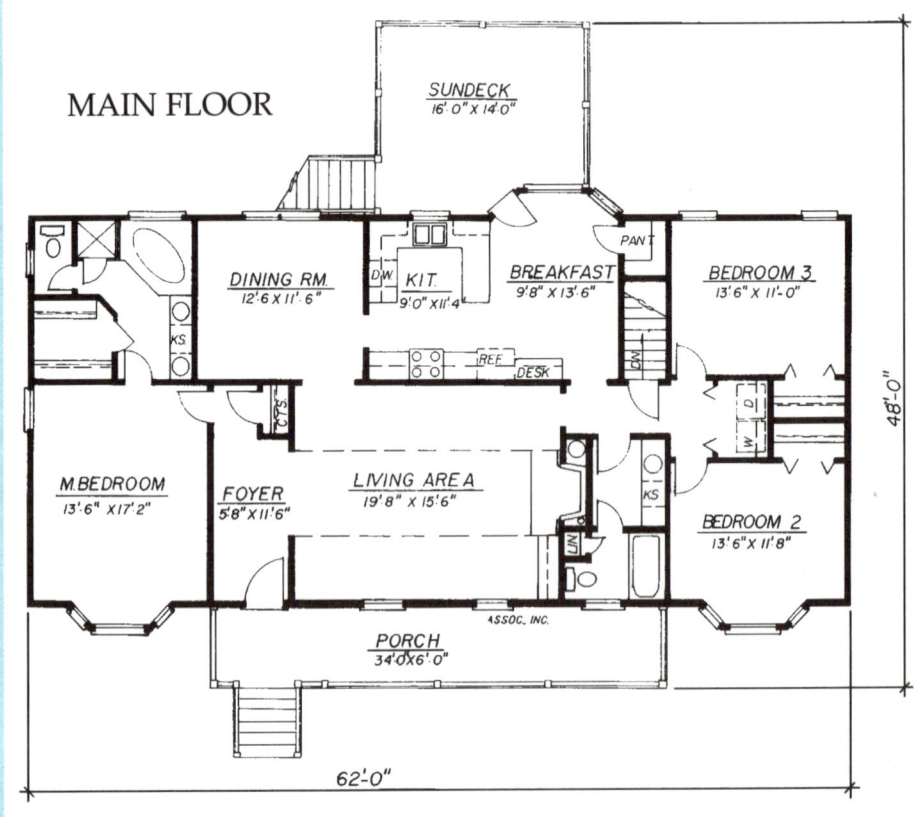

- SUNDECK 16'0" x 14'0"
- DINING RM. 12'6" x 11'6"
- KIT. 9'0" x 12'4"
- BREAKFAST 9'8" x 13'6"
- BEDROOM 3 13'6" x 11'-0"
- M. BEDROOM 13'6" x 17'2"
- FOYER 5'8" x 11'6"
- LIVING AREA 19'8" x 15'6"
- BEDROOM 2 13'6" x 11'8"
- PORCH 34'0" x 6'0"

62'-0" x 48'-0"

An *EXCLUSIVE DESIGN* By Jannis Vann & Associates, Inc.

DESIGN NO. 92615

PRICE CODE D

TRADITIONAL OUTSIDE WITH UNIQUE INSIDE

No. 92615

- This plan features:
— Three bedrooms
— Two full baths

- Gables, brick quoins, a wing wall, a front door with sidelights, and an arched transom enhance elevation

- Formal Living and Dining Room accented by vaulted ceilings, decorative windows, columns, and custom moldings

- Open Great Room with corner fireplace, skylights and atrium door to rear yard

- Efficient Kitchen with walk-in pantry and peninsula counter easily serving the Breakfast area and Great Room

- French doors lead into superb Master Bedroom with a walk-in closet and lavish bath

MAIN FLOOR — 2,277 SQ. FT.
BASEMENT — 2,132 SQ. FT.
GARAGE — 456 SQ. FT.

TOTAL LIVING AREA: 2,277 SQ. FT.

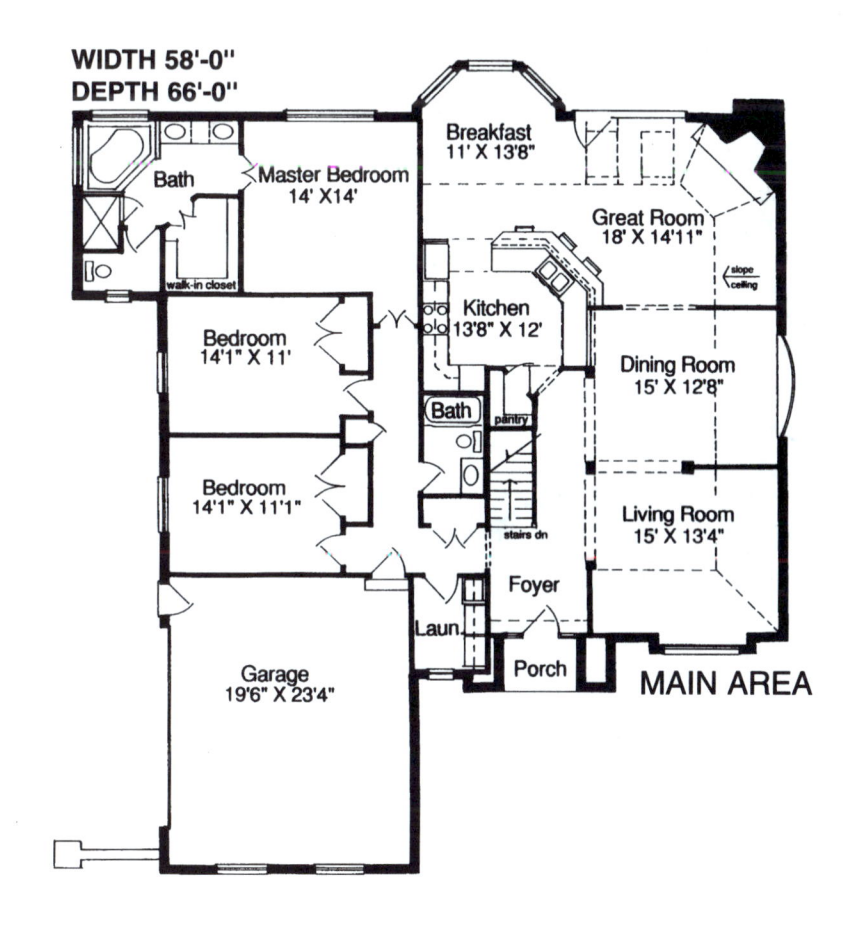

WIDTH 58'-0"
DEPTH 66'-0"

- Bath
- Master Bedroom 14' X 14'
- Breakfast 11' X 13'8"
- Great Room 18' X 14'11"
- walk-in closet
- Bedroom 14'1" X 11'
- Kitchen 13'8" X 12'
- Dining Room 15' X 12'8"
- Bath
- pantry
- Bedroom 14'1" X 11'1"
- Living Room 15' X 13'4"
- stairs dn
- Foyer
- Laun
- Garage 19'6" X 23'4"
- Porch

MAIN AREA

No materials list available

DESIGN NO. 99290

PRICE CODE E

Unique angles and lots of light

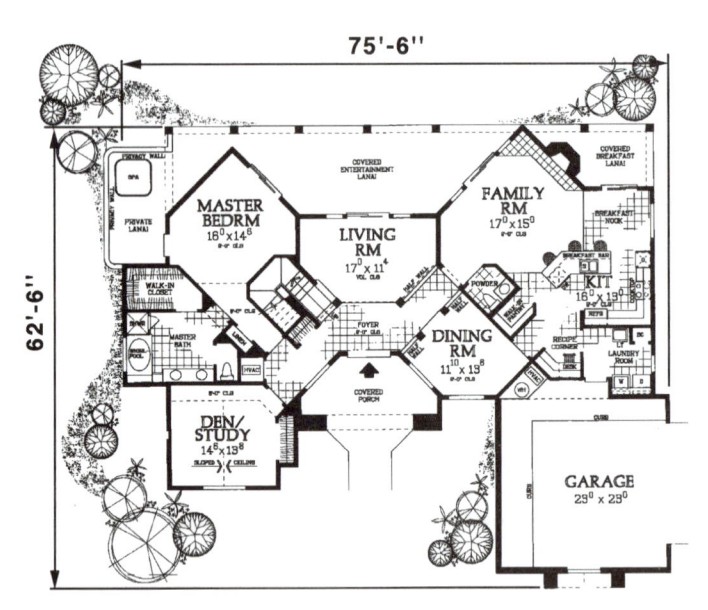

No. 99290

■ This plan features:

— Three or four bedrooms

— Two full and one half baths

■ Arched portico creates impressive entrance into easy-care Foyer leading to all areas of gracious home

■ Unusual angles and windows highlight the formal Living and Dining rooms

■ Expansive Family Room with angled fireplace opens to Covered Lanai, Kitchen and Breakfast Nook

■ Dream Kitchen offers every option an owner could want: breakfast bar/work island, walk-in pantry, recipe corner, laundry room, garage entry and breakfast lanai

■ Master Bedroom suite opens to private lanai with a spa and a plush Master Bath with a whirlpool window tub

FIRST FLOOR — 2,137 SQ. FT.
SECOND FLOOR — 671 SQ. FT.

TOTAL LIVING AREA: 2,808 SQ. FT.

FIRST FLOOR

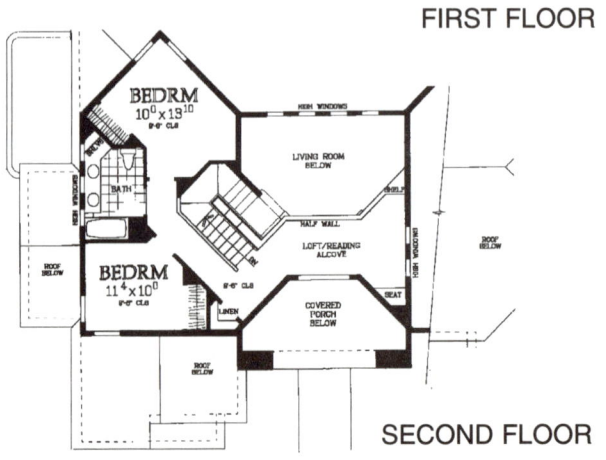

SECOND FLOOR

DESIGN NO. 93021

PRICE CODE A

An open concept home

No. 93021

- This plan features:
— Three bedrooms
— Two full baths
- An angled Entry creating the illusion of space
- Two square columns that flank the bar and separate the Kitchen from the Living Room
- A Dining Room that may service both formal and informal occasions
- A Master Bedroom with a large walk-in closet
- A large Master Bath with double vanities, linen closet and whirlpool tub/shower combination
- Two additional bedrooms that share a full bath

MAIN AREA — 1,282 SQ. FT.
GARAGE — 501 SQ. FT.

**TOTAL LIVING AREA:
1,282 SQ. FT.**

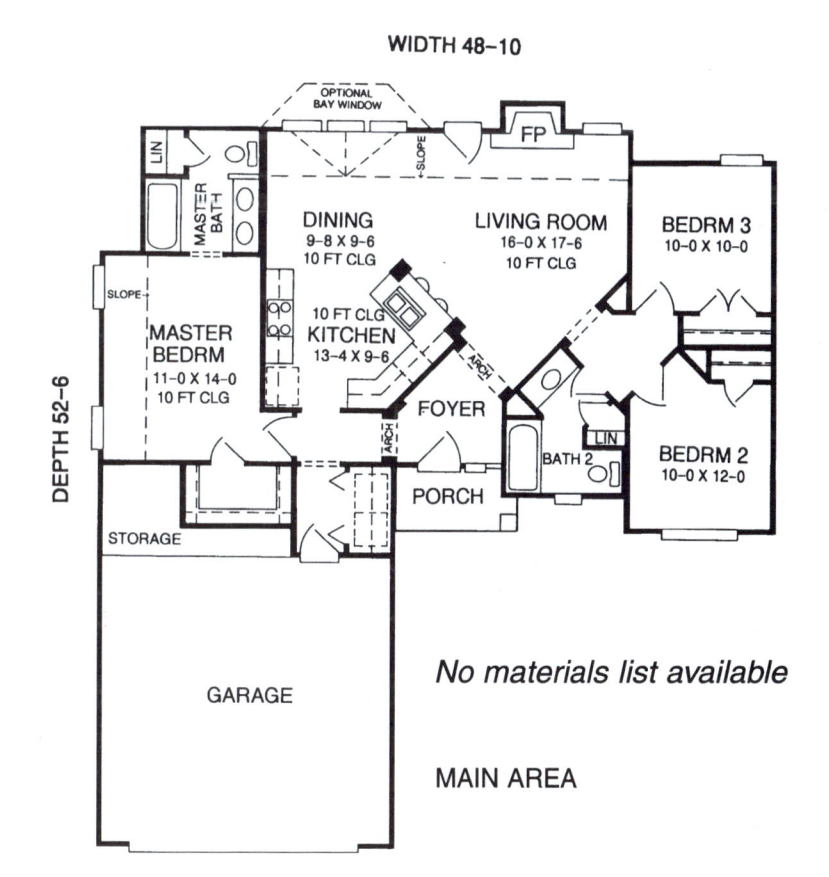

WIDTH 48-10
DEPTH 52-6

OPTIONAL BAY WINDOW
FP
LIN
MASTER BATH
DINING 9-8 X 9-6 10 FT CLG
LIVING ROOM 16-0 X 17-6 10 FT CLG
BEDRM 3 10-0 X 10-0
SLOPE
MASTER BEDRM 11-0 X 14-0 10 FT CLG
KITCHEN 13-4 X 9-6 10 FT CLG
FOYER
BATH 2
LIN
BEDRM 2 10-0 X 12-0
STORAGE
PORCH
GARAGE

No materials list available

MAIN AREA

DESIGN NO. 92537

PRICE CODE E

DETAILS DISTINGUISH THIS HOME DESIGN

No. 92537

- This plan features:
— Four bedrooms
— Three full and one half baths
- Gracious entrance into Open Foyer is highlighted by an arched window and banister staircase
- Formal Living and Dining rooms conveniently located off Foyer
- Expansive Den accented by a decorative ceiling over hearth fireplace and access to back yard
- Hub Kitchen with peninsula counter/snackbar, two pantries, a bright Breakfast area, Utility room, and Garage entry
- Spacious Master Bedroom suite enhanced by a large bath with two walk-in closets and vanities
- Three additional bedrooms, one with a private bath, share second floor
- An optional crawl space or slab foundation available, please specify when ordering

FIRST FLOOR — 1,809 SQ. FT.
SECOND FLOOR — 730 SQ. FT.
GARAGE — 533 SQ. FT.

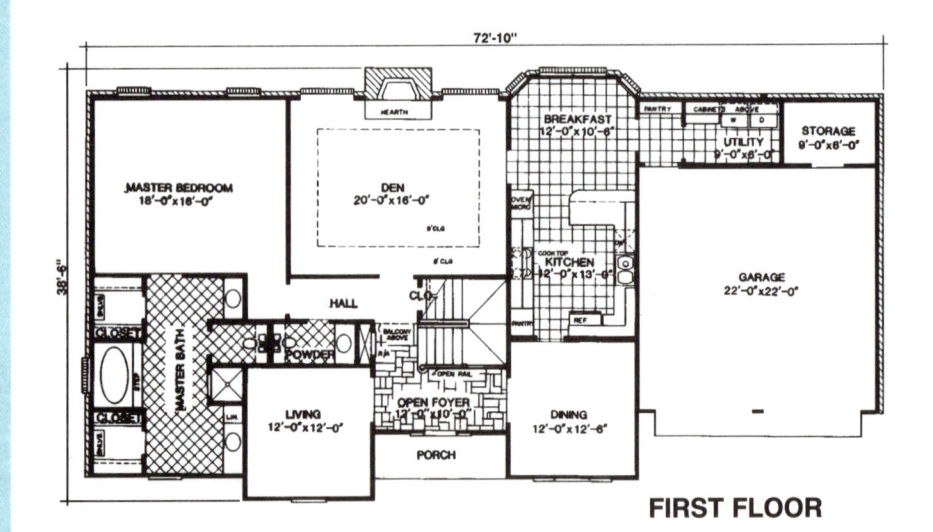

FIRST FLOOR

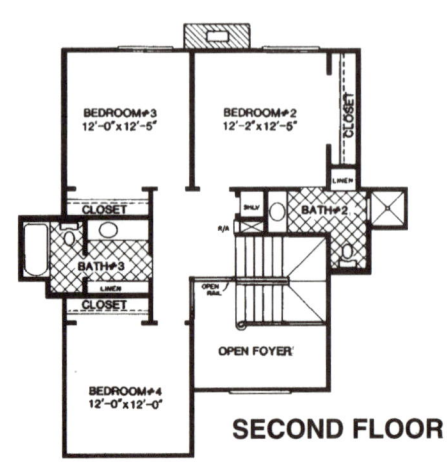

SECOND FLOOR

TOTAL LIVING AREA:
2,539 SQ. FT.

DESIGN NO. 99284

PRICE CODE C

Lots of Views and Breezes

No. 99284

■ This plan features:

— Three bedrooms

— Two full baths

■ Garden entry and large windows appealing to all

■ Kitchen directly off Foyer with work island/cooktop, serving counter/snackbar and adjoining Service Entry

■ Sloped ceiling tops fireplace and sliding glass doors to Terrace in Living/Dining room area

■ Master Bedroom enhanced by outdoor access, his-n-her walk-in closets and a pampering bath with two vanities and a whirlpool tub

■ Two additional bedrooms share a double vanity bath

MAIN AREA — 2,189 SQ. FT.
GARAGE — 480 SQ. FT.

TOTAL LIVING AREA: 2,189 SQ. FT.

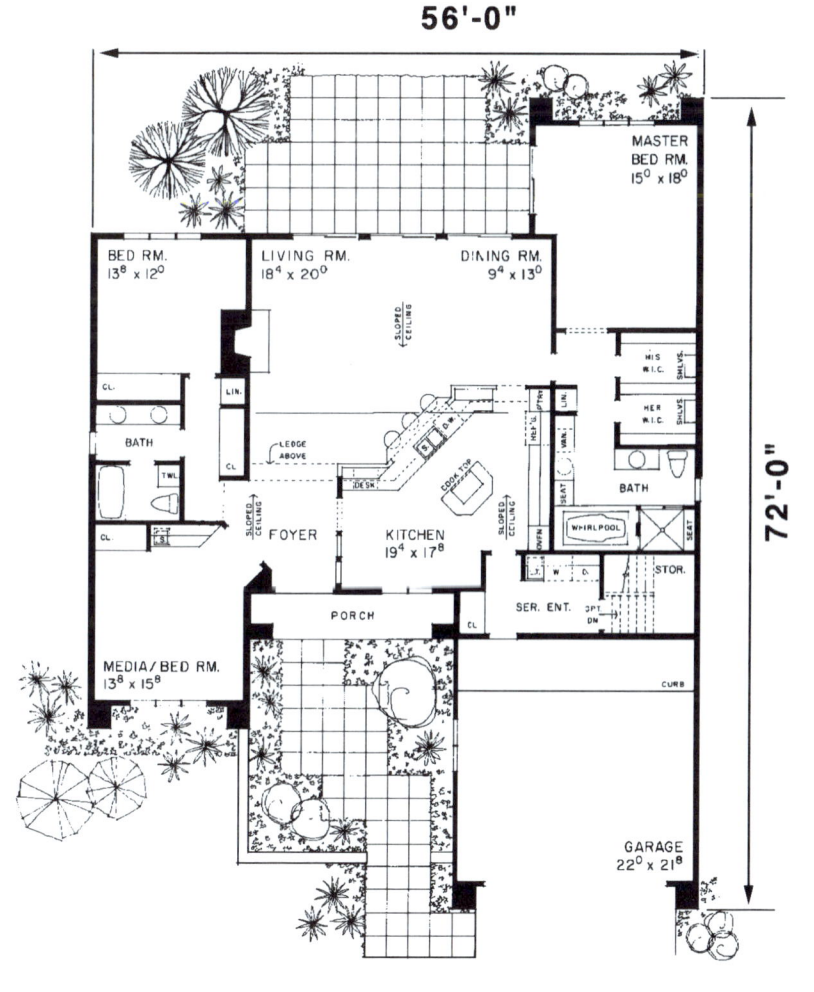

56'-0"

72'-0"

- MASTER BED RM. 15⁰ x 18⁰
- BED RM. 13⁸ x 12⁰
- LIVING RM. 18⁴ x 20⁰
- DINING RM. 9⁴ x 13⁰
- KITCHEN 19⁴ x 17⁸
- MEDIA/BED RM. 13⁸ x 15⁸
- GARAGE 22⁰ x 21⁸

MAIN AREA

DESIGN NO. 92649

PRICE CODE B

MULTIPLE GABLES AND A COZY PORCH

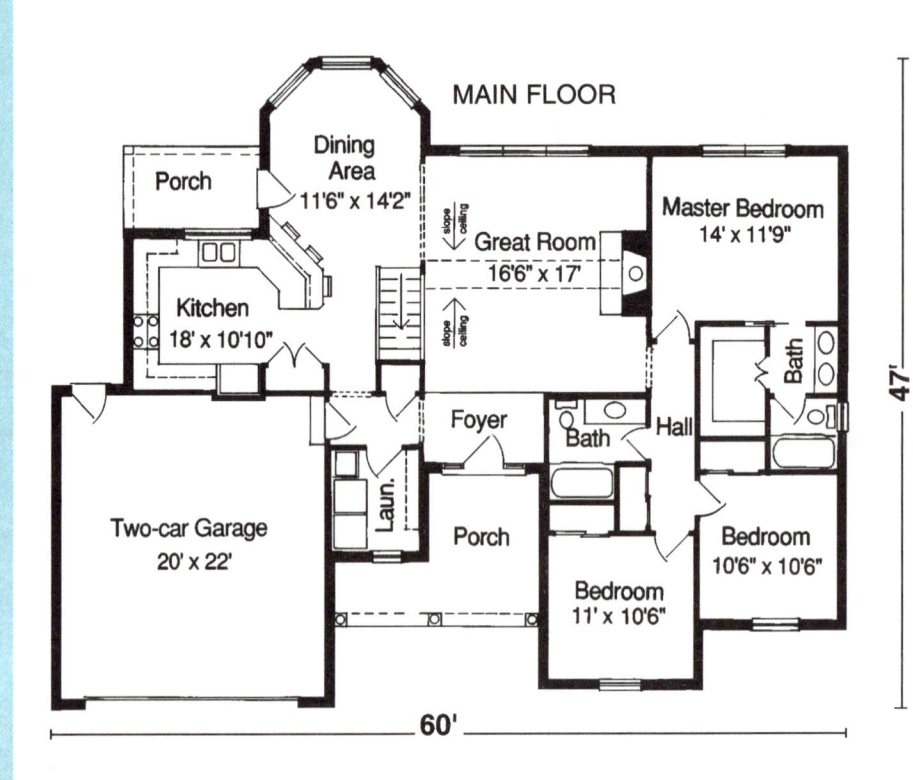

No. 92649

- This plan features:
- — Three bedrooms
- — Two full baths
- Multiple gables and a cozy front porch
- A Foyer area that leads to a bright and cheery Great Room capped by a sloped ceiling and highlighted by a fireplace
- The Dining Area includes double hung windows and angles adding light and dimension to the room
- A functional Kitchen providing an abundance of counter space with additional room provided by a breakfast bar
- A Master Bedroom Suite with a walk-in closet and private bath
- Two additional bedrooms share a full bath in the hall

MAIN FLOOR — 1,508 SQ. FT.
BASEMENT — 1,429 SQ. FT.
GARAGE — 440 SQ. FT.

TOTAL LIVING AREA: 1,508 SQ. FT.

MAIN FLOOR

- Dining Area 11'6" x 14'2"
- Porch
- Great Room 16'6" x 17'
- Master Bedroom 14' x 11'9"
- Kitchen 18' x 10'10"
- Foyer
- Bath
- Hall
- Bath
- Two-car Garage 20' x 22'
- Laun.
- Porch
- Bedroom 11' x 10'6"
- Bedroom 10'6" x 10'6"

60' × 47'

No materials list available

DESIGN NO. 92623

PRICE CODE E

LUXURY PERSONIFIED

No. 92623

- This plan features:
— Four bedrooms
— Two full and one half baths
- A tray ceiling in the formal Living Room and Dining Room with corner columns
- An island Kitchen which includes a corner sink with windows to either side
- A sunken Family Room with a cozy fireplace
- A luxurious Master Suite with double walk-in closets, sloped ceiling and private Master Bath
- Three additional bedrooms that share a skylit full bath with laundry chute located close by

FIRST FLOOR — 1,365 SQ. FT.
SECOND FLOOR — 1,288 SQ. FT.
BASEMENT — 1,217 SQ. FT.
GARAGE — 491 SQ. FT.

TOTAL LIVING AREA: 2,653 SQ. FT.

No materials list available

FIRST FLOOR

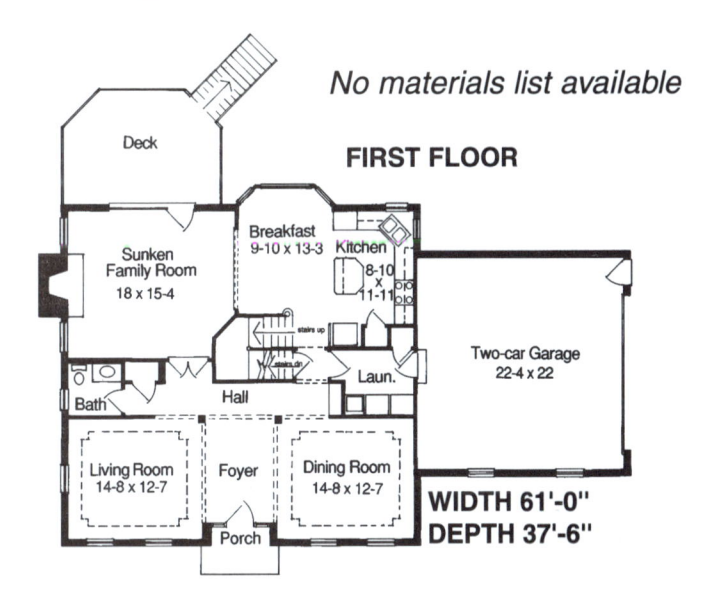

- Deck
- Sunken Family Room 18 x 15-4
- Breakfast 9-10 x 13-3
- Kitchen 8-10 x 11-11
- Two-car Garage 22-4 x 22
- Bath
- Hall
- Laun.
- Living Room 14-8 x 12-7
- Foyer
- Dining Room 14-8 x 12-7
- Porch

WIDTH 61'-0"
DEPTH 37'-6"

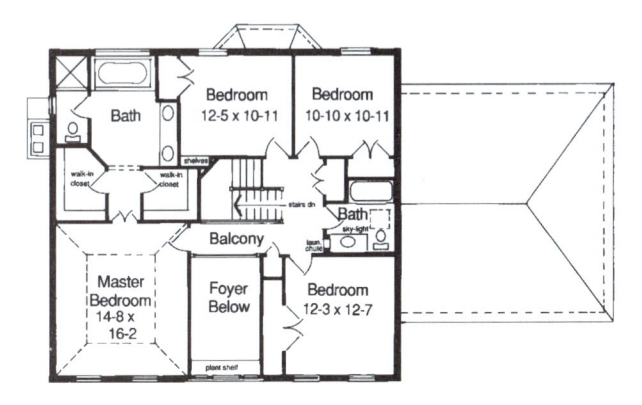

SECOND FLOOR

- Bath
- Bedroom 12-5 x 10-11
- Bedroom 10-10 x 10-11
- walk-in closet
- walk-in closet
- Bath
- Balcony
- Master Bedroom 14-8 x 16-2
- Foyer Below
- Bedroom 12-3 x 12-7

DESIGN NO. 93050

PRICE CODE D

AN OPEN CONCEPT FLOOR PLAN

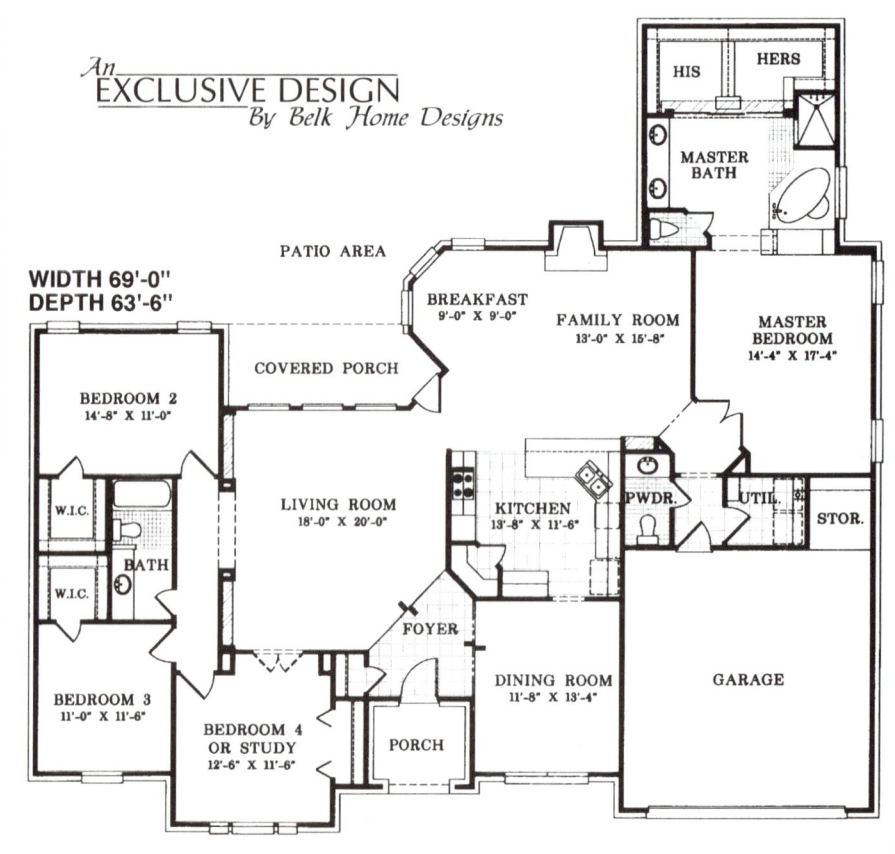

An EXCLUSIVE DESIGN By Belk Home Designs

No. 93050

- This plan features:
— Four bedrooms
— Two full and one half baths
- The Kitchen, Breakfast Room and the Family Room are adjacent to one another and open to one another.
- A well-appointed Kitchen with ample cabinet space and a peninsula counter.
- An expansive Living Room with A stupendous fireplace on the center of the rear wall
- A private Master Suite with a large Master Bath
- An oval tub, separate shower, compartmented toilet, double vanity and his-n-her walk-in closets in the Master bath
- Two additional bedrooms with walk-in closets and a full hall bath in close proximity

MAIN FLOOR — 2,511 SQ. FT.
GARAGE — 469 SQ. FT.

TOTAL LIVING AREA: 2,511 SQ. FT.

WIDTH 69'-0"
DEPTH 63'-6"

MAIN FLOOR

No materials list available

DESIGN NO. 99289

PRICE CODE F

Indoor-Outdoor Living Design

No. 99289

- This plan features:
— Four or five bedrooms
— Three full and one half baths
- Formal Living and Dining rooms either side of two-story Entry Art Gallery
- Country Kitchen includes convenient snack bar and a built-in pantry along with an eating area and formal Dining Room nearby
- Central Family Great Room highlighted by large hearth fireplace between built-ins topped by large cupulo
- Private Master Suite with a sitting area, a walk-in closet and a luxurious Master Bath
- A Guest-Studio attached to separate garage for additional guests and privacy

MAIN FLOOR — 3,278 SQ. FT.

TOTAL LIVING AREA: 3,278 SQ. FT.

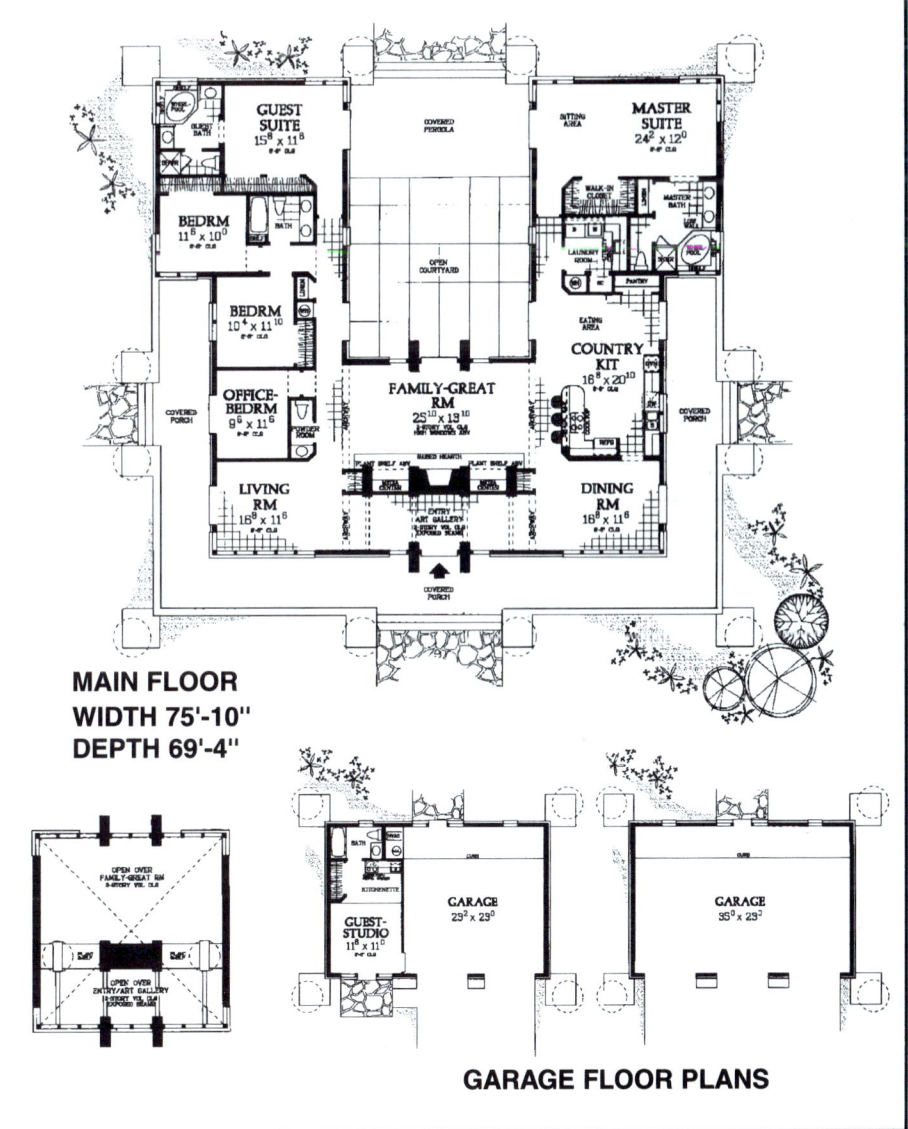

MAIN FLOOR
WIDTH 75'-10"
DEPTH 69'-4"

GARAGE FLOOR PLANS

DESIGN NO. 93202

PRICE CODE A

Compact and comfortable

No. 93202

- This plan features:
  — Three bedrooms
  — Two full baths
- Arched window highlights front entrance, Foyer and staircase
- Spacious Living Area with focal point fireplace and Deck access
- Efficient, U-shaped Kitchen easily serves bright Dining Room and Deck
- Private Master Bedroom with walk-in closet and double vanity bath with a raised tub
- Two additional bedrooms with ample closets, share a full bath
- Lower level with Garage, Storage and future Playroom

MAIN FLOOR — 1,447 SQ. FT.
BASEMENT — 950 SQ. FT.
GARAGE — 400 SQ. FT.

TOTAL LIVING AREA: 1,447 SQ. FT.

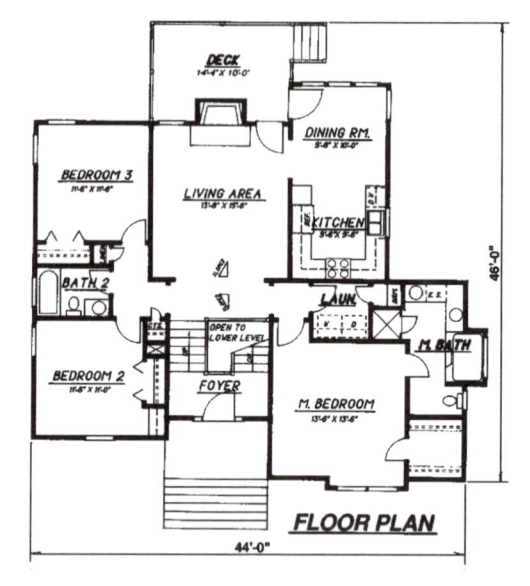

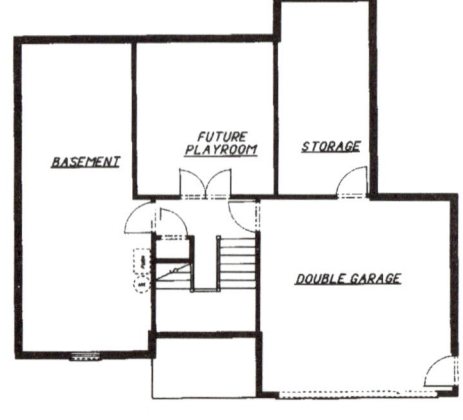

FLOOR PLAN

LOWER LEVEL

An EXCLUSIVE DESIGN *By Jannis Vann & Associates, Inc.*

DESIGN NO. 92644

PRICE CODE C

DISTINCTIVE DETAIL AND DESIGN

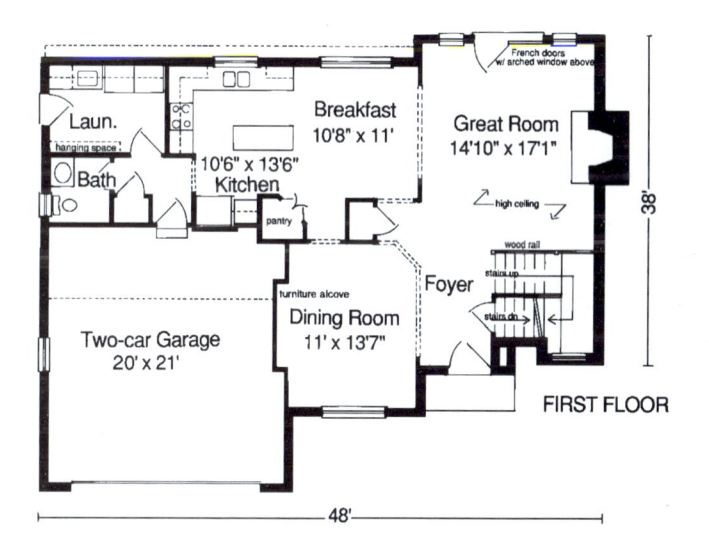

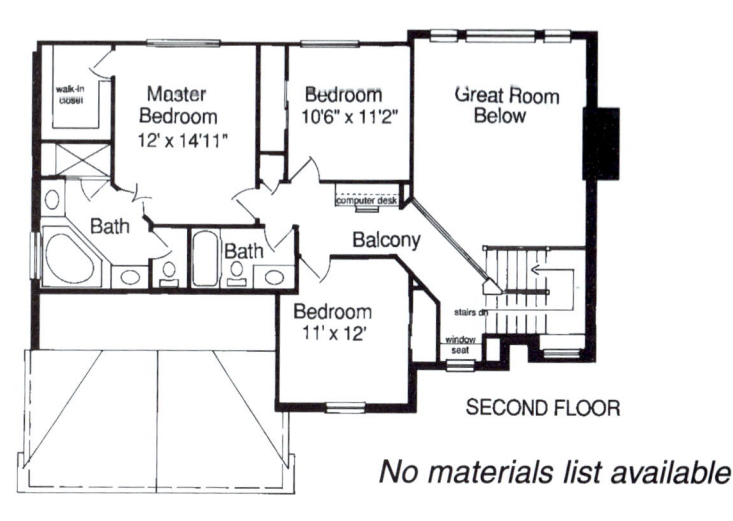

No. 92644

■ This plan features:

— Three bedrooms

— Two full and one half baths

■ Impressive pilaster entry into open Foyer with landing staircase highlighted by decorative windows

■ Great Room accented by hearth fireplace and French doors with arched window above and topped by a high ceiling

■ Formal Dining Room enhanced by furniture alcove and decorative window

■ Efficient, L-shaped Kitchen with work island, walk-in pantry, bright breakfast area

■ Quiet Master Bedroom offers a walk-in closet, and plush bath

■ Two additional bedrooms share a full bath and Computer Desk

FIRST FLOOR — 1,036 SQ. FT.
SECOND FLOOR — 861 SQ. FT.
GARAGE — 420 SQ. FT.

TOTAL LIVING AREA: 1,897 SQ. FT.

FIRST FLOOR

SECOND FLOOR

No materials list available

DESIGN NO. 92504

PRICE CODE F

TRADITIONAL ELEGANCE

No. 92504

- This plan features:
— Four bedrooms
— Three full and one half baths

- A elegant entrance leading into a two-story Foyer with an impressive staircase highlighted by a curved window

- A spacious Den with a hearth fireplace, built-in book shelves, a wetbar and a wall of windows viewing the backyard

- A large, efficient Kitchen, a bright Breakfast area, and access to the Dining Room, Utility Room, walk-in pantry and Garage

- A grand Master Suite with decorative ceilings, a private Porch, an elaborate Bath and two walk-in closets

- Three additional bedrooms on the second floor with walk-in closets, sharing adjoining, full baths and a ideal Children's Den

- This plan is available with a slab or crawlspace foundation. Please specify when ordering.

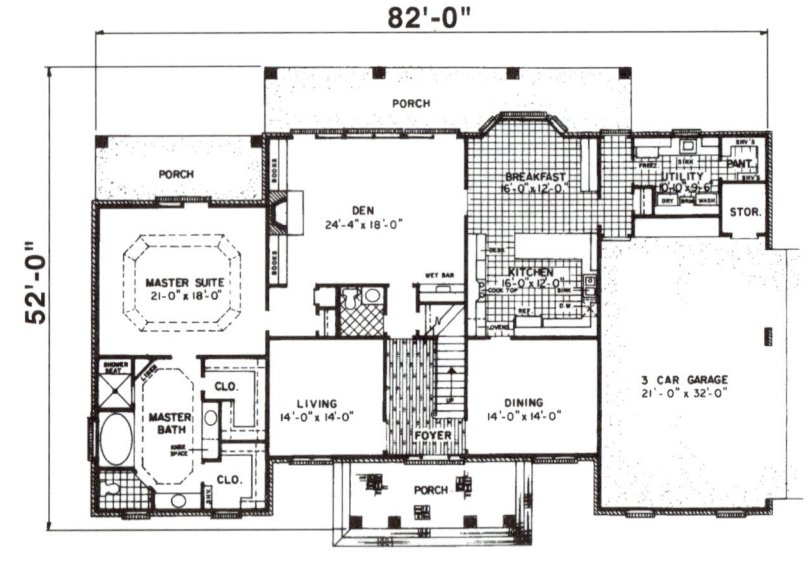

FIRST FLOOR PLAN

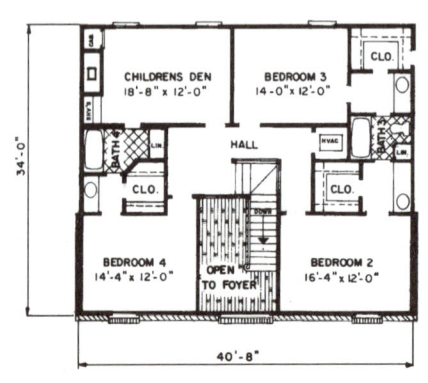

SECOND FLOOR PLAN

FIRST FLOOR — 2,553 SQ. FT.
SECOND FLOOR — 1,260 SQ. FT.
GARAGE — 714 SQ. FT.

TOTAL LIVING AREA: 3,813 SQ. FT.

DESIGN NO. 94716

PRICE CODE B

GREAT GREEK REVIVAL

An EXCLUSIVE DESIGN
By United Design Associates

No. 94716

■ This plan features:

— Three bedrooms

— Two full and one half baths

■ Formality & function combine in an open & comfortable floor plan

■ Entry Portico leads into a Dining area defined by columns and two-story Great room with a cozy fireplace and Patio access

■ Convenient Kitchen with a peninsula counter serving bright Breakfast area

■ Secluded Master suite enhanced by a decorative ceiling, walk-in closet and plush bath with a whirlpool tub

■ Two more bedrooms with walk-in closets and an adjoining bath

FIRST FLOOR — 1,318 SQ. FT.
SECOND FLOOR — 452 SQ. FT.
GARAGE — 431 SQ. FT.

TOTAL LIVING AREA: 1,770 SQ. FT.

HIGH WIND LOAD ENGINEERING AVAILABLE
SEE PAGE 246 FOR DETAILS

SECOND FLOOR
- Bed 10'0" x 12'0"
- Bed 10'0" x 12'0"
- open to below

FIRST FLOOR
No. 94716
- Mstr 14'8" x 15'
- Patio
- Brk 11'0" x 9'0"
- Great 17'8" x 17'9"
- Kit 11'0" x 12'4"
- Gar 19'7" x 21'6"
- Din 12'4" x 10'4"
- Por
- 53'-6"
- 44'-0"

DESIGN NO. 93043

PRICE CODE E

Four bedroom brick traditional

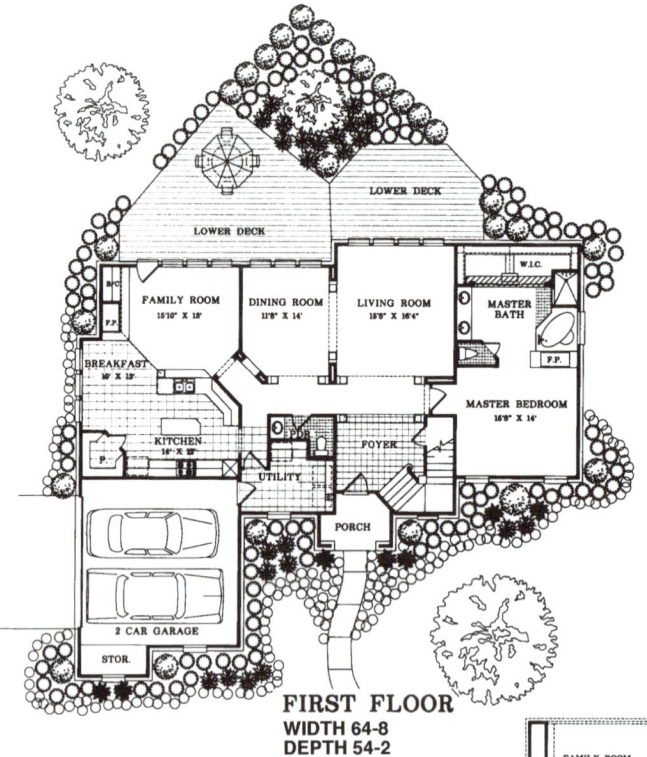

No. 93043

- This plan features:
- — Four bedrooms
- — Two full and one half baths
- Arched entry into pillared Foyer with angled staircase
- Formal Living and Dining rooms enhanced by pillars and expansive views of rear grounds
- Country-size Kitchen offers work island, large walk-in pantry, bright Breakfast area, serving counter to Family Room, and adjoining Utility/Garage entry
- Private first floor Master Bedroom boasts a fireplace and lavish bath with a corner whirlpool tub
- Three additional bedrooms on second floor share a double vanity bath

First floor — 1,910 sq. ft.
Second floor — 834 sq. ft.
Garage — 489 sq. ft.

Total living area: 2,744 sq. ft.

FIRST FLOOR
WIDTH 64-8
DEPTH 54-2

No materials list available

SECOND FLOOR

DESIGN NO. 92646

PRICE CODE D

A TOUCH OF OLD WORLD CHARM

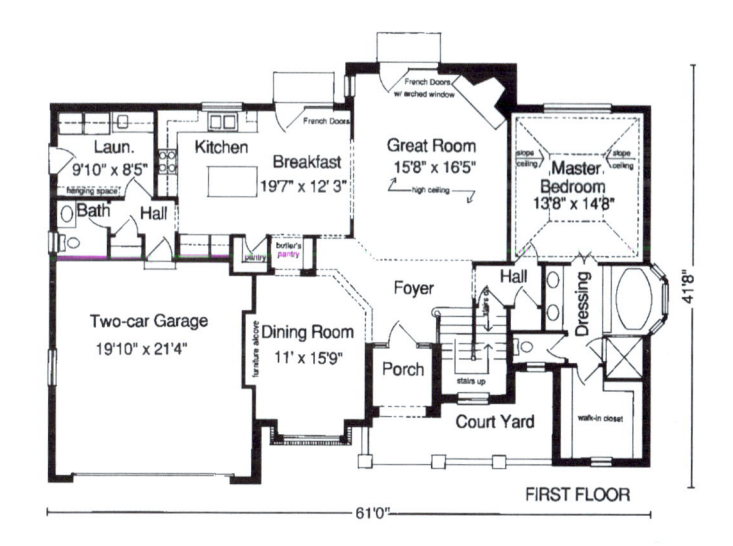

No. 92646

■ This plan features:

— Four bedrooms

— Two full and one half baths

■ Authentic balustrade railings and front courtyard greet one and all

■ High ceiling in Great Room tops corner fireplace and French doors with arched window

■ Formal Dining Room enhanced by a decorative window and furniture alcove

■ Country Kitchen with work island, two pantrys, Breakfast area with French door to rear yard, Laundry and Garage entry

■ Master Bedroom wing offers a sloped ceiling, plush bath and a huge walk-in closet

■ Three additional bedrooms share second floor, balcony and double vanity bath

FIRST FLOOR — 1,595 SQ. FT.
SECOND FLOOR — 725 SQ. FT.
BASEMENT — 1,471 SQ. FT.
GARAGE — 409 SQ. FT.

TOTAL LIVING AREA: 2,320 SQ. FT.

No materials list available

DESIGN NO. 92636

PRICE CODE C

FAMILY-SIZED DESIGN

No. 92636

- This plan features:
- — Three bedrooms
- — Two full and one half baths
- Inviting Porch leads into central Foyer and banister staircase
- Formal Living and Dining Rooms enhanced by decorative windows
- Expansive Family Room with cozy fireplace and bright bay window
- L-shaped Kitchen with work island and Breakfast area with sliding glass door to rear yard
- Handy half bath, Laundry and Garage entry off Kitchen
- Private Master Bedroom with plush bath and walk-in closet
- Two additional bedrooms with ample closets share a full bath

FIRST FLOOR — 1,113 SQ. FT.
SECOND FLOOR — 835 SQ. FT.
BONUS — 245 SQ. FT.

TOTAL LIVING AREA: 1,948 SQ. FT.

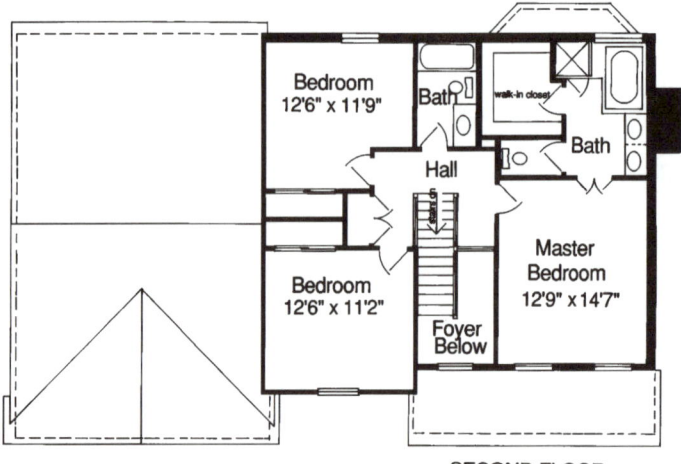

SECOND FLOOR

- Bedroom 12'6" x 11'9"
- Bedroom 12'6" x 11'2"
- Master Bedroom 12'9" x 14'7"
- Hall
- Bath
- Bath
- walk-in closet
- Foyer Below

No materials list available

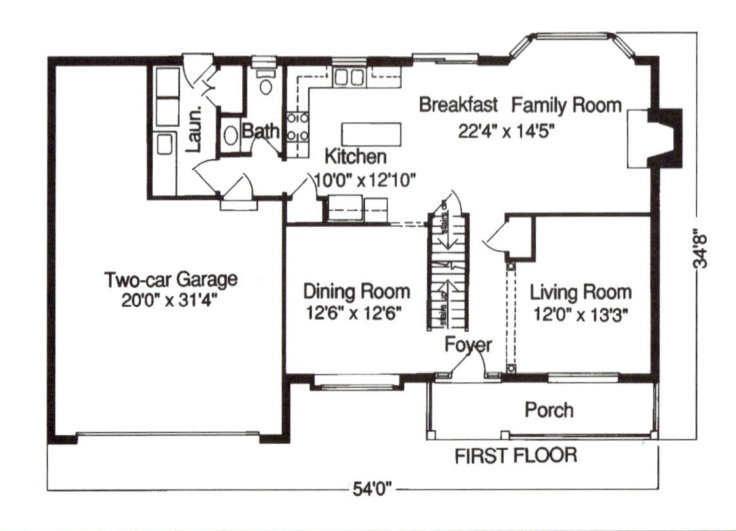

FIRST FLOOR

- Laun.
- Bath
- Kitchen 10'0" x 12'10"
- Breakfast
- Family Room 22'4" x 14'5"
- Two-car Garage 20'0" x 31'4"
- Dining Room 12'6" x 12'6"
- Living Room 12'0" x 13'3"
- Foyer
- Porch

54'0" × 34'8"

DESIGN NO. 92538

PRICE CODE F

LAVISH ACCOMMODATIONS

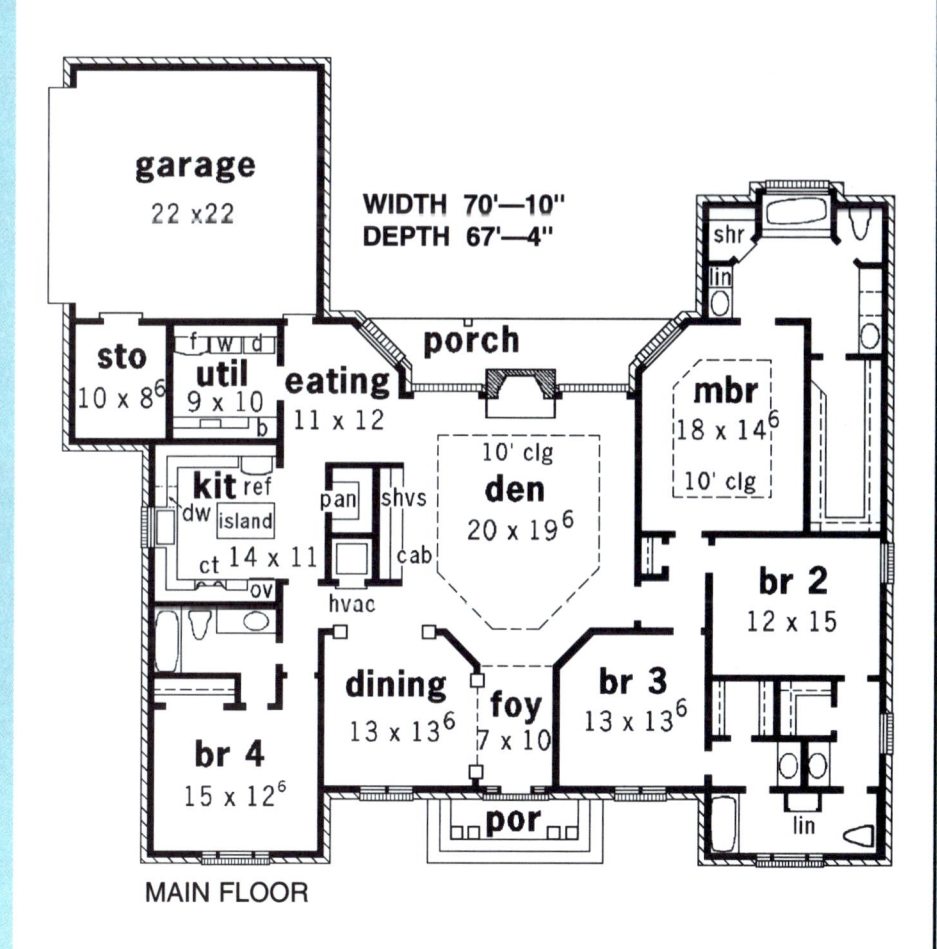

No. 92538

■ This plan features:

— Four bedrooms

— Three full baths

■ A central Den with a large fireplace, built-in shelves and cabinets and a decorative ceiling

■ Columns defining the entrance to the formal Dining Room

■ An island Kitchen that includes a walk-in pantry

■ An informal Breakfast Room

■ A Master Bedroom enhanced by a decorative ceiling and a walk-in closet as well as a luxurious Master Bath

■ Four additional bedrooms, each with private access to a full bath, two of which have walk-in closets

■ An optional crawl space or slab foundation — please specify when ordering

MAIN FLOOR — 2,733 SQ. FT.
GARAGE AND STORAGE — 569 SQ. FT.

TOTAL LIVING AREA: 2,733 SQ. FT.

WIDTH 70'—10"
DEPTH 67'—4"

MAIN FLOOR

DESIGN NO. 92631

PRICE CODE C

Traditional two-story with special details

No. 92631

- This plan features:
- — Four bedrooms
- — Two full and one half baths
- Front entrance into two-story Foyer with a plant shelf and lovely railing staircase
- Expansive Great Room with corner fireplace and access to rear yard topped by two-story ceiling
- Efficient Kitchen with peninsula counter, walk-in pantry, Breakfast bay and access to Deck, Laundry, Garage entry and formal Dining Room
- Secluded Master Bedroom offers a sloped ceiling and lavish bath with walk-in closet

FIRST FLOOR — 1,511 SQ. FT.
SECOND FLOOR — 646 SQ. FT.
BASEMENT — 1,479 SQ. FT.
GARAGE — 475 SQ. FT.

TOTAL LIVING AREA: 2,157 SQ. FT.

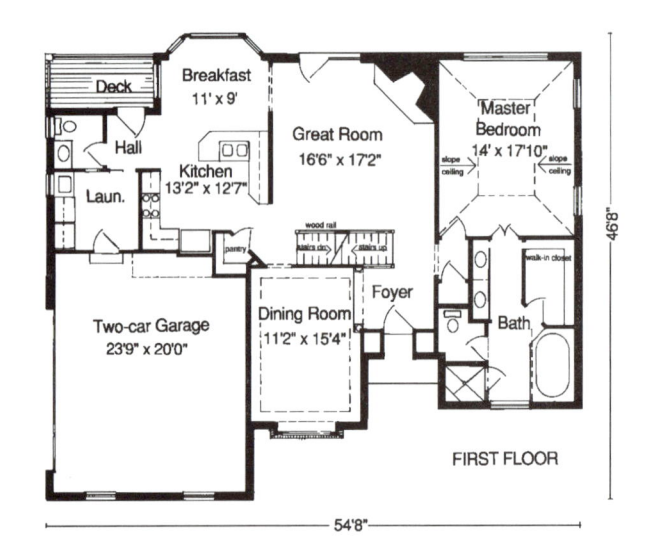

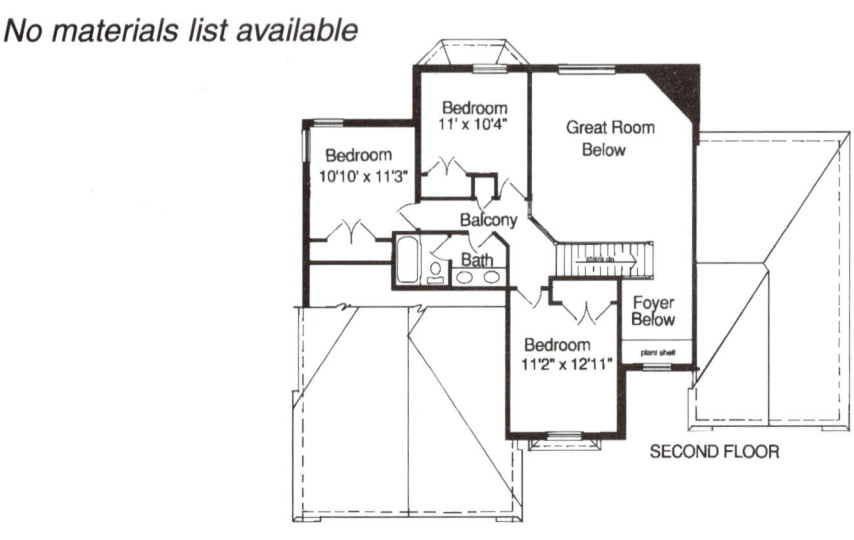

FIRST FLOOR

- Deck
- Breakfast 11' x 9'
- Hall
- Kitchen 13'2" x 12'7"
- Laun.
- Great Room 16'6" x 17'2"
- Master Bedroom 14' x 17'10"
- Bath
- Two-car Garage 23'9" x 20'0"
- Dining Room 11'2" x 15'4"
- Foyer

54'8" x 46'8"

No materials list available

SECOND FLOOR

- Bedroom 10'10" x 11'3"
- Bedroom 11' x 10'4"
- Great Room Below
- Balcony
- Bath
- Bedroom 11'2" x 12'11"
- Foyer Below

DESIGN NO. 93279

PRICE CODE A

Open Living Spaces

An EXCLUSIVE DESIGN
By Jannis Vann & Associates, Inc.

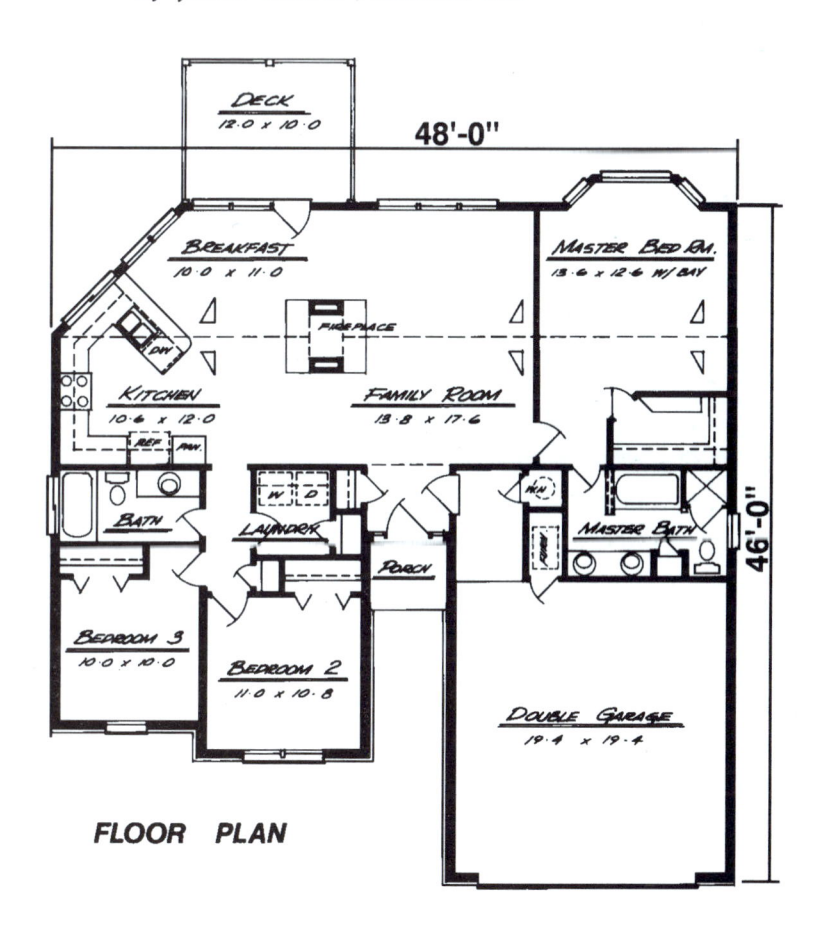

TOTAL LIVING AREA:
1,388 SQ. FT.

No. 93279

- This plan features:
— Three bedrooms
— Two full baths
- A Family Room, Kitchen and Breakfast Area that all connect to form a great space
- A central, double fireplace adding warmth and atmosphere to the Family Room, Kitchen and the Breakfast area
- An efficient Kitchen that is highlighted by a peninsula counter and doubles as a snack bar
- A Master Suite that includes a walk-in closet, a double vanity, separate shower and tub bath
- Two additional bedrooms sharing a full hall bath
- A wooden deck that can be accessed from the Breakfast Area
- An optional crawl space or slab foundation available, please specify when ordering

MAIN FLOOR — 1,388 SQ. FT.
GARAGE — 400 SQ. FT.

FLOOR PLAN

48'-0" × 46'-0"

- Deck 12.0 × 10.0
- Breakfast 10.0 × 11.0
- Master Bed Rm. 13.6 × 12.6 w/ Bay
- Kitchen 10.6 × 12.0
- Family Room 13.8 × 17.6
- Bedroom 3 10.0 × 10.0
- Bedroom 2 11.0 × 10.8
- Double Garage 19.4 × 19.4

DESIGN NO. 93041

PRICE CODE E

Two-story Entry Adds Grace

No. 93041

■ This plan features:

— Five bedrooms

— Two full and one half baths

■ A stucco designed accented by an arched, two-story Entry

■ All major living areas are located with views to the rear grounds

■ The Kitchen, Breakfast Room and Family Room are adjacent and open to one another

■ An island cooktop and double sinks, along with an abundance of storage space making the Kitchen even more convenient

■ The Master Suite with an angled whirlpool tub, separate shower and his-and-her vanities

■ Three additional bedrooms located on the second floor

FIRST FLOOR — 1,974 SQ. FT.
SECOND FLOOR — 1,060 SQ. FT.
GARAGE — 531 SQ. FT.

TOTAL LIVING AREA: 3,034 SQ. FT.

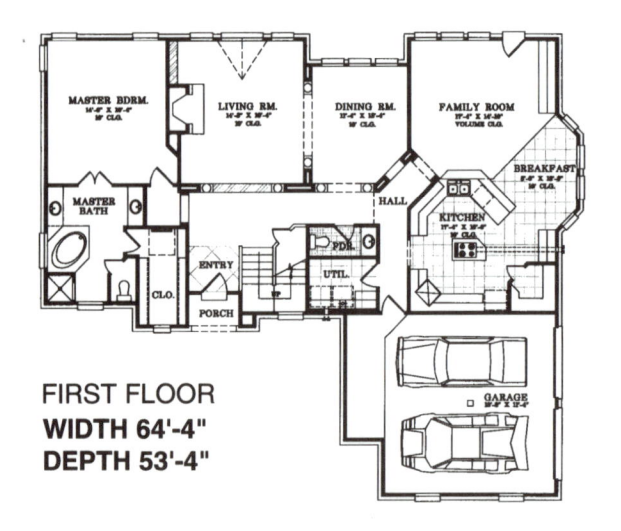

FIRST FLOOR
WIDTH 64'-4"
DEPTH 53'-4"

SECOND FLOOR

No materials list available

DESIGN NO. 92634

PRICE CODE D

ELEGANT ELEVATION

No. 92634

■ This plan features:

— Four bedrooms

— Two full and one half baths

■ A wide-apron staircase and plant shelf highlight open Foyer

■ An arched entrance frames formal Living Room with high ceiling

■ Decorative bay window enhances formal Dining Room

■ Expansive Family Room with focal point fireplace and view of rear yard

■ Hub Kitchen with Breakfast area, Garage entry, Laundry, and peninsula counter/snackbar

■ Comfortable Master Bedroom with sloped ceiling, large walk-in closet and plush bath

FIRST FLOOR — 1,309 SQ. FT.
SECOND FLOOR — 1,119 SQ. FT.
BASEMENT — 1,277 SQ. FT.
GARAGE — 452 SQ. FT.

TOTAL LIVING AREA: 2,428 SQ. FT.

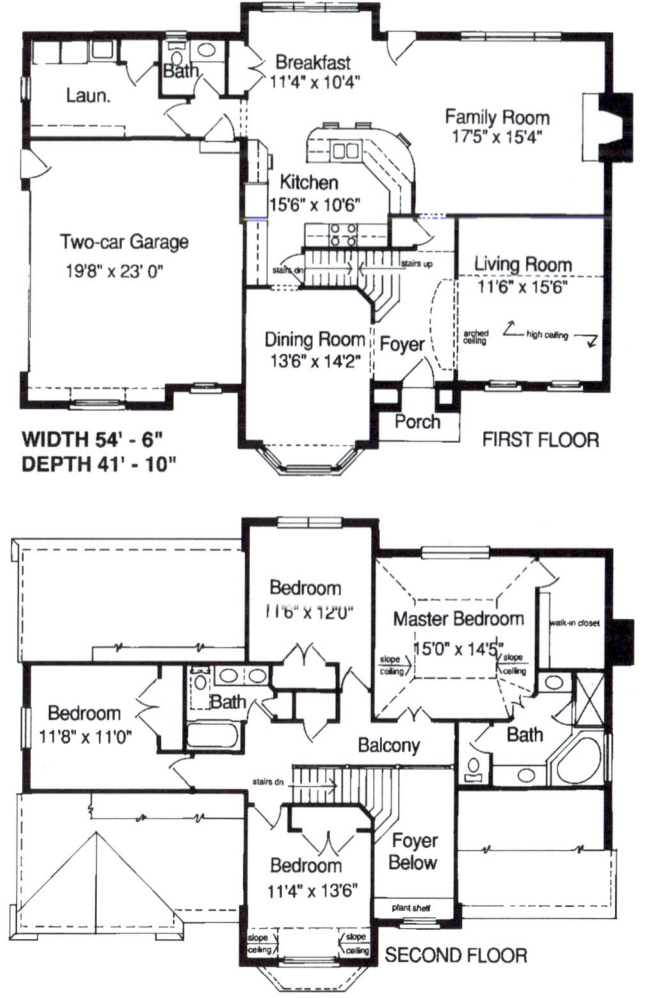

WIDTH 54' - 6"
DEPTH 41' - 10"

FIRST FLOOR

- Bath
- Laun.
- Breakfast 11'4" x 10'4"
- Family Room 17'5" x 15'4"
- Kitchen 15'6" x 10'6"
- Two-car Garage 19'8" x 23'0"
- Living Room 11'6" x 15'6"
- Dining Room 13'6" x 14'2"
- Foyer
- Porch

SECOND FLOOR

- Bedroom 11'6" x 12'0"
- Master Bedroom 15'0" x 14'5"
- Bedroom 11'8" x 11'0"
- Bath
- Balcony
- Bath
- Bedroom 11'4" x 13'6"
- Foyer Below

No materials list available

DESIGN NO. 92628

PRICE CODE C

VERSATILITY AND CHARM

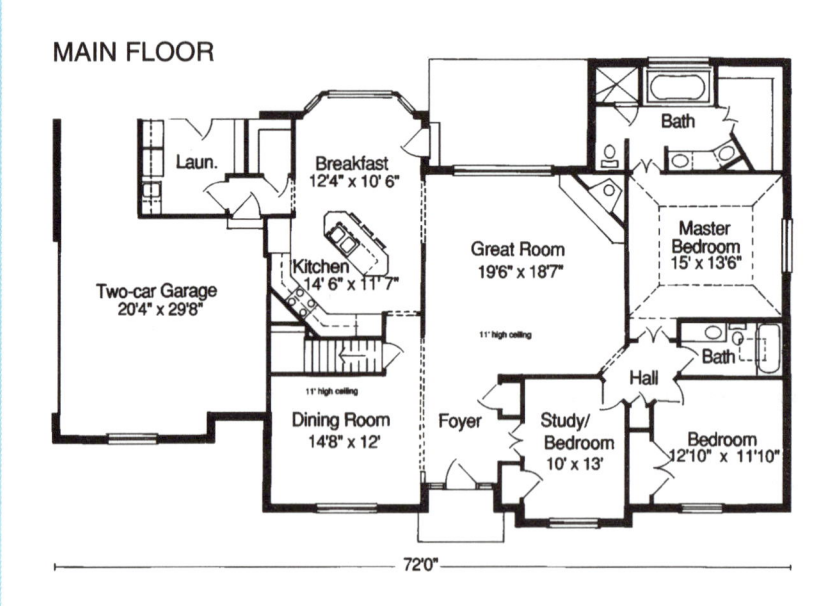

No. 92628

- This plan features:
— Three bedrooms
— Two full baths
- A spacious Great Room with a corner fireplace and tall transom windows
- A formal Dining Room that allows for easy expansion of your entertaining area
- An optional Study or Bedroom that provides flexibility for the living space
- A large island that expands the Kitchen and offers an abundance of counter space
- A bright and cheery Breakfast Bay for informal dining
- Eleven-foot ceilings featured in the Great Room and Dining Room
- A sloped ceiling and an ultra bath in the Master Suite

MAIN FLOOR — 1,998 SQ. FT.
GARAGE — 488 SQ. FT.

TOTAL LIVING AREA:
1,998 SQ. FT.

MAIN FLOOR

No materials list available

DESIGN NO. 94721

PRICE CODE E

CLASSIC VICTORIAN

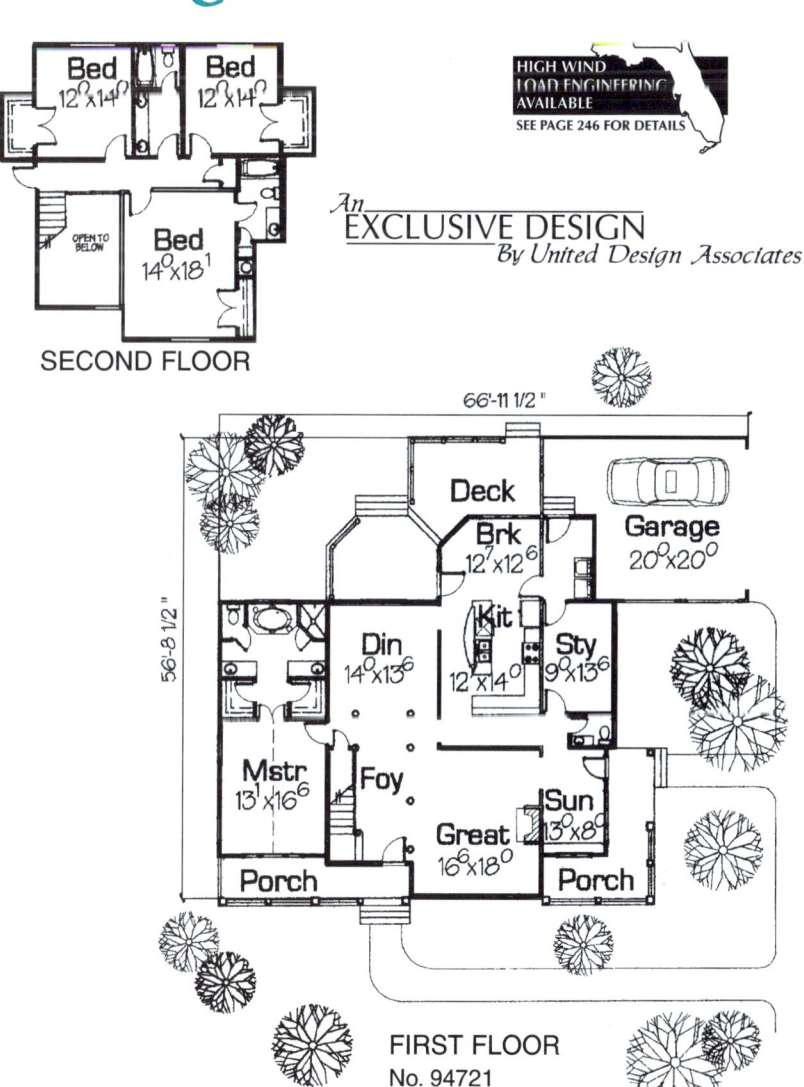

No. 94721

■ This plan features:

— Four bedrooms

— Three full and one half baths

■ Large open areas that are bright and free flowing

■ Great room accented by a fireplace and large front window

■ Sun Room off of the Great room viewing the porch

■ Dining Room in close proximity to the Kitchen

■ Efficient Kitchen flows into informal Breakfast Nook

■ Private first floor Master Suite highlighted by a plush Master Bath

■ Three bedrooms on the second floor, two with walk-in closets and one with a private bath

FIRST FLOOR—1,868 SQ. FT.
SECOND FLOOR—964 SQ. FT.
GARAGE—460 SQ. FT.

TOTAL LIVING AREA: 2,832 SQ. FT.

HIGH WIND LOAD ENGINEERING AVAILABLE
SEE PAGE 246 FOR DETAILS

An EXCLUSIVE DESIGN
By United Design Associates

SECOND FLOOR
- Bed 12'×14'
- Bed 12'×14'
- Bed 14'⁰×18'¹

FIRST FLOOR
No. 94721

- 66'-11 1/2"
- 56'-8 1/2"
- Deck
- Brk 12'⁷×12'⁶
- Garage 20'⁰×20'⁰
- Din 14'⁰×13'⁶
- Kit 12'×14'
- Sty 9'⁰×13'⁶
- Mstr 13'¹×16'⁶
- Foy
- Great 16'⁶×18'⁰
- Sun 13'×8'
- Porch
- Porch

DESIGN NO. 94216

PRICE CODE D

CLASSIC CONTEMPORARY SPANISH STYLE

No. 94216

■ This plan features:

— Three bedrooms

— Two full and one half baths

■ Double arches shelter Entry into Foyer and open Living/Dining Room with Verandah access

■ Spacious Kitchen with island cooktop, built-in pantry, Utility and Garage entry serves peninsula snackbar, Nook and Dining area

■ Comfortable Master Suite with Verandah access, two walk-in closets and vanities, and a corner tub

■ French doors access Study with tray ceiling above alcove of arched windows

■ Two additional bedrooms with ample closets share a full bath

MAIN FLOOR — 2,582 SQ. FT.
GARAGE — 695 SQ. FT.

TOTAL LIVING AREA: 2,582 SQ. FT.

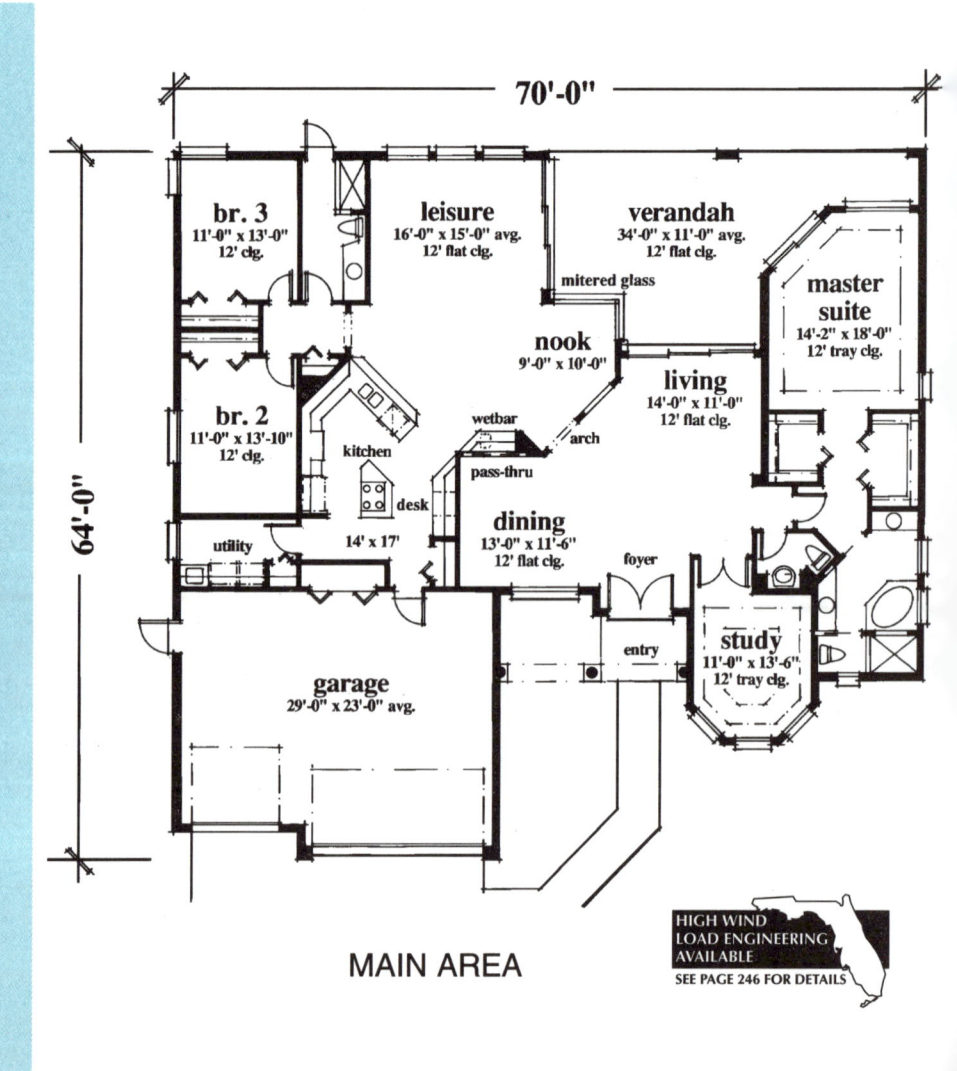

MAIN AREA

HIGH WIND LOAD ENGINEERING AVAILABLE
SEE PAGE 246 FOR DETAILS

DESIGN NO. 92647

PRICE CODE C

PLENTY OF ROOM TO GROW

No. 92647

- This plan features:
- — Three or Four bedrooms
- — Two full and one half baths
- Fieldstone and wood siding accent Porch entrance into open Foyer with lovely landing staircase
- Sunken Great Room with large fireplace, built-in entertainment center and access to rear yard
- Hub Kitchen with built-in pantry, serving counter, bright Breakfast area and adjoining Dining Room, Laundry and Garage entry
- Corner Master bedroom with walk-in closet, pampering bath with double vanity and whirlpool tub topped by sloped ceiling
- Two or three additional bedrooms share a full bath and a study/computer area

FIRST FLOOR — 1,065 SQ. FT.
SECOND FLOOR — 833 SQ. FT.
BONUS ROOM — 254 SQ. FT.
GARAGE — 652 SQ. FT.

TOTAL LIVING AREA: 1,898 SQ. FT.

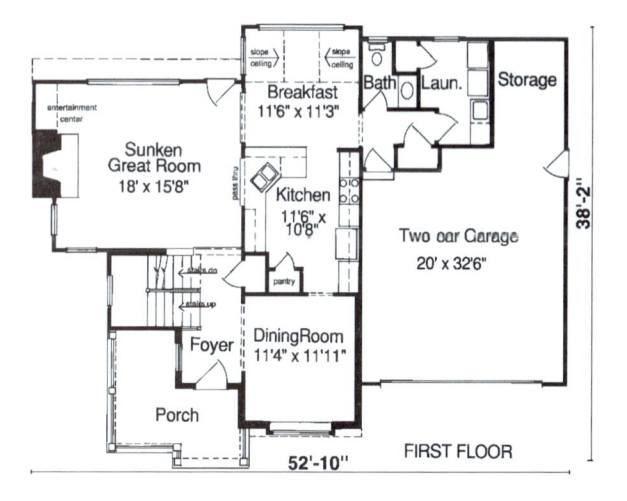

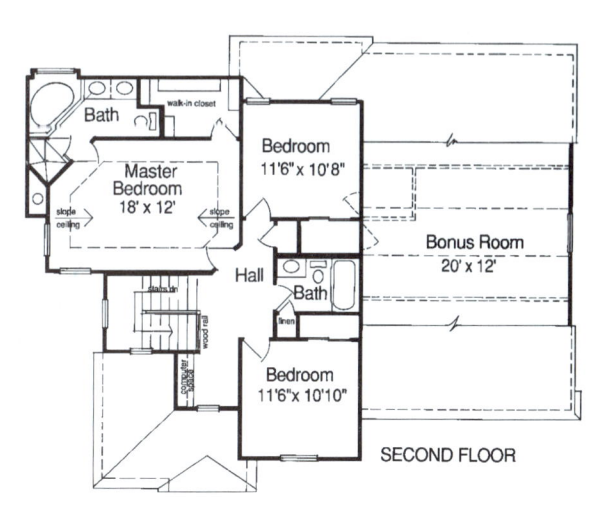

No materials list available

DESIGN NO. 92651

PRICE CODE D

Eye-catching turret adds to master suite

No. 92651

- This plan features:
- — Four bedrooms
- — Three full and one half baths
- Sheltered entry surrounded by glass leads into open Foyer and Great Room with high ceiling, hearth fireplace and atrium door to back yard
- Columns frame entrance to conveniently located Dining Room
- Efficient Kitchen with built-in pantry, work island and bright Breakfast area accesses Laundry, backyard and Garage
- Master Bedroom wing with a sitting area, walk-in closet and private bath with corner window tub and double vanity

FIRST FLOOR — 1,710 SQ. FT.
SECOND FLOOR — 693 SQ. FT.
BASEMENT — 1,620 SQ. FT.
GARAGE — 467 SQ. FT.

TOTAL LIVING AREA: 2,403 SQ. FT.

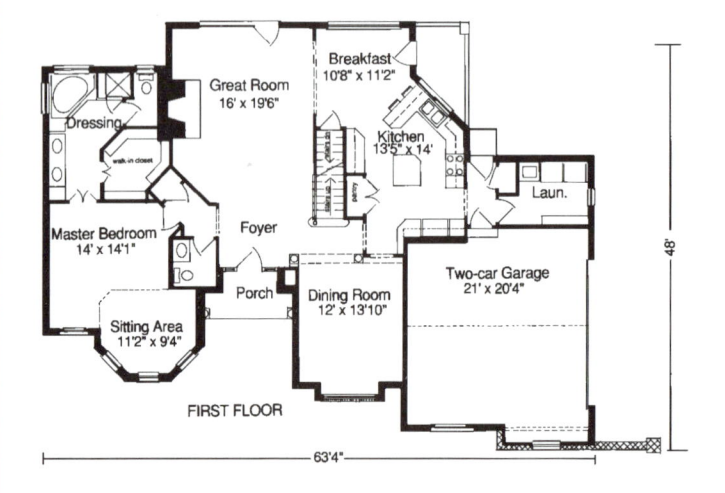

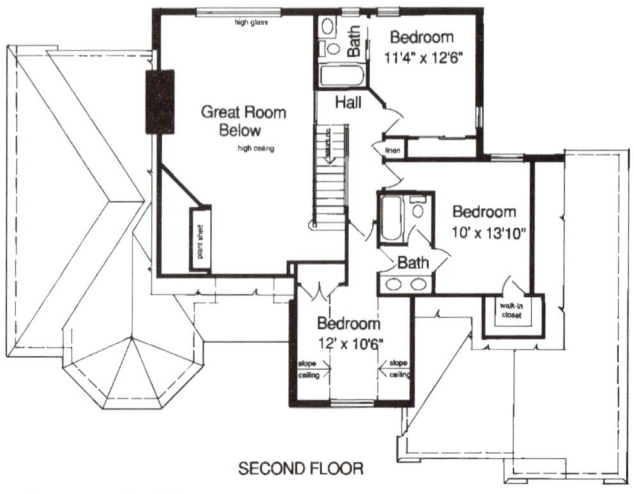

No materials list available

DESIGN NO. 92608

PRICE CODE C

GREAT FOR EMPTY NESTERS OR FAMILIES WITH TEENS

No. 92608

■ This plan features:

— Three bedrooms

— Two full and one half baths

■ Two-story Foyer with an open staircase, balcony and dormer window

■ A grand sunken Great Room with a cathedral ceiling, built-ins

■ Dramatic views from the octagon-shaped, formal Dining Room

■ Kitchen with a central work island, built-in pantry, a pass-thru to Dining Room and a bright, bay windowed Breakfast area

■ A first floor, private Master Suite with walk-in closet, and a plush Bath with an oversized shower and raised, corner window tub

■ Three more bedrooms share a full hall bath and a Bonus Room

FIRST FLOOR — 1,557 SQ. FT.
SECOND FLOOR — 512 SQ. FT.
OPTIONAL BONUS — 280 SQ. FT.

TOTAL LIVING AREA: 2,069 SQ. FT.

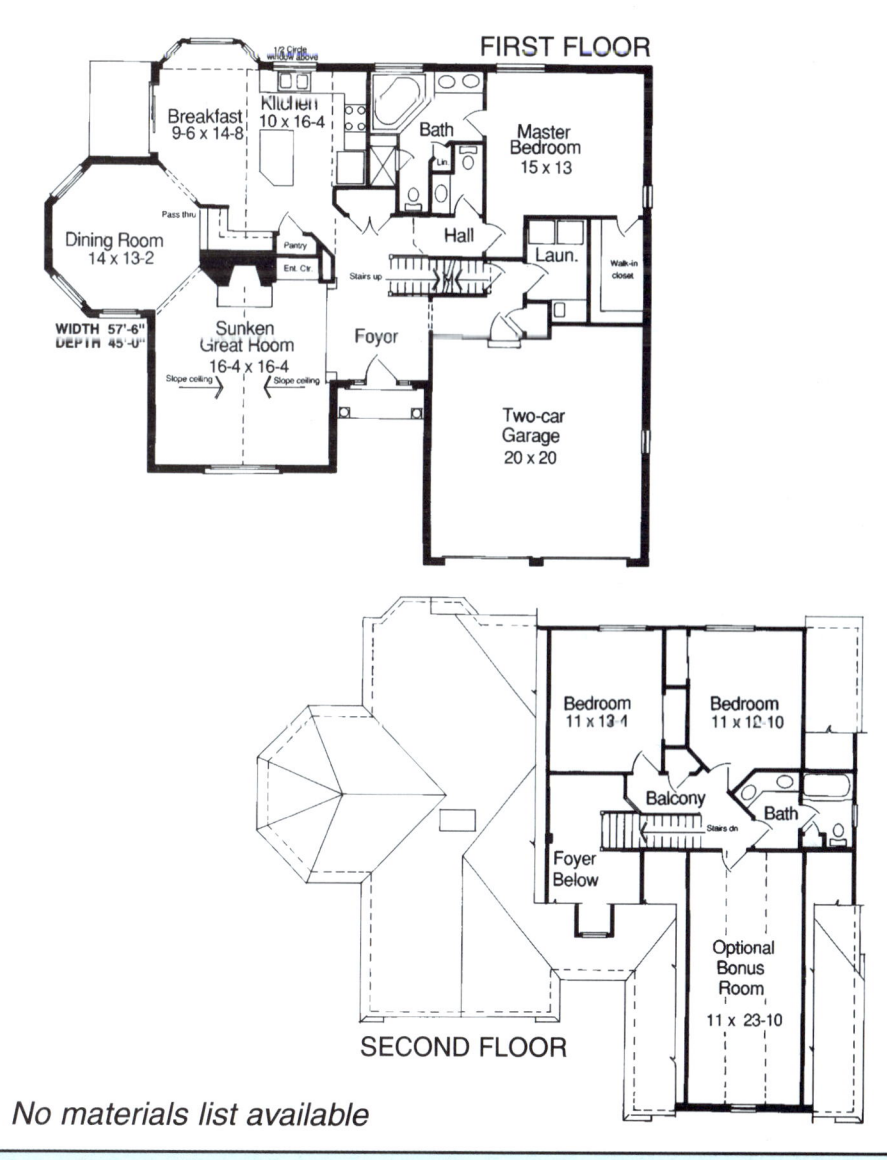

No materials list available

DESIGN NO. 94726

PRICE CODE C

A CLASSIC CHARMER

No. 94726

■ This plan features:

— Three bedrooms

— Two full and one half baths

■ The portico entry leads into the formal Dining room, which is defined by columns from the Great room

■ The two-story Great room has an expansive view to the outside and a cozy fireplace

■ The spacious Kitchen has a snack bar, and serves the all the eating areas with ease

■ The first floor Master suite includes a tray ceiling, walk-in closet and a whirlpool tub

■ Two additional bedrooms share an adjoining bath and enjoy the second floor balcony overlooking the Great Room

■ An optional crawl space or slab foundation available, please specify when ordering

FIRST FLOOR — 1,381 SQ. FT.
SECOND FLOOR — 453 SQ. FT.
GARAGE — 423 SQ. FT.

TOTAL LIVING AREA: 1,834 SQ. FT.

HIGH WIND LOAD ENGINEERING AVAILABLE
SEE PAGE 246 FOR DETAILS

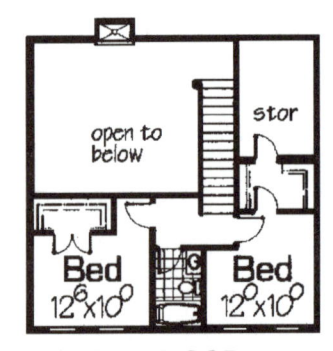

SECOND FLOOR
- open to below
- stor
- Bed 12⁶x10⁰
- Bed 12⁰x10⁰

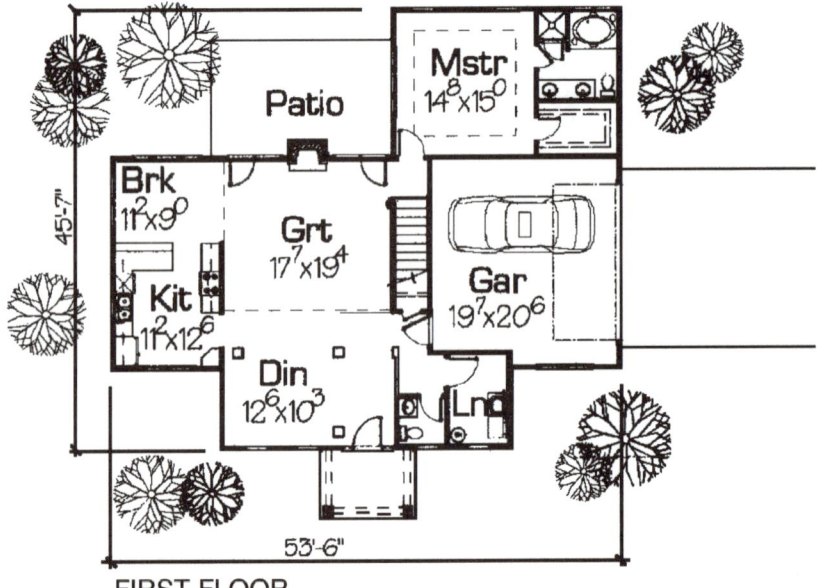

FIRST FLOOR
No. 94726

- Brk 11²x9⁰
- Patio
- Mstr 14⁸x15⁰
- Kit 11²x12⁶
- Grt 17⁷x19⁴
- Gar 19⁷x20⁶
- Din 12⁶x10³
- Lnd
- 45'-7"
- 53'-6"

An EXCLUSIVE DESIGN
By United Design Associates

178

DESIGN NO. 93231

PRICE CODE B

Design is clean and convenient

No. 93231

■ This plan features:

— Three bedrooms

— Two full baths

■ Arched entrance into Foyer and central Living Area with fireplace and access to Patio/Sundeck

■ Kitchen with peninsula counter/snackbar, convenient to formal Dining Room, Breakfast alcove, Laundry and Garage entry

■ Private Master Bedroom with decorative ceiling, walk-in closet and lavish bath with corner whirlpool tub and two vanities

■ Two additional bedrooms share a double vanity bath

■ An optional crawl space or slab foundation available, please specify when ordering

Main floor — 1,781 sq. ft.
Garage — 558 sq. ft.

Total living area:
1,781 sq. ft.

No materials list available

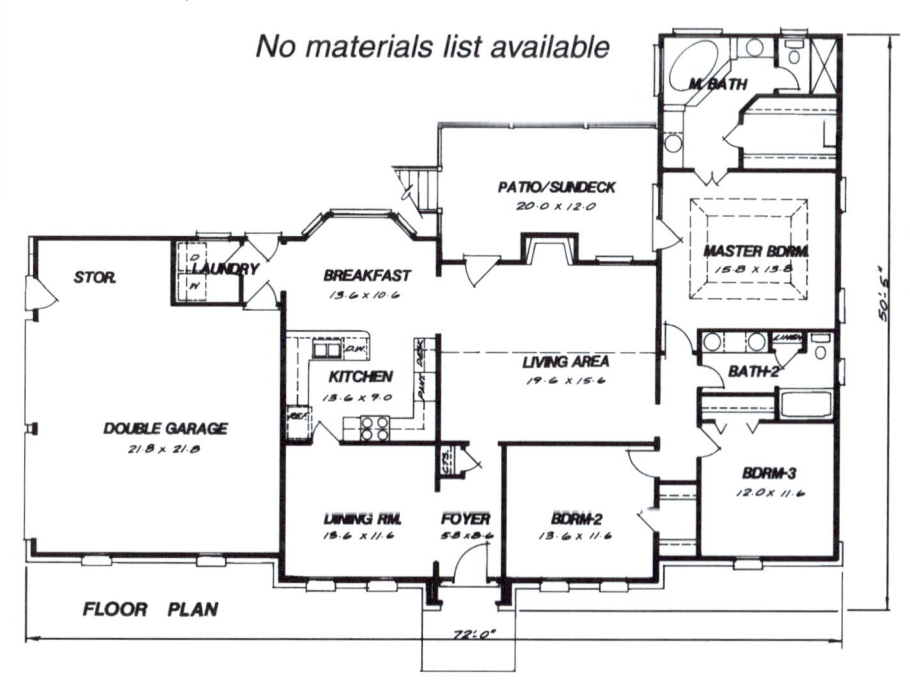

An
EXCLUSIVE DESIGN
By Jannis Vann & Associates, Inc.

DESIGN NO. 91814

PRICE CODE B

WIDE OPEN LIVING AREAS

No. 91814

- This plan features:
- — Three bedrooms
- — Two full baths
- Adaptable for barrier-free living
- An efficient Kitchen with double sink peninsula counter, that also serves as an eating bar
- A covered Porch and a Patio with decorative columns and half-round windows
- A large Master Bedroom with a Patio, double sinks, walk-in closet, spa tub, and a shower
- Two additional bedrooms that share a full hall bath
- An optional crawl space or slab foundation — please specify when ordering

MAIN AREA — 1,785 SQ. FT.
GARAGE — 672 SQ. FT.

TOTAL LIVING AREA: 1,785 SQ. FT.

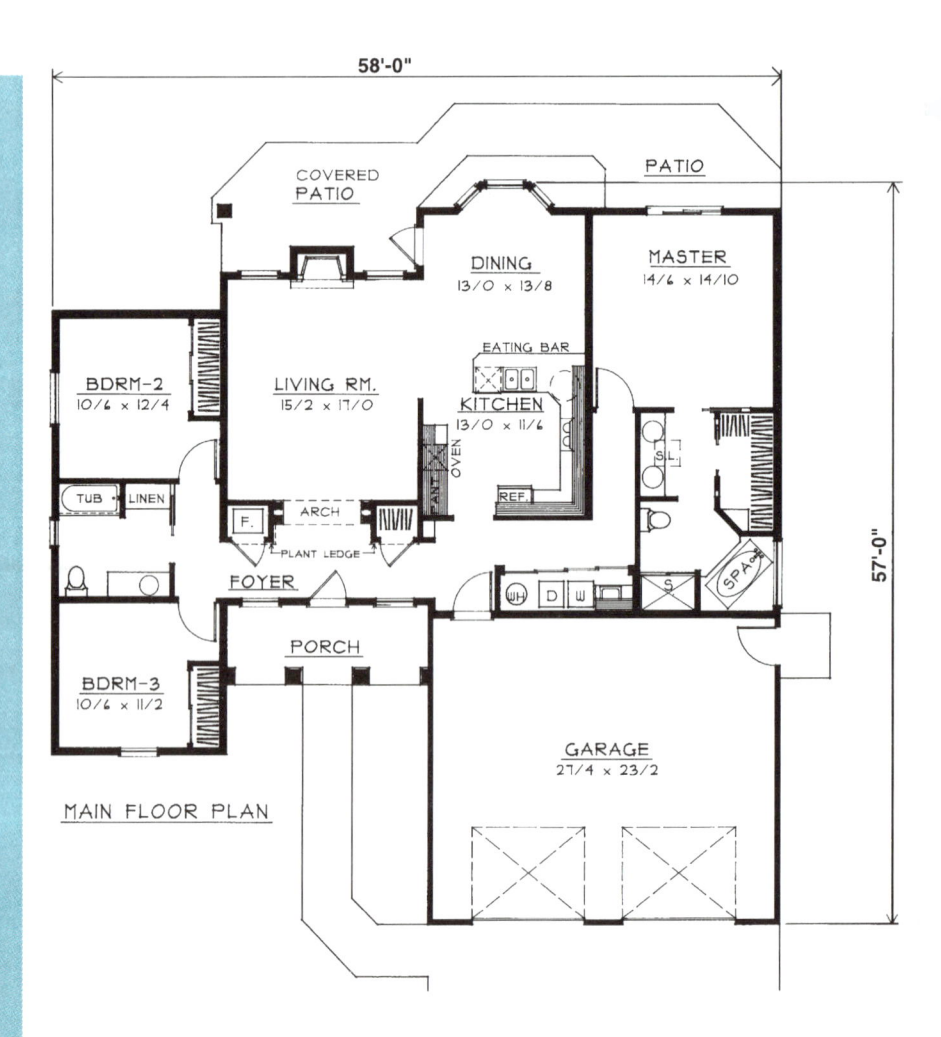

DESIGN NO. 93013

PRICE CODE D

Two-Story Glass Entry

No. 93013

- This plan features:
- — Three bedrooms
- — Two full and one half baths
- A Living Room and Dining Room with openings defined by traditional square columns
- A large fireplace to add warmth and interest to the Living Room
- An ample Kitchen with cooktop island, built-in pantry, angled double sink, and eating bar
- A Master Suite with a lavish Master Bath equipped with oval tub, step-in shower, and double vanity
- Two additional bedrooms with walk-in closets that share a full hall bath

FIRST FLOOR — 1,831 SQ. FT.
SECOND FLOOR — 632 SQ. FT.
GARAGE — 525 SQ. FT.

TOTAL LIVING AREA: 2,463 SQ. FT.

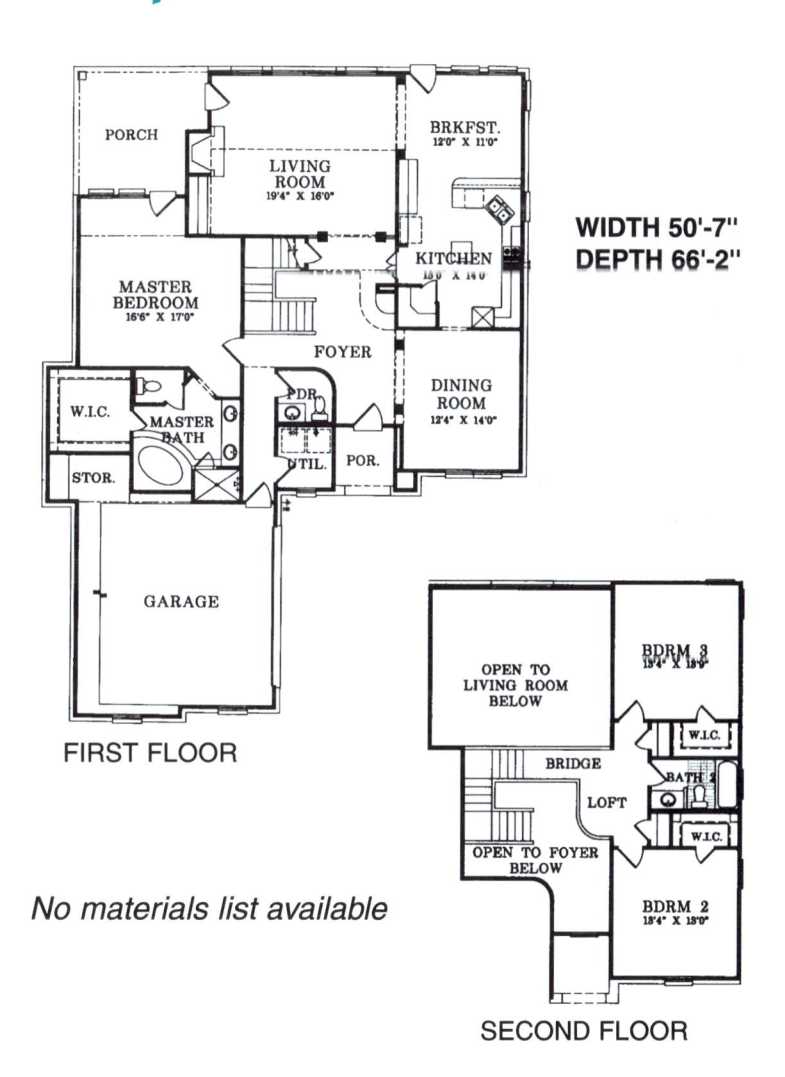

WIDTH 50'-7"
DEPTH 66'-2"

FIRST FLOOR

- PORCH
- LIVING ROOM 19'4" X 16'0"
- BRKFST. 12'0" X 11'0"
- KITCHEN 13'0" X 14'0"
- MASTER BEDROOM 16'6" X 17'0"
- FOYER
- DINING ROOM 12'4" X 14'0"
- W.I.C.
- MASTER BATH
- PDR
- UTIL.
- POR.
- STOR.
- GARAGE

SECOND FLOOR

- OPEN TO LIVING ROOM BELOW
- BRIDGE
- LOFT
- OPEN TO FOYER BELOW
- BDRM 3 19'4" X 13'0"
- W.I.C.
- BATH 2
- W.I.C.
- BDRM 2 13'4" X 13'0"

No materials list available

DESIGN NO. 90983

PRICE CODE A

ATTRACTIVE ROOF LINES

No. 90983

■ This plan features:

— Three bedrooms

— One full and one three quarter baths

■ An open floor plan shared by the sunken Living Room, Dining and Kitchen areas

■ An unfinished daylight Basement which will provide future bedrooms, a bathroom and laundry facilities

■ A Master Suite with a big walk-in closet and a private bath featuring a double shower

MAIN FLOOR — 1,396 SQ. FT.
BASEMENT — 1,396 SQ. FT.
GARAGE — 389 SQ. FT.
WIDTH — 48'-0"
DEPTH — 54'-0"

TOTAL LIVING AREA: 1,396 SQ. FT.

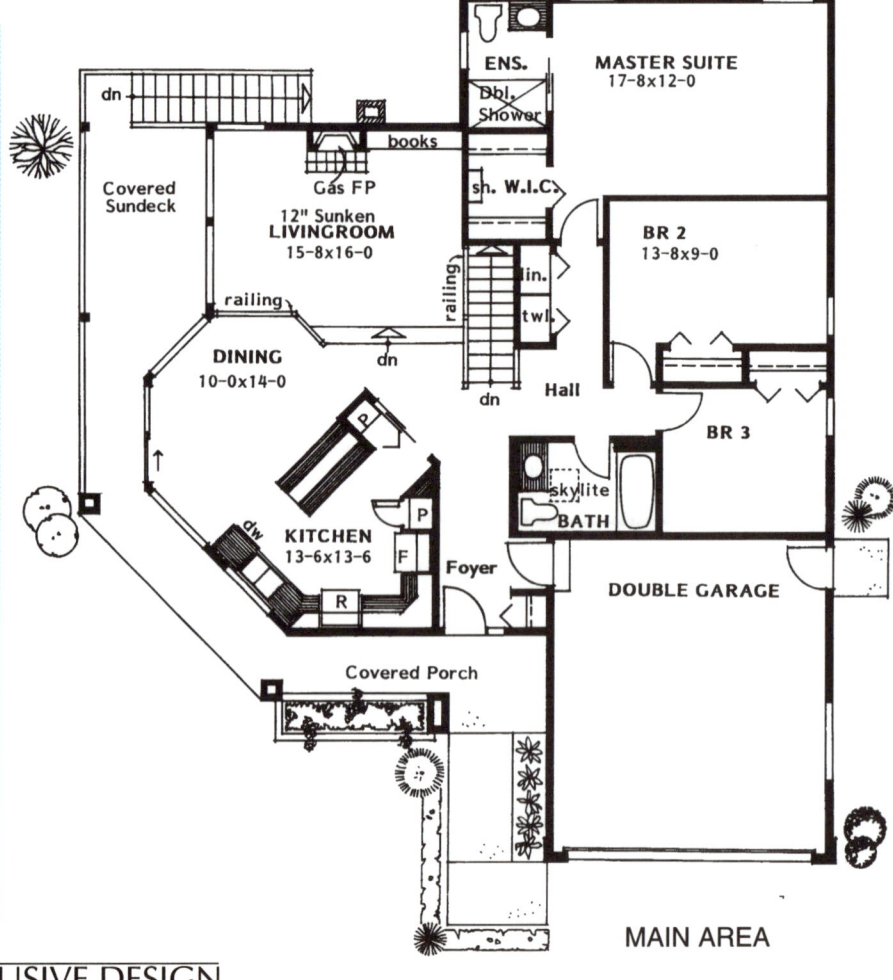

MAIN AREA

An EXCLUSIVE DESIGN By Westhome Planners, Ltd.

DESIGN NO. 92539

PRICE CODE D

ARCHES ADD AMBIENCE

No. 92539

- This plan features:
— Four bedrooms
— Two full and one half baths
- Arched two-story entrance highlighted by a lovely arched window
- Expansive Den offers hearth fireplace between book shelves, raised ceiling and access to rear yard
- Efficient Kitchen with peninsula counter, built-in pantry, Breakfast bay, Garage entry, laundry and adjoining Dining room
- Private Master Bedroom enhanced by a large walk-in closet and plush bath
- Three second floor bedrooms with walk-in closets share a double vanity bath
- This plan is available with a slab or crawlspace foundation. Please specify when ordering.

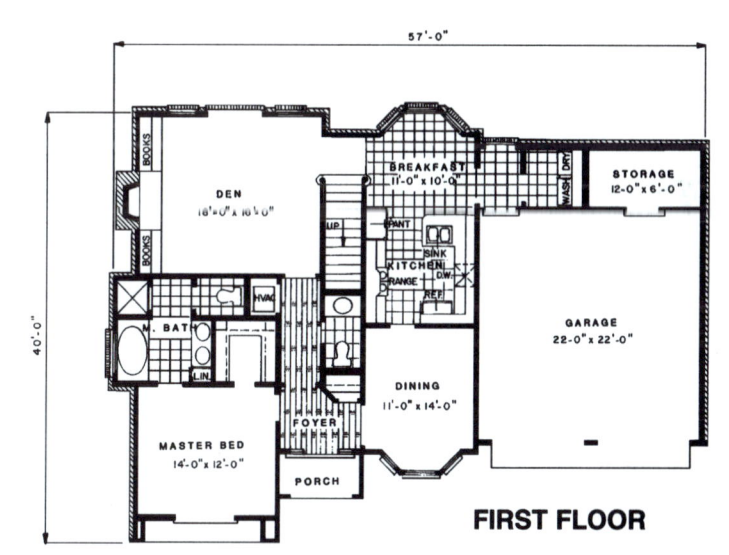

FIRST FLOOR — 1,250 SQ. FT.
SECOND FLOOR — 783 SQ. FT
GARAGE AND STORAGE — 555 SQ. FT.

TOTAL LIVING AREA: 2,033 SQ. FT.

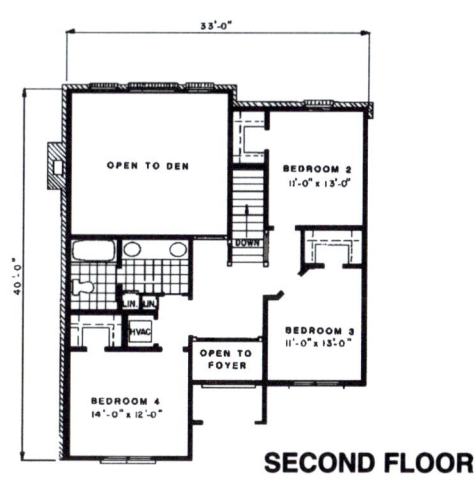

FIRST FLOOR

SECOND FLOOR

DESIGN NO. 92505

PRICE CODE F

No. 92505

■ This plan features:

— Four bedrooms

— Three and one half baths

■ Elegant columns rising up two floors through the balcony providing an unusual entrance

■ Den with highlights such as; a two-story fireplace that is framed by sliding doors leading to a covered Porch

■ A vaulted ceiling adding a spacious feeling to the gourmet Kitchen that also includes a cooktop snackbar, a built-in pantry, and a separate Breakfast area

■ A cozy, private Sitting area with a vaulted ceiling providing quiet moments in the Master Suite

■ A Master Bath with his-n-her walk-in closets, separate vanities and linen closets, an over-sized shower and a whirlpool tub

■ An optional crawl space or slab foundation available, please specify when ordering

Stucco & Brick Unite

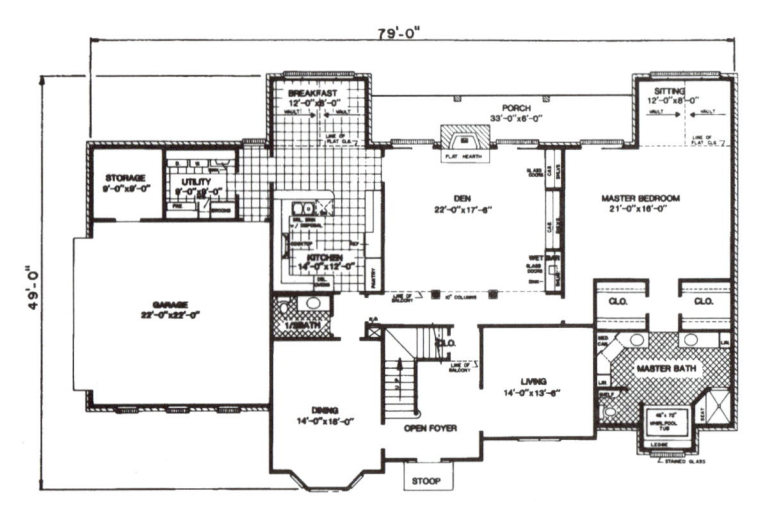

FIRST FLOOR PLAN

SECOND FLOOR PLAN

FIRST FLOOR — 2,442 SQ. FT.
SECOND FLOOR — 1,062 SQ. FT.
GARAGE — 565 SQ. FT.

TOTAL LIVING AREA: 3,504 SQ. FT.

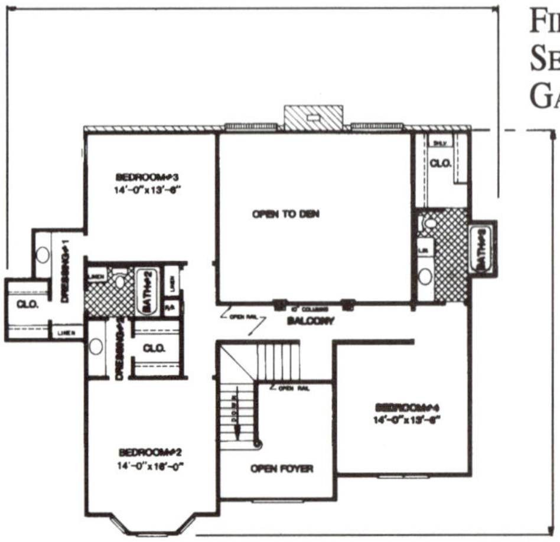

DESIGN NO. 91607

PRICE CODE B

DAYTIME DELIGHT

No. 91607

■ This plan features:

— Three bedrooms

— Two full baths

■ A large, vaulted ceiling in the Living Room and Dining Room, that flows together and is accentuated by huge windows

■ A centrally-located Kitchen with a double sink, and ample cabinet and counter space

■ A glass-walled eating Nook with access to a covered Porch

■ A vaulted ceiling in the Family Room, with a focal point fireplace

■ An exciting Master Suite with a vaulted ceiling, a walk-in closet and a private double-vanity bath

■ Two additional bedrooms, one with French doors, served by a full hall bath

MAIN AREA — 1,653 SQ. FT.

TOTAL LIVING AREA:
1,653 SQ. FT.

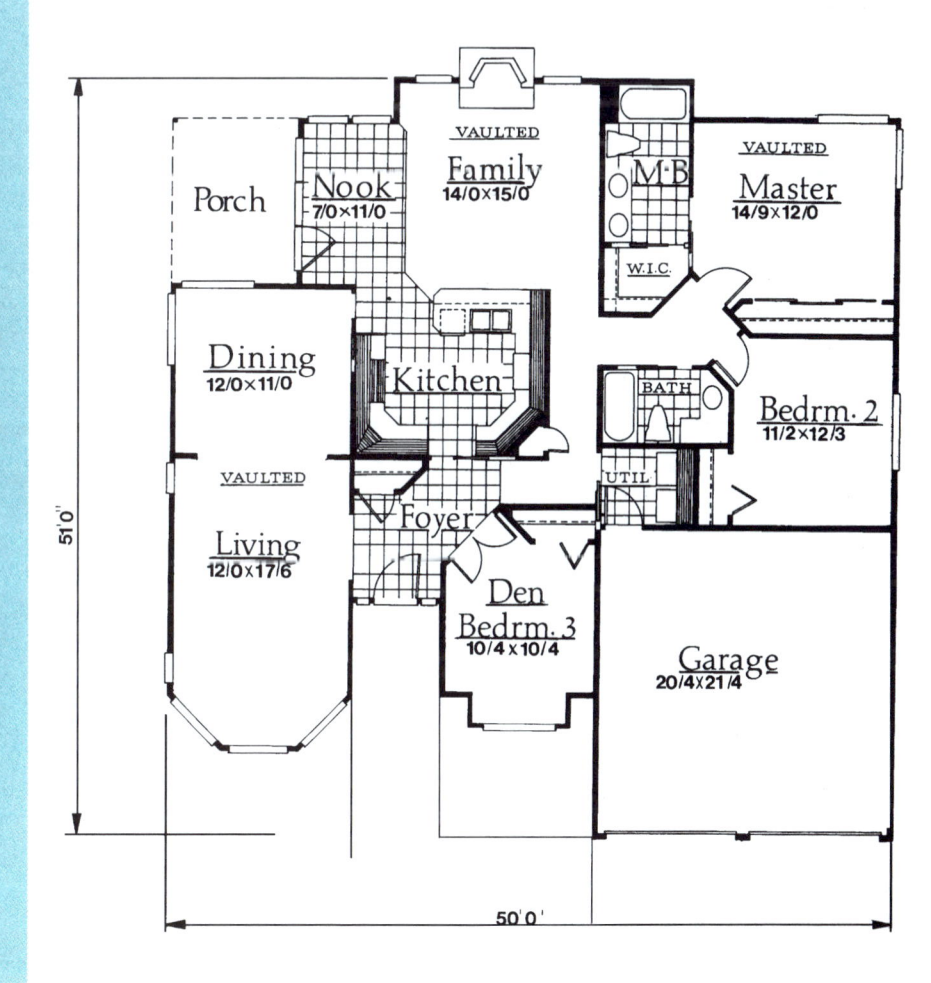

DESIGN NO. 91418

PRICE CODE B

CAREFREE COMFORT

No. 91418

- This plan features:
— Three bedrooms
— Two full baths
- A dramatic vaulted Foyer
- A range top island Kitchen with a sunny eating Nook surrounded by a built-in planter
- A vaulted ceiling in the Great Room with a built-in bar and corner fireplace
- A bayed Dining Room that combines with the Great Room for a spacious feeling
- A Master Bedroom with a private reading nook, vaulted ceiling, walk-in closet, and a well-appointed private Bath
- Two additional bedrooms sharing a full hall bath
- An optional basement, crawl space or slab foundation — please specify when ordering

MAIN AREA — 1,665 SQ. FT.
GARAGE — 2-CAR

TOTAL LIVING AREA: 1,665 SQ. FT.

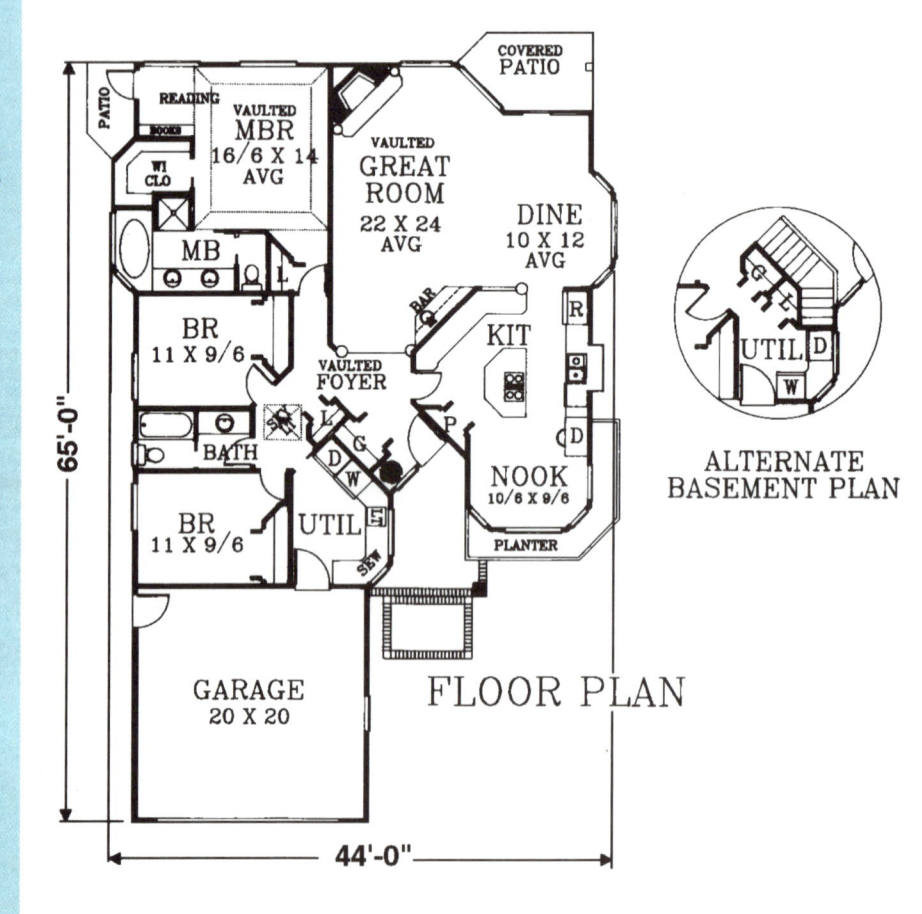

FLOOR PLAN

ALTERNATE BASEMENT PLAN

DESIGN NO. 90449

PRICE CODE D

CLASSIC COLONIAL STYLE

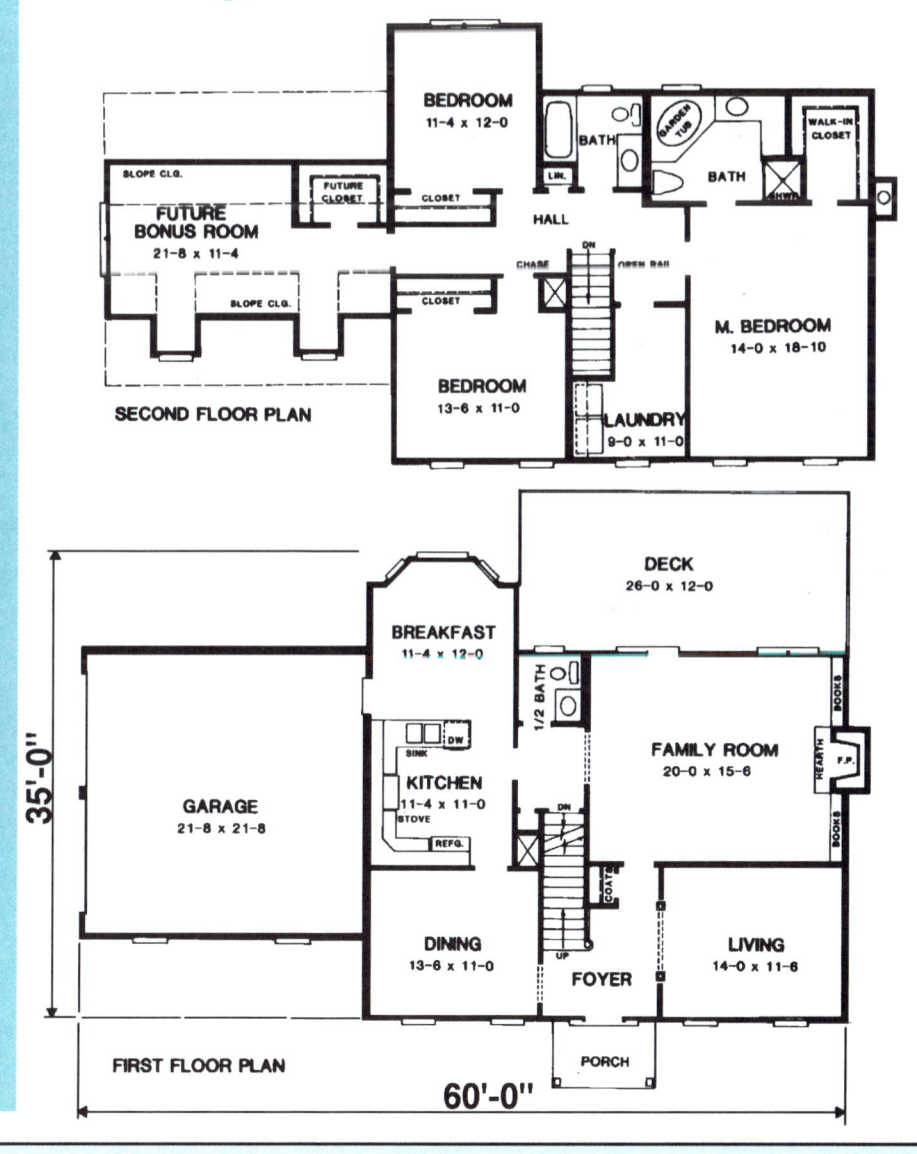

No. 90449

■ This plan features:

— Three bedrooms

— Two full and one half baths

■ A large Family Room with a fireplace and built-in book shelves having French doors leading to an outdoor deck

■ A spacious, efficient Kitchen open to the Breakfast Room which has a sunny bay

■ A Master Suite with a large private bath including a garden tub and separate shower

■ A second floor laundry convenient to the bedrooms

■ An optional bonus room so the house can expand with your family

■ An optional basement or crawl space foundation — please specify when ordering

FIRST FLOOR — 1,138 SQ. FT.
SECOND FLOOR — 1,124 SQ. FT.
OPTIONAL BONUS — 284 SQ. FT.
BASEMENT — 1,124 SQ. FT.
GARAGE — 484 SQ. FT.

TOTAL LIVING AREA: 2,262 SQ. FT.

SECOND FLOOR PLAN

- FUTURE BONUS ROOM 21-8 x 11-4
- BEDROOM 11-4 x 12-0
- M. BEDROOM 14-0 x 18-10
- BEDROOM 13-6 x 11-0
- LAUNDRY 9-0 x 11-0

FIRST FLOOR PLAN

- GARAGE 21-8 x 21-8
- BREAKFAST 11-4 x 12-0
- KITCHEN 11-4 x 11-0
- DECK 26-0 x 12-0
- FAMILY ROOM 20-0 x 15-6
- DINING 13-6 x 11-0
- LIVING 14-0 x 11-6
- FOYER
- PORCH

35'-0" x 60'-0"

DESIGN NO. 92635

PRICE CODE A

CHARMING TWO-STORY

No. 92635

■ This plan features:

— Three bedrooms

— Two full and one half baths

■ Inviting entrance framed by windows and lantern lights

■ Great Room highlighted by front box window and rear atrium door

■ Efficient U-shaped Kitchen/Breakfast area with large decorative window adjoins Great Room, Laundry and Garage

■ Spacious Master Bedroom with decorative window offers a walk-in closet and private bath

■ Two additional bedrooms share a full bath

FIRST FLOOR — 748 SQ. FT.
SECOND FLOOR — 705 SQ. FT.
BASEMENT — 744 SQ. FT.
GARAGE — 396 SQ. FT.

TOTAL LIVING AREA: 1,453 SQ. FT.

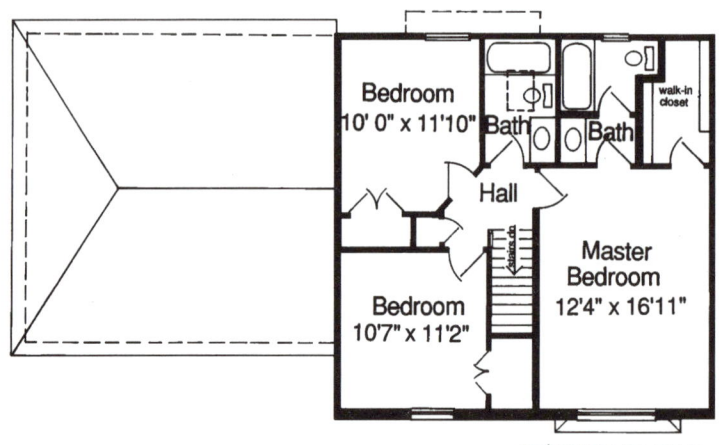

No materials list available

Bedroom 10'0" x 11'10"
Bedroom 10'7" x 11'2"
Master Bedroom 12'4" x 16'11"
walk-in closet

SECOND FLOOR

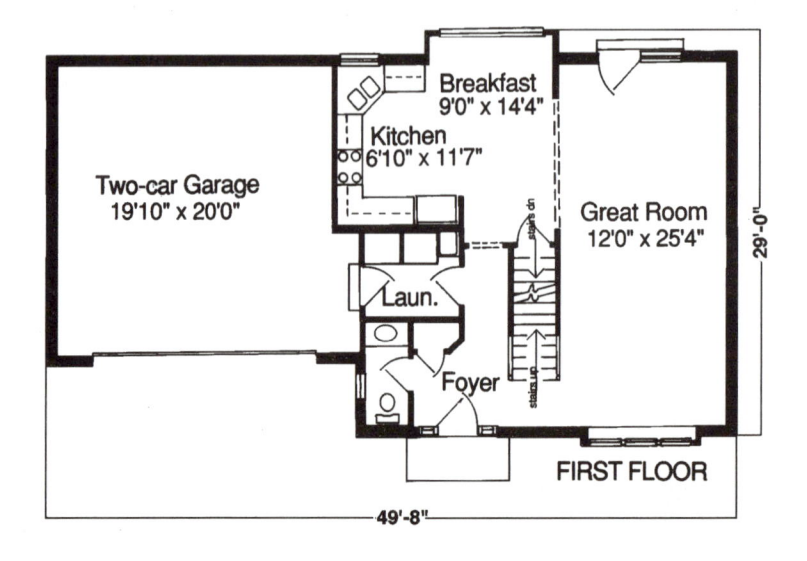

Breakfast 9'0" x 14'4"
Kitchen 6'10" x 11'7"
Two-car Garage 19'10" x 20'0"
Great Room 12'0" x 25'4"
Laun.
Foyer

FIRST FLOOR

49'-8"
29'-0"

DESIGN NO. 92616

PRICE CODE E

DISTINGUISHED FOUR BEDROOM

No. 92616

- This plan features:
— Four bedrooms
— Two full and one half baths
- Central Foyer opens to formal Living and Dining rooms
- Efficient, L-shaped Kitchen with work island/snack bar, Breakfast area and access to Laundry, Den, Family Room, Dining Room and Garage
- Sunken Family Room with a cozy fireplace and access to rear yard
- Master Bedroom wing offers a plush bath with double vanity and whirlpool tub
- Three additional bedrooms with ample closets share a double vanity bath

FIRST FLOOR — 1,516 SQ. FT.
SECOND FLOOR — 1,148 SQ. FT.
GARAGE — 440 SQ. FT.

TOTAL LIVING AREA: 2,664 SQ. FT.

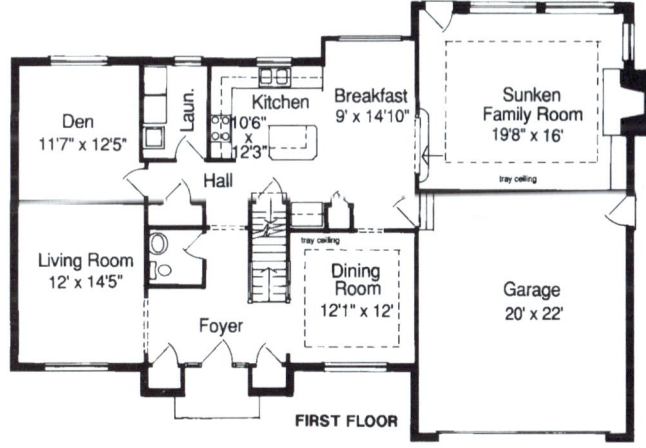

WIDTH 59'-6"
DEPTH 40'-0"

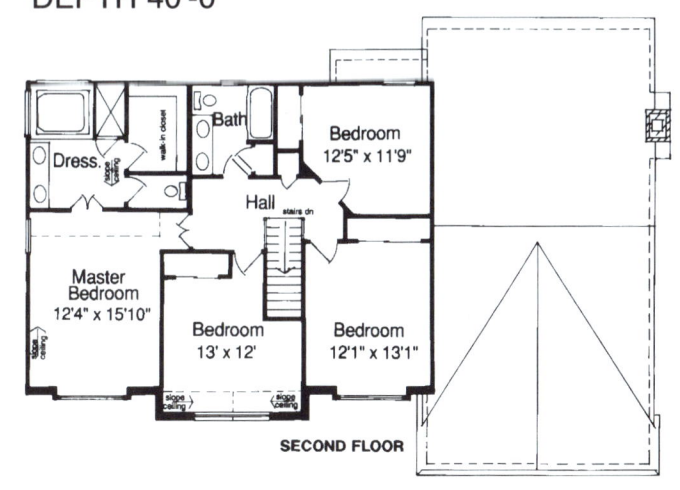

First Floor:
- Den 11'7" x 12'5"
- Laun.
- Kitchen 10'6" x 12'3"
- Breakfast 9' x 14'10"
- Sunken Family Room 19'8" x 16" (tray ceiling)
- Hall
- Living Room 12' x 14'5"
- Dining Room 12'1" x 12' (tray ceiling)
- Foyer
- Garage 20' x 22'

Second Floor:
- Dress.
- Bath
- Bedroom 12'5" x 11'9"
- Hall (stairs dn)
- Master Bedroom 12'4" x 15'10"
- Bedroom 13' x 12'
- Bedroom 12'1" x 13'1"

No materials list available

DESIGN NO. 92643

PRICE CODE D

EXCITING ARCHED ACCENTS GIVE IMPACT

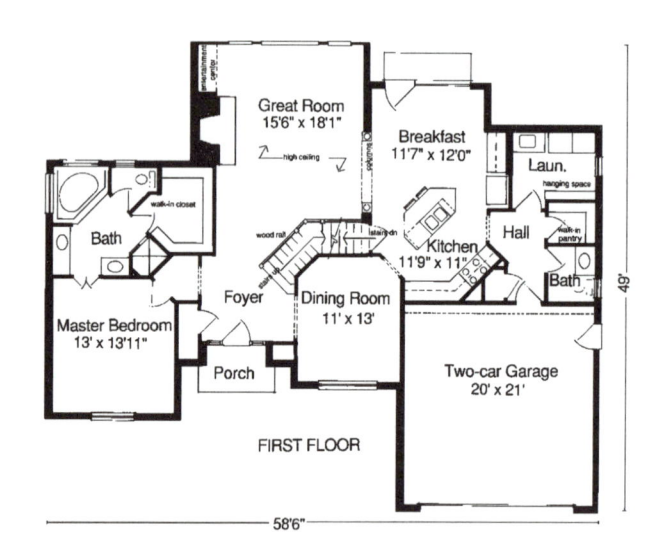

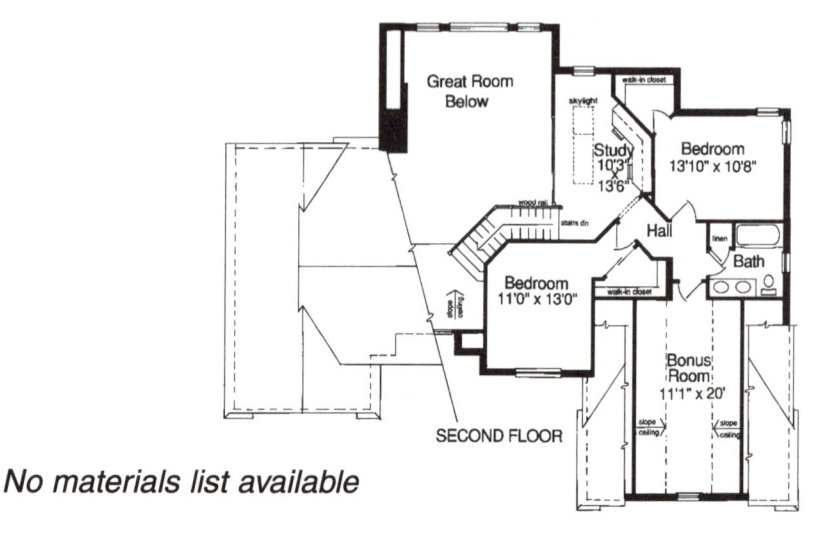

No. 92643

- This plan features:
— Three bedrooms
— Two full and one half baths
- Keystone arch accents entrance into open Foyer with lovely angled staircase and sloped ceiling
- Great Room enhanced by an entertainment center, hearth fireplace and a wall of windows
- Efficient, angled Kitchen offers work island/snackbar, Breakfast area next to Dining Room, Laundry, Bath and Garage entry
- Master Bedroom wing features a lavish Bath with two vanities, large walk-in closet and corner window tub
- Two second floor bedrooms with walk-in closets share a skylit Study, double vanity bath and a Bonus Room

FIRST FLOOR — 1,542 SQ. FT.
SECOND FLOOR — 667 SQ. FT.
BONUS ROOM — 236 SQ. FT.
BASEMENT — 1,470 SQ. FT.
GARAGE — 420 SQ. FT.

TOTAL LIVING AREA: 2,209 SQ. FT.

No materials list available

DESIGN NO. 94736

PRICE CODE B

Southern coastal cottage

No. 94736

- This plan features:
- — Three bedrooms
- — Two full baths
- Southern coastal cottage design offers a vaulted Great room, Dining area and Kitchen
- An inviting front porch is the perfect spot for relaxation
- A romantic fireplace highlights the Great room which flows into the Dining room and Kitchen
- Interior architectural columns define the Dining room
- The Master suite is located in a private rear location and includes a tray ceiling, walk-in closet and a luxurious bath
- Two additional bedrooms share the full bath in the hall

MAIN FLOOR — 1,504 SQ. FT.
GARAGE — 406 SQ. FT.

TOTAL LIVING AREA: 1,504 SQ. FT.

HIGH WIND LOAD ENGINEERING AVAILABLE
SEE PAGE 246 FOR DETAILS

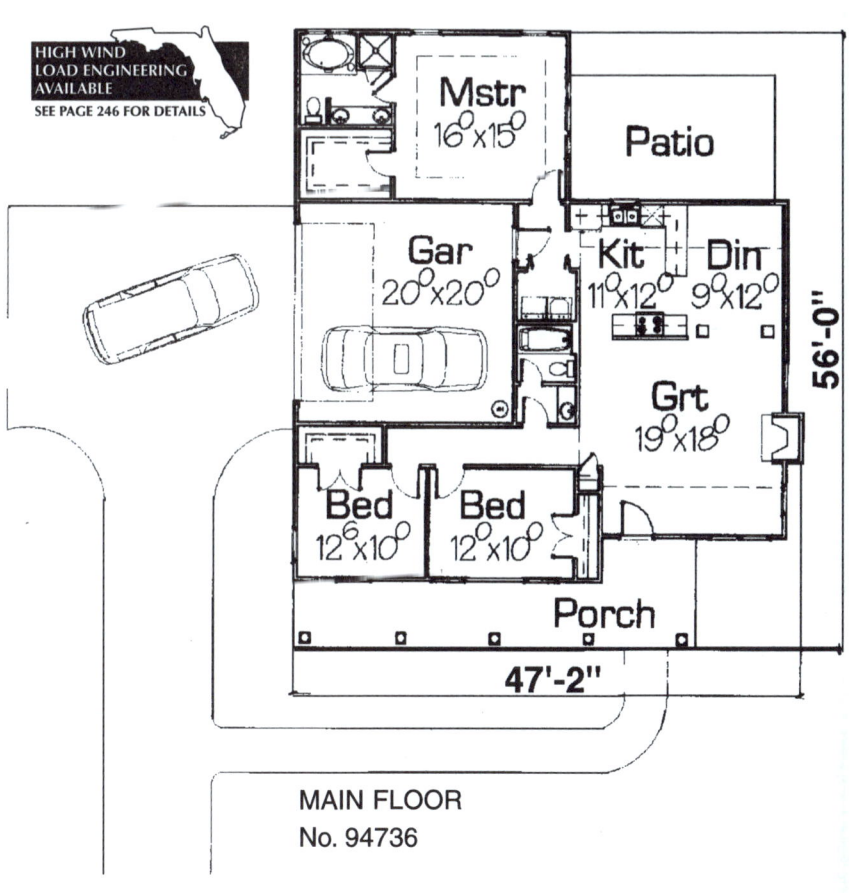

Mstr 16'0"x15'0"
Patio
Gar 20'0"x20'0"
Kit 11'0"x12'0"
Din 9'0"x12'0"
Grt 19'0"x18'0"
Bed 12'6"x10'0"
Bed 12'0"x10'0"
Porch
56'-0"
47'-2"

MAIN FLOOR
No. 94736

An EXCLUSIVE DESIGN
By United Design Associates

DESIGN NO. 93708

PRICE CODE D

Tailored for a view to the side

An **EXCLUSIVE DESIGN**
By *Building Science Associates*

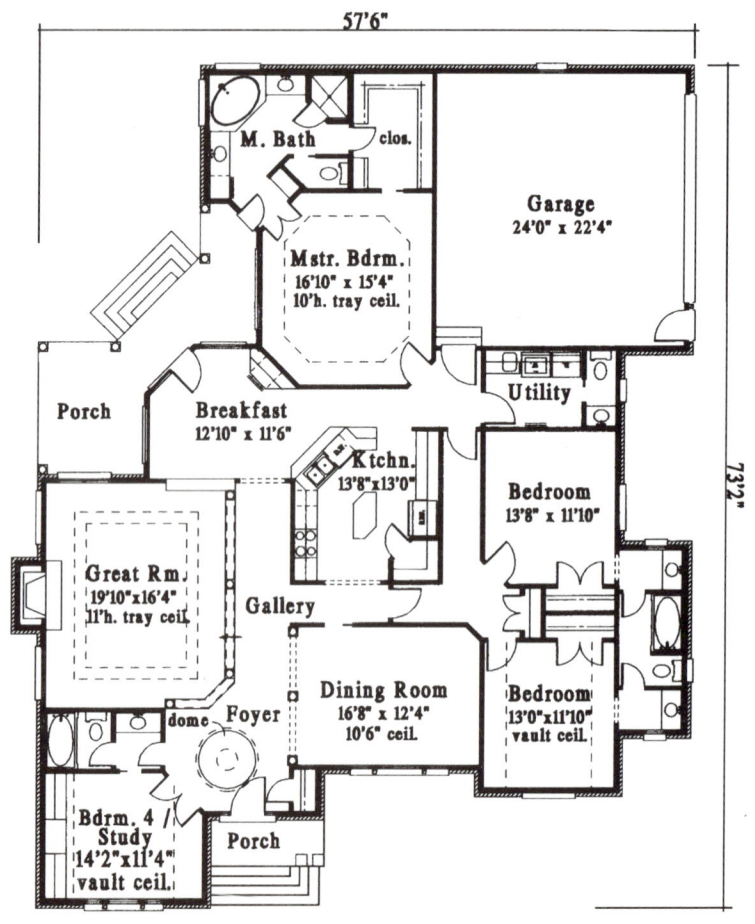

No. 93708

■ This plan features:

— Three/Four bedrooms

— Three full and one half baths

■ A sheltered entrance with windows over the door and a side light

■ A large entry Foyer highlighted by a ceiling dome and French doors leading to the private study

■ An elegant formal Dining Room with a high ceiling and a columned and arched entrance

■ A sunken Great room with a high tray ceiling and arched and columned openings and a fireplace enhancing the room

■ A tray ceiling and lavish bath pamper the owner in the Master Suite

■ Two additional bedrooms that share a split vanity bath

MAIN FLOOR — 2,579 SQ. FT.
GARAGE — 536 SQ. FT.

**TOTAL LIVING AREA:
2,579 SQ. FT.**

Main Level Floor Plan

No materials list available

DESIGN NO. 94235

PRICE CODE E

Curved glass study

No. 94235

■ This plan features:
— Three bedrooms
— Two full and one half baths

■ Detailed pillars enhance glass entrance into expansive Living area with sliding glass doors to Verandah

■ Large arch frames entrance to Dining Room from Gallery

■ Ideal Kitchen with two islands, built-in pantry and planning desk, a greenhouse Nook and Leisure area with a fireplace

■ Private Master Suite offers an AM kitchen, Verandah access, walk-in closet and lavish bath

■ Two additional bedrooms with large closets, share a full bath

MAIN FLOOR — 2,762 SQ. FT.
GARAGE — 605 SQ. FT.

TOTAL LIVING AREA: 2,762 SQ. FT.

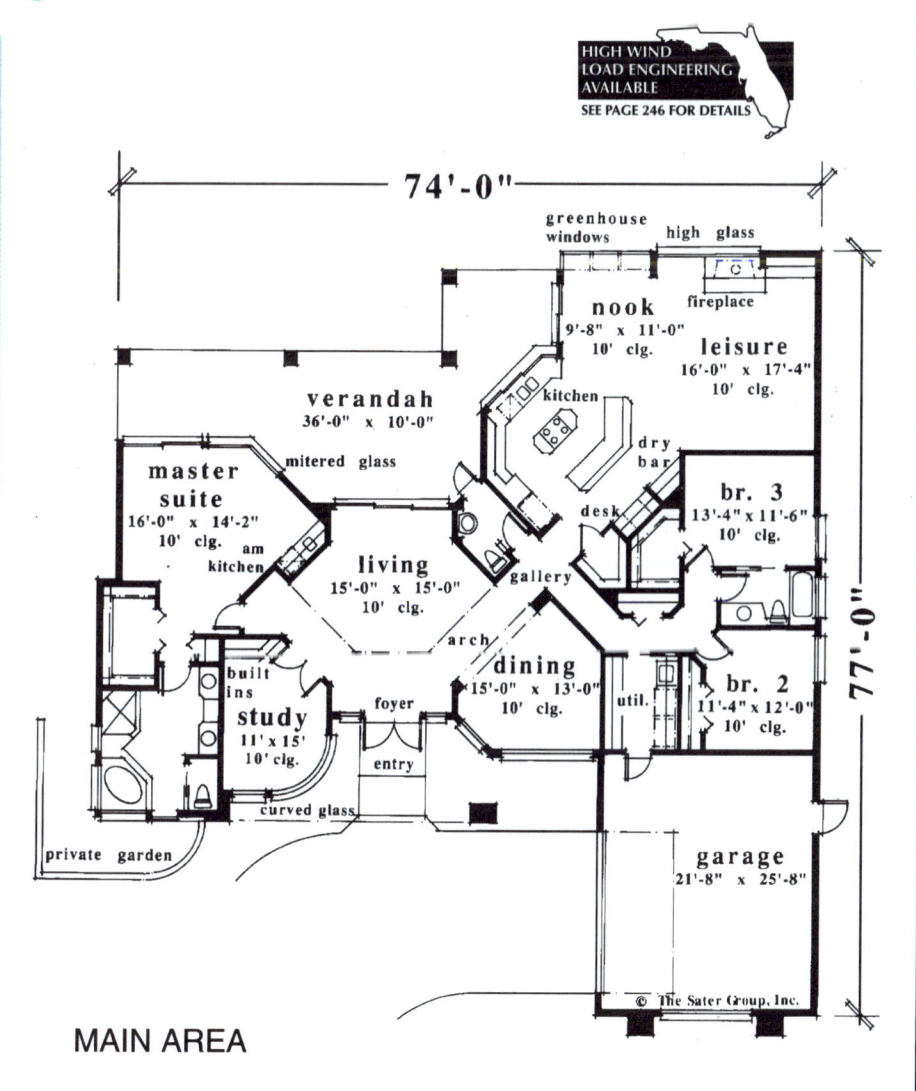

HIGH WIND LOAD ENGINEERING AVAILABLE
SEE PAGE 246 FOR DETAILS

74'-0"
77'-0"

greenhouse windows — high glass — fireplace

nook 9'-8" x 11'-0" 10' clg.

leisure 16'-0" x 17'-4" 10' clg.

verandah 36'-0" x 10'-0"
mitered glass
kitchen
dry bar

master suite 16'-0" x 14'-2" 10' clg.
am kitchen

br. 3 13'-4" x 11'-6" 10' clg.

desk
gallery

living 15'-0" x 15'-0" 10' clg.

arch

built ins

study 11' x 15' 10' clg.

dining 15'-0" x 13'-0" 10' clg.

foyer
entry
curved glass

util.

br. 2 11'-4" x 12'-0" 10' clg.

private garden

garage 21'-8" x 25'-8"

© The Sater Group, Inc.

MAIN AREA

DESIGN NO. 94232

PRICE CODE E

Secluded Master Suite

No. 94232

■ This plan features:

— Four bedrooms

— Two full baths

■ Stucco and brick exterior accent gracious entrance into pillar Foyer

■ Arches and pillars separate Dining Room and Grand Room with built-ins, fireplace and glass access to Veranda

■ Hub Kitchen with work island, serving counter, walk-in pantry, glass Nook, Leisure area and Utility/Garage Entry

■ Master Suite enhanced by his and her closets, a plush bath and access to Veranda

■ Three additional bedrooms with ample closets share a double vanity bath

MAIN FLOOR — 2,659 SQ. FT.
GARAGE — 474 SQ. FT.

TOTAL LIVING AREA: 2,659 SQ. FT.

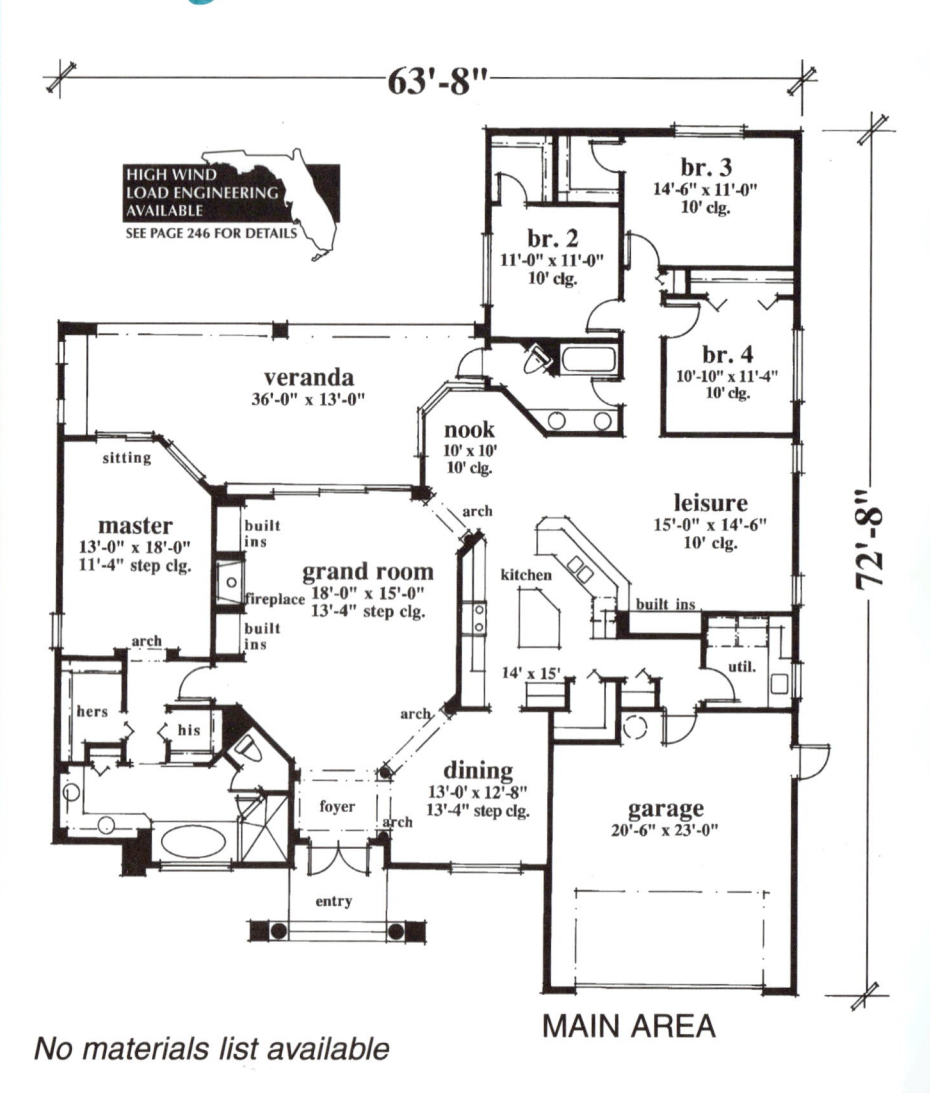

HIGH WIND LOAD ENGINEERING AVAILABLE
SEE PAGE 246 FOR DETAILS

63'-8"
72'-8"

veranda 36'-0" x 13'-0"
sitting
master 13'-0" x 18'-0" 11'-4" step clg.
hers
his
built ins
nook 10' x 10' 10' clg.
br. 2 11'-0" x 11'-0" 10' clg.
br. 3 14'-6" x 11'-0" 10' clg.
br. 4 10'-10" x 11'-4" 10' clg.
grand room 18'-0" x 15'-0" 13'-4" step clg.
fireplace
built ins
arch
kitchen
14' x 15'
leisure 15'-0" x 14'-6" 10' clg.
built ins
util.
arch
foyer
dining 13'-0" x 12'-8" 13'-4" step clg.
garage 20'-6" x 23'-0"
entry

MAIN AREA

No materials list available

DESIGN NO. 94607

PRICE CODE C

FRONT PORCH CATCHES BREEZES

No. 94607

- This plan features:
— Three bedrooms
— Two full and one half baths
- Full front Porch shelters full length windows and front entrance
- Foyer features powder room and a lovely landing staircase
- A formal Dining Room entertains easily with adjoining Kitchen and Living Room
- Spacious Living Room with hearth fireplace and access to Wood Deck below vaulted ceiling
- An efficient Kitchen easily serves Breakfast and Dining area
- Private first floor bedroom offers a double vanity bath
- An optional crawl space or slab foundation — please specify when ordering
- Right reading reverse is available for this plan

FIRST FLOOR — 1,244 SQ. FT.
SECOND FLOOR — 636 SQ. FT.

TOTAL LIVING AREA: 1,880 SQ. FT.

WIDTH 40'-6"
DEPTH 50'-0"

FIRST FLOOR

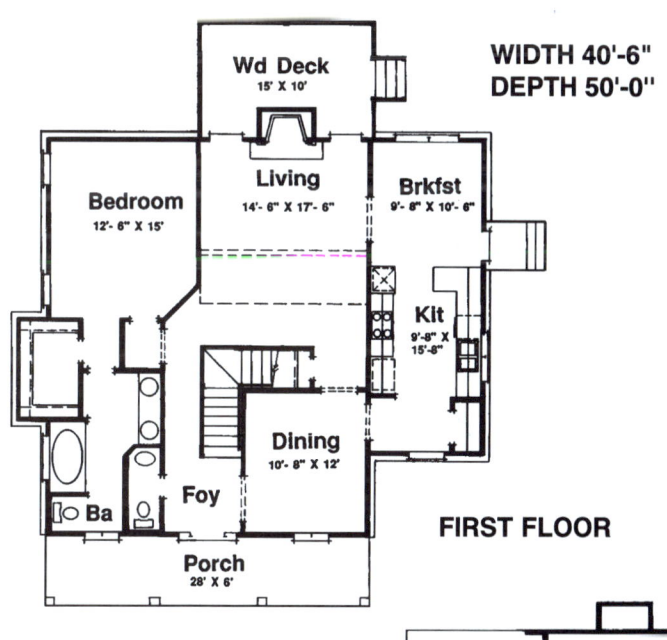

- Wd Deck 15' X 10'
- Living 14'-6" X 17'-6"
- Brkfst 9'-6" X 10'-6"
- Bedroom 12'-6" X 15'
- Kit 9'-8" X 15'-8"
- Dining 10'-8" X 12'
- Foy
- Ba
- Porch 28' X 6'

No materials list available

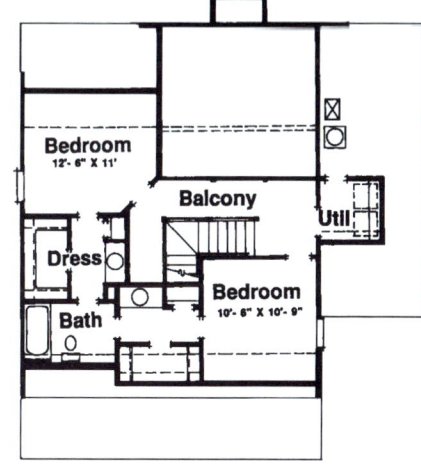

SECOND FLOOR

- Bedroom 12'-6" X 11'
- Balcony
- Util
- Dress
- Bath
- Bedroom 10'-6" X 10'-9"

DESIGN NO. 93107

PRICE CODE C

Charming brick home

No. 93107

■ This plan features:

— Three bedrooms

— Two full baths

■ A covered entrance leading into a spacious Living Room with a fireplace and an airy Dining Room with access to the Patio

■ An island Kitchen, open to the Dining Room, offering ample storage and easy access to the Laundry area and the Garage

■ A Master Bedroom with a walk-in closet, access to the Patio and a plush bath offering a window tub, a step-in shower and a double vanity

■ Two additional bedrooms, with decorative windows, sharing a full hall bath

MAIN FLOOR — 1,868 SQ. FT.
BASEMENT — 1,868 SQ. FT.
GARAGE — 782 SQ. FT.

TOTAL LIVING AREA: 1,868 SQ. FT.

No materials list available

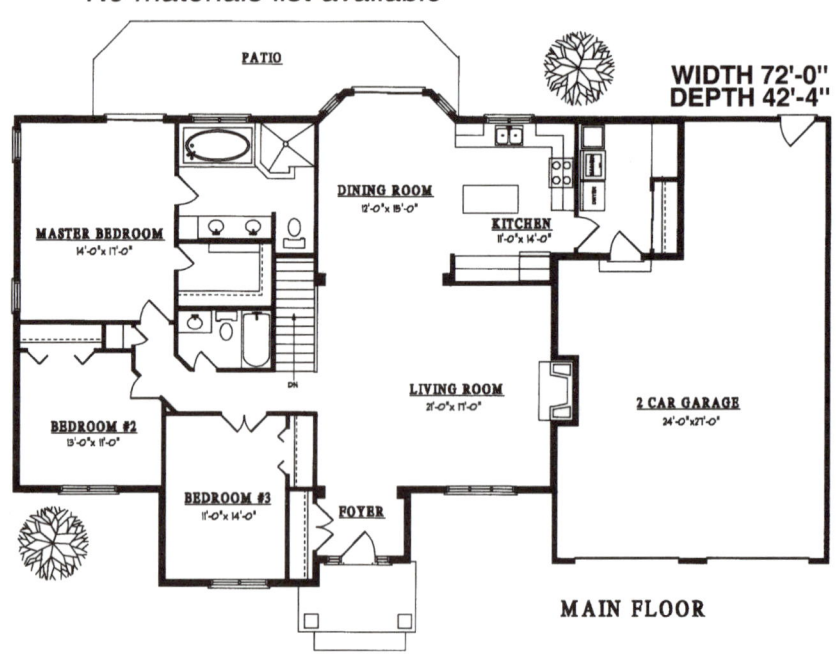

WIDTH 72'-0"
DEPTH 42'-4"

MAIN FLOOR

RIGHT READING REVERSE available for this plan

DESIGN NO. 92210

PRICE CODE F

Stunning Manor for Elegant Living

No. 92210

■ This plan features:

— Four bedrooms

— Two full and one half baths

■ Curved Porch leads into spacious Entry with double, curved staircase

■ Formal Library and Dining Room flank Entry for easy entertaining

■ Expansive Family Room offers an entertainment center, and access to Covered Patio

■ Country-size Kitchen with a work island/snackbar, Dining area, Utility and Garage entry

■ Luxurious Master Bedroom suite with private Study and skylight bath with a whirlpool tub

■ Three additional bedrooms, two with walk-in closets and one with a private bath

First floor — 2,745 sq. ft.
Second floor — 2,355 sq. ft.

Total living area: 5,100 sq. ft.

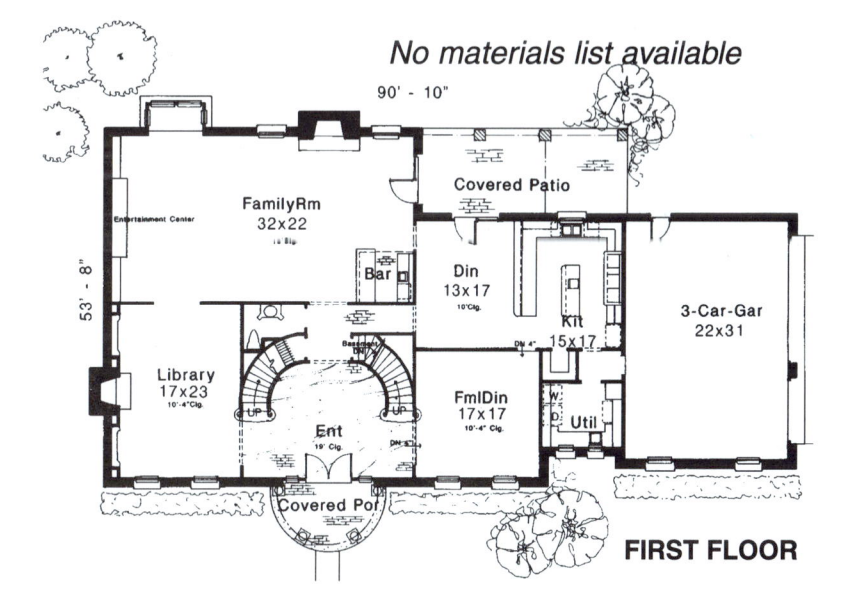

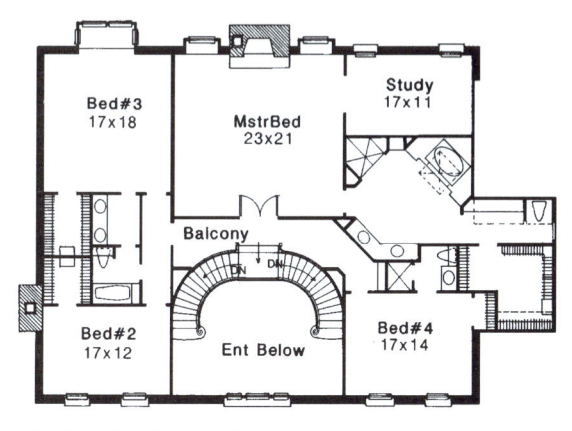

No materials list available

FIRST FLOOR

SECOND FLOOR

DESIGN NO. 94227

PRICE CODE F

CURVED FLOATING STAIRCASE

No materials list available

HIGH WIND LOAD ENGINEERING AVAILABLE
SEE PAGE 246 FOR DETAILS

No. 94227

■ This plan features:

— Three bedrooms

— Five full baths

■ Grand palladian entrance leads into two-story Foyer and a floating, curved staircase

■ Open Living and Leisure rooms with sliding glass doors to Veranda

■ Large Kitchen boasts a long serving counter/snackbar, glass eating Nook, a large walk-in closet and adjoining Dining area

■ Two Master Suites, on first and second floor, offer outdoor access and luxurious baths

■ French doors open to Study with book shelves and outdoor access

■ Guest bedroom and Bonus bedroom with walk-in closets, balconies and private baths

FIRST FLOOR — 2,618 SQ. FT.
SECOND FLOOR — 1,945 SQ. FT.
GARAGE — 633 SQ. FT.

TOTAL LIVING AREA: 4,563 SQ. FT.

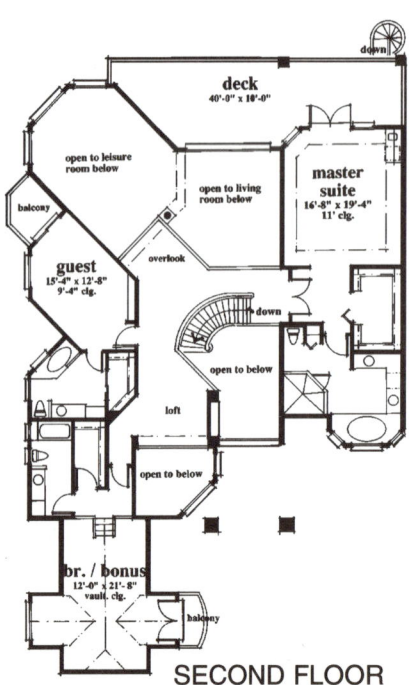

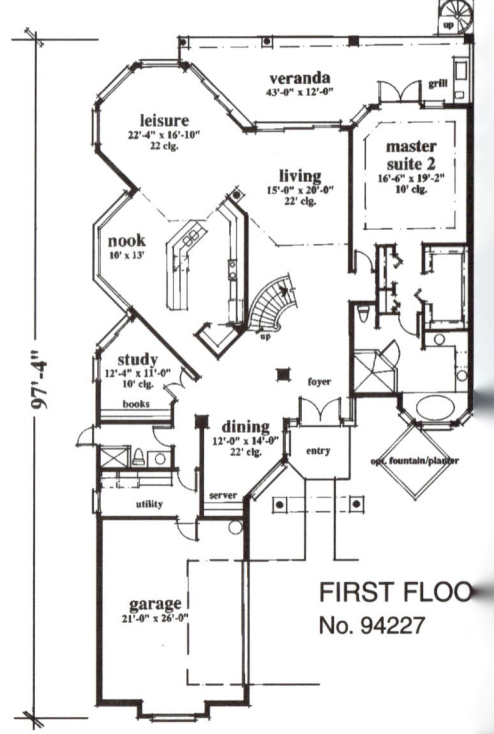

SECOND FLOOR

FIRST FLOOR
No. 94227

DESIGN NO. 94244

PRICE CODE F

Southern Contemporary

No. 94244

■ This plan features:

— Three bedrooms

— Three full and one half baths

■ Impressive Entry into Foyer enhanced by planters, columns and arches

■ Stepped ceilings top formal Living and Dining rooms

■ Unique circular Study enhanced by a turret ceiling

■ Family Kitchen with a large walk-in pantry, work island and serving counter easily serves Lanai, Leisure and Dining rooms

■ Expansive views in Master Suite in addition to his-n-hers closets and a lavish bath with a circular shower

■ Two additional bedrooms with private baths and Lanai access

MAIN FLOOR — 3,866 SQ. FT.
GARAGE — 683 SQ. FT.

TOTAL LIVING AREA: 3,866 SQ. FT.

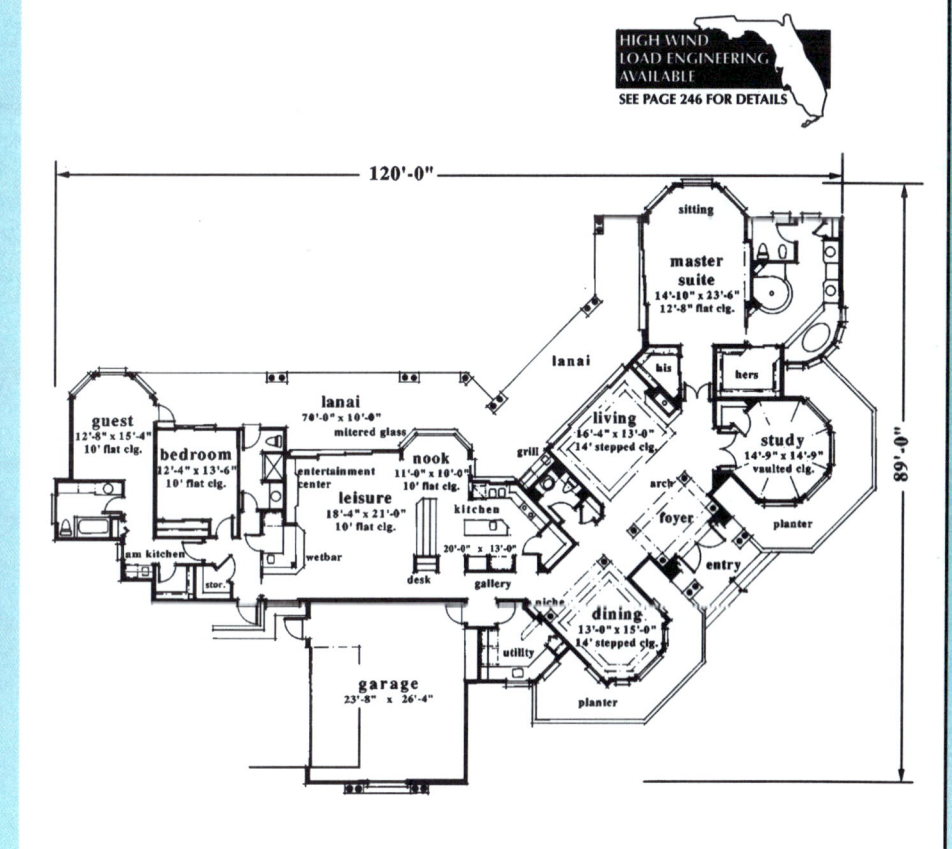

HIGH WIND LOAD ENGINEERING AVAILABLE
SEE PAGE 246 FOR DETAILS

MAIN FLOOR

No materials list available

DESIGN NO. 94740

PRICE CODE B

No 94740

- This plan features:
- — Three bedrooms
- — Two full baths
- Inviting front porch of this home leads directly into the main living areas
- The open Dining room and Great room have vaulted ceilings, a two-way fireplace and French doors to the patio
- The Master suite is positioned to the rear of the home and offers a walk-in closet
- Two additional bedrooms share the full bath in the hall

MAIN FLOOR — 1,775 SQ. FT.
GARAGE — 422 SQ. FT.

TOTAL LIVING AREA: 1,775 SQ. FT.

1NVITING FRONT PORCH

HIGH WIND LOAD ENGINEERING AVAILABLE
SEE PAGE 246 FOR DETAILS

Mstr 15'9"x15'0"
Patio
Gar 20'0"x20'0"
Grt 16'0"x20'0"
Keep 14'0"x11'6"
Bed 11'3"x10'0"
Bed 12'0"x9'9"
Foy
Din 12'0"x12'0"
Kit 14'0"x12'0"
Porch
52'-0"
59'-9"

MAIN FLOOR
No. 94740

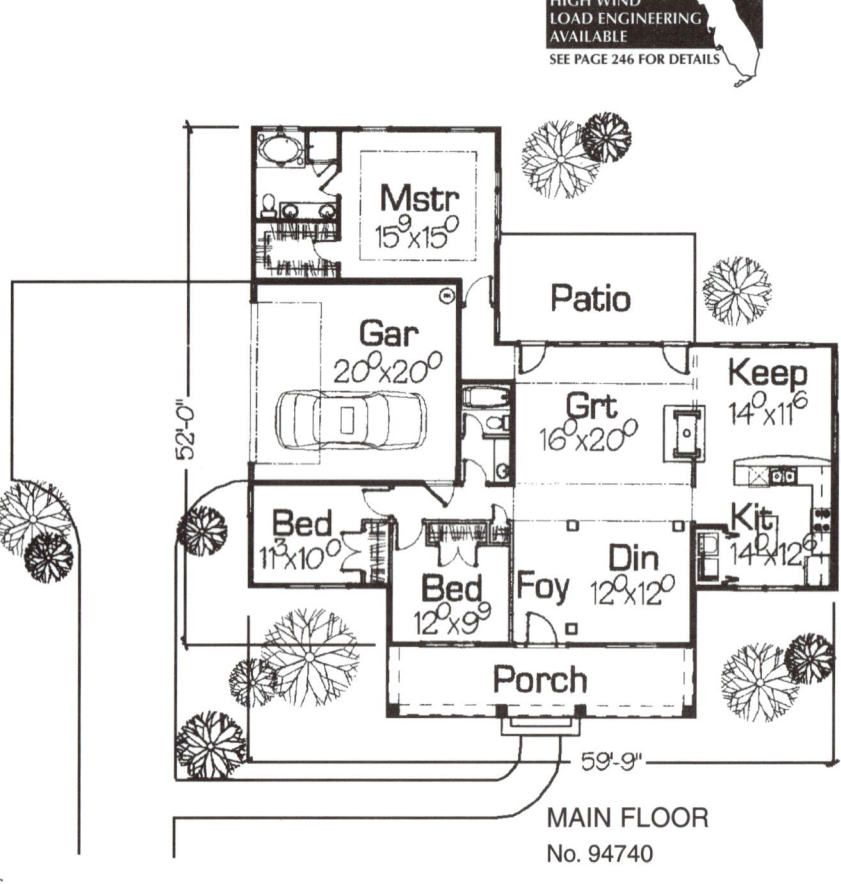

An EXCLUSIVE DESIGN *By United Design Associates*

DESIGN NO. 94744

PRICE CODE E

MEDITERRANEAN VILLA STYLE

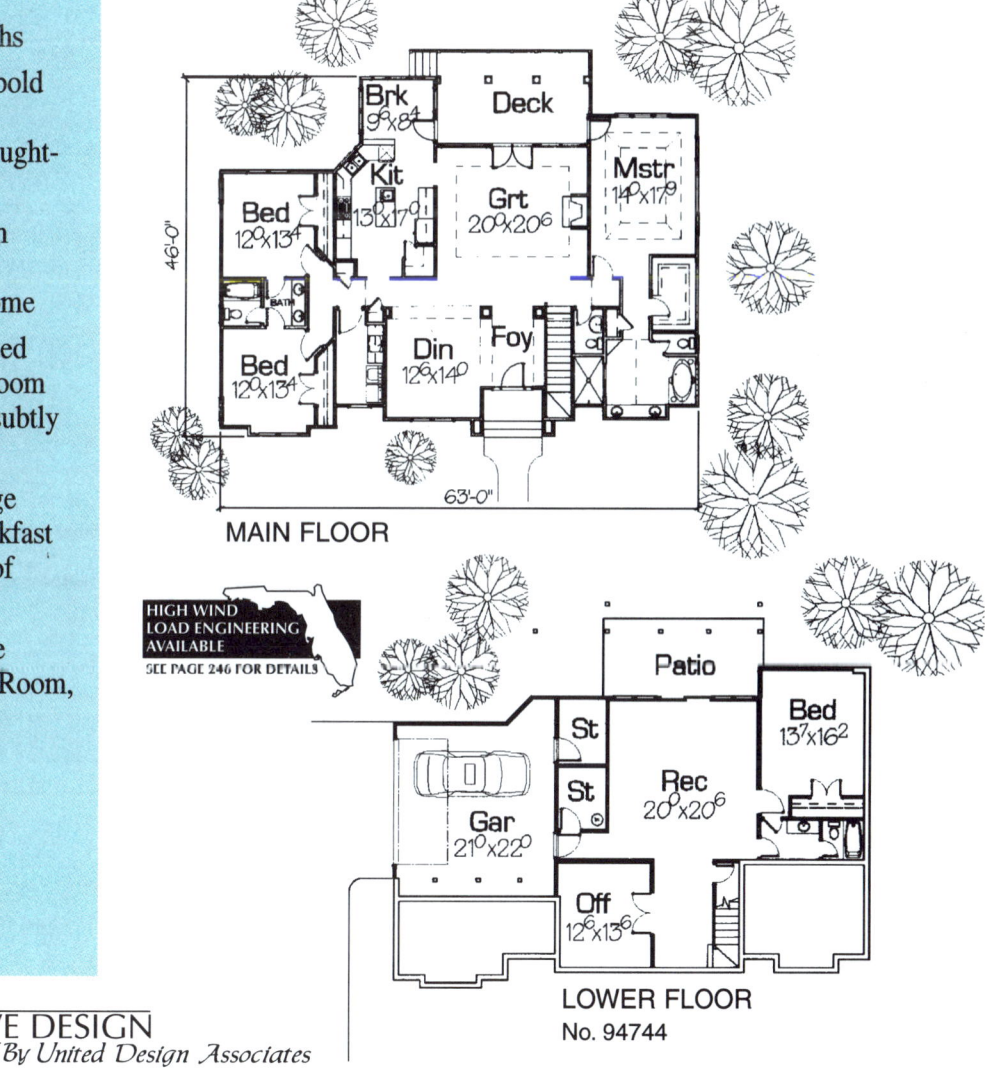

No. 94744

- This plan features:
  — Four bedrooms
  — Three full and one half baths
- This plan incorporates the bold architectural elements of a Spanish Mission with a thoughtful open layout
- Volume ceilings in the main living areas and beautiful windows throughout the home
- The Dining room is separated from the Foyer and Great room with a set of columns that subtly define the respective areas
- Designer Kitchen has a large island, a pantry, and a Breakfast nook that takes advantage of views from all sides
- Basement level includes the Garage, a large Recreation Room, an Office and a Guest Suite

MAIN FLOOR — 2,282 SQ. FT.
LOWER LEVEL — 1,184 SQ. FT.
GARAGE — 565 SQ. FT.

TOTAL LIVING AREA: 3,466 SQ. FT.

HIGH WIND LOAD ENGINEERING AVAILABLE
SEE PAGE 246 FOR DETAILS

MAIN FLOOR

LOWER FLOOR
No. 94744

An EXCLUSIVE DESIGN
By United Design Associates

DESIGN NO. 93704

PRICE CODE D

Yesterday's style for today's lifestyle

No. 93704

- This plan features:
- — Three bedrooms
- — Two full and one half baths
- Front Porch shelters entrance into Foyer, Great room and Study
- Great room with inviting fireplace opens to formal Dining Room
- Spacious Kitchen with work island, built-in pantry and serving/snackbar for Breakfast area and Porch
- Master Bedroom adjoins Study, pampering bath and Utility area
- Two second floor bedrooms with double closets, share a double vanity bath and study alcove

FIRST FLOOR — 1,748 SQ. FT.
SECOND FLOOR — 558 SQ. FT.
GARAGE — 440 SQ. FT.

TOTAL LIVING AREA: 2,306 SQ. FT.

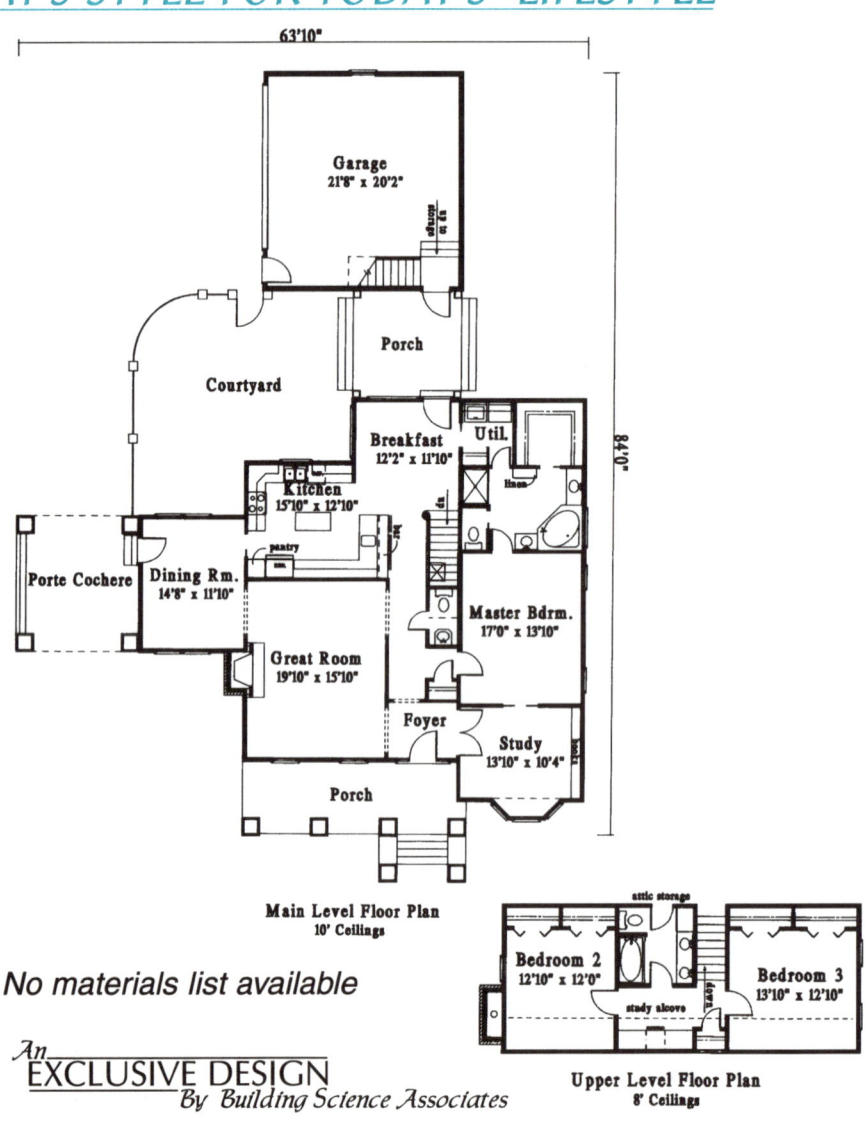

No materials list available

Main Level Floor Plan
10' Ceilings

- Garage 21'8" x 20'2"
- Porch
- Courtyard
- Breakfast 12'2" x 11'10"
- Util.
- Kitchen 15'10" x 12'10"
- Porte Cochere
- Dining Rm. 14'8" x 11'10"
- pantry
- Master Bdrm. 17'0" x 13'10"
- Great Room 19'10" x 15'10"
- Foyer
- Study 13'10" x 10'4"
- Porch

63'10" x 84'0"

Upper Level Floor Plan
8' Ceilings

- Bedroom 2 12'10" x 12'0"
- attic storage
- study alcove
- Bedroom 3 13'10" x 12'10"

An **EXCLUSIVE DESIGN** *By Building Science Associates*

DESIGN NO. 92613

PRICE CODE E

No. 92613

- This plan features:
— Three bedrooms
— Two full and two half baths
- A classic design with decorative stucco, keystone arches and boxed windows surrounding a broad, pillar entrance
- A sloped ceiling in the Great Room accenting a wall of windows, a great hearth fireplace and an entertainment center
- An elegant formal Dining Room with a tray ceiling highlighting the decorative, boxed window
- An efficient, island Kitchen opening to the Patio through an atrium door and a spacious Breakfast Room
- The Master Bedroom Suite with a luxurious bath and an over-sized walk-in closet
- A second floor with two additional bedrooms sharing a full-hall bath and a Bonus Room

FIRST FLOOR — 2,192 SQ. FT.
SECOND FLOOR — 654 SQ. FT.

TOTAL LIVING AREA: 2,846 SQ. FT.

Classic European Styling

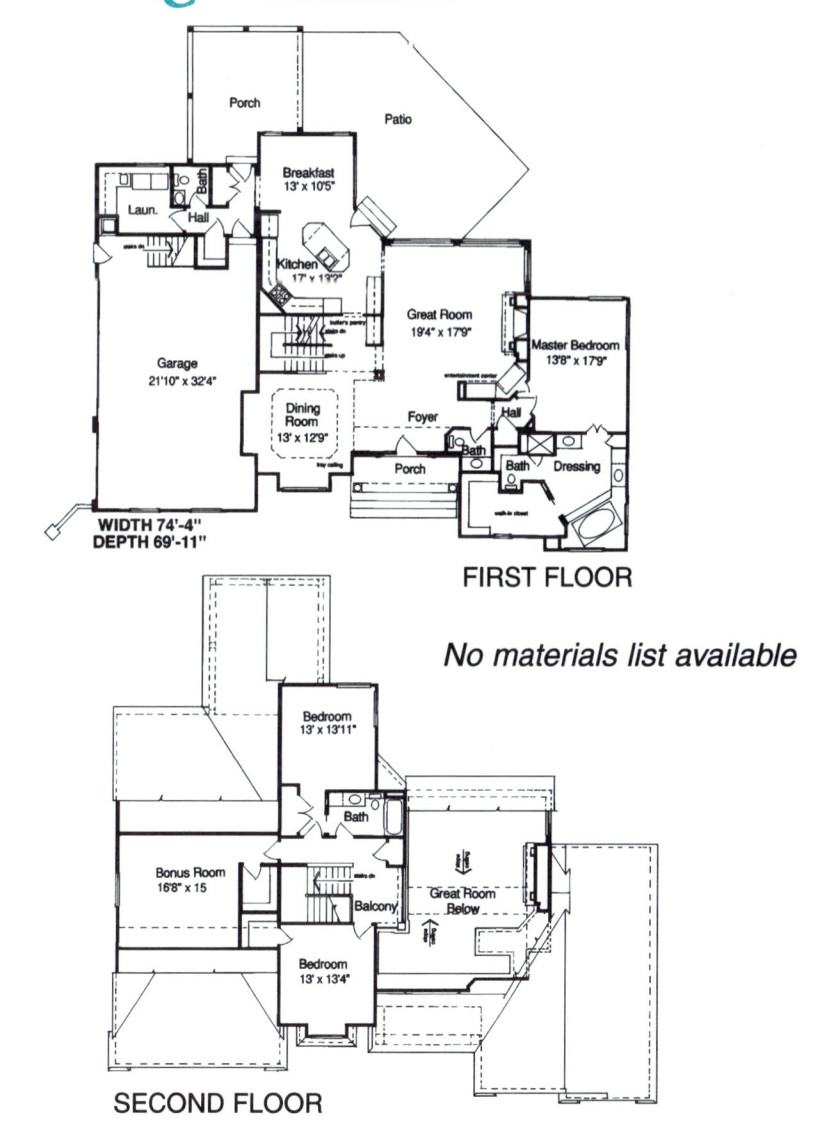

WIDTH 74'-4"
DEPTH 69'-11"

FIRST FLOOR

No materials list available

SECOND FLOOR

DESIGN NO. 94600

PRICE CODE D

Functional Floor Plan

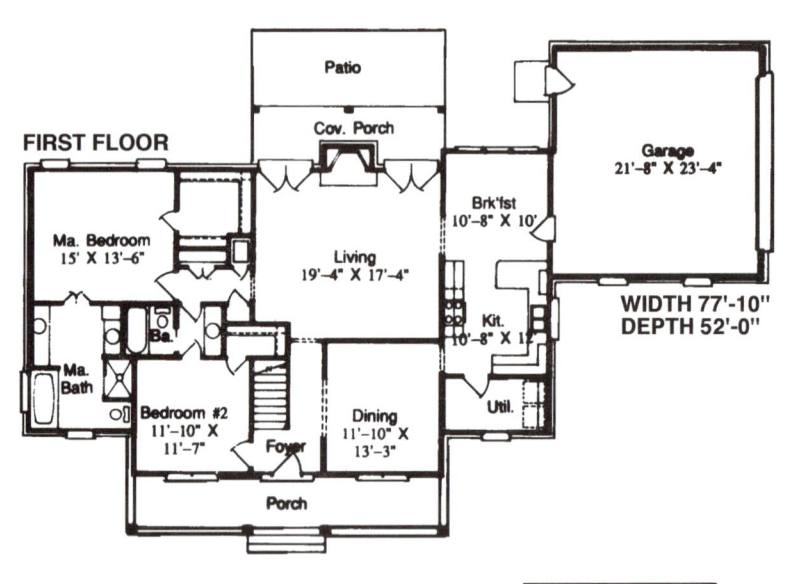

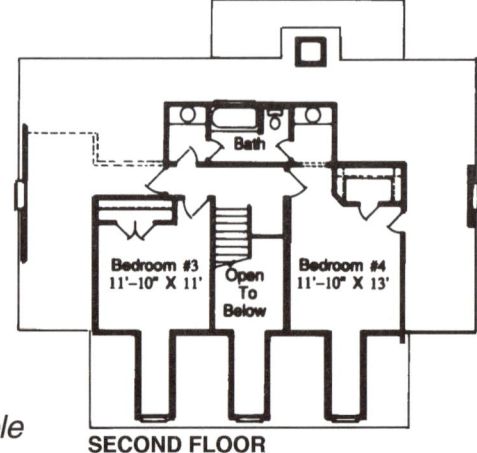

No. 94600

■ This plan features:

— Four bedrooms

— Three full baths

■ Expansive Living Room with hearth fireplace between French doors leading to Covered Porch and Patio

■ Efficient Kitchen with peninsula counter, bright Breakfast area and adjoining Utility, Dining Room and Garage entry

■ Private Master Bedroom wing with a large walk-in closet and plush bath with two vanities

■ First floor bedroom with another walk-in closet and full bath access, offers multiple uses

■ Two additional bedrooms on second floor with dormers and large closets, share a full bath with separate vanities

■ An optional crawl space or slab foundation — please specify when ordering

FIRST FLOOR — 1,685 SQ. FT.
SECOND FLOOR — 648 SQ. FT.
GARAGE — 560 SQ. FT.

TOTAL LIVING AREA: 2,333 SQ. FT.

No materials list available

FIRST FLOOR

- Patio
- Cov. Porch
- Ma. Bedroom 15' X 13'-6"
- Living 19'-4" X 17'-4"
- Brk'fst 10'-8" X 10'
- Garage 21'-8" X 23'-4"
- Kit. 10'-8" X 12'
- Ma. Bath
- Bedroom #2 11'-10" X 11'-7"
- Foyer
- Dining 11'-10" X 13'-3"
- Util.
- Porch

WIDTH 77'-10"
DEPTH 52'-0"

SECOND FLOOR

- Bath
- Bedroom #3 11'-10" X 11'
- Open To Below
- Bedroom #4 11'-10" X 13'

DESIGN NO. 93100

PRICE CODE B

Stylish Single-Level

No. 93100

- This plan features:
— Three bedrooms
— Two full and one half baths
- A well appointed, U-shaped Kitchen separated from the Dining Room by a peninsula counter
- A spacious Living Room, enhanced by a focal point fireplace
- An elegant Dining Room with a bay window that opens to a screen porch, expanding living space
- A Master Suite with a walk-in closet and private Master Bath
- Two family bedrooms that share a full hall-bath

MAIN FLOOR — 1,642 SQ. FT.
GARAGE — 591 SQ. FT.
BASEMENT — 1,642 SQ. FT.

TOTAL LIVING AREA: 1,642 SQ. FT.

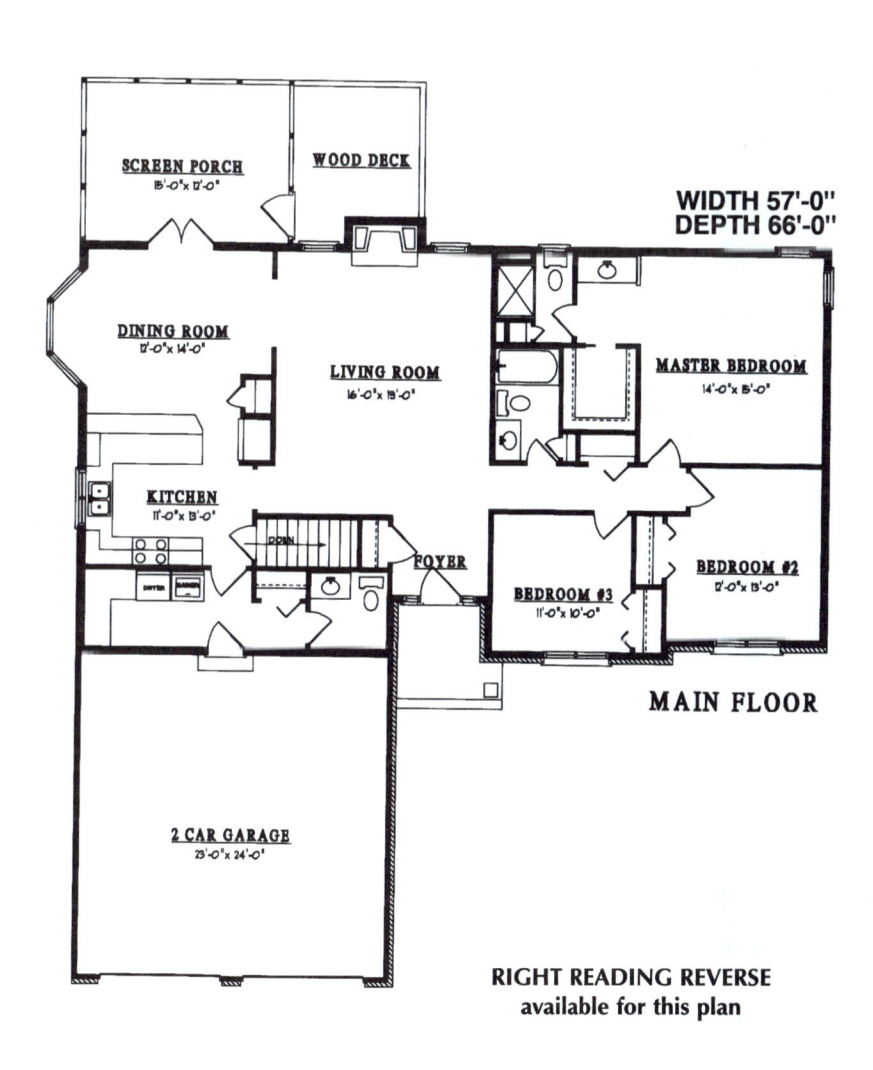

WIDTH 57'-0"
DEPTH 66'-0"

MAIN FLOOR

RIGHT READING REVERSE available for this plan

DESIGN NO. 94208

PRICE CODE B

Compact and convenient ranch

MAIN AREA

No. 94208
■ This plan features:
— Three bedrooms
— Two full baths
■ Impressive Portico entry into Foyer with a decorative ceiling and formal Dining Room
■ Spacious Great room with built-in entertainment center and cozy fireplace, opens through double French doors onto Veranda
■ Efficient Kitchen with a walk-in pantry, serving/snack bar, and eating Nook with bay window
■ Plush Master Suite with French doors to the Veranda, two walk-in closets and full bath
■ Two additional bedrooms, with large closets share a full bath

MAIN FLOOR — 1,795 SQ. FT.
GARAGE — 465 SQ. FT.

TOTAL LIVING AREA: 1,795 SQ. FT.

HIGH WIND LOAD ENGINEERING AVAILABLE
SEE PAGE 246 FOR DETAILS

78'-0"
48'-0"

verandah 54'-8" x 10'-0"
nook 10'-6" x 8'-4"
br. 2 11'-4" x 15'-0" 10' clg.
great room 16'-4" x 17'-0" 10' clg.
fireplace
enter. center
kitchen
master suite 13'-0" x 15'-6" 10' clg.
utility
garage 21'-6" x 21'-4"
br. 3 12'-8" x 11'-6" 10' clg.
foy.
dining 13'-6" x 13'-0" 10' clg.
his   hers
entry

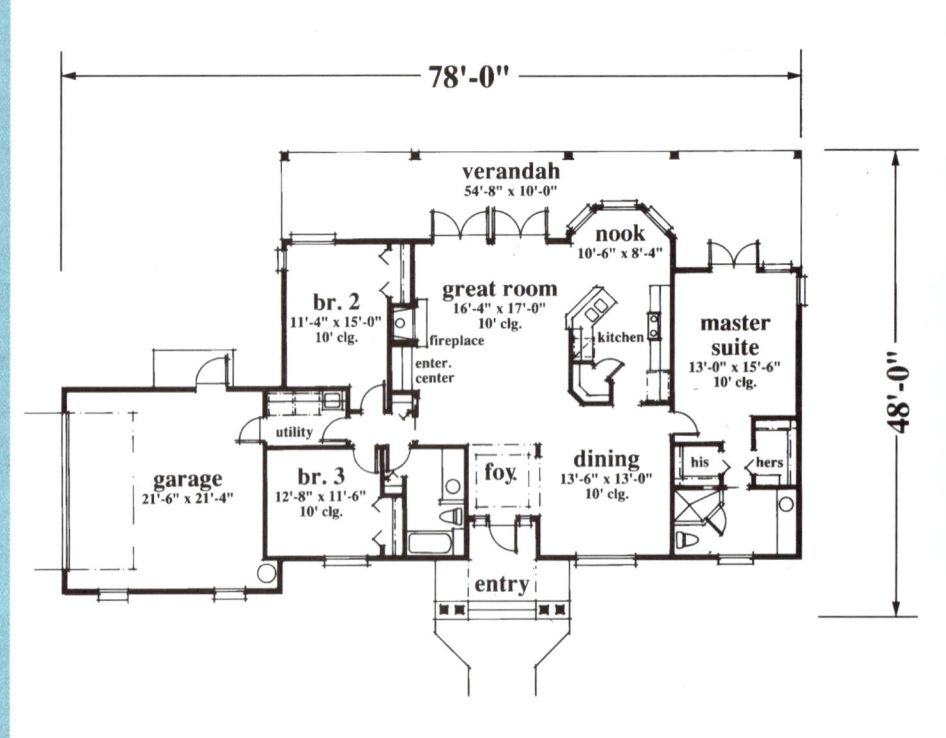

No materials list available

DESIGN NO. 94233

PRICE CODE D

Soft Arches Accent Country Design

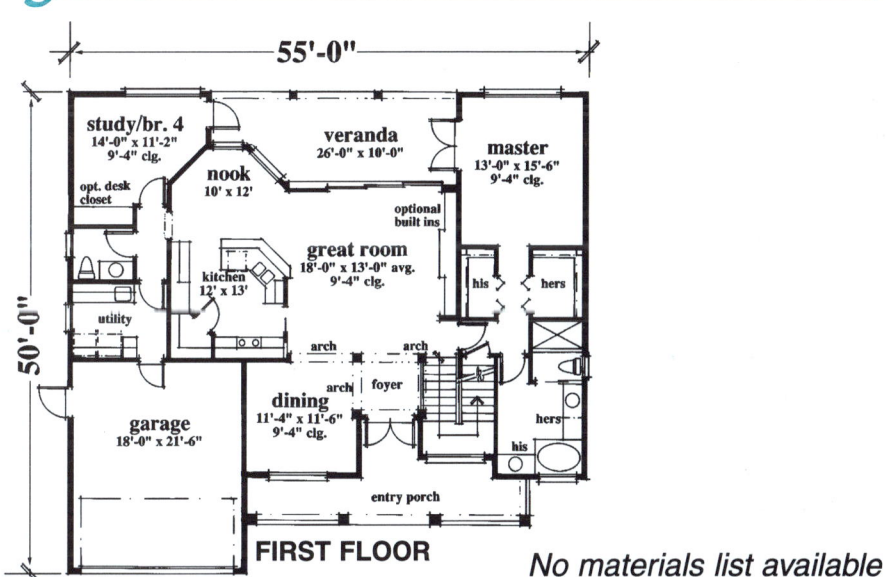

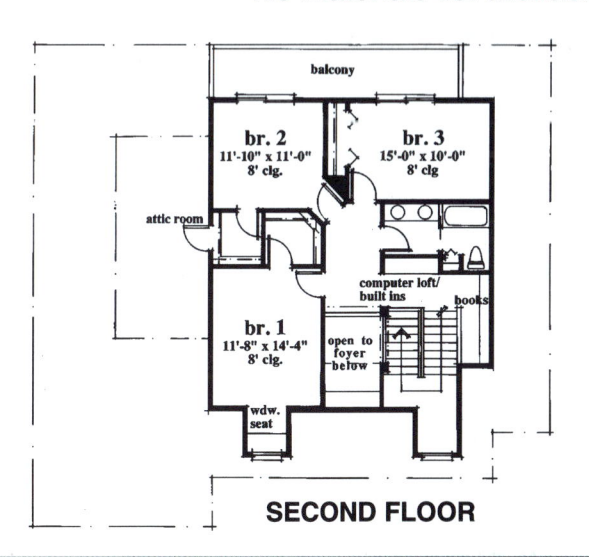

No. 94233

■ This plan features:

— Four or five bedrooms

— Two full and one half baths

■ Entry Porch with double dormers and doors

■ Pillared arches frame Foyer, Dining Room and Great Room

■ Open Great Room with optional built-ins and sliding glass doors to Verandah

■ Compact Kitchen with walk-in pantry and a counter/snackbar

■ Comfortable Master Suite with his-n-her closets and vanities and a garden tub

■ Corner Study/Bedroom with Lanai access offers multiple uses

■ An optional basement or slab foundation — please specify when ordering

FIRST FLOOR — 1,676 SQ. FT.
SECOND FLOOR — 851 SQ. FT.
GARAGE — 304 SQ. FT.

TOTAL LIVING AREA: 2,527 SQ. FT.

No materials list available

HIGH WIND LOAD ENGINEERING AVAILABLE
SEE PAGE 246 FOR DETAILS

FIRST FLOOR

- study/br. 4 — 14'-0" x 11'-2" — 9'-4" clg.
- veranda — 26'-0" x 10'-0"
- master — 13'-0" x 15'-6" — 9'-4" clg.
- nook — 10' x 12'
- great room — 18'-0" x 13'-0" avg. — 9'-4" clg.
- kitchen — 12' x 13'
- dining — 11'-4" x 11'-6" — 9'-4" clg.
- garage — 18'-0" x 21'-6"
- utility, foyer, entry porch
- 55'-0" × 50'-0"

SECOND FLOOR

- balcony
- br. 2 — 11'-10" x 11'-0" — 8' clg.
- br. 3 — 15'-0" x 10'-0" — 8' clg.
- br. 1 — 11'-8" x 14'-4" — 8' clg.
- attic room
- computer loft/built ins
- books
- open to foyer below
- wdw. seat

DESIGN NO. 92516

PRICE CODE D

DISTINCTIVE EUROPEAN DESIGN

No. 92516

■ This plan features:

— Three bedrooms

— Two full baths

■ Foyer leading into a grand Living Room, topped by a vaulted ceiling, a fireplace between built-in cabinets and a wall of glass leading to a covered Porch

■ A gourmet Kitchen with a peninsula counter/snackbar and a built-in pantry, that is central to the Dining Room, the bay window Breakfast area, the Utility Room and the Garage

■ A large Master Bedroom, crowned by a raised ceiling, with French doors leading to a covered Porch, a luxurious bath and a walk-in closet

■ An optional crawl space or slab foundation — please specify when ordering

MAIN FLOOR — 1,887 SQ. FT.
GARAGE & STORAGE — 524 SQ. FT.

TOTAL LIVING AREA: 1,887 SQ. FT.

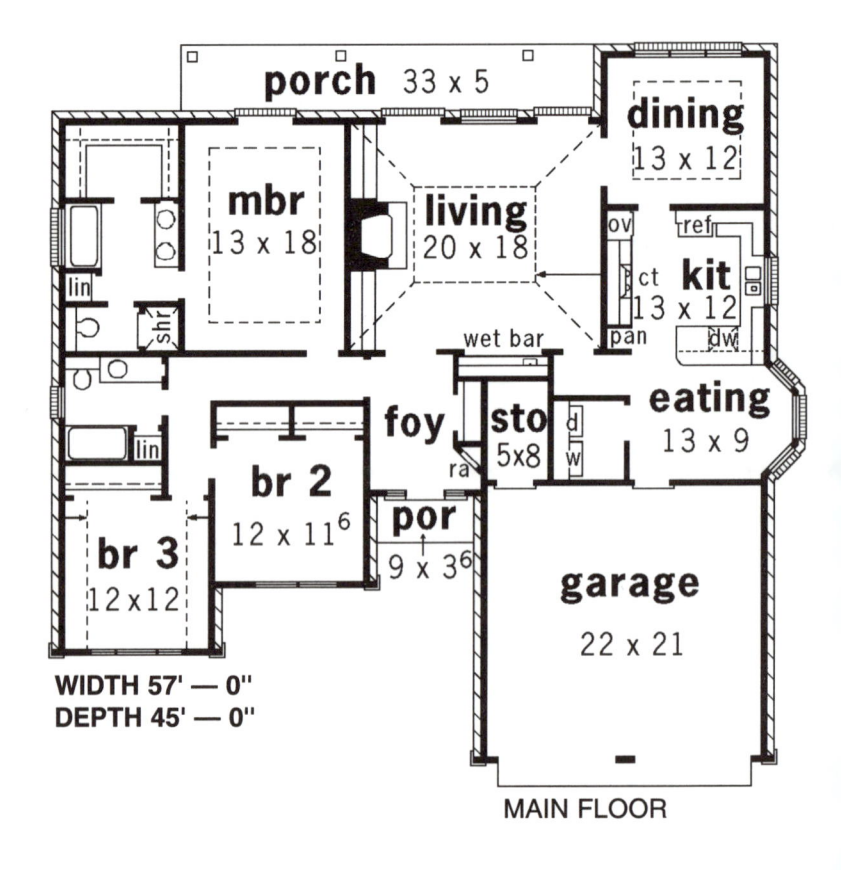

WIDTH 57' — 0"
DEPTH 45' — 0"

MAIN FLOOR

DESIGN NO. 92520

PRICE CODE B

GREAT ROOM IS CENTER OF ACTIVITY

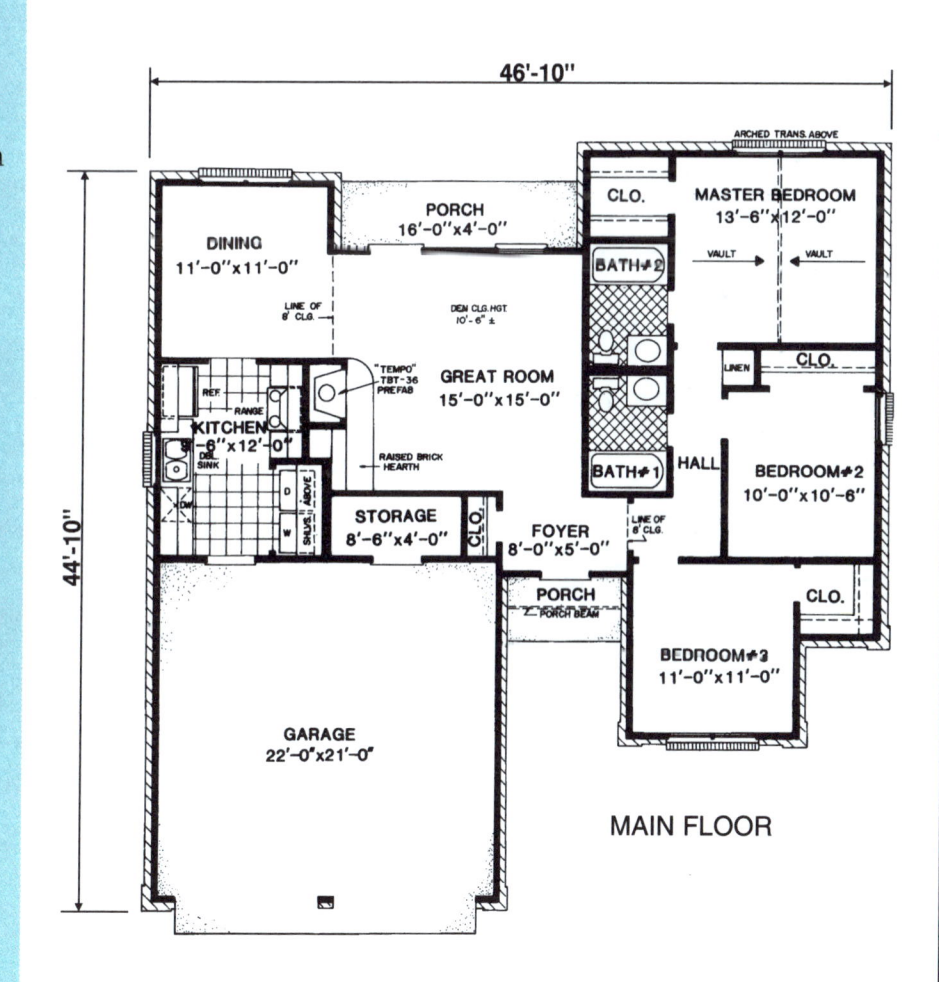

No. 92520

- This plan features:
— Three bedrooms
— Two full baths
- Sheltered entry leads into open Foyer and Great Room beyond
- Raised, brick hearth and wood bin enhance fireplace in spacious Great Room with access to back Porch
- Formal Dining Room adjoins Great Room and Kitchen for easy entertaining
- Efficient Kitchen with laundry alcove and Garage entrance
- Vaulted ceiling tops arched transom window in the Master Bedroom with private bath and walk-in closet
- Two additional bedrooms with ample closet space, share a full bath
- An optional crawl space or slab foundation is available — please specify when ordering

MAIN FLOOR — 1,208 SQ. FT.
GARAGE — 2-CAR

TOTAL LIVING AREA: 1,208 SQ. FT.

MAIN FLOOR

- Overall: 46'-10" x 44'-10"
- Dining: 11'-0" x 11'-0"
- Porch: 16'-0" x 4'-0"
- Master Bedroom: 13'-6" x 12'-0"
- Great Room: 15'-0" x 15'-0"
- Kitchen: 8'-6" x 12'-0"
- Storage: 8'-6" x 4'-0"
- Foyer: 8'-0" x 5'-0"
- Bedroom #2: 10'-0" x 10'-6"
- Bedroom #3: 11'-0" x 11'-0"
- Garage: 22'-0" x 21'-0"

DESIGN NO. 93263

PRICE CODE B

Arched keystones add to appeal

No. 93263

- This plan features:
- — Four bedrooms
- — Two full baths
- Sheltered entry leads into Living Area with focal point fireplace, Dining Room with lovely bay window and access to Deck
- Efficient Kitchen with peninsula serving counter for glass Breakfast area, built-in pantry, Laundry and Garage entry
- Secluded Master Bedroom with decorative ceiling offers walk-in closet and plush bath with double vanity and window tub
- Three additional bedrooms with ample closets share a full bath

MAIN FLOOR — 1,625 SQ. FT.
BASEMENT — 1,579 SQ. FT.
GARAGE — 406 SQ. FT.

TOTAL LIVING AREA: 1,625 SQ. FT.

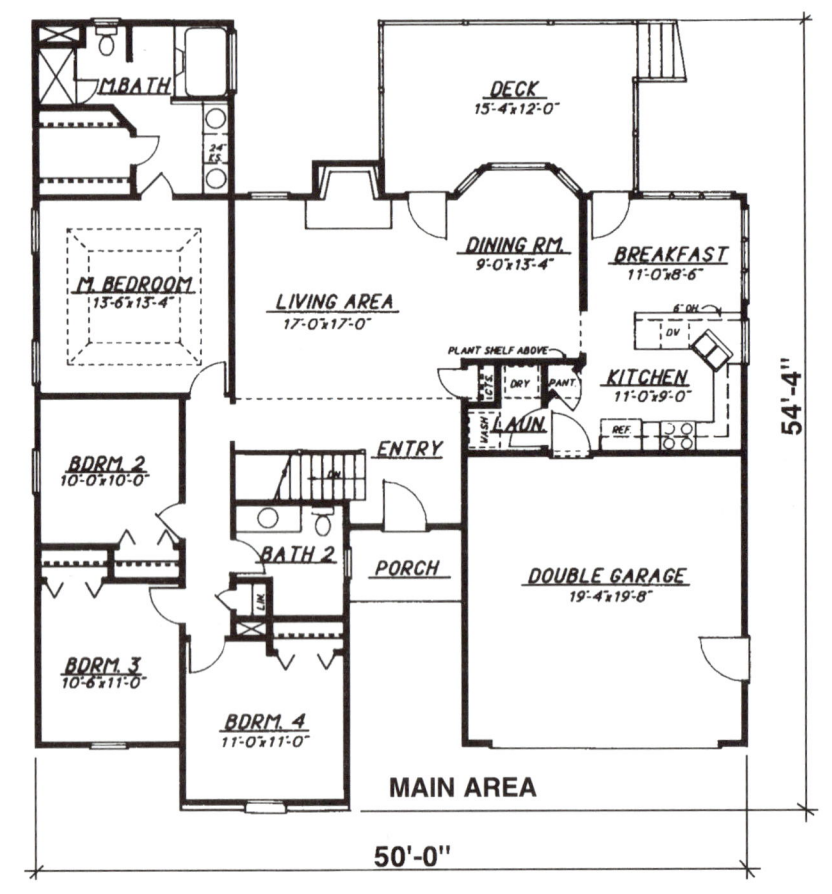

An *Exclusive Design* By Jannis Vann & Associates, Inc.

No materials list available

210

DESIGN NO. 99277

PRICE CODE D

Impressive Curving Staircase

No. 99277

■ This plan features:

— Three bedrooms

— Two full and one half baths

■ Covered porch leads into two-story Foyer and open Living and Dining rooms separated by curved staircase

■ Expansive Family Room with two-sided fireplace, wetbar, glass shelves and access to Covered Porch and Terrace beyond

■ Efficient, U-shaped Kitchen with built-in pantry and glass eating Nook

■ Spacious Master Bedroom with three closets, private Deck and luxurious bath

■ Two additional bedrooms share a double vanity bath

FIRST FLOOR — 1,336 SQ. FT.
SECOND FLOOR — 1,186 SQ. FT.
GARAGE — 655 SQ. FT.

TOTAL LIVING AREA: 2,522 SQ. FT.

WIDTH 58'-9"
DEPTH 54'-10"

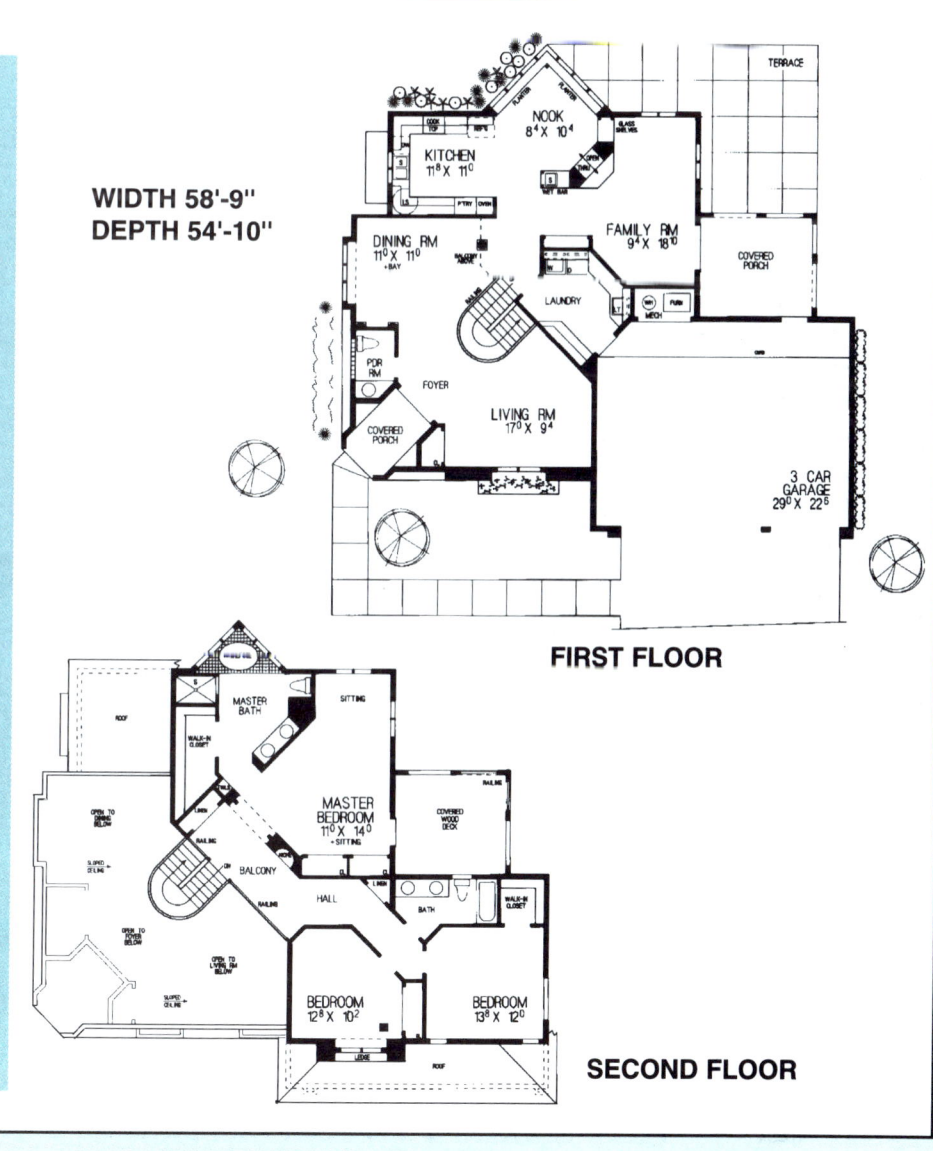

FIRST FLOOR

SECOND FLOOR

DESIGN NO. 92220

PRICE CODE C

SOUTHERN HOSPITALITY

No. 92220

- This plan features:
— Three bedrooms
— Two full baths
- Welcoming Covered Veranda catches breezes
- Easy-care, tiled Entry leads into Great Room with fieldstone fireplace and atrium door to another Covered Veranda topped by a cathedral ceiling
- A bright Kitchen/Dining Room includes a stovetop island/snackbar, built-in pantry and desk and access to Covered Veranda
- Vaulted ceiling crowns Master Bedroom that offers a plush bath and huge walk-in closet
- Two additional bedrooms with ample closets share a double vanity bath

MAIN FLOOR — 1,830 SQ. FT.
GARAGE — 759 SQ. FT.

TOTAL LIVING AREA:
1,830 SQ. FT.

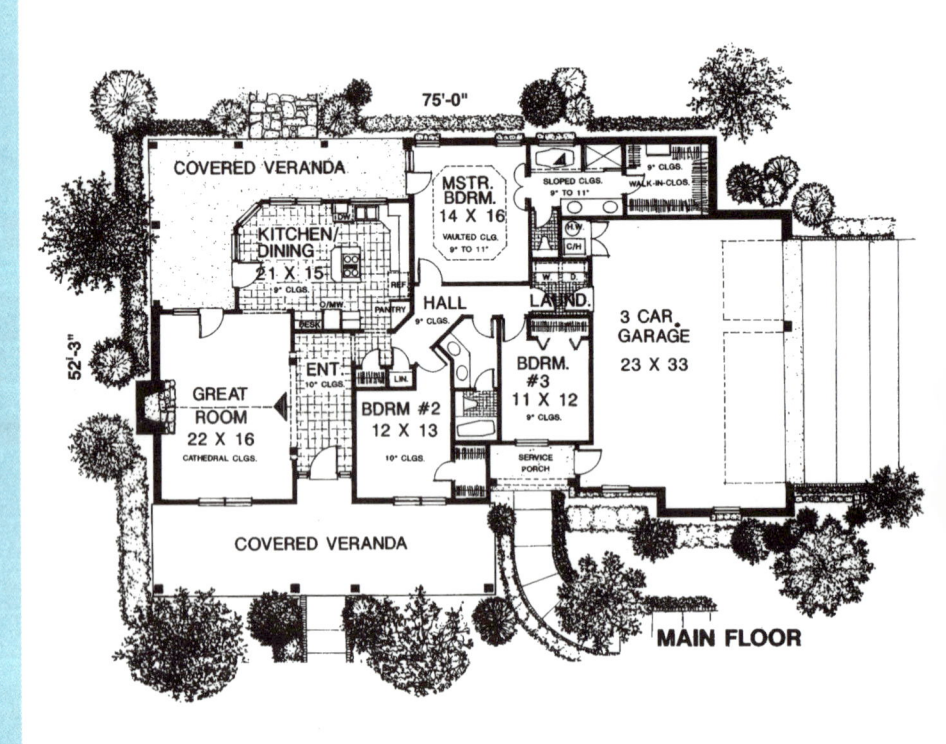

No materials list available

DESIGN NO. 94745

PRICE CODE B

CLASSICALLY STYLED

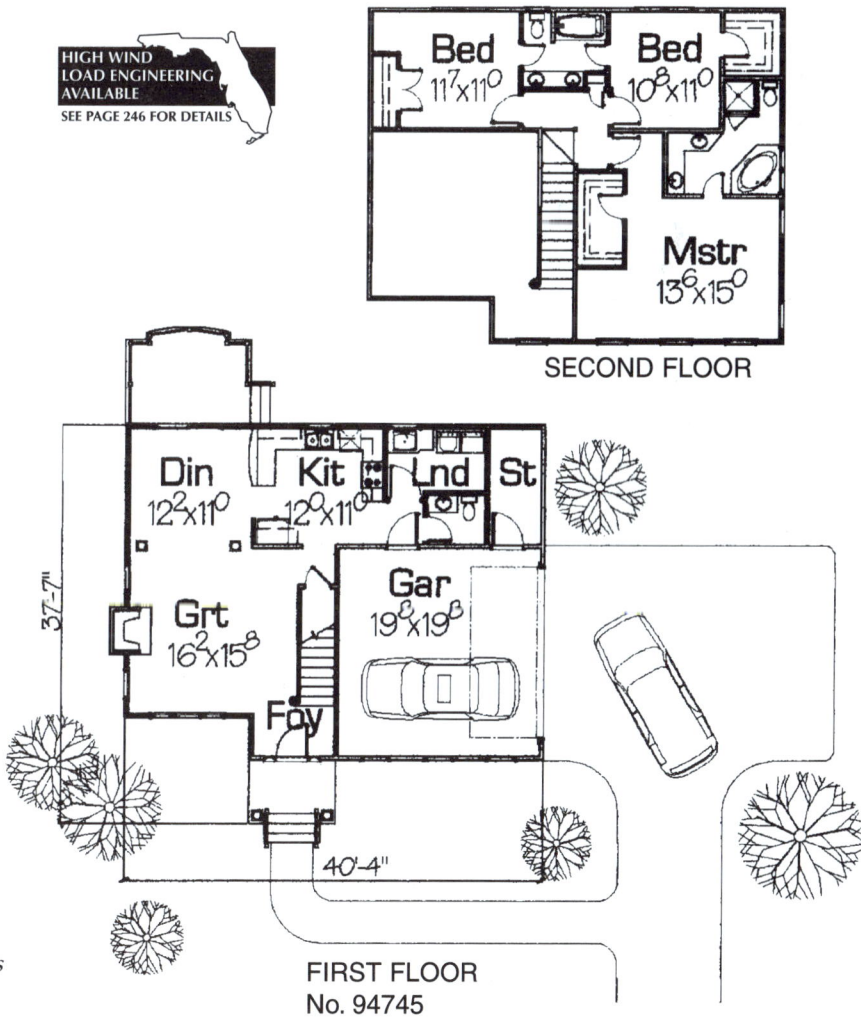

No. 94745

- This plan features:
- — Three bedrooms
- — Two full and one half baths
- This plan has a vaulted Foyer with an open staircase and a Great room with stunning transom windows to let in light
- The upstairs Master suite includes a tray ceiling, walk-in closet and a bath with a separate shower and garden tub
- The Kitchen and open Dining area face the rear of the home and offering extensive views
- A side entry garage includes a large storage area perfect for the lawnmower, weed eater and children's bicycles

FIRST FLOOR — 769 SQ. FT.
SECOND FLOOR — 872 SQ. FT.
GARAGE — 462 SQ. FT.

TOTAL LIVING AREA: 1,641 SQ. FT.

HIGH WIND LOAD ENGINEERING AVAILABLE
SEE PAGE 246 FOR DETAILS

An **EXCLUSIVE DESIGN** *By United Design Associates*

DESIGN NO. 94608

PRICE CODE C

PILLARS PLEASE THE EYE

No. 94608

■ This plan features:

— Three bedrooms

— Two full and one half baths

■ Front Porch leads into a two-story Foyer with banister staircase

■ An expansive Family Room with a cozy fireplace, large windows and access to Covered Porch

■ A hub Kitchen efficiently serves formal Dining Room and bright Breakfast area

■ Exclusive Master Bedroom offers a walk-in closet and lavish bath with double vanity

■ Two additional bedrooms with large closets share a full bath

■ An optional crawl space or slab foundation — please specify when ordering

FIRST FLOOR — 1,395 SQ. FT.
SECOND FLOOR — 676 SQ. FT.
GARAGE — 489 SQ. FT.

TOTAL LIVING AREA: 2,071 SQ. FT.

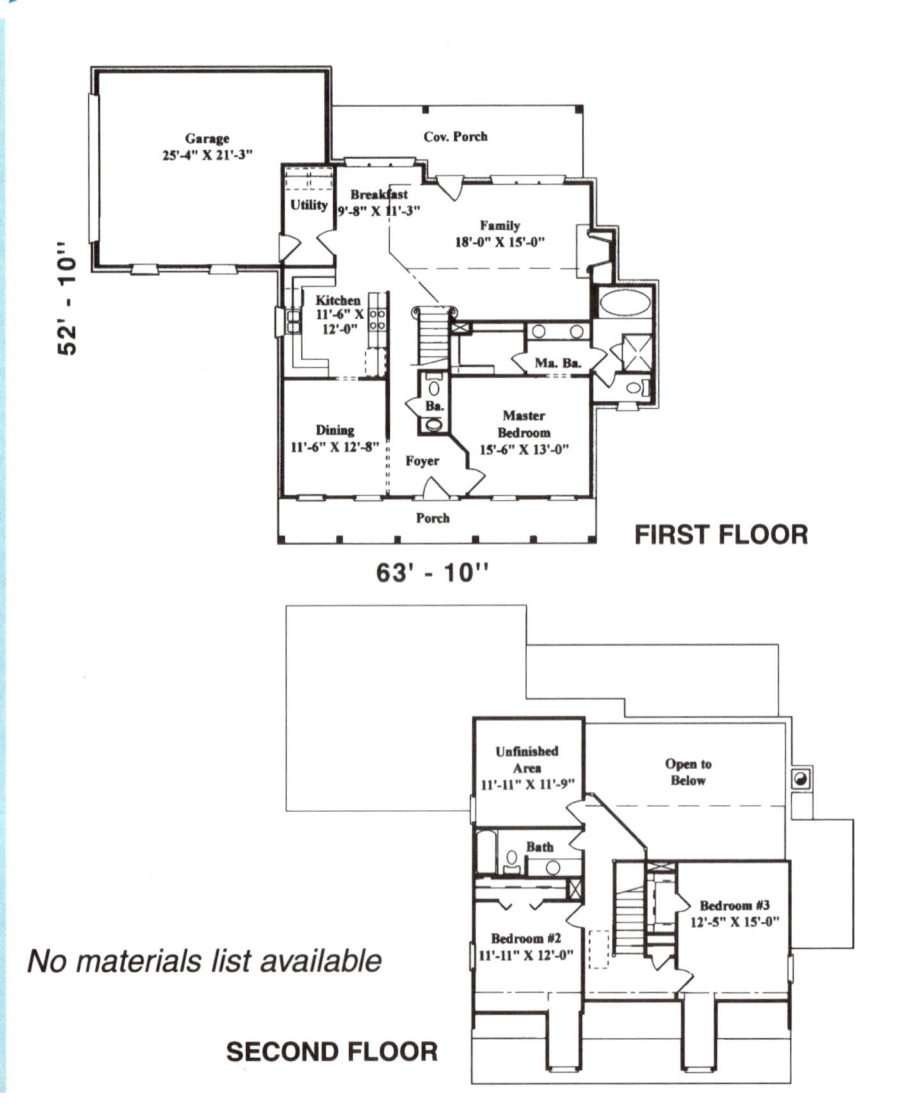

Garage 25'-4" X 21'-3"
Cov. Porch
Utility
Breakfast 9'-8" X 11'-3"
Family 18'-0" X 15'-0"
Kitchen 11'-6" X 12'-0"
Ma. Ba.
Dining 11'-6" X 12'-8"
Ba.
Foyer
Master Bedroom 15'-6" X 13'-0"
Porch

52' - 10"
63' - 10"

FIRST FLOOR

Unfinished Area 11'-11" X 11'-9"
Open to Below
Bath
Bedroom #2 11'-11" X 12'-0"
Bedroom #3 12'-5" X 15'-0"

No materials list available

SECOND FLOOR

DESIGN NO. 92610

PRICE CODE C

SUNKEN GREAT ROOM IS ONE OF THE MANY HIGHLIGHTS

No. 92610

- This plan features:
  — Three bedrooms
  — Two full and one half baths
- An arched front entrance framed by a decorative stone and brick exterior, and a unique turret room
- A sunken Great Room, centrally located, with a huge, hearth fireplace
- An efficient, island Kitchen, corner sink, ample counter and cabinet space, and a bright bay windowed Breakfast area
- A formal Dining Room with an expansive, bay window and pocket doors
- A quiet wing for the Master Bedroom suite with a sloped ceiling and a plush Bath
- Two additional bedrooms on the second floor sharing a full bath with a double vanity

FIRST FLOOR — 1,626 SQ. FT.
SECOND FLOOR — 475 SQ. FT.

TOTAL LIVING AREA: 2,101 SQ. FT.

No materials list available

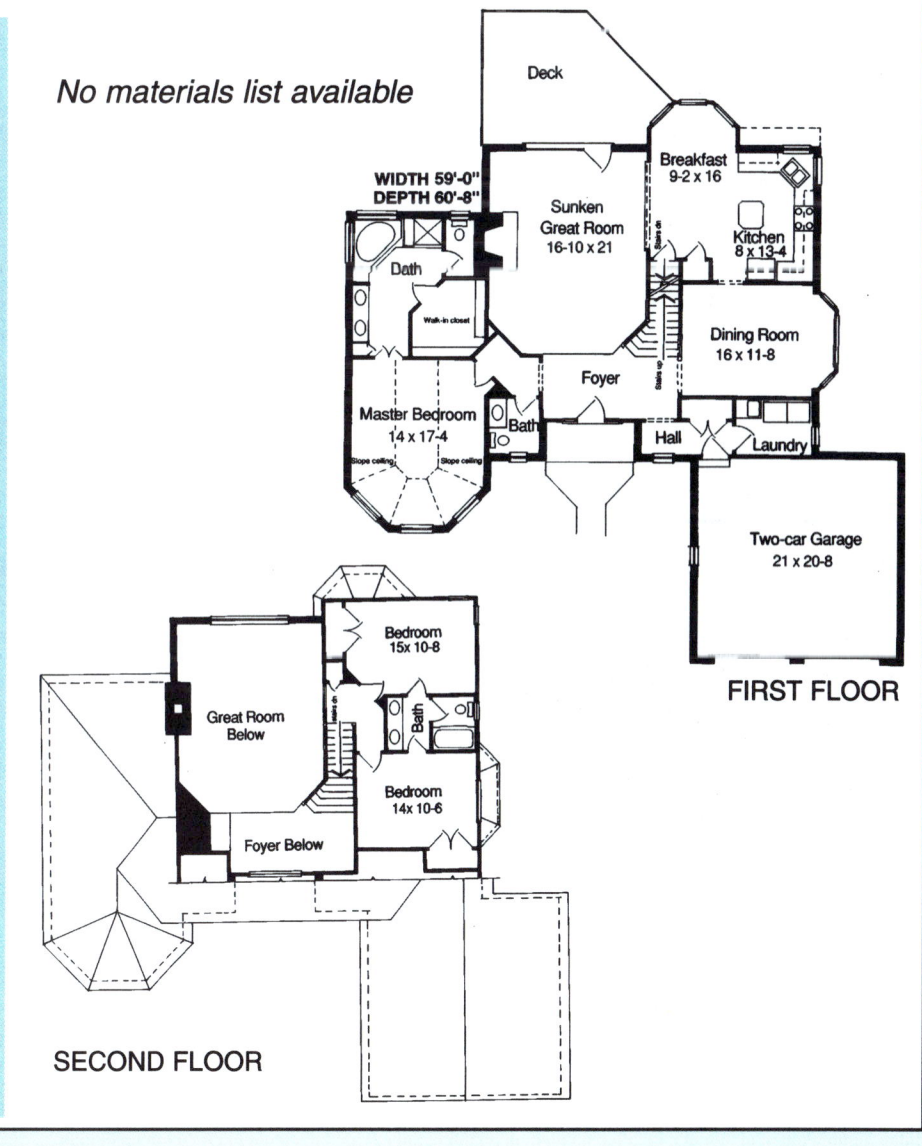

WIDTH 59'-0"
DEPTH 60'-8"

FIRST FLOOR

- Deck
- Sunken Great Room 16-10 x 21
- Breakfast 9-2 x 16
- Kitchen 8 x 13-4
- Bath
- Walk-in closet
- Dining Room 16 x 11-8
- Foyer
- Master Bedroom 14 x 17-4
- Bath
- Hall
- Laundry
- Two-car Garage 21 x 20-8

SECOND FLOOR

- Great Room Below
- Bedroom 15 x 10-8
- Bath
- Bedroom 14 x 10-6
- Foyer Below

DESIGN NO. 93707

PRICE CODE E

A GRAND ENTRANCE

No materials list available

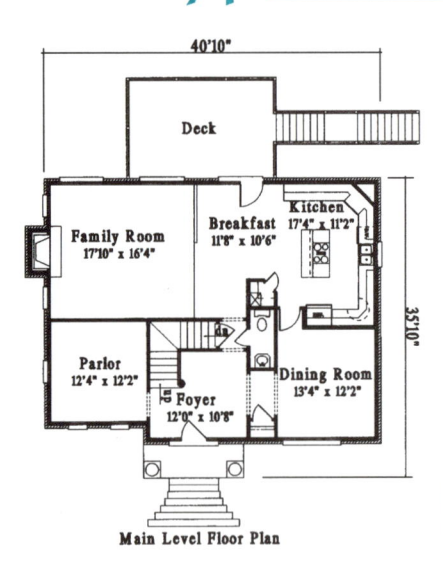

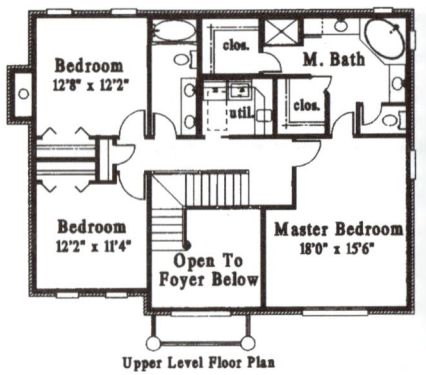

No. 93707

■ This plan features:

— Three bedrooms

— Three full and one half baths

■ A rich exterior with a dramatic entry porch leading to an impressive two-story Foyer

■ A formal Parlor which could be used for a home office or study

■ A large Family Room highlighted by a fireplace and flowing easily from the Breakfast Room

■ A large Kitchen containing a walk-in pantry, island/bar, an abundance of cabinet storage and counter space.

■ A Master Suite with his and her walk-in closets, separate vanities, compartmented toilet, whirlpool tub and separate shower

■ Two additional bedrooms that share a double vanitied hall bath

FIRST FLOOR — 1,210 SQ. FT.
SECOND FLOOR — 1,039 SQ. FT.
LOWER LEVEL — 464 SQ. FT.

TOTAL LIVING AREA: 2,713 SQ. FT.

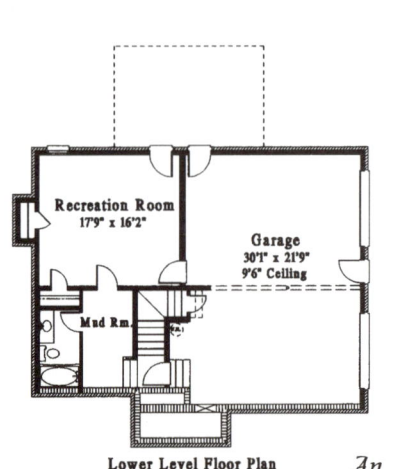

An EXCLUSIVE DESIGN *By Building Science Associates*

DESIGN NO. 94245

PRICE CODE F

MASTER SUITE WITH A VIEW

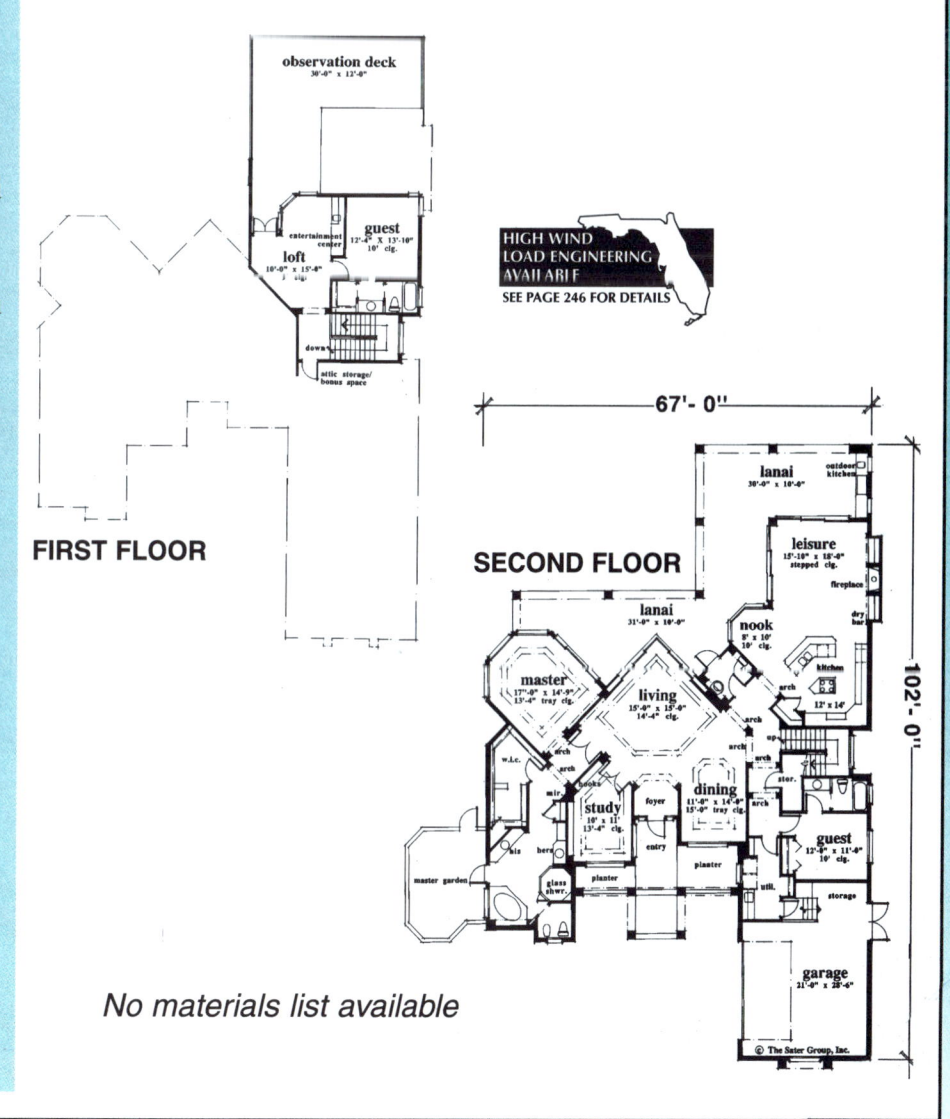

No. 94245

This plan features:

— Three bedrooms

— Three full and one half baths

- Gracious Entry between planters leads into Foyer and Living Room angled for views and Lanai access
- Decorative ceiling and windows highlight Study and Dining Room
- Expansive Kitchen with cooktop island, walk-in pantry, angled serving counter/snackbar and bay Nook
- Open Leisure Room with fireplace, built-ins and sliding glass doors to Lanai with outdoor Kitchen
- Bright and beautiful Master suite with a huge walk-in closet and lavish bath
- Two Guest rooms with large closets and private baths

FIRST FLOOR — 2,894 SQ. FT.
SECOND FLOOR — 568 SQ. FT.
GARAGE — 598 SQ. FT.

TOTAL LIVING AREA: 3,462 SQ. FT.

FIRST FLOOR

SECOND FLOOR

No materials list available

DESIGN NO. 94246

PRICE CODE F

No. 94246

- This plan features:
- Four bedrooms
- Three full and one half baths
- Portico Entry way opens up to a unique courtyard plan, expanding living areas to the lovely outdoors with an optional pool
- Octagon-shaped Grand Salon overlooks Lanai and opens to formal Dining area
- An efficient Kitchen with a walk-in pantry, built-in desk, island sink and expansive snackbar
- Open Leisure room with a high ceiling, sliding glass doors to Lanai and Courtyard
- Master wing has a large bedroom with a stepped ceiling, a bayed sitting area, glass doors to a Lanai, built-ins and a lavish bath area
- Private Guest House offers luxurious accommodations

FIRST FLOOR — 2,853 SQ. FT.
SECOND FLOOR — 627 SQ. FT.
GUEST HOUSE — 312 SQ. FT.
GARAGE — 777 SQ. FT.

TOTAL LIVING AREA: 3,792 SQ. FT.

SEPARATE GUEST QUARTERS

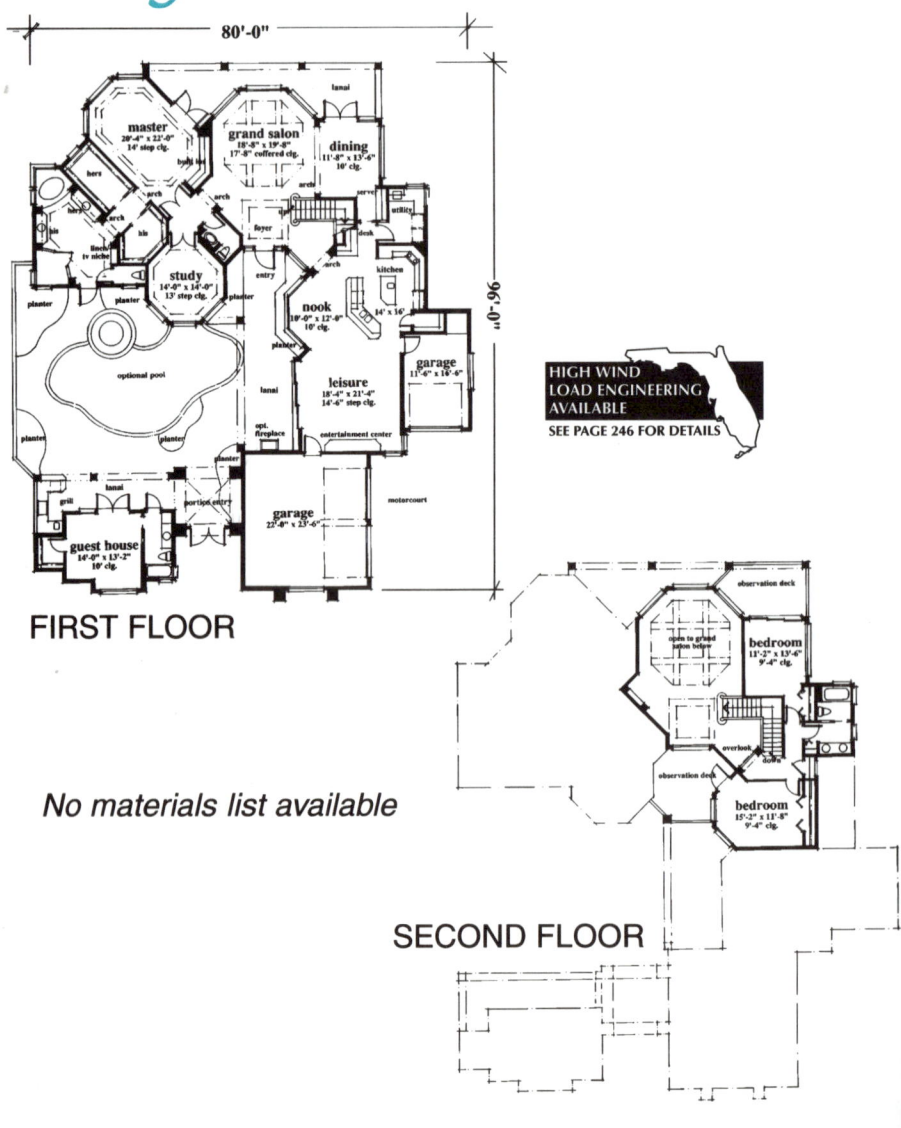

FIRST FLOOR

HIGH WIND LOAD ENGINEERING AVAILABLE
SEE PAGE 246 FOR DETAILS

No materials list available

SECOND FLOOR

DESIGN NO. 24650

PRICE CODE E

Impressive Two Story Foyer

No. 24650

■ This plan features:

— Four bedrooms

— Two full and one half baths

■ A two story Foyer with an angled staircase

■ An open layout between the formal Living Room and the formal Dining Room

■ A well-appointed, island Kitchen equipped with a double sink, a walk-in pantry and ample cabinet and counter space

■ An expansive Family Room enhanced by a cozy fireplace and a bumped out window

■ A luxurious Master Suite with Bath and two walk-in closets

■ Three additional bedrooms that share a double vanity hall bath

FIRST FLOOR — 1,435 SQ. FT.
SECOND FLOOR — 1,462 SQ.FT.
BONUS ROOM — 347 SQ. FT.
GARAGE — 616 SQ. FT.

TOTAL LIVING AREA: 2,897 SQ. FT.

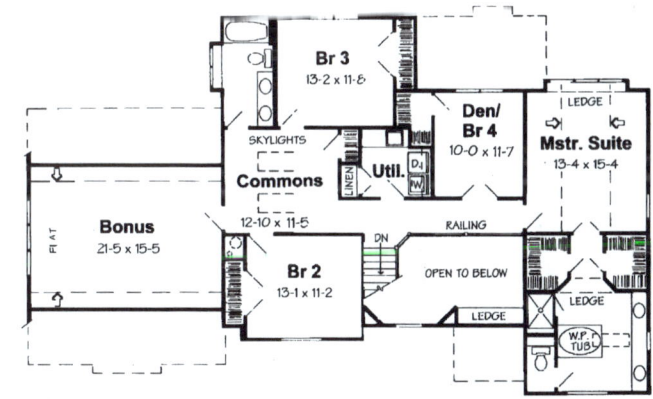

No materials list available

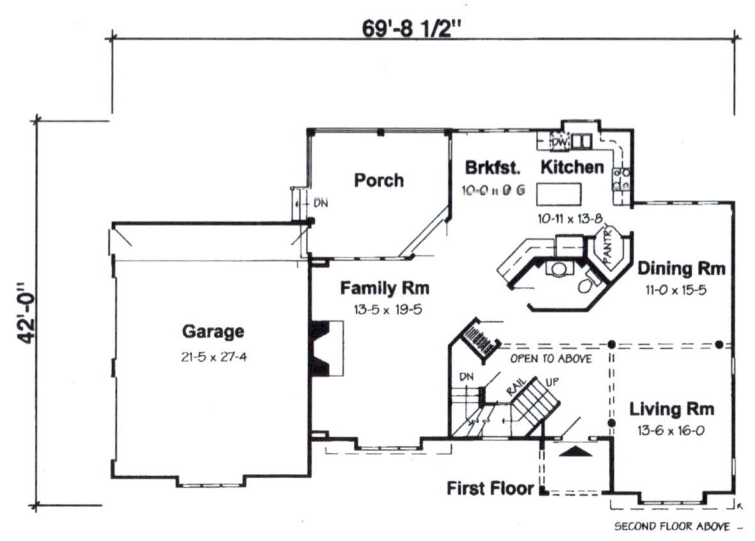

An **EXCLUSIVE DESIGN** By Plan One Homes, Inc.

DESIGN NO. 92281

PRICE CODE A

Small yet sophisticated

No. 92281

- This plan features:
- Three bedrooms
- Two full baths
- A tile Entry into a spacious Great Room highlighted by a triple window and a cozy fireplace between built-in shelving
- An efficient U-shaped Kitchen with ample work and storage space
- The Master Bedroom suite features an Sitting Area with window seats and an elegant bath with a garden window tub

MAIN FLOOR — 1,360 SQ. FT.
GARAGE — 380 SQ. FT.

TOTAL LIVING AREA: 1,360 SQ. FT.

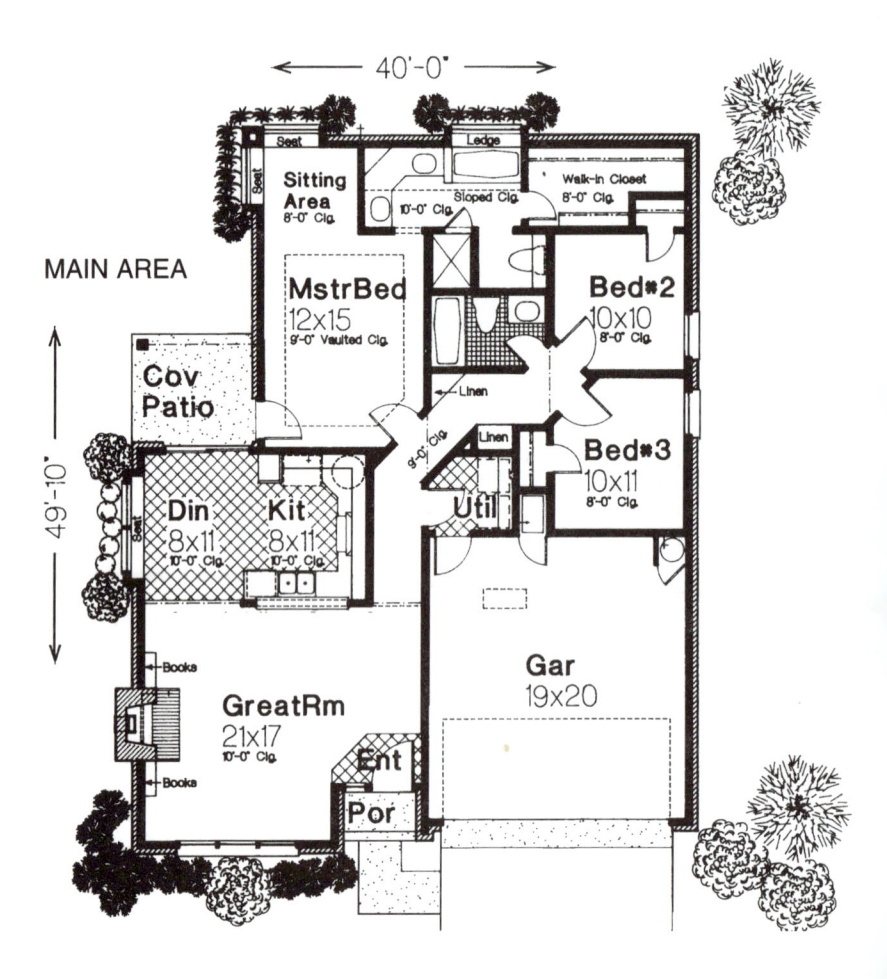

MAIN AREA

40'-0"
49'-10"

Sitting Area 8'-0" Clg.
Walk-In Closet 8'-0" Clg.
MstrBed 12x15 9'-0" Vaulted Clg.
Bed #2 10x10 8'-0" Clg.
Cov Patio
Bed #3 10x11 8'-0" Clg.
Din 8x11 10'-0" Clg.
Kit 8x11 10'-0" Clg.
Util
GreatRm 21x17 10'-0" Clg.
Gar 19x20
Ent
Por

No materials list available

DESIGN NO. 94243

PRICE CODE E

Impressive Entryway

No. 94243
- This plan features:
- Three or four bedrooms
- Two full and one half baths
- Three different exterior adaptations, each with its own special character and charm
- Double door leads into curved Living/Dining area and Veranda beyond
- An efficient Kitchen with an angled serving counter/snackbar, eating Nook and Leisure area with a fireplace
- Large Master Suite access to Veranda, two walk-in closets and a deluxe bath with two vanities
- French doors lead into bright Study/Bedroom with walk-in closet
- Two additional bedrooms share a double vanity bath

MAIN AREA — 2,998 SQ. FT.
GARAGE — 632 SQ. FT.

TOTAL LIVING AREA: 2,998 SQ. FT.

64'-8" × 83'-0"

- leisure 18'-0" x 18'-0" 10' clg.
- nook 8'-0" x 10'-0"
- veranda 20'-0" x 10'-0"
- master suite 17'-8" x 18'-0" 13' clg.
- kitchen 15' x 13'
- dining 13'-0" x 16'-0" 13' clg.
- living 13'-0" x 16'-0" 13' clg.
- br. 2 12'-4" x 12'-0" 10' clg.
- br. 3 12'-4" x 12'-0" 8' clg.
- br.4/study 19'-4" x 12'-6"
- garage 24'-8" x 22'-0"
- window seat (Elev. "B" only)

MAIN AREA

HIGH WIND LOAD ENGINEERING AVAILABLE
SEE PAGE 246 FOR DETAILS

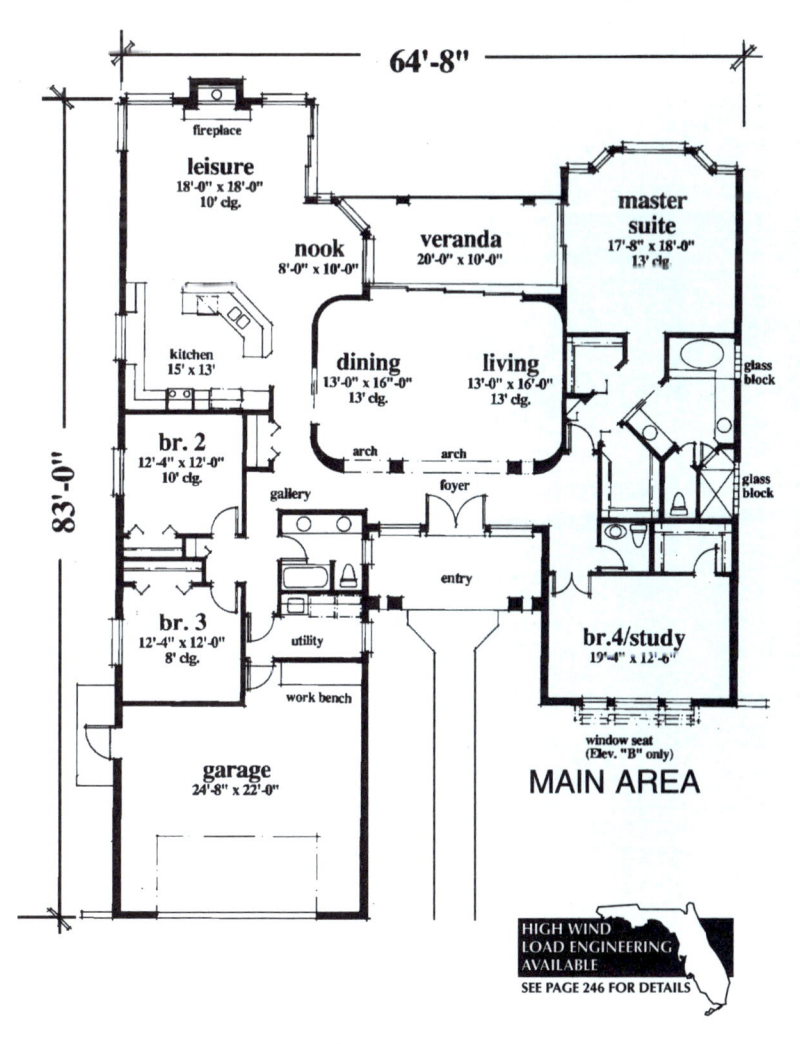

No materials list available

DESIGN NO. 94602

PRICE CODE B

Quoins and Arch Window Accents

No. 94602

- This plan features:
- — Three bedrooms
- — Two full bathrooms
- Sheltered entry leads into pillared Foyer defining Living and Dining room areas
- A cozy fireplace and access to Covered Porch featured in Living Room
- Efficient Kitchen offers a work island and bright Breakfast area
- Master Bedroom wing enhanced by a luxurious bath with a walk-in closet, double vanity and spa tub
- An optional crawl space or slab foundation — please specify when ordering

Main area —1,704 sq. ft.

Total living area: 1,704 sq. ft.

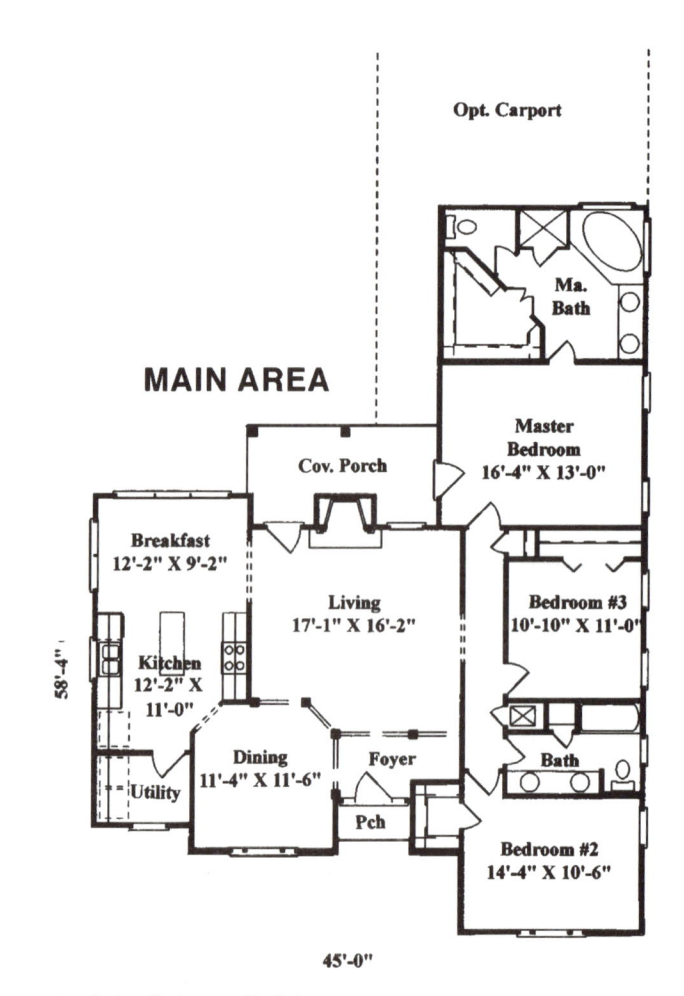

No materials list available

222

DESIGN NO. 93213

PRICE CODE C

Imposing and Practical Design

No. 93213

- This plan features:
— Three bedrooms
— Two full and one half baths
- Two-story keystone entrance with sidelights leads into Foyer
- Bay windows illuminate formal Dining and Living Rooms elegantly
- Expansive Family Room with cozy fireplace and a wall of windows with access to Patio
- Efficient, U-shaped Kitchen convenient to both formal and informal dining areas
- Private Master Bedroom crowned by decorative ceiling, features two vanities and garden tub bath
- Two additional bedrooms, full bath and convenient laundry closet complete second floor
- An optional basement or slab foundation — please specify when ordering

FIRST FLOOR — 1,126 SQ. FT.
SECOND FLOOR — 959 SQ. FT
BASEMENT — 458 SQ. FT.
GARAGE — 627 SQ. FT.

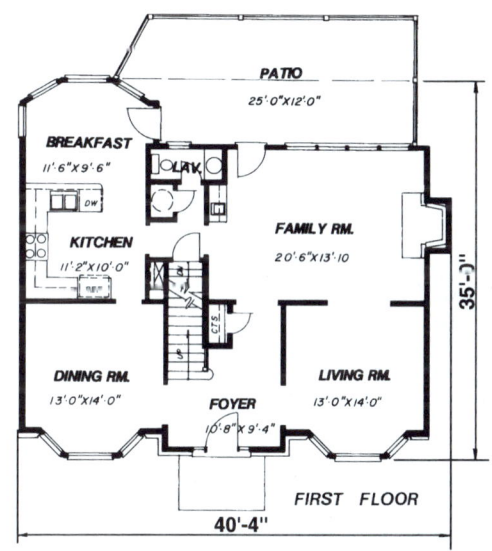

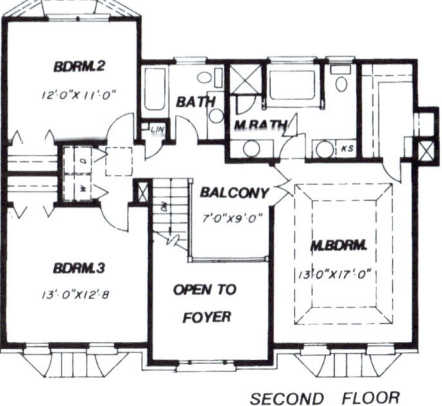

TOTAL LIVING AREA:
2,085 SQ. FT.

No materials list available

An **EXCLUSIVE DESIGN**
By Jannis Vann & Associates, Inc.

DESIGN NO. 93262

PRICE CODE B

ATTENTION TO DETAILS

No. 93262

- This plan features:
— Three bedrooms
— Two full baths
- Beautiful detailing around the windows and the doors, adding to its curb appeal
- A large Living Room with a focal point fireplace in the center of the outside wall, and direct access to the rear yard
- A Master Suite located at the opposite end of the house from the secondary bedrooms, insuring privacy
- A decorative ceiling in the Master Bedroom and a private Master Bath and walk-in closet
- An optional Slab Crawlspace foundation available — please specify when ordering

FIRST FLOOR — 1,708 SQ. FT.
GARAGE — 400 SQ. FT.

TOTAL LIVING AREA: 1,708 SQ. FT.

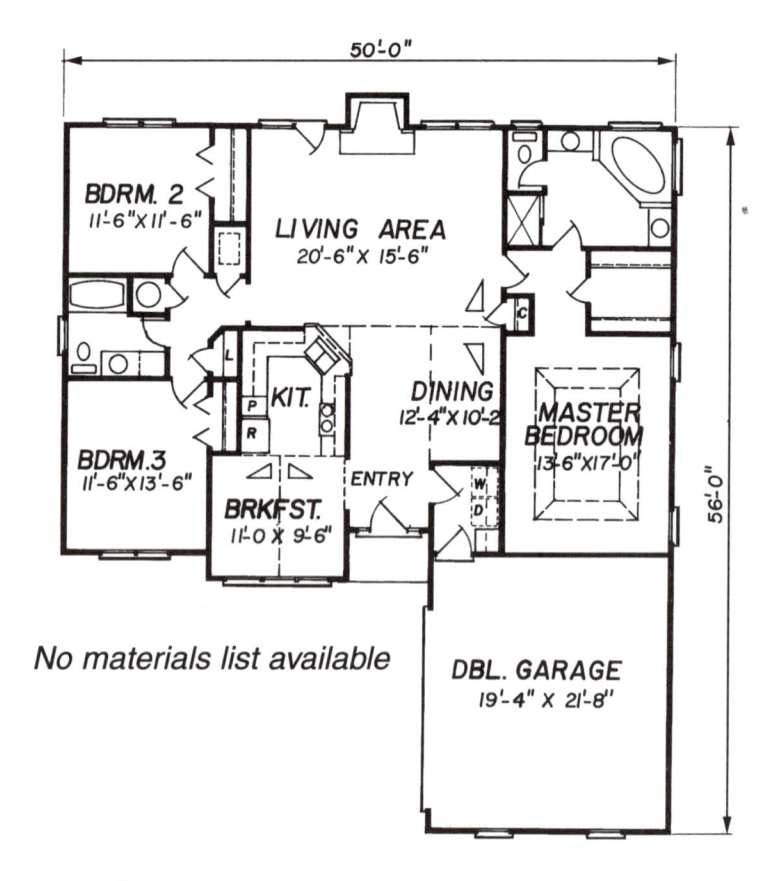

No materials list available

An EXCLUSIVE DESIGN
By Jannis Vann & Associates, Inc.

DESIGN NO. 94236

PRICE CODE D

LEISURE LIVING

HIGH WIND LOAD ENGINEERING AVAILABLE
SEE PAGE 246 FOR DETAILS

No. 94236

- This plan features:
— Three bedrooms
— Two full baths
- A raised entry with glass above the double doors warmly welcomes one and all
- Open formal Living space fronts the lanai while an octagon-shaped Dining Room with a tray ceiling views a garden area
- An arched doorway leads to an efficient Kitchen, sunlit Nook and a comfortable Leisure area with a fireplace and entertainment center
- A private Master Suite with sitting area and a plush bath
- Two additional bedrooms and a full bath
- Options for a fourth bedroom and an outdoor bath area

MAIN FLOOR — 2,282 SQ. FT.
GARAGE — 628 SQ. FT.

TOTAL LIVING AREA: 2,282 SQ. FT.

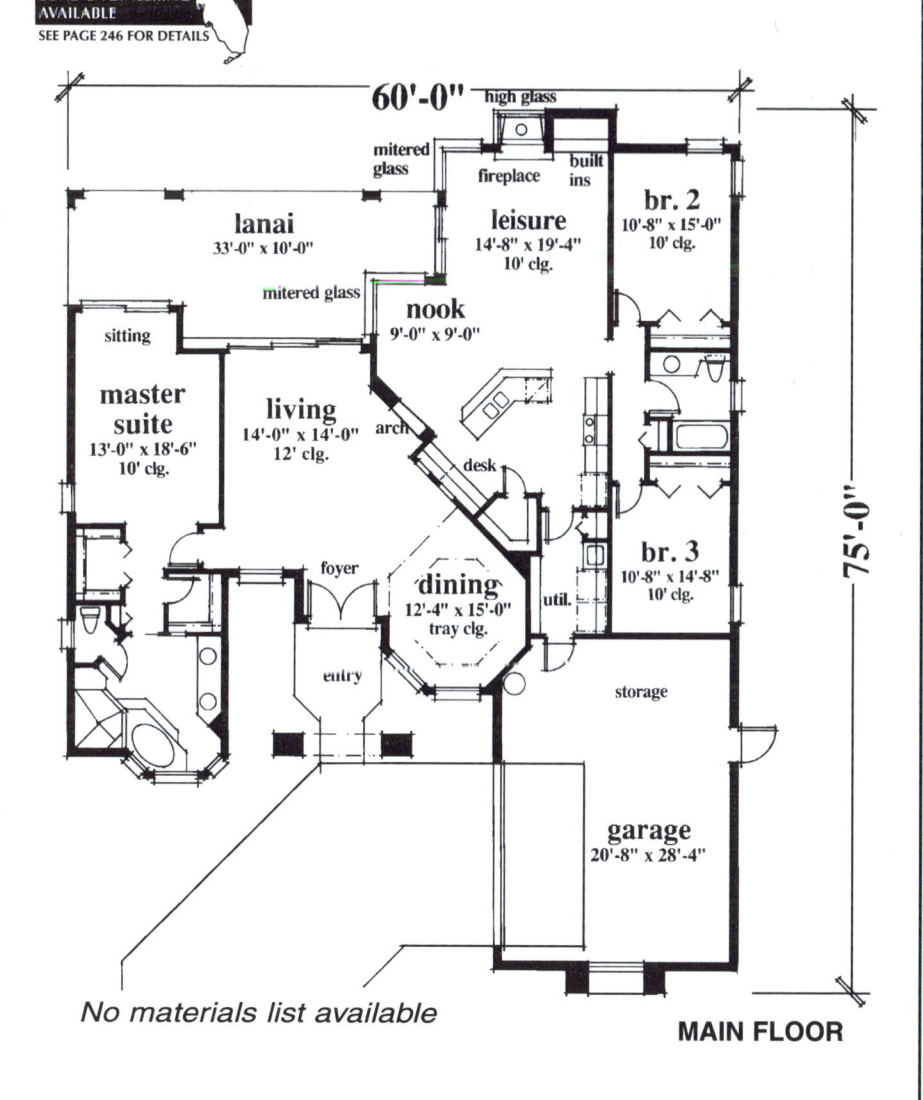

Floor plan dimensions

60'-0" wide × 75'-0" deep

- lanai 33'-0" x 10'-0"
- leisure 14'-8" x 19'-4" 10' clg.
- br. 2 10'-8" x 15'-0" 10' clg.
- nook 9'-0" x 9'-0"
- master suite 13'-0" x 18'-6" 10' clg.
- living 14'-0" x 14'-0" 12' clg.
- br. 3 10'-8" x 14'-8" 10' clg.
- dining 12'-4" x 15'-0" tray clg.
- garage 20'-8" x 28'-4"

No materials list available

MAIN FLOOR

DESIGN NO. 94224

PRICE CODE F

CASCADING ARCHES ADD ELEGANCE

No. 94224

- This plan features:
— Three bedrooms
— Two full and three quarter baths
- Raised entry welcomes guests in
- Cascading arches frame Foyer, Dining Room ceiling and Living Room fireplace
- Spacious Kitchen with walk-in pantry, efficient work island and peninsula counter serves eating Nook with skylit atrium, and Dining Room easily
- Expansive Leisure Room with a built-in entertainment center, wet bar and access to Lanai
- Master Suite enhanced by a sitting area, access to Lanai, cascading arches, two walk-in closets and a plush bath
- Two additional bedrooms with walk-in closets and access to a full bath

MAIN FLOOR — 4,028 SQ. FT.
GARAGE — 660 SQ. FT.

TOTAL LIVING AREA: 4,028 SQ. FT.

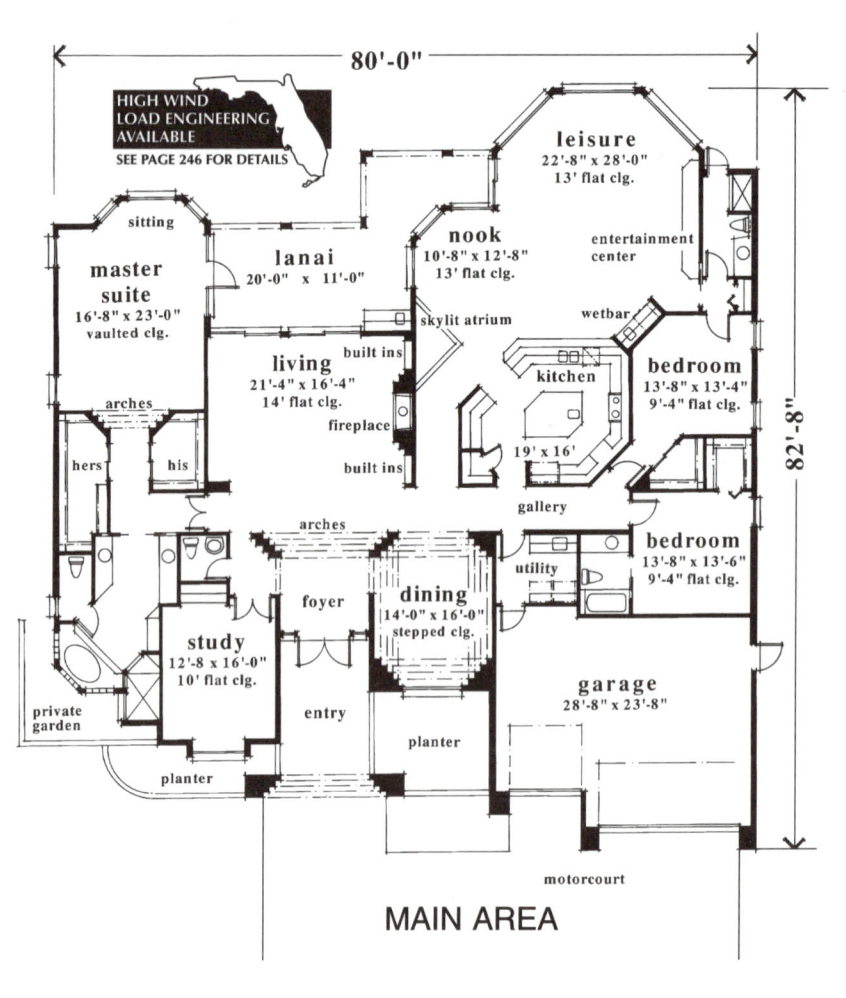

MAIN AREA

- master suite 16'-8" x 23'-0" vaulted clg.
- sitting
- lanai 20'-0" x 11'-0"
- nook 10'-8" x 12'-8" 13' flat clg.
- leisure 22'-8" x 28'-0" 13' flat clg.
- entertainment center
- living 21'-4" x 16'-4" 14' flat clg.
- skylit atrium
- wetbar
- kitchen 19' x 16'
- bedroom 13'-8" x 13'-4" 9'-4" flat clg.
- hers / his
- arches
- fireplace
- built ins
- gallery
- bedroom 13'-8" x 13'-6" 9'-4" flat clg.
- study 12'-8" x 16'-0" 10' flat clg.
- foyer
- arches
- utility
- dining 14'-0" x 16'-0" stepped clg.
- garage 28'-8" x 23'-8"
- private garden
- planter
- entry
- planter
- motorcourt

80'-0" x 82'-8"

HIGH WIND LOAD ENGINEERING AVAILABLE
SEE PAGE 246 FOR DETAILS

No materials list available

DESIGN NO. 94749

PRICE CODE B

SOUTHERN COASTAL STYLING

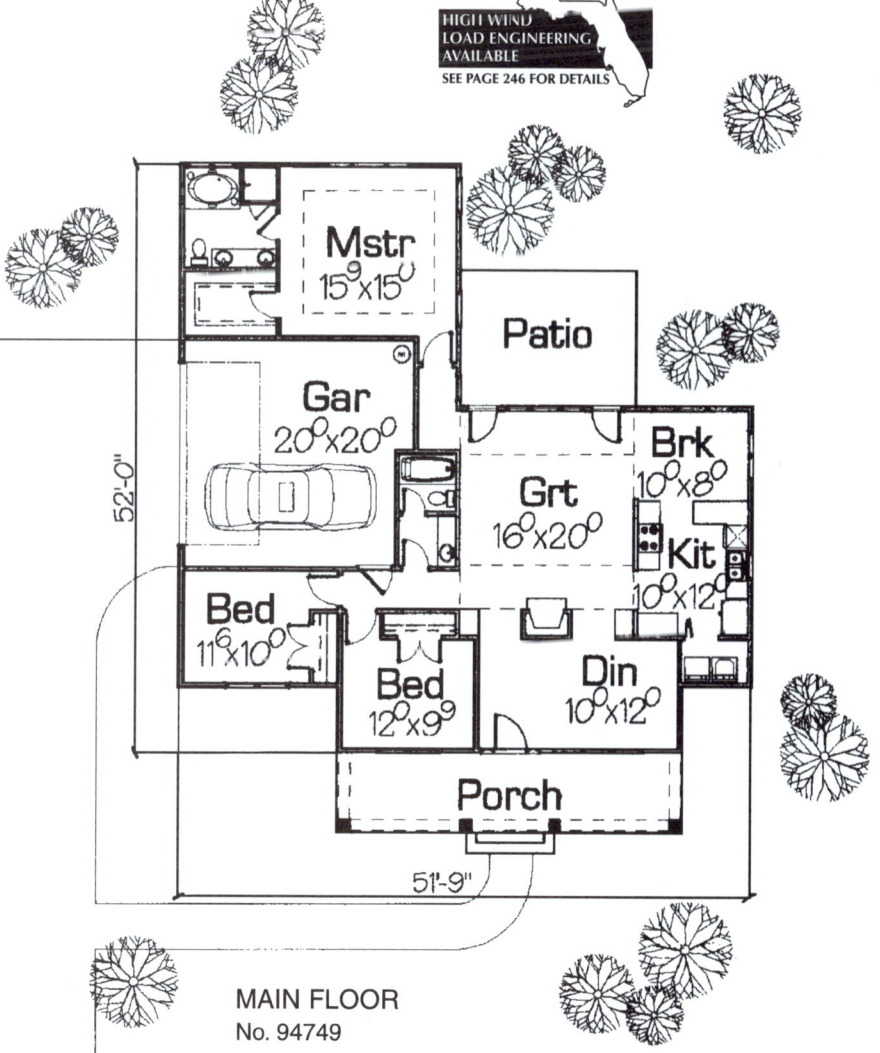

HIGH WIND LOAD ENGINEERING AVAILABLE
SEE PAGE 246 FOR DETAILS

No. 94749

■ This plan features:

— Three bedrooms

— Two full baths

■ The Great room is topped by a twelve foot vaulted ceiling and is highlighted by windows plus a fireplace

■ The Breakfast room takes advantage of a corner location which offers beautiful views of the outside

■ An efficient Kitchen with extended counter/snack bar

■ The Master suite is separated from the secondary bedrooms providing privacy

■ The L-shaped layout provides for a private patio extending from the main living areas, and complements the elegant front porch

MAIN FLOOR — 1,589 SQ. FT.
GARAGE — 410 SQ. FT.

TOTAL LIVING AREA: 1,589 SQ. FT.

An EXCLUSIVE DESIGN
By United Design Associates

MAIN FLOOR
No. 94749

DESIGN NO. 10507

PRICE CODE C

Central courtyard features pool

No. 10507

■ This plan features:

— Three bedrooms

— One full and one three quarter baths

■ A central courtyard complete with a pool

■ A secluded Master Bedroom accented by a skylight, a spacious walk-in closet, and a private bath

■ A convenient Kitchen easily serving the patio for comfortable outdoor entertaining

■ A detached two-car Garage

MAIN AREA — 2,194 SQ. FT.
GARAGE — 576 SQ. FT.

TOTAL LIVING AREA: 2,194 SQ. FT.

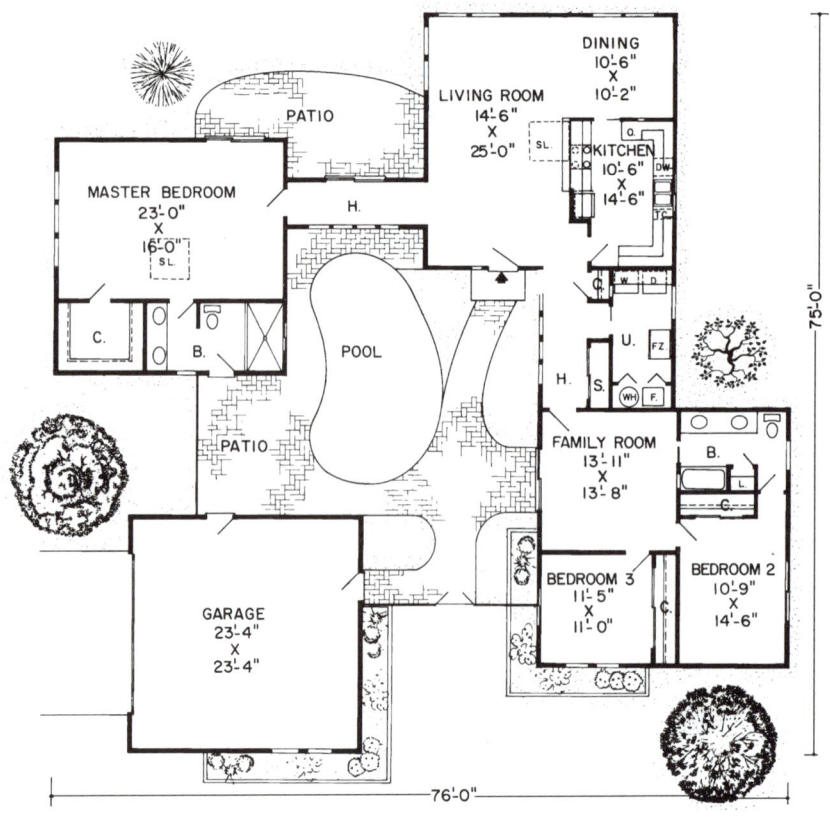

MAIN AREA

DESIGN NO. 94621

PRICE CODE E

DIGNIFIED AND DISTINGUISHED

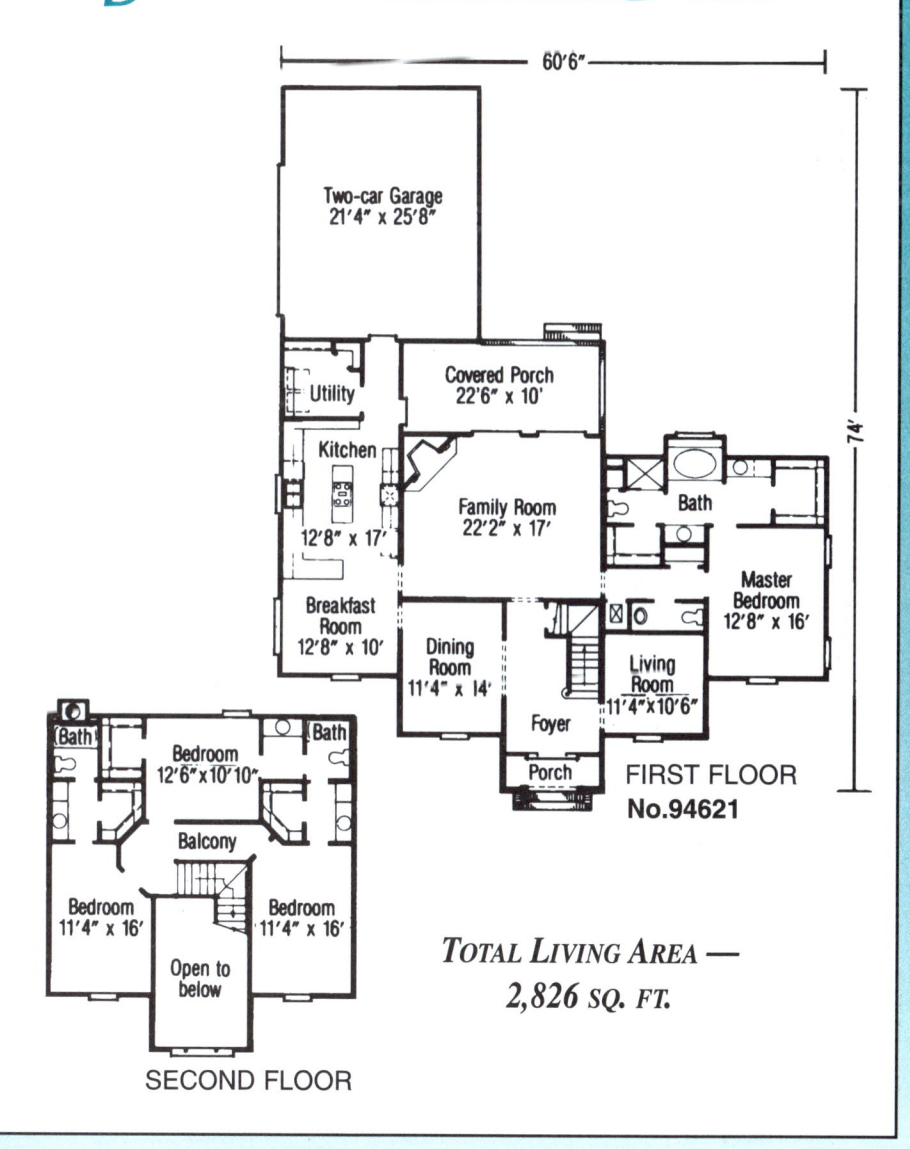

- This plan features:
— Four bedrooms
— Three full and one half baths
- The covered porch opens into a two story foyer with grand staircase
- A formal Living room and Dining room are located off the foyer
- The large Family room features a corner fireplace and access to a covered porch
- The Kitchen has an island with a cooktop and ample counter space
- A Breakfast nook is located next to the Kitchen
- The Master bedroom has it's own private bath with whirlpool tub
- Upstairs find three more bedrooms all with walk in closets and two full baths
- An optional slab or a crawl space foundation available, please specify when ordering
- No materials list is available for this plan

FIRST FLOOR — 1,904 SQ. FT
SECOND FLOOR — 922 SQ. FT
GARAGE — 572 SQ. FT

FIRST FLOOR
No. 94621

SECOND FLOOR

TOTAL LIVING AREA — 2,826 SQ. FT.

DESIGN NO. 99269

PRICE CODE D

SOUTHERN PLANTATION STYLE

No. 99269

■ This plan features:

— Three bedrooms

— Two full and one half baths

■ Imposing columns highlight elevation and entrance into central Foyer

■ Expansive Drawing Room with huge fireplace and access to Garden Terrace

■ Open Family Room with a sliding glass door to Terrace

■ Efficient Kitchen with serving counter/snackbar, Laundry and Garage entry

■ Corner Master Bedroom offers a large closet and double vanity bath with a whirlpool window tub

■ Two additional bedrooms share a double vanity bath

FIRST FLOOR — 1,507 SQ. FT.
SECOND FLOOR — 976 SQ. FT.
GARAGE — 454 SQ. FT.

TOTAL LIVING AREA: 2,483 SQ. FT.

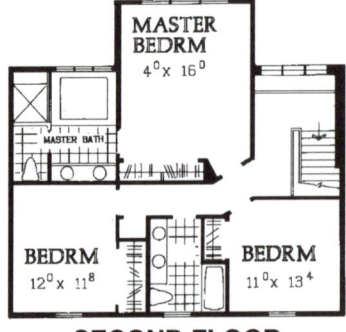

SECOND FLOOR

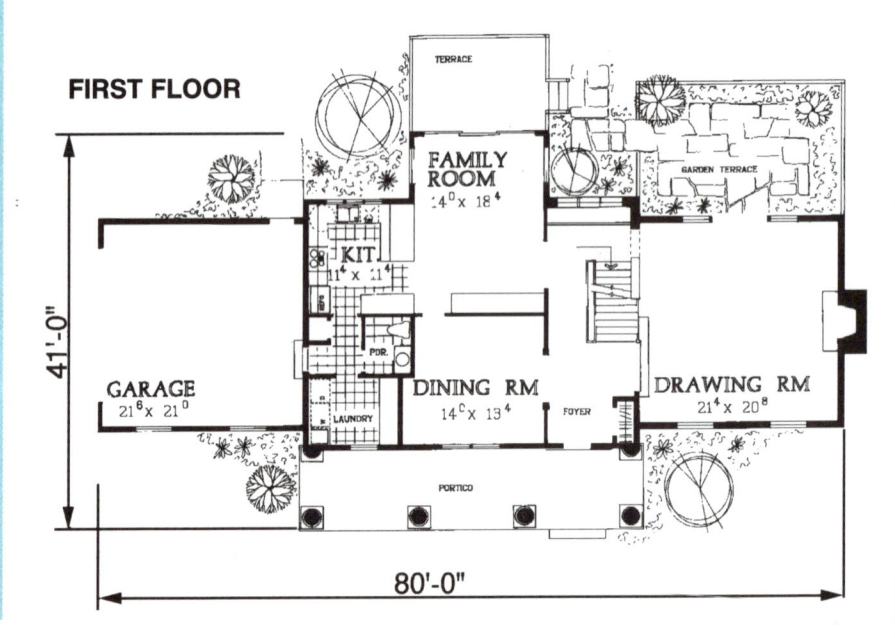

- MASTER BEDRM 4'0" x 16'0"
- BEDRM 12'0" x 11'8"
- BEDRM 11'0" x 13'4"

FIRST FLOOR

- GARAGE 21'6" x 21'0"
- FAMILY ROOM 14'0" x 18'4"
- KIT 11'4" x 11'4"
- DINING RM 14'0" x 13'4"
- DRAWING RM 21'4" x 20'8"

41'-0" × 80'-0"

DESIGN NO. 94241

PRICE CODE F

SEPARATE GUEST SUITE

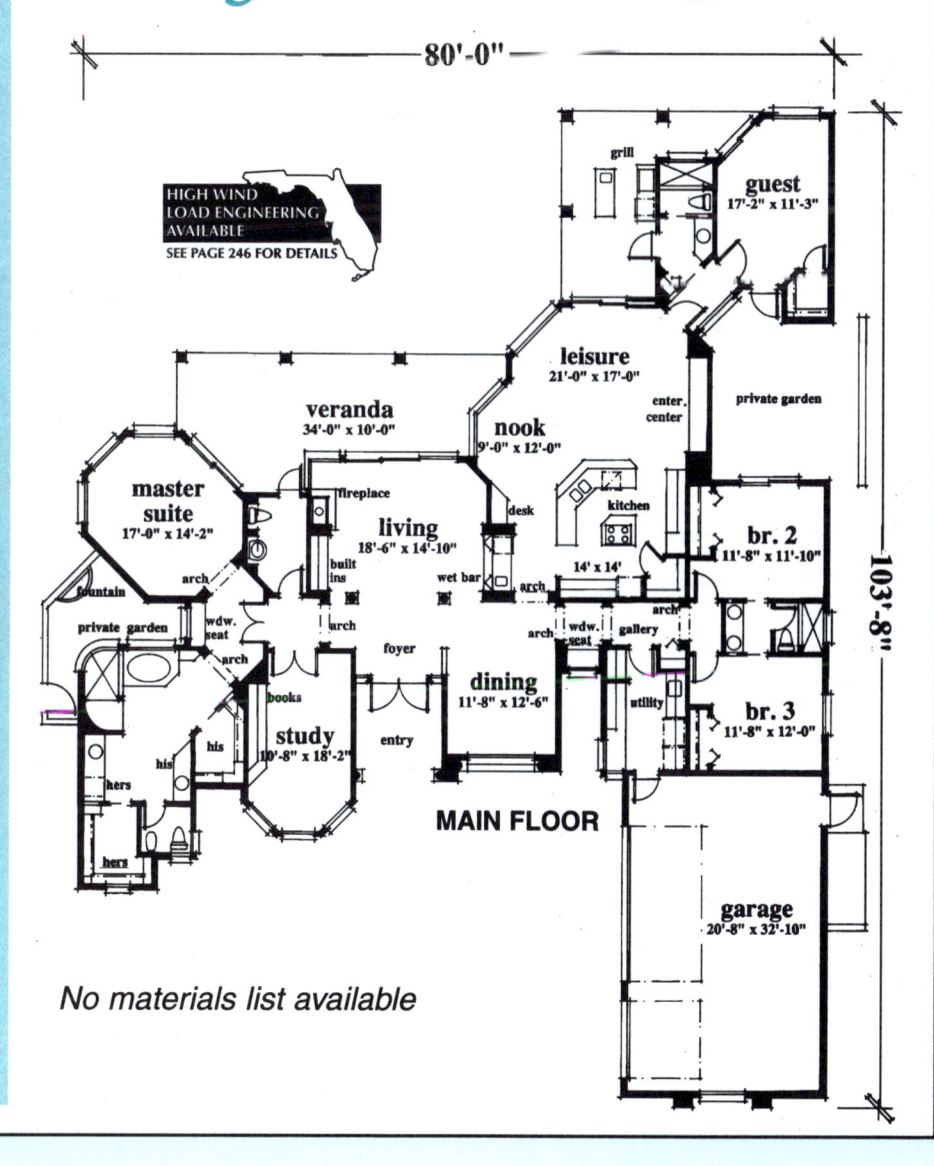

No. 94241

- This plan features:
— Four bedrooms
— Three full and one half baths
- Elegant entry with double door into Foyer and Living room accented with columns, fireplace, built-ins and glass doors to Veranda
- Open and efficient Kitchen with cooktop island, walk-in pantry, serving counter/snackbar, eating Nook and Leisure area with an entertainment center
- Private Master Suite with octagon sleeping area, private garden and lavish bath
- Guest Suite offers a full bath and access to a Private Garden and Grill Patio
- Two additional bedrooms with ample closets, have private access to a double vanity bath

MAIN FLOOR — 3,265 SQ. FT.
GARAGE — 830 SQ. FT.

TOTAL LIVING AREA: 3,265 SQ. FT.

HIGH WIND LOAD ENGINEERING AVAILABLE
SEE PAGE 246 FOR DETAILS

80'-0"
103'-8"

grill
guest 17'-2" x 11'-3"
leisure 21'-0" x 17'-0"
private garden
veranda 34'-0" x 10'-0"
nook 9'-0" x 12'-0"
enter. center
master suite 17'-0" x 14'-2"
fireplace
living 18'-6" x 14'-10"
desk
kitchen
br. 2 11'-8" x 11'-10"
built ins
wet bar
14' x 14'
private garden
fountain
arch
wdw. seat
arch
arch
wdw. seat
gallery
arch
books
foyer
dining 11'-8" x 12'-6"
utility
br. 3 11'-8" x 12'-0"
his
hers
study 10'-8" x 18'-2"
entry
garage 20'-8" x 32'-10"

MAIN FLOOR

No materials list available

DESIGN NO. 94234

PRICE CODE E

Roof Balustrade Crowns Grand Home

No. 94234

- This plan features:
— Four bedrooms
— Two full and one half baths

- Covered Entry Porch and access to Foyer and Dining Room

- Arched entrances enhance Parlor, Dining and Grand rooms, and Master Suite

- Country-size Kitchen with a work island/eating counter, large walk-in pantry and glass eating Nook

- Master Suite highlighted by bay window, his-n-hers closets, and a plush bath

- Three second floor bedrooms share a loft and full bath

- An optional basement or slab foundation — please specify when ordering

FIRST FLOOR — 2,240 SQ. FT.
SECOND FLOOR — 943 SQ. FT.

TOTAL LIVING AREA: 3,183 SQ. FT.

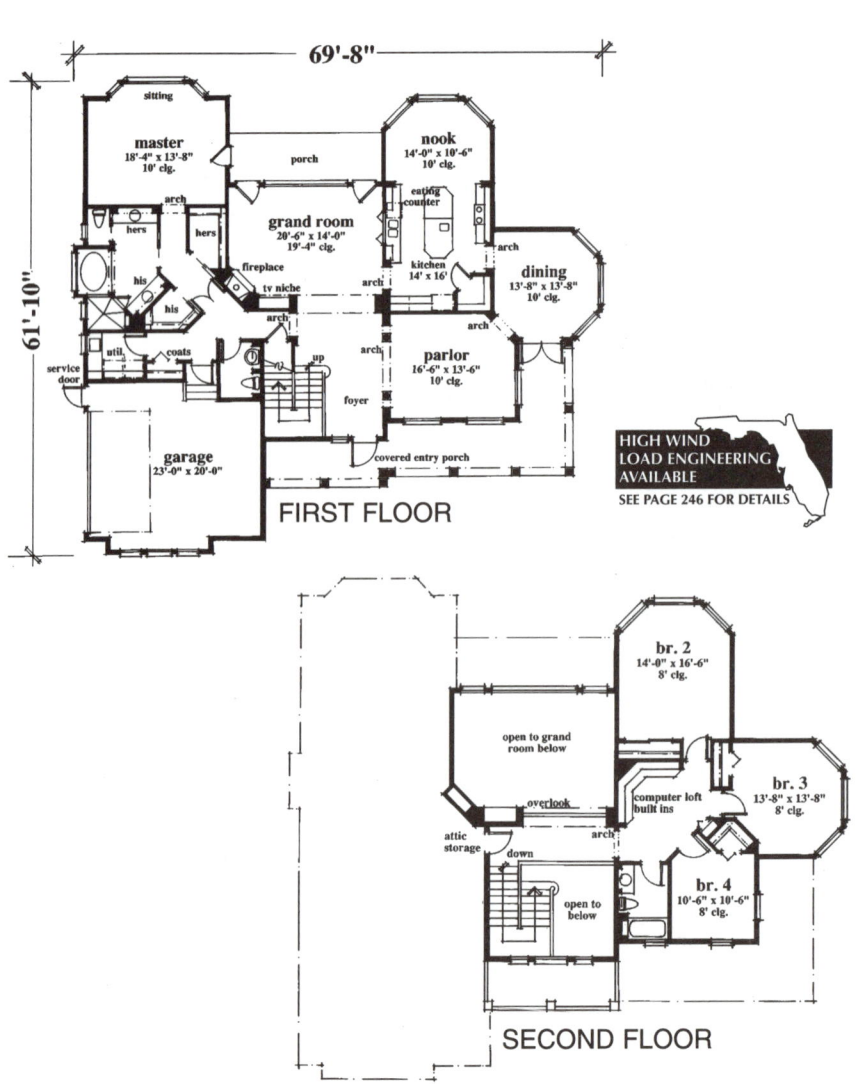

HIGH WIND LOAD ENGINEERING AVAILABLE
SEE PAGE 246 FOR DETAILS

FIRST FLOOR

SECOND FLOOR

DESIGN NO. 92534

PRICE CODE F

Elegance Enhanced by Arched Windows

No. 92534

■ This plan features:

— Four bedrooms

— Three full and one half baths

■ Impressive stucco details and multiple roof lines provide eye appeal

■ Spacious Foyer flanked by formal Living and Dining rooms

■ Large Den offers hearth fireplace, built-ins, wetbar and access to rear grounds

■ Efficient Kitchen with peninsula counter/snackbar, Breakfast bay, Garage entry, pantry and Utility Room

■ Corner Master Bedroom suite with a luxurious Master Bath and two walk-in closets

■ An optional crawl space or slab foundtion available, please specify when ordering

FIRST FLOOR — 2,380 SQ. FT.
SECOND FLOOR — 1,504 SQ. FT.
GARAGE — 806 SQ. FT.

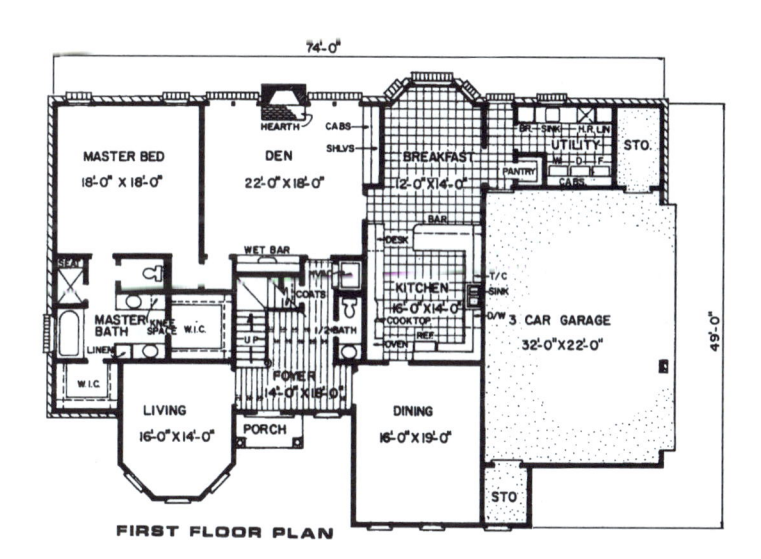

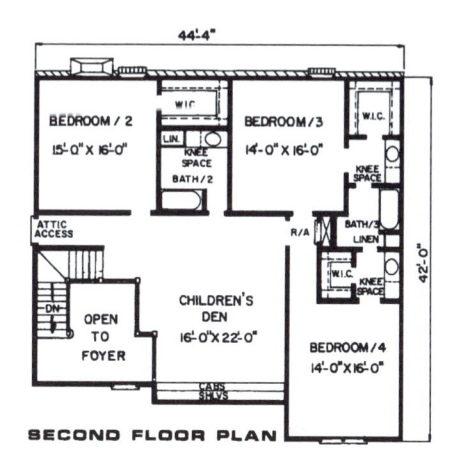

TOTAL LIVING AREA: 3,884 SQ. FT.

TOWERING WINDOWS ENHANCE ELEGANCE
DESIGN NO. 93034

- This plan features:
  — Four bedrooms
  — Three full baths
- Designed for a corner or pie-shaped lot
- Spectacular split staircase highlights Foyer
- Expansive Great Room with hearth fireplace opens to formal Dining Room and Patio
- Quiet Study easily another bedroom or home office
- Secluded Master Bedroom suite offers private Porch, two walk-in closets and vanities, and a corner whirlpool tub
- Three second floor bedrooms with walk-in closets, share a balcony and double-vanity bath

FIRST FLOOR — 1,966 SQ. FT.
SECOND FLOOR — 872 SQ. FT.
GARAGE — 569 SQ. FT.

TOTAL LIVING AREA: 2,838 SQ. FT.

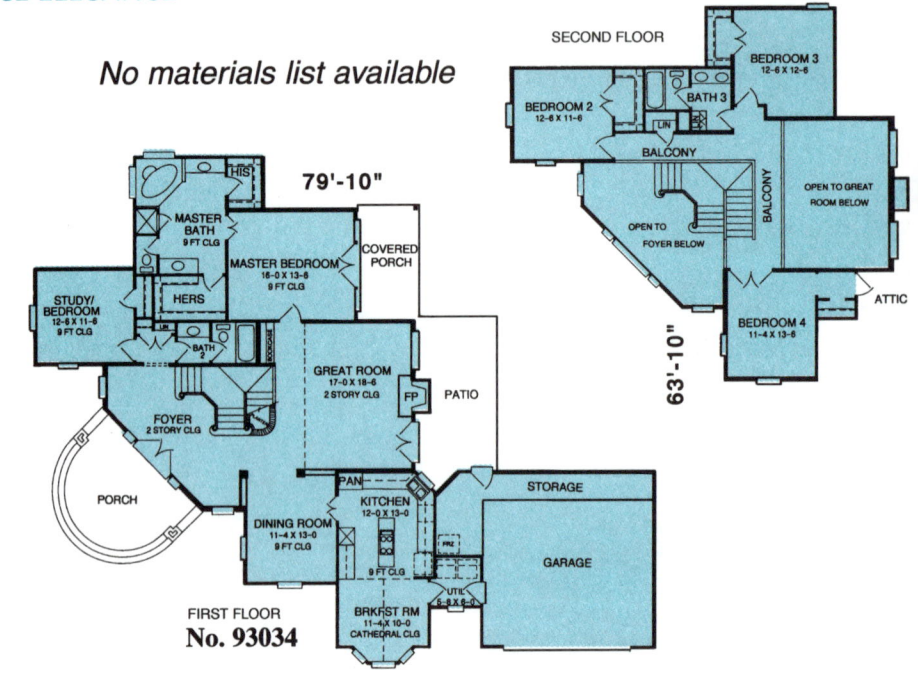

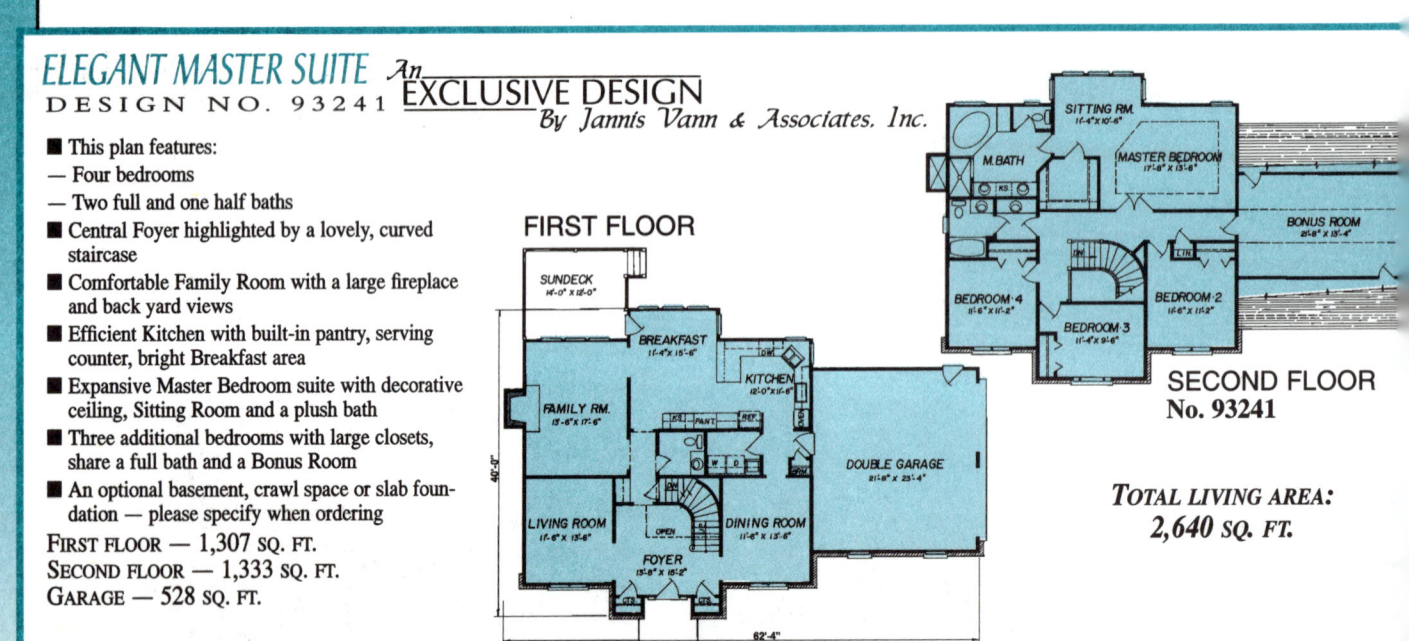

No materials list available

PRICE CODE E

ELEGANT MASTER SUITE
DESIGN NO. 93241

An EXCLUSIVE DESIGN *By Jannis Vann & Associates, Inc.*

- This plan features:
  — Four bedrooms
  — Two full and one half baths
- Central Foyer highlighted by a lovely, curved staircase
- Comfortable Family Room with a large fireplace and back yard views
- Efficient Kitchen with built-in pantry, serving counter, bright Breakfast area
- Expansive Master Bedroom suite with decorative ceiling, Sitting Room and a plush bath
- Three additional bedrooms with large closets, share a full bath and a Bonus Room
- An optional basement, crawl space or slab foundation — please specify when ordering

FIRST FLOOR — 1,307 SQ. FT.
SECOND FLOOR — 1,333 SQ. FT.
GARAGE — 528 SQ. FT.

TOTAL LIVING AREA: 2,640 SQ. FT.

PRICE CODE A

FOR FIRST TIME BUYERS
DESIGN NO. 93048

- This plan features:
  — Three bedrooms
  — Two full baths
- An efficiently designed Kitchen with a corner sink, ample counter space and a peninsula counter
- A sunny Breakfast Room with a convenient hide-away laundry center
- An expansive Family Room that includes a corner fireplace and direct access to the Patio
- A private Master Suite with a walk-in closet and a double vanity Bath
- Two additional bedrooms, both with walk-in closets, that share a full hall bath

MAIN AREAD — 1,310 SQ. FT.
GARAGE — 449 SQ. FT.

TOTAL LIVING AREA:
1,310 SQ. FT.

No materials list available

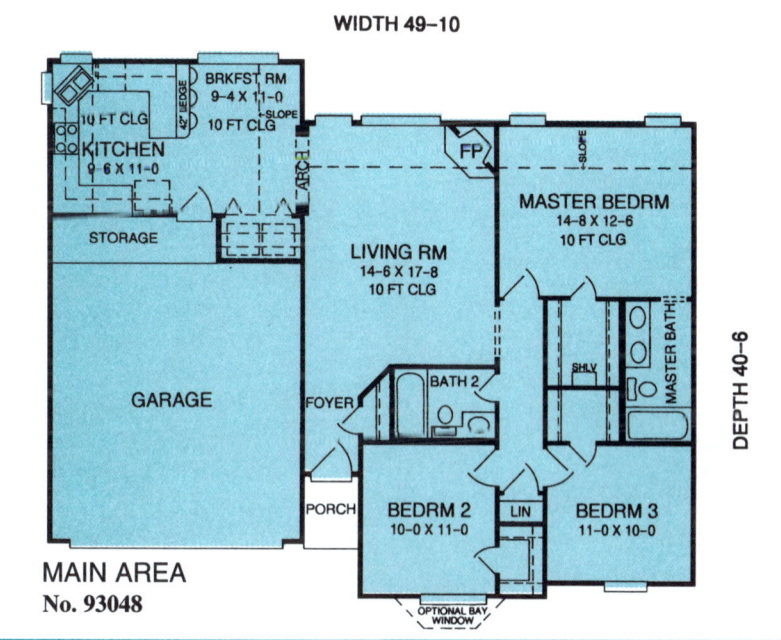

MAIN AREA
No. 93048

WIDTH 49-10
DEPTH 40-6

PRICE CODE E

STUCCO OPULENCE
DESIGN NO. 93270

- This plan features:
  — Four bedrooms
  — Three full (plus one future) and two half baths
- A fantastic two-story Living Room that includes a fireplace
- An expansive Kitchen with a cooktop island/snack bar and Breakfast Nook, as well as a Keeping Room
- A private sitting area, luxuriant Master Bath, as well as his-and-her walk-in closets in the Master Suite
- A Library located across from the Master Suite, convenient for working late nights at home
- Three additional bedrooms on the second floor that have easy access to full hall baths

FIRST FLOOR — 2,329 SQ. FT.
SECOND FLOOR — 1,259 SQ. FT.
FINISHED STAIRCASE — 68 SQ. FT.
BASEMENT — 1,806 SQ. FT.
GARAGE — 528 SQ. FT.

TOTAL LIVING AREA: 3,656 SQ. FT.

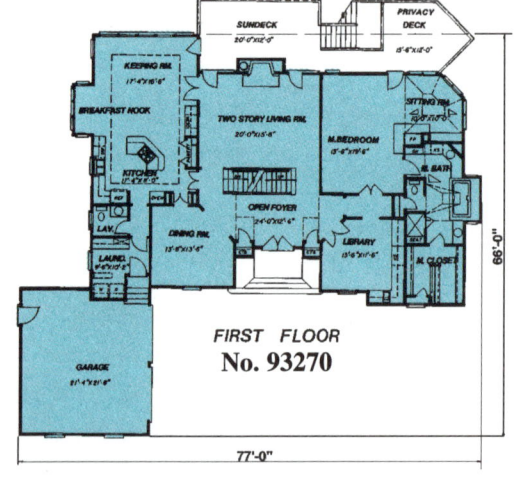

An **EXCLUSIVE DESIGN** *By Jannis Vann & Associates, Inc.*

No materials list available

PRICE CODE F

FOCAL POINT WINDOW HIGHLIGHTS BALCONY
DESIGN NO. 93215

- This plan features:
  — Three or four bedrooms
  — Two full and one half baths
- Open Living Dining Room provides easy entertaining
- Efficient, U-shaped Kitchen with built-in pantry, peninsula counter and bright Breakfast area
- Comfortable Family Room with focal point fireplace and access to Sundeck/Patio
- Master Bedroom with walk-in closet and private bath
- Two additional bedrooms with ample closets share a full bath
- An optional basement, crawl space or slab foundation — please specify when ordering

FIRST FLOOR — 949 SQ. FT.
SECOND FLOOR — 1,038 SQ. FT.
BONUS ROOM — 232 SQ. FT.
BASEMENT — 949 SQ. FT.
GARAGE — 484 SQ. FT.

TOTAL LIVING AREA: 1,987 SQ. FT.

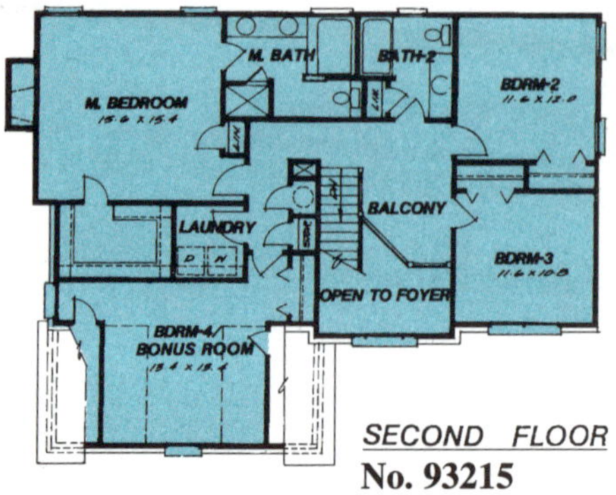

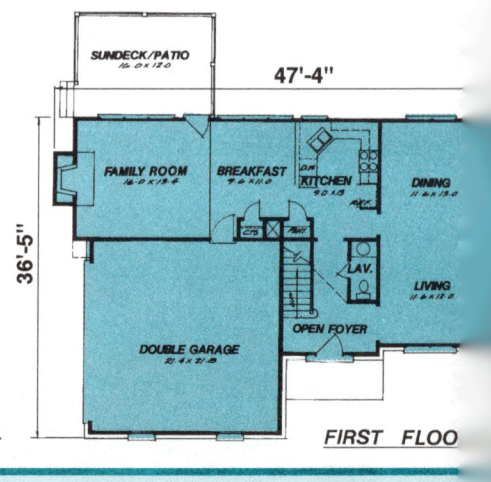

An **EXCLUSIVE DESIGN** *By Jannis Vann & Associates, Inc.*

PRICE CODE D

TWO-STORY FOYER ADDS TO ELEGANCE

DESIGN NO. 93240

- This plan features:
— Four bedrooms
— Two full and one half baths
- Formal Dining and Living Rooms to either side of the Foyer
- Family Room enhanced by fireplace and access to Sundeck
- Country-sized Kitchen with bright Breakfast area, adjoins Dining Room and Utility/Garage entry
- French doors lead into plush Master Bedroom with decorative ceiling and large Master Bath
- Three additional bedrooms with ample closets share a full bath and Bonus Room
- An optional basement, crawl space or slab foundation — please specify when ordering

First floor — 1,277 sq. ft.
Second floor — 1,177 sq. ft.
Bonus room — 392 sq. ft.
Basement — 1,261 sq. ft.
Garage — 572 sq. ft.

Total living area: 2,454 sq. ft.

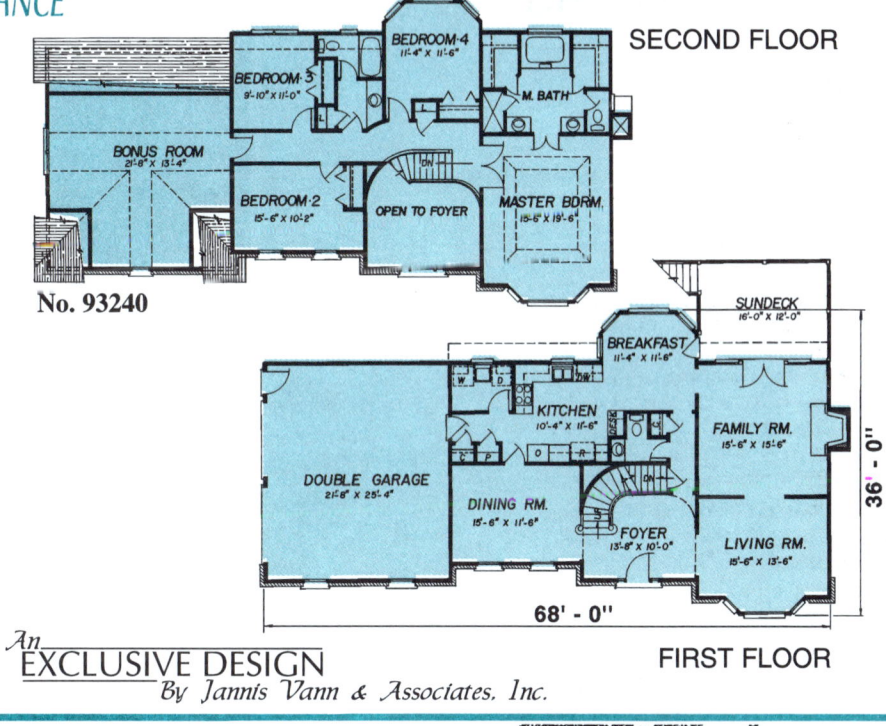

An **EXCLUSIVE DESIGN** *By Jannis Vann & Associates, Inc.*

SECOND FLOOR

No. 93240

FIRST FLOOR

PRICE CODE C

EXPANSIVE REAR VIEWS
DESIGN NO. 93054

■ This plan features:
— Four bedrooms
— Three full and one half baths
■ Impressive arched entrance leads into two-story Foyer and graceful landing staircase
■ Arches define entry into Living, Dining and Keeping rooms and frame expansive views of back yard
■ Hub Kitchen offers walk-in pantry, Utility area, Garage entry, bright Breakfast Room and a large serving counter
■ A vaulted ceiling crowns a wall of windows in Master Bedroom and a coffered ceiling tops the lavish Master Bath
■ Three additional bedrooms, one with a private bath, have over-sized closets

FIRST FLOOR — 1,421 SQ. FT.
SECOND FLOOR — 1,446 SQ. FT.
GARAGE — 510 SQ. FT.

TOTAL LIVING AREA: 2,867 SQ. FT.

PRICE CODE E

RIGHT READING REVERSE available for this plan

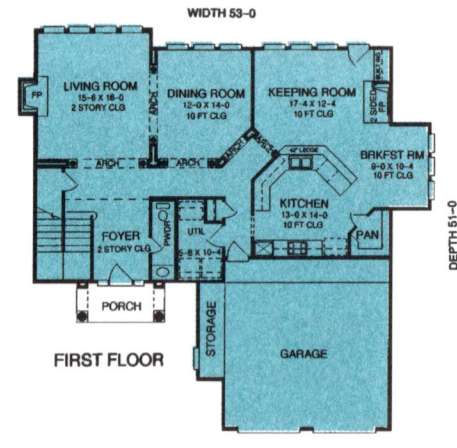

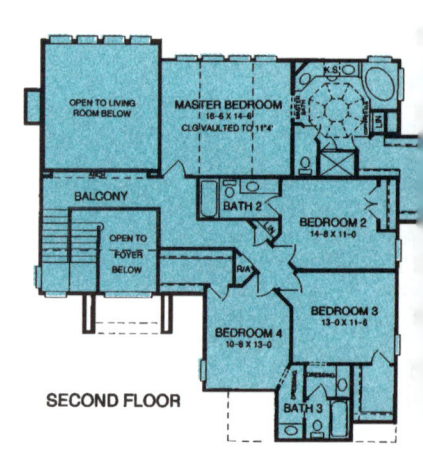

No materials list available

FRENCH FLAVOR ADDS STYLE
DESIGN NO. 94616

■ This plan features:
— Five bedrooms
— Three full baths
■ Wrap-around front Porch provides comfortable outdoor living
■ Central Foyer flanked by formal Living and Dining rooms
■ Efficient, U-shaped Kitchen with cooktop island, peninsula counter serving Breakfast area, Utility room and Garage entry
■ An optional Slab or Crawl space foundation— Please specify when ordering

FIRST FLOOR — 2,135 SQ. FT.
SECOND FLOOR — 538 SQ. FT.
UNFINISHED PLAYROOM — 225 SQ. FT.
GARAGE — 436 SQ. FT.

TOTAL LIVING AREA: 2,673 SQ. FT.

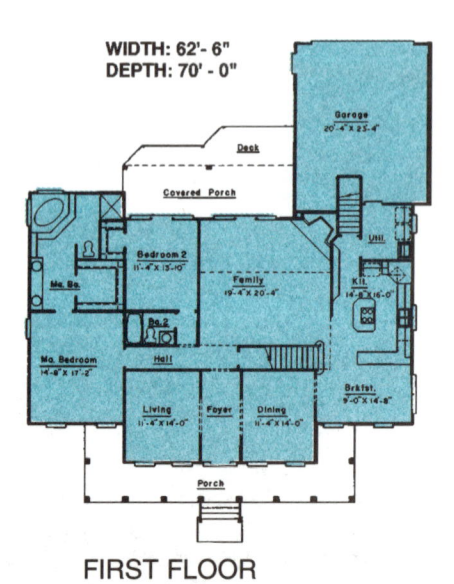

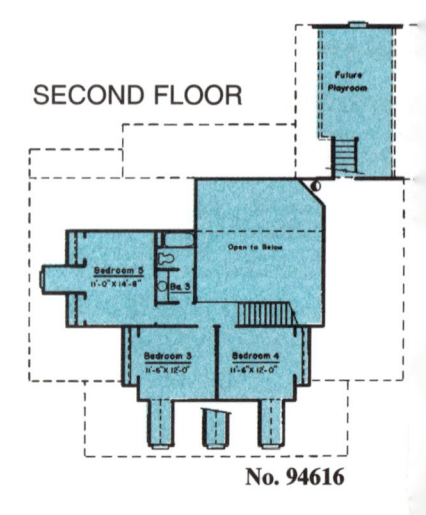

No materials list available

SOUTHERN COUNTRY FLAIR
DESIGN NO. 94619

This plan features:
- Four bedrooms
- Two full baths
- Great wrap-around front Porch leads into the central Foyer and a formal Dining room
- Spacious Family Room with a tray ceiling topping the corner fireplace and access to the Covered Porch
- Efficient, country Kitchen with a peninsula counter/eating bar, a glass Breakfast area and a nearby Utility room
- Master Bedroom suite with a decorative ceiling and a lavish Master Bath with two vanities and walk-in closets and an atrium tub
- Three additional bedrooms share a double vanity bath
- An optional Slab or Crawl space foundation— Please specify when ordering

MAIN FLOOR — 2,355 SQ. FT.
GARAGE — 553 SQ. FT.

TOTAL LIVING AREA:
2,355 SQ. FT.

No materials list available

MAIN FLOOR
No. 94619

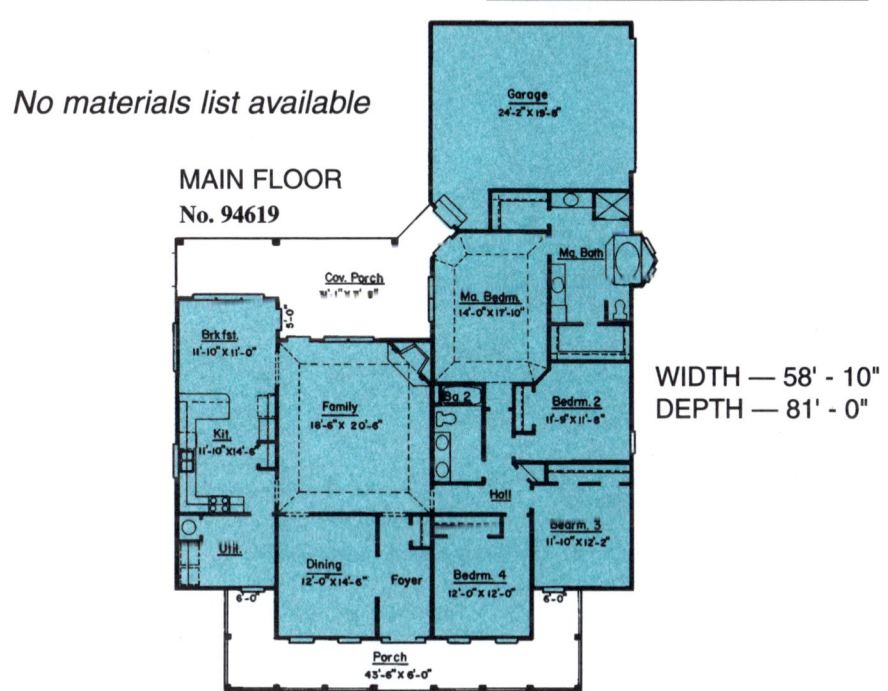

WIDTH — 58' - 10"
DEPTH — 81' - 0"

PRICE CODE D

PRICE CODE E

CLASSIC AMERICAN DESIGN
DESIGN NO. 94708

- This plan features:
  — Four bedrooms
  — Three full and one half baths
- Pillar entry leads into Foyer and Living Room, enhanced by a cozy fireplace
- Bright, spacious Family Room opens to Living and Dining rooms
- Formal Dining Room highlighted by curved window
- Hub Kitchen with Breakfast area, Deck and Garage access and Dining Room serving counter
- Cozy fireplace, lavish bath and large walk-in closet enhance the Master Suite
- Three additional bedrooms with ample closets and easy access to full baths

FIRST FLOOR — 1,089 SQ. FT.
SECOND FLOOR — 1,367 SQ. FT.
GARAGE — 543 SQ. FT.

TOTAL LIVING AREA: 2,456 SQ. FT.

FIRST FLOOR

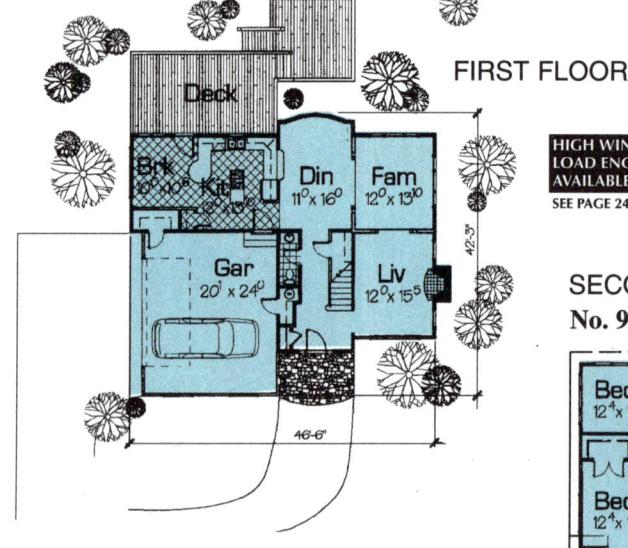

SECOND FLOOR
No. 94708

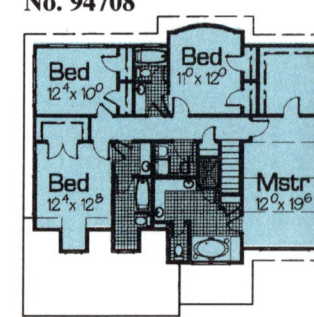

An EXCLUSIVE DESIGN *By United Design Associates*

AT HOME OFFICE OPTION
DESIGN NO. 94711

- This plan features:
  — Three or four bedrooms
  — Three full baths
- Sheltered entrance leads into an open Foyer, Dining and Great Room with cozy fireplace
- Quiet corner Living Room highlighted by decorative windows
- Hub Kitchen with work island, serving counter, Breakfast bay and access to Porch, Dining area, Laundry and Garage
- Corner Master suite enhanced by decorative ceiling, a huge walk-in closet and plush bath
- An optional crawl space or slab foundation — please specify when ordering

MAIN FLOOR — 2,378 SQ. FT.
GARAGE — 539 SQ. FT.

TOTAL LIVING AREA: 2,378 SQ. FT.

MAIN AREA

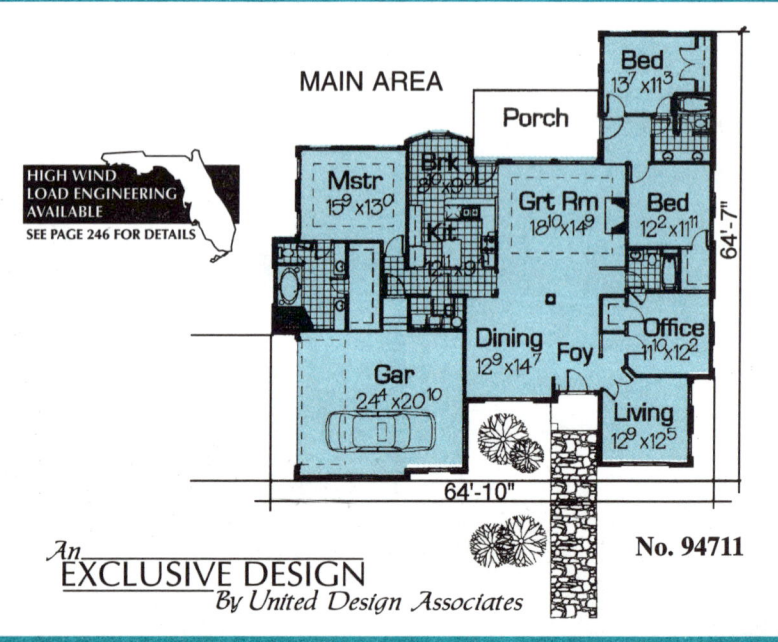

No. 94711

An EXCLUSIVE DESIGN *By United Design Associates*

PRICE CODE C

ONE-STORY HOME BRIMMING WITH AMENITIES

DESIGN NO. 94805

- This plan features:
— Three bedrooms
— Two full baths
- Pleasant country look with double dormer windows and wrap-around Porch
- Foyer opens to Dining Room and Activity Room enhanced by tray ceiling, corner fireplace and Sun Deck access
- Kitchen/Breakfast Room topped by a sloped ceiling, offers an angular serving counter and lots of storage space
- Secluded Master Bedroom graced with twin walk-in closets and a garden tub bath
- Two additional bedrooms with easy access to full bath

MAIN AREA — 2,079 SQ. FT.
BASEMENT — 2,079 SQ. FT.
GARAGE — 438 SQ. FT.

TOTAL LIVING AREA: 2,079 SQ. FT.

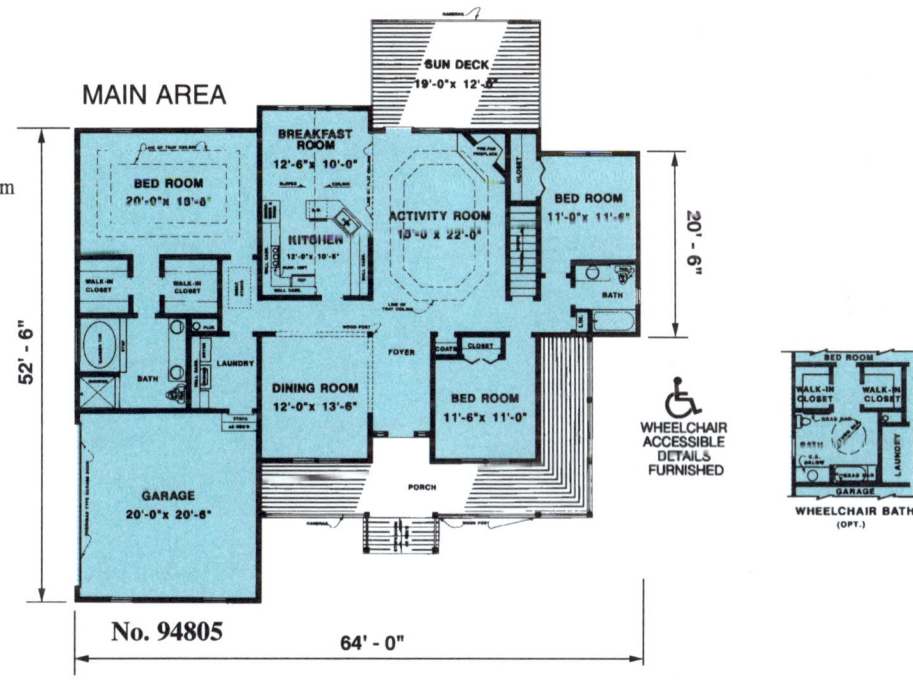

MAIN AREA

WHEELCHAIR ACCESSIBLE DETAILS FURNISHED

WHEELCHAIR BATH (OPT.)

No. 94805 64' - 0" 52' - 6"

PRICE CODE D

TRADITIONAL BRICK
DESIGN NO. 94706

- This plan features:
  — Four bedrooms
  — Three full and one half baths
- Front Foyer opens to Library and Dining Room highlighted by decorative windows
- Great Room with focal point fireplace opens to Solarium and Deck
- Efficient Kitchen with work island and serving counter for bright Breakfast area
- Corner Master suite offers a tray ceiling and plush bath with two vanities
- An optional full basement or 1/2 basement, 1/2 crawl space combination foundation — please specify when ordering

FIRST FLOOR — 2,586 SQ. FT.
SECOND FLOOR — 584 SQ. FT.
LOWER FLOOR — 805 SQ. FT.
GARAGE — 450 SQ. FT.

TOTAL LIVING AREA: 3,975 SQ. FT.

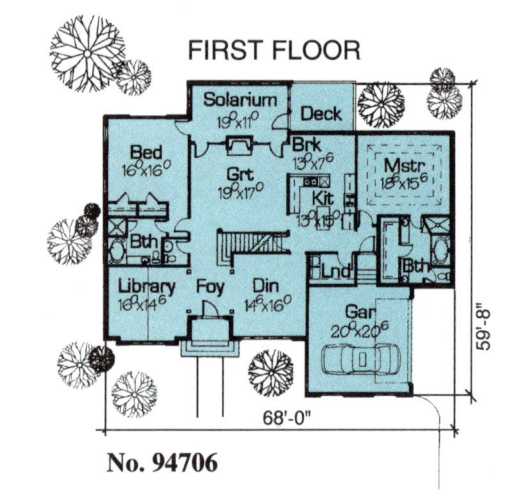

No. 94706

HIGH WIND LOAD ENGINEERING AVAILABLE
SEE PAGE 246 FOR DETAILS

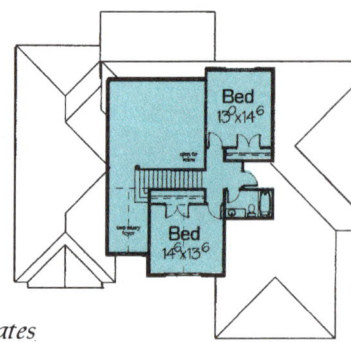

An EXCLUSIVE DESIGN *By United Design Associates*

PRICE CODE F

APPEALING ARCHES
DESIGN NO. 94620

- This plan features:
  — Four bedrooms
  — Three full baths
- Porch shades triple French door highlighting Foyer, Living and Dining rooms
- Expansive Family Room with focal point fireplace and French doors to Covered Porch
- Efficient, U-shaped Kitchen with work island
- Private Master Bedroom offers a pampering bath with two walk-in closets, a double vanity and garden window tub
- An optional crawl space or slab foundation — please specify when ordering

FIRST FLOOR — 2,159 SQ. FT.
SECOND FLOOR — 710 SQ. FT.
GARAGE — 475 SQ. FT.

TOTAL LIVING AREA: 2,869 SQ. FT.

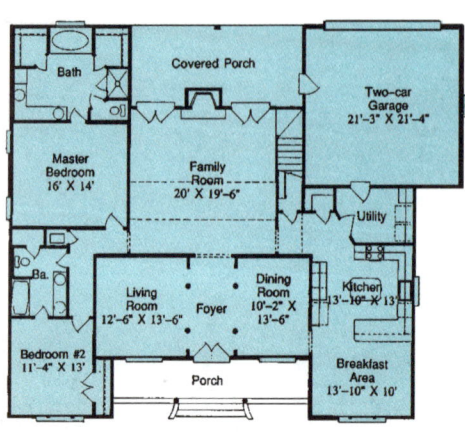

No. 94620

No materials list available

WIDTH 62'-4"
DEPTH 53'-0"

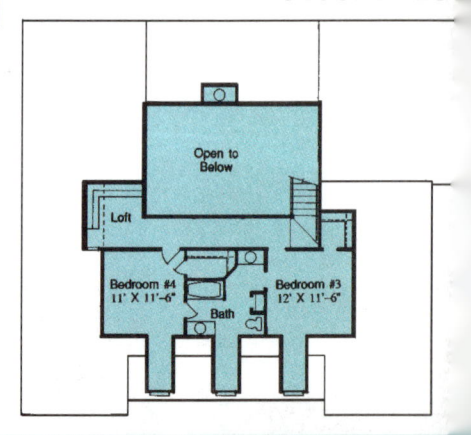

PRICE CODE C

LOTS OF LIGHT CAPTURED BY HIGH CEILINGS
DESIGN NO. 94712

- This plan features:
  — Three bedrooms
  — Two full baths
- Arched entrance leads into grand Great Room, with windows filling a fifteen foot ceiling above a two-way fireplace, separating the Dining area
- Efficient Kitchen with a work island, serving counter, bright Breakfast area and access to Deck, Laundry and Garage
- Private Master Bedroom enhanced by windows filling thirteen foot high ceiling, and double vanity bath
- Two additional bedrooms with large closets, share a full bath

MAIN AREA — 2,069 SQ. FT.
GARAGE — 417 SQ. FT.

**TOTAL LIVING AREA:
2,069 SQ. FT.**

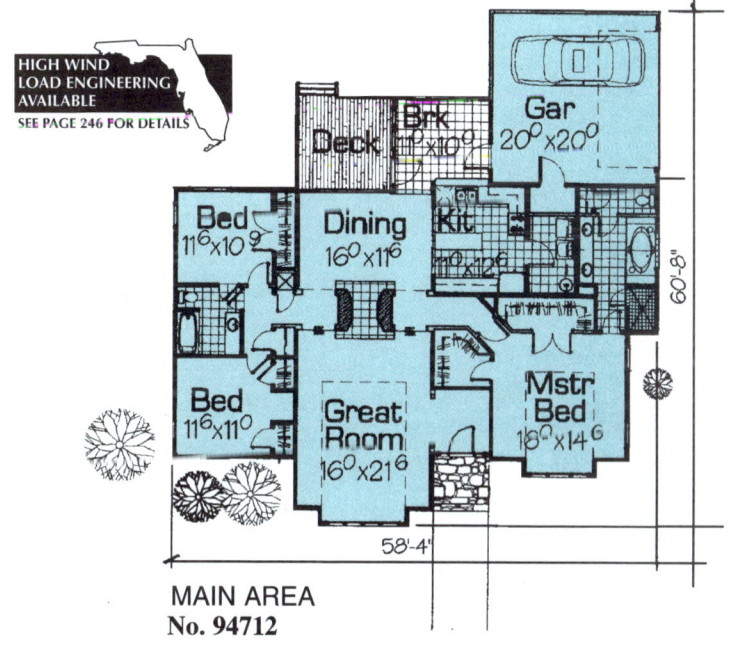

An EXCLUSIVE DESIGN
By United Design Associates

HIGH WIND LOAD ENGINEERING AVAILABLE
SEE PAGE 246 FOR DETAILS

**MAIN AREA
No. 94712**

PRICE CODE E

COTTAGE INFLUENCES ADD CHARM
DESIGN NO. 94614

- This plan features:
  — Three or four bedrooms
  — Three full and one half baths
- Cozy porch entrance into Foyer with banister staircase and coat closet
- Expansive Great Room with focal point fireplace and access to Covered Porch and Deck
- Cooktop island in Kitchen easily serves Breakfast bay and formal Dining Room
- Large Master Suite with access to Covered Porch, walk-in closet and double vanity bath
- Study/Guest Bedroom with private access to a full bath, offers many uses
- Two second floor bedrooms with dormers, private vanities and walk-in closets
- An optional crawl space or slab foundation available, please specify when ordering

FIRST FLOOR — 1,916 SQ. FT.
SECOND FLOOR — 617 SQ. FT.
GARAGE — 516 SQ. FT.

Width = 66' - 0"
Depth = 66' - 0"

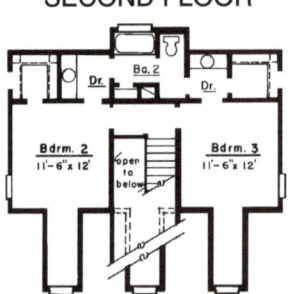

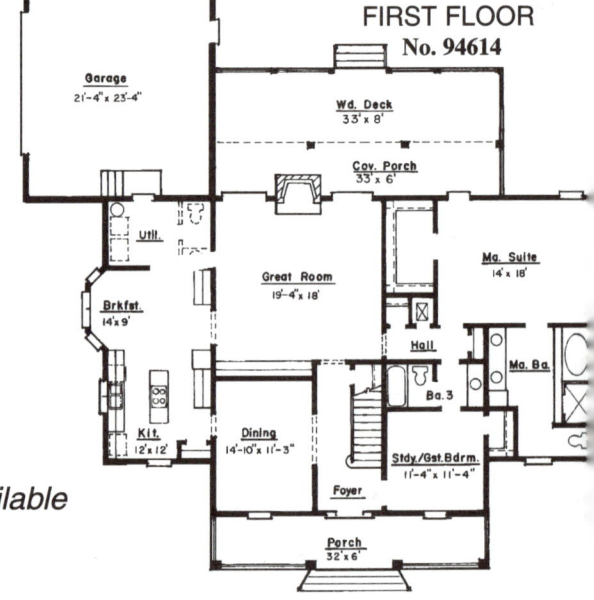

No materials list available

TOTAL LIVING AREA: 2,533 SQ. FT.

PRICE CODE D

GRAND LIVING ROOM
DESIGN NO. 92200

- This plan features:
  — Four bedrooms
  — Three full and one half baths
- Impressive Porch and Entry leads into front-to-back Living Room with focal point fireplace and vaulted ceiling
- Easy entertaining with formal Dining Room adjoining Living Room
- An efficient U-shaped island Kitchen with an island cooktop opens to Family Room/Dining Area with corner fireplace
- A quiet Study with built-in book shelves
- Secluded Master Bedroom offers a private Patio and plush bath with two walk-in closets, a double vanity and a raised tub
- Three additional bedrooms, one with a private bath, on second floor

FIRST FLOOR — 2,283 SQ. FT.
SECOND FLOOR — 855 SQ. FT.

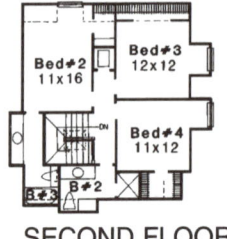

No materials list available

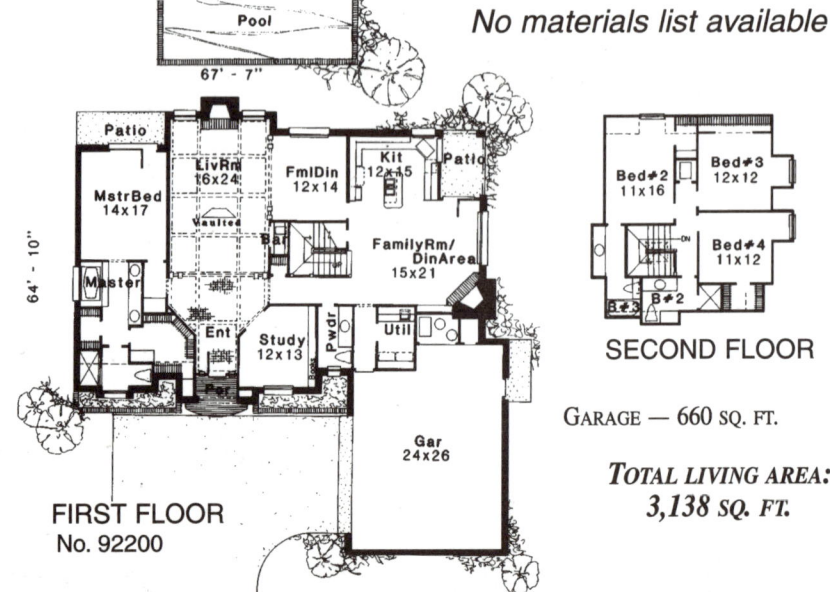

GARAGE — 660 SQ. FT.

TOTAL LIVING AREA: 3,138 SQ. FT.

SOUTHERN APPEAL

DESIGN NO. 94617

- This plan features:
- Four bedrooms
- Three full baths
- Large windows, shutters, and wide country Porch ideal design for warm climate
- Expansive Family Room with landing staircase, fireplace and French doors to Covered Porch
- Country Kitchen with cook top island/eating bar, built-in pantry, Utility room and a bright Breakfast area
- Formal Dining Room overlooking front Porch conveniently located
- Corner Master Bedroom suite offers a pampering bath and large walk-in closet
- Two additional bedrooms with dormers and walk-in closets, share a full bath
- Game Room over Garage offers multiple uses
- An optional crawl space or slab foundation available, please specify when ordering

FIRST FLOOR — 1,977 SQ. FT.
SECOND FLOOR — 687 SQ. FT.
GAME ROOM — 346 SQ. FT.
GARAGE AND STORAGE — 487 SQ. FT.

No materials list available

WIDTH: 69'- 6"
DEPTH: 69'- 8 1/2"

TOTAL LIVING AREA: 2,664 SQ. FT.

PRICE CODE E

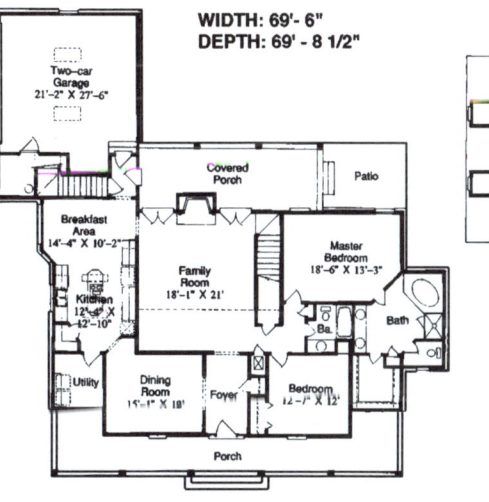

FIRST FLOOR
No. 94617

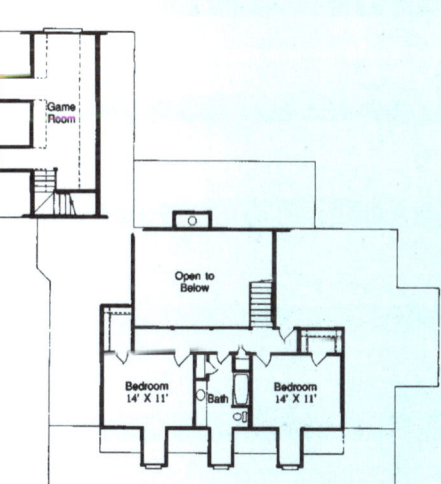

SECOND FLOOR

Hurricane Engineering for Florida!

The Garlinghouse Company has teamed with The Sater Design Collection and United Design Associates, not only to supply our Sunbelt Home Plans publication with stunning home designs, but to provide structural wind load engineering services for the Florida building market. We are now able to provide high wind load engineering for any design from The Sater Design Collection and United Design Associates that appears in this publication.

Our extensive engineering packages will come to you complete with 3 sets of signed and sealed blueprints along with the modified reproducible vellums. Many localities will require energy calculations in addition to the engineered plans. The energy calculations can often be obtained from a reputable HVAC contractor free of charge as an incentive to use their service or we can provide them for a fee of $150.00. Check with your local building department to find out your exact requirements before ordering.

The Sater Design Collection, from Bonita Springs, Florida and United Design Associates from Auburn, AL will help make building your dream home a reality. Through this exclusive offer, we are able to provide these high wind load engineering services at very reasonable prices.

Price Code	High Wind Load Engineering Fees
A	$650
B	$775
C	$900
D	$1025
E	$1150
F	$1275
G	$1400
H	$1525

NOTE: High wind load engineering pricing is in addition to the cost of a reproducible vellum and is only available for plans with this symbol...

Once you have placed your order, please allow 7-10 additional business days for delivery after we have received all of your applicable site information. This includes a copy of your site plan and legal description of your property.

High wind load engineering is a custom professional service and is locally specific. Please note that all fees for this service are non-refundable upon commencement of any engineering. The above pricing includes shipping from The Sater Design Collection or United Design Associates to you.

We are proud to offer these engineering services to you at these very competitive rates.

Seismic Engineering for California!

The Garlinghouse Company has teamed with Parker Resnick Structural Engineering, a premiere Engineering firm in Southern California, to provide structural engineering services to the Southwestern Sunbelt market. We are now able to provide structural and seismic engineering for any plan that appears in this publication. Seismic engineering can be provided with, or without, specific soils information, depending on your local building needs.

Our extensive engineering packages will come to you complete with 3 sets of stamped and signed blueprints, 1 set of reproducible vellums, and 3 sets of stamped and signed structural calculations!

Parker Resnick Structural Engineering, located in Los Angeles California will help make building your dream home a reality. Through this exclusive offer, we are able to provide these services at very reasonable prices.

Price Code	Without Specific Soils Information	With Specific Soils Information
A	$1020	$1500
B	$1080	$1590
C	$1160	$1720
D	$1250	$1840
E	$1360	$2000
F	$1490	$2200
G	$1620	$2400
H	$1760	$2600

NOTE: Seismic engineering pricing is in addition to the cost of a reproducible vellum.

You will be required to provide all applicable soils reports (if they are required in your area) before any specific foundation engineering can begin. Once we have received your order or approved soils reports, please allow 10-14 additional business days for delivery. Check with your local building department to find out your exact requirements before placing your order.

The above pricing includes shipping from Parker Resnick Structural Engineering to you. All plan check revisions, site visits or field questions will be billable at $100.00 per hour. Site visit billing will include travel time. Seismic engineering is a custom professional service and is locally specific. Please note that all fees for this service are non-refundable upon commencement of any engineering.

We are proud to offer these engineering services to you at these very competitive rates.

TOP SELLING GARAGE PLANS

Save money by Doing-It-Yourself using our Easy-To-Follow plans. Whether you intend to build your own garage or contract it out to a building professional, the Garlinghouse garage plans provide you with everything you need to price out your project and get started. Put our 90+ years of experience to work for you. *Order now!!*

No. 06016C — $86.00
Apartment Garage With One Bedroom

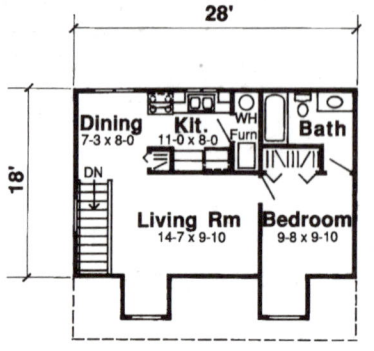

- 24' x 28' Overall Dimensions
- 544 Square Foot Apartment
- 12/12 Gable Roof with Dormers
- Slab or Stem Wall Foundation Options

No. 06015C — $86.00
Apartment Garage With Two Bedrooms

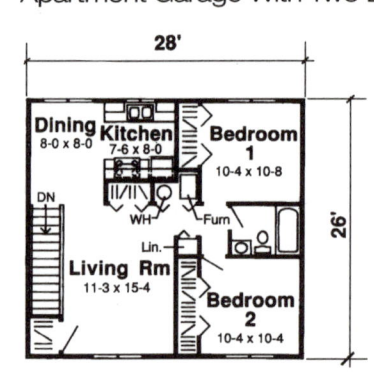

- 26' x 28' Overall Dimensions
- 728 Square Foot Apartment
- 4/12 Pitch Gable Roof
- Slab or Stem Wall Foundation Options

No. 06012C — $54.00
30' Deep Gable &/or Eave Jumbo Garages

- 4/12 Pitch Gable Roof
- Available Options for Extra Tall Walls, Garage & Personnel Doors, Foundation, Window, & Sidings
- Package contains 4 Different Sizes
  - 30' x 28'
  - 30' x 32'
  - 30' x 36'
  - 30' x 40'

No. 06013C — $68.00
Two-Car Garage With Mudroom/Breezeway

- Attaches to Any House
- 24' x 24' Eave Entry
- Available Options for Utility Room with Bath, Mudroom, Screened-In Breezeway, Roof, Foundation, Garage & Personnel Doors, Window, & Sidings

No. 06001C — $48.00
12', 14' & 16' Wide-Gable 1-Car Garages
- Available Options for Roof, Foundation, Window, Door, & Sidings
- Package contains 8 Different Sizes
- 12' x 20' Mini-Garage
- 14' x 20'
- 14' x 22'
- 14' x 24'
- 16' x 20'
- 16' x 22'
- 16' x 24'
- 16' x 26'

No. 06003C — $48.00
24' Wide-Gable 2-Car Garages
- Available Options for Side Shed, Roof, Foundation, Garage & Personnel Doors, Window, & Sidings
- Package contains 5 Different Sizes
- 24' x 22'
- 24' x 24'
- 24' x 26'
- 24' x 28'
- 24' x 32'

No. 06007C — $60.00
Gable 2-Car Gambrel Roof Garages
- Interior Rear Stairs to Loft Workshop
- Front Loft Cargo Door With Pulley Lift
- Available Options for Foundation, Garage & Personnel Doors, Window, & Sidings
- Package contains 5 Different Sizes
- 22' x 26'
- 22' x 28'
- 24' x 28'
- 24' x 30'
- 24' x 32'

No. 06006C — $48.00
22' & 24' Deep Eave 2 & 3-Car Garages
- Can Be Built Stand-Alone or Attached to House
- Available Options for Roof, Foundation, Garage & Personnel Doors, Window, & Sidings
- Package contains 6 Different Sizes
- 22' x 28'
- 22' x 30'
- 22' x 32'
- 24' x 30'
- 24' x 32'
- 24' x 36'

No. 06002C — $48.00
20' & 22' Wide-Gable 2-Car Garages
- Available Options for Roof, Foundation, Garage & Personnel Doors, Window, & Sidings
- Package contains 7 Different Sizes
- 20' x 20'
- 20' x 22'
- 20' x 24'
- 20' x 28'
- 22' x 22'
- 22' x 24'
- 22' x 28'

No. 06008C — $60.00
Eave 2 & 3-Car Clerestory Roof Garages
- Interior Side Stairs to Loft Workshop
- Available Options for Engine Lift, Foundation, Garage & Personnel Doors, Window, & Sidings
- Package contains 4 Different Sizes
- 24' x 26'
- 24' x 28'
- 24' x 32'
- 24' x 36'

Here's What You Get

- Three complete sets of drawings for each plan ordered

- Detailed step-by-step instructions with easy-to-follow diagrams on how to build your garage (not available with apartment garages)

- For each garage style, a variety of size and garage door configuration options

- Variety of roof styles and/or pitch options for most garages

- Complete materials list

- Choice between three foundation options:
  Monolithic Slab, Concrete Stem Wall or Concrete Block Stem Wall

- Full framing plans, elevations and cross-sectionals for each garage size and configuration

Build-It-Yourself PROJECT PLAN

GARLINGHOUSE

Order Information For Garage Plans:
All garage plan orders contain three complete sets of drawings with instructions and are priced as listed next to the illustratio
Additional sets of plans may be obtained for $10.00 each with your original order. UPS shipping is used unless otherwise requeste
Please include the proper amount for shipping.

Garage Order Form

Order Code No. **G8SB2**

Please send me 3 complete sets of the following GARAGE PLAN:

Item no. & description	Price
_____	$ _____

Additional Sets

_____ (@ $10.00 each) $ _____

Shipping Charges: UPS-$3.75, First Class- $4.50 $ _____

Subtotal: $ _____

Resident sales tax: KS-6.15%, CT-6% $ _____
(NOT REQUIRED FOR OTHER STATES)

Total Enclosed: $ _____

My Billing Address is:
Name _____
Address _____
City _____
State _____ Zip _____
Daytime Phone No. _____

My Shipping Address is:
Name _____
Address _____
(UPS will not ship to P.O. Boxes)
City _____
State _____ Zip _____

For Faster Service...Charge It!
U.S. & Canada Call
1(800)235-5700
All foreign residents call 1(860)343-5977

❏ Mastercard   ❏ Visa

Card # |_|_|_|_|_|_|_|_|_|_|_|_|_|_|_|_|

Signature _____ Exp. ___/___

If paying by credit card, to avoid delays:
billing address must be as it appears on credit card statement

or FAX us at (860) 343-5984

Send your order to:
(With check or money order payable in U.S. funds only)
The Garlinghouse Company
P.O. Box 1717
Middletown, CT 06457

No C.O.D. orders accepted; U.S. funds only. UPS will not ship to Post Office boxes, FPO boxes, APO boxes, Alaska or Hawaii.
Canadian orders must be shipped First Class.

Prices subject to change without notice.

Ignoring Copyright Laws Can Be
A $1,000,000 Mistake

Recent changes in the US copyright laws allow for statutory penalties of up to **$100,000** per incident for copyright infringement involving any of the copyrighted plans found in this publication. The law can be confusing. So, for your own protection, take the time to understand what you can and cannot do when it comes to home plans.

••• WHAT YOU CANNOT DO •••

You Cannot Duplicate Home Plans

Purchasing a set of blueprints and making additional sets by reproducing the original is **illegal**. If you need multiple sets of a particular home plan, then you must purchase them.

You Cannot Copy Any Part of a Home Plan to Create Another

Creating your own plan by copying even part of a home design found in this publication is called "creating a derivative work" and is **illegal** unless you have permission to do so.

You Cannot Build a Home Without a License

You must have specific permission or license to build a home from a copyrighted design, even if the finished home has been changed from the original plan. It is **illegal** to build one of the homes found in this publication without a license.

What Garlinghouse Offers

Home Plan Blueprint Package

By purchasing a single or multiple set package of blueprints from Garlinghouse, you not only receive the physical blueprint documents necessary for construction, but you are also granted a license to build one, and only one, home. You can also make simple modifications, including minor non-structural changes and material substitutions, to our design, as long as these changes are made directly on the blueprints purchased from Garlinghouse and no additional copies are made.

Home Plan Vellums

By purchasing vellums for one of our home plans, you receive the same construction drawings found in the blueprints, but printed on vellum paper. Vellums can be erased and are perfect for making design changes. They are also semi-transparent making them easy to duplicate. But most importantly, the purchase of home plan vellums comes with a broader license that allows you to make changes to the design (ie, create a hand drawn or CAD derivative work), to make an unlimited number of copies of the plan, and to build one home from the plan.

License To Build Additional Homes

With the purchase of a blueprint package or vellums you automatically receive a license to build one home and only one home, respectively. If you want to build more homes than you are licensed to build through your purchase of a plan, then additional licenses may be purchased at reasonable costs from Garlinghouse. Inquire for more information.

Everything You Need...
...to Make Your Dream Come True

You pay only a fraction of the original cost for home designs by respected professionals.

You've Picked Your Dream Home!

You can already see it standing on your lot... you can see yourselves in your new home... enjoying family, entertaining guests, celebrating holidays. All that remains ahead are the details. That's where we can help. Whether you plan to build-it-yourself, be your own contractor, or hand your plans over to an outside contractor, your Garlinghouse blueprints provide the perfect beginning for putting yourself in your dream home right away.

We even make it simple for you to make professional design modifications. We can also provide a materials list for greater economy.

My grandfather, L.F. Garlinghouse, started a tradition of quality when he founded this company in 1907. For over 90 years, homeowners and builders have relied on us for accurate, complete, professional blueprints. Our plans help you get results fast... and save money, too! These pages will give you all the information you need to order. So get started now... I know you'll love your new Garlinghouse home!

Sincerely,

EXTERIOR ELEVATIONS

Elevations are scaled drawings of the front, rear, left and right sides of a home. All of the necessary information pertaining to the exterior finish materials, roof pitches and exterior height dimensions of your home are defined.

CABINET PLANS

These plans, or in some cases elevations, will detail the layout of the kitchen and bathroom cabinets at a larger scale. This gives you an accurate layout for your cabinets or an ideal starting point for a modified custom cabinet design. Available for most plans in our collection.

TYPICAL WALL SECTION

This section is provided to help your builder understand the structural components and material used to construct the exterior walls of your home. This section will address insulation, roof components, and interior and exterior wall finishes. Your plans will be designed with either 2x4 2x6 exterior walls, but most professional contractors can easily adapt the plans to the wall thickness you require. Available for most plans in our collection.

FIREPLACE DETAILS

If the home you have chosen includes a fireplace, the fireplace detail will show typical methods to construct the firebox, hearth and flue chase for masonry units, or a wood frame chase for a zero-clearance unit. Available for most plans in our collection.

FOUNDATION PLAN

These plans will accurately dimension the footprint of your home including load bearing points and beam placement if applicable. The foundation style will vary from plan to plan. Your local climatic conditions will dictate whether a basement, slab or crawlspace is best suited for your area. In most cases, if your plan comes with one foundation style, a professional contractor can easily adapt the foundation plan to an alternate style.

ROOF PLAN

The information necessary to construct the roof will be included with your home plans. Some plans will reference roof trusses, while many others contain schematic framing plans. These framing plans will indicate the lumber sizes necessary for the rafters and ridgeboards based on the designated roof loads.

TYPICAL CROSS SECTION

A cut-away cross-section through the entire home shows your building contractor the exact correlation of construction components at all levels of the house. It will help to clarify the load bearing points from the roof all the way down to the basement.

DETAILED FLOOR PLANS

The floor plans of your home accurately dimension the positioning of all walls, doors, windows, stairs and permanent fixtures. They will show you the relationship and dimensions of rooms, closets and traffic patterns. Included is the schematic of the electrical layout. This layout is clearly represented and does not hinder the clarity of other pertinent information shown. All the details will help your builder properly construct your new home.

STAIR DETAILS

If stairs are an element of the design you have chosen, then a cross-section of the stairs will be included in your home plans. This gives your builders the essential reference points that they need for headroom clearance, and riser and tread dimensions. Available for most plans in our collection.

TYPICAL WALL SECTION

TYPICAL CROSS SECTION

DETAILED FLOOR PLANS

ROOF PLAN

FOUNDATION PLAN

FIREPLACE DETAILS

CABINET PLANS

STAIR DETAILS

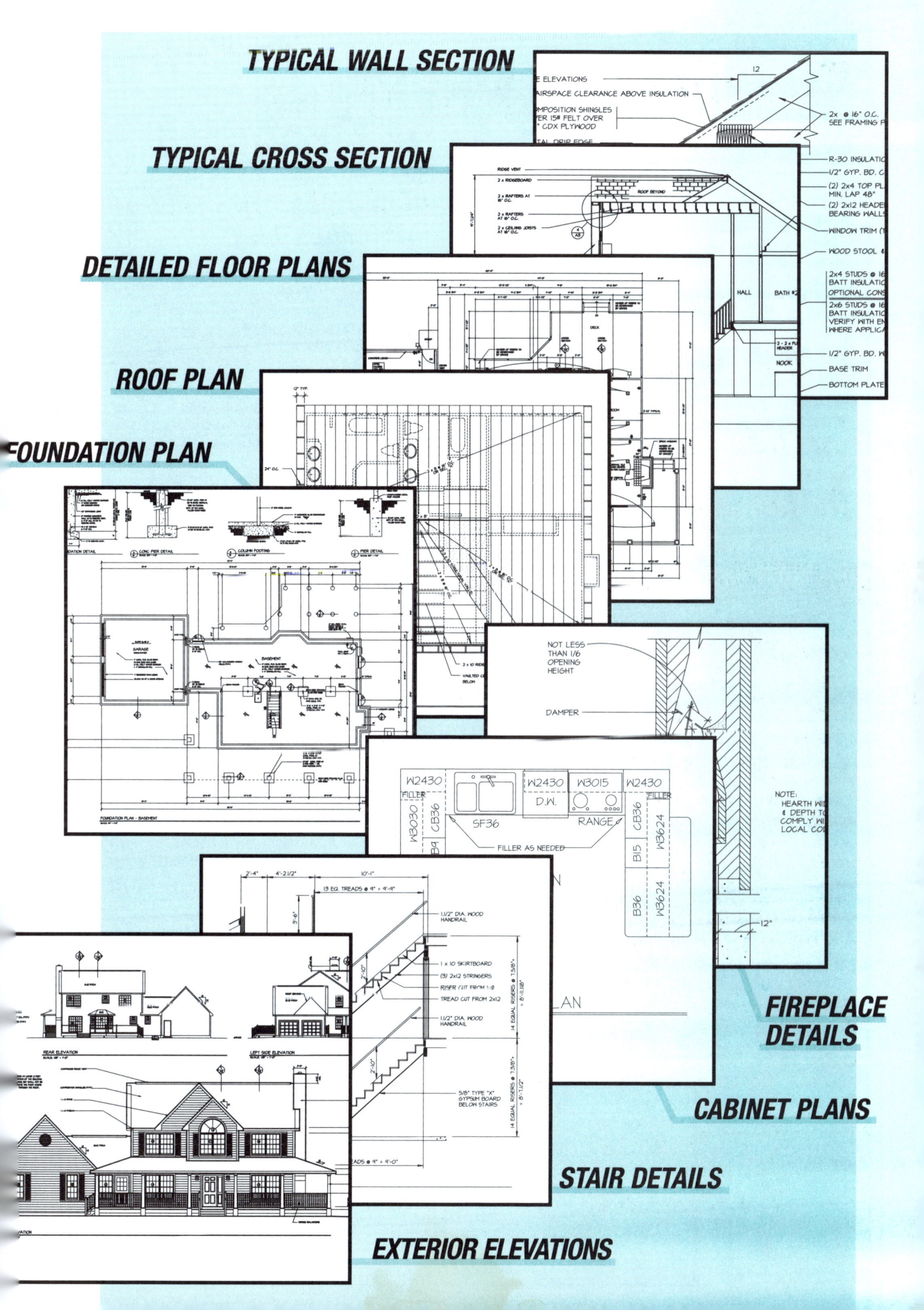

EXTERIOR ELEVATIONS

Garlinghouse Options & Extras ...Make Your Dream A Home

Reversed Plans Can Make Your Dream Home Just Right!

"That's our dream home...if only the garage were on the other side!"
You could have exactly the home you want by flipping it end-for-end. Check it out by holding your dream home page of this book up to a mirror. Then simply order your plans "reversed." We'll send you one full set of mirror-image plans (with the writing backwards) as a master guide for you and your builder.

The remaining sets of your order will come as shown in this book so the dimensions and specifications are easily read on the job site...but most plans in our collection come stamped "REVERSED" so there is no construction confusion.

We can only send reversed plans with multiple-set orders. There is a $50 charge for this service.

Some plans in our collection are available in Right Reading Reverse. Right Reading Reverse plans will show your home in reverse, with the writing on the plan being readable. This easy-to-read format will save you valuable time and money. Please contact our Customer Service Department at (860) 343-5977 to check for Right Reading Reverse availability. (There is a $125 charge for this service.)

Specifications & Contract Form

We send this form to you free of charge with your home plan order. The form is designed to be filled in by you or your contractor with the exact materials to use in the construction of your new home. Once signed by you and your contractor it will provide you with peace of mind throughout the construction process.

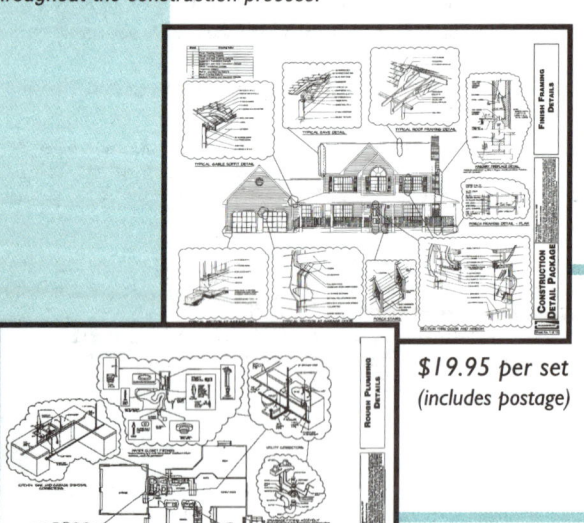

$19.95 per set
(includes postage)

Remember To Order Your Materials List

It'll help you save money. Available at a modest additional charge, the Materials List gives the quantity, dimensions, and specifications for the major materials needed to build your home. You will get faster, more accurate bids from your contractors and building suppliers — and avoid paying for unused materials and waste. Materials Lists are available for all home plans except as otherwise indicated, but can only be ordered with a set of home plans. Due to differences in regional requirements and homeowner or builder preferences... electrical, plumbing and heating/air conditioning equipment specifications are not designed specifically for each plan. However, non-plan specific detailed typical prints of residential electrical, plumbing and construction guidelines can be provided. Please see below for additional information.

Detail Plans Provide Valuable Information About Construction Techniques

Because local codes and requirements vary greatly, we recommend that you obtain drawings and bids from licensed contractors to do your mechanical plans. However, if you want to know more about techniques — and deal more confidently with subcontractors — we offer these remarkably useful detail sheets. These detail sheets will aid in your understanding of these technical subjects. **The detail sheets are not specific to any one home plan and should be used only as a general reference guide.**

RESIDENTIAL CONSTRUCTION DETAILS

Ten sheets that cover the essentials of stick-built residential home construction. Details foundation options — poured concrete basement, concrete block, or monolithic concrete slab. Shows all aspects of floor, wall and roof framing. Provides details for roof dormers, overhangs, chimneys and skylights. Conforms to requirements of Uniform Building code or BOCA code. Includes a quick index and a glossary of terms.

RESIDENTIAL PLUMBING DETAILS

Eight sheets packed with information detailing pipe installation methods, fittings, and sized. Details plumbing hook-ups for toilets, sinks, washers, sump pumps, and septic system construction. Conforms to requirements of National Plumbing code. Color coded with a glossary of terms and quick index.

RESIDENTIAL ELECTRICAL DETAILS

Eight sheets that cover all aspects of residential wiring, from simple switch wiring to service entrance connections. Details distribution panel layout with outlet and switch schematics, circuit breaker and wiring installation methods, and ground fault interrupter specifications. Conforms to requirements of National Electrical Code. Color coded with a glossary of terms.

GARLINGHOUSE

Order Code No. **H8SB2**

Order Form

Plan prices guaranteed until 4/14/99 — After this date call for updated pricing

___ set(s) of blueprints for plan #_____ $_____

___ Vellum & Modification kit for plan #_____ $_____

___ Additional set(s) @ $35 each for plan #_____ $_____

___ Mirror Image Reverse @ $50 each $_____

___ Right Reading Reverse @ $125 each $_____

___ Materials list for plan #_____ $_____

___ Detail Plans @ $19.95 each
    ❑ Construction ❑ Plumbing ❑ Electrical $_____

High Wind Load Engineering (see page 246) $_____

Seismic Engineering (see page 247) $_____

Shipping (see charts on opposite page) $_____

Subtotal $_____

Sales Tax (CT residents add 6% sales tax, KS residents add 6.15% sales tax) (Not required for all states) $_____

TOTAL AMOUNT ENCLOSED $_____

Send your check, money order or credit card information to:
(No C.O.D.'s Please)

Please submit all United States & Other Nations orders to:
Garlinghouse Company
P.O. Box 1717
Middletown, CT. 06457

Please Submit all Canadian plan orders to:
Garlinghouse Company
102 Ellis Street
Penticton, BC V2A 4L5

ADDRESS INFORMATION:

NAME:_____

STREET:_____

CITY:_____

STATE:_____ ZIP:_____

DAYTIME PHONE:_____

Credit Card Information

Charge To: ❑ Visa   ❑ Mastercard

Card # |_|_|_|_|_|_|_|_|_|_|_|_|_|_|_|_|

Signature _____ Exp. _____

Payment must be made in U.S. funds. Foreign Mail Orders: Certified bank checks in U.S. funds only

TERMS OF SALE FOR HOME PLANS: All home plans sold through this publication are copyright protected. Reproduction of these home plans, either in whole or in part, including any direct copying and/or preparation of derivative works thereof, for any reason without the prior written permission of The L.F. Garlinghouse Co., Inc., is strictly prohibited. The purchase of a set of home plans in no way transfers any copyright or other ownership interest in it to the buyer except for a limited license to use that set of home plans for the construction of one, and only one, dwelling unit. The purchase of additional sets of that home plan at a reduced price from the original set or as a part of a multiple set package does not entitle the buyer a license to construct more than one dwelling unit.

IMPORTANT INFORMATION TO READ BEFORE YOU PLACE YOUR ORDER

How Many Sets Of Plans Will You Need?

The Standard 8-Set Construction Package
Our experience shows that you'll speed every step of construction and avoid costly building errors by ordering enough sets to go around. Each tradesperson wants a set — the general contractor and all subcontractors; foundation, electrical, plumbing, heating/air conditioning and framers. Don't forget your lending institution, building department and, of course, a set for yourself.

The Minimum 4-Set Construction Package
If you're comfortable with arduous follow-up, this package can save you a few dollars by giving you the option of passing down plan sets as work progresses. You might have enough copies to go around if work goes exactly as scheduled and no plans are lost or damaged by subcontractors. But for only $50 more, the 8-set package eliminates these worries.

The Single Study Set
We offer this set so you can study the blueprints to plan your dream home in detail. As with all of our plans, they are stamped with a copyright warning. Remember, one set is never enough to build your home. In pursuant to copyright laws, it is *illegal* to reproduce any blueprint.

Our Reorder and Exchange Policies:

If you find after your initial purchase that you require additional sets of plans you may purchase them from us at special reorder prices (please call for pricing details) provided that you reorder within 6 months of your original order date. There is a $28 reorder processing fee that is charged on all reorders. For more information on reordering plans please contact our Customer Service Department at (860) 343-5977.

We want you to find your dream home from our wide selection of home plans. However, if for some reason you find that the plan you have purchased from us does not meet your needs, then you may exchange that plan for any other plan in our collection. We allow you sixty days from your original invoice date to make an exchange. At the time of the exchange you will be charged a processing fee of 15% of the total amount of your original order plus the difference in price between the plans (if applicable) plus the cost to ship the new plans to you. Call our Customer Service Department at (860) 343-5977 for more information. Please Note: Reproducible vellums can only be exchanged if they are unopened.

Important Shipping Information

Please refer to the shipping charts on the order form for service availability for your specific plan number. Our delivery service must have a street address or Rural Route Box number — never a post office box. (PLEASE NOTE: Supplying a P.O. Box number *only* will delay the shipping of your order.) Use a work address if no one is home during the day.

Orders being shipped to APO or FPO must go via First Class Mail. Please include the proper postage.

For our International Customers, only Certified bank checks and money orders are accepted and must be payable in U.S. currency. For speed, we ship international orders Air Parcel Post. Please refer to the chart for the correct shipping cost.

Important Canadian Shipping Information

To our friends in Canada, we have a plan design affiliate in Kitchener, Ontario. This relationship will help you avoid the delays and charges associated with shipments from the United States. Moreover, our affiliate is familiar with the building requirements in your community and country. We prefer payments in U.S. Currency. If you, however, are sending Canadian funds please add 40% to the prices of the plans and shipping fees.

An Important Note About Building Code Requirements:

All plans are drawn to conform to one or more of the industry's major national building standards. However, due to the variety of local building regulations, your plan may need to be modified to comply with local requirements — snow loads, energy loads, seismic zones, etc. Do check them fully and consult your local building officials.

A few states require that all building plans used be drawn by an architect registered in that state. While having your plans reviewed and stamped by such an architect may be prudent, laws requiring non-conforming plans like ours to be completely redrawn forces you to unnecessarily pay very large fees. If your state has such a law, we strongly recommend you contact your state representative to protest.

The rendering, floor plans, and technical information contained within this publication are not guaranteed to be totally accurate. Consequently, no information from this publication should be used either as a guide to constructing a home or for estimating the cost of building a home. Complete blueprints must be purchased for such purposes.

BEFORE ORDERING PLEASE READ ALL ORDERING INFORMATION

Please submit all Canadian plan orders to:
Garlinghouse Company
102 Ellis Street, Penticton, BC V2A 4L5
Canadian Customers: 1-800-361-7526/Fax: 1-250-493-7526
Customer Service: 1-250-493-0942

ORDER TOLL FREE — 1-800-235-5700
Monday-Friday 8:00 a.m. to 8:00 p.m. Eastern Time
or FAX your Credit Card order to 1-860-343-5984
All foreign residents call 1-800-343-5977

Please have ready: 1. Your credit card number 2. The plan number 3. The order code number ⇨ **H8SB2**

Garlinghouse 1998 Blueprint Price Code Schedule

Additional sets with original order $35

PRICE CODE	A	B	C	D	E	F	G	H
8 SETS OF SAME PLAN	$385	$425	$470	$510	$550	$595	$635	$675
4 SETS OF SAME PLAN	$335	$375	$420	$460	$500	$545	$585	$625
1 SINGLE SET OF PLANS	$285	$325	$370	$410	$450	$495	$535	$575
VELLUMS	$495	$540	$590	$635	$680	$730	$775	$820
MATERIALS LIST	$50	$50	$55	$55	$60	$60	$65	$65

Shipping — (Plans 1-84999)

	1-3 Sets	4-6 Sets	7+ & Vellums
Standard Delivery (UPS 2-Day)	$15.00	$20.00	$25.00
Overnight Delivery	$30.00	$35.00	$40.00

Shipping — (Plans 85000-99999)

	1-3 Sets	4-6 Sets	7+ & Vellums
Ground Delivery (7-10 Days)	$9.00	$18.00	$20.00
Express Delivery (3-5 Days)	$15.00	$20.00	$25.00

International Shipping & Handling

	1-3 Sets	4-6 Sets	7+ & Vellums
Regular Delivery Canada (7-10 Days)	$14.00	$17.00	$20.00
Express Delivery Canada (5-6 Days)	$35.00	$40.00	$45.00
Overseas Delivery Airmail (2-3 Weeks)	$45.00	$52.00	$60.00

Index

- RRR — Right Reading Reverse Available
- ML — Materials List Available
- WL — Hurricane Engineering Available

Plan	Pg.	Price	Option	Plan	Pg.	Price	Option	Plan	Pg.	Price	Option	Plan	Pg.	Price	Option	Plan	Pg.	Price	Option
9828	36	E	ML	92523	84	A	ML	93041	170	E		94215	82	D	WL	94622	24	E	
10108	33	D	ML	92531	87	B	ML	93043	164	E		94216	174	F	ML/WL	94701	120	E	WL
10507	228	C	ML	92534	233	F	ML	93048	235	A		94218	98	D	WL	94705	112	D	ML/WL
24650	219	E		92536	66	C	ML	93049	61	D		94219	1	E	WL	94706	242	F	ML/WL
90423	65	B	ML	92537	154	D	ML	93050	158	D		94220	8	F	WL	94707	106	D	ML/WL
90436	70	E	ML	92538	167	E	ML	93054	238	E	RRR	94221	19	F	WL	94708	240	D	ML/WL
90441	134	C	ML	92539	183	C	ML	93100	205	B	ML/RRR	94222	6	F	WL	94709	124	D	ML/WL
90443	92	E	ML	92608	177	C		93107	196	C	RRR	94223	2	F	WL	94710	97	B	ML/WL
90444	71	D	ML	92609	39	B		93202	160	A	ML	94224	226	F	WL	94711	240	D	ML/WL
90448	50	C	ML	92610	215	C		93205	85	D	ML	94225	27	F	WL	94712	243	C	ML/WL
90449	187	D	ML	92613	203	E		93206	90	E	ML	94226	28	F	WL	94713	123	C	ML/WL
90450	67	D	ML	92615	151	D		93212	86	C		94227	198	F	WL	94714	115	C	ML/WL
90983	182	A	ML	92616	189	E		93213	223	C		94228	14	F	WL	94715	139	E	ML/WL
91418	186	B	ML	92623	157	E		93215	237	D	ML	94229	10	F	WL	94716	163	B	ML/WL
91607	185	B	ML	92625	64	B		93216	74	C	ML	94230	31	F	WL	94721	173	E	ML/WL
91814	180	B	ML	92626	94	C		93219	83	B	ML	94231	32	E	WL	94726	178	C	ML/WL
92200	244	E		92628	172	C		93220	89	B	ML	94232	194	E	WL	94736	191	B	ML/WL
92202	108	F		92629	100	C		93222	79	A	ML	94233	207	D	WL	94740	200	B	ML/WL
92207	54	E		92630	49	B		93227	102	B	ML	94234	232	E	ML/WL	94744	201	E	ML/WL
92209	60	F		92631	168	C		93228	99	C		94235	193	E	ML/WL	94745	213	B	ML/WL
92210	197	F		92632	53	B		93231	179	B		94236	225	D	WL	94749	227	B	ML/WL
92219	38	F		92634	171	D		93240	237	D	ML	94237	72	F	ML/WL	94801	48	B	ML
92220	212	C		92635	188	A		93241	234	E	ML	94238	78	D	WL	94803	125	B	ML
92237	63	F		92636	166	C		93253	107	D	ML	94239	21	F	WL	94804	127	C	ML
92238	37	B		92642	138	C		93261	150	B	ML	94240	75	B	WL	94805	241	C	ML
92257	52	D		92643	190	D		93262	224	B		94241	231	F	WL	94806	109	C	ML
92265	65	F		92644	161	C		93263	210	B		94242	51	E	WL	94808	81	F	ML
92269	95	E		92646	165	D		93266	88	C		94243	221	E	WL	94809	30	E	ML
92273	43	F		92647	175	C		93269	76	B	ML	94244	199	F	WL	99208	132	C	ML
92274	105	F		92649	156	B		93270	236	F		94245	217	F	WL	99239	147	F	ML
92275	91	E		92651	176	D		93279	169	A	ML	94246	218	F	WL	99250	148	C	ML
92277	57	E		92702	68	A		93311	73	C		94247	46	E	WL	99269	230	D	ML
92279	62	E		92703	128	B		93702	103	B		94600	204	D		99270	136	E	ML
92281	220	A		92704	133	A		93704	202	D		94601	114	B		99271	142	E	ML
92283	101	B		92705	129	C		93707	216	E		94602	222	C		99272	146	E	ML
92286	40	A		93000	18	C		93708	192	D		94603	41	B		99275	143	E	ML
92288	77	F		93013	181	D		94200	20	B	WL	94607	195	C	RRR	99276	130	D	ML
92401	56	F		93015	149	A		94201	22	A	ML/WL	94608	214	C		99277	211	D	ML
92403	116	F		93018	145	A		94202	16	F	ML/WL	94610	29	D		99278	141	F	ML
92404	80	D	ML	93021	153	A		94203	15	B	WL	94611	29	E		99280	131	C	ML
92405	44	B		93025	23	A	ML	94204	12	B	WL	94612	96	D		99281	135	C	ML
92415	35	D		93026	34	A		94205	11	C	ML/WL	94613	31	E		99283	140	C	ML
92503	69	A	ML	93027	47	A		94206	58	D	WL	94614	244	D		99284	155	C	ML
92504	162	F	ML	93029	55	C		94208	206	B	WL	94615	110	E		99285	113	B	ML
92505	184	F	ML	93030	42	C		94209	4	E	WL	94616	238	E		99286	111	B	ML
92509	122	D	ML	93031	26	C		94210	27	E	WL	94617	245	E		99287	121	D	ML
92513	117	C	ML	93032	59	D		94211	25	C	ML/WL	94618	119	C		99288	144	E	ML
92516	208	C	ML	93034	234	E		94212	104	E	ML/WL	94619	239	D		99289	159	F	ML
92517	137	C	ML	93035	93	B		94213	17	E	WL	94620	242	E		99290	152	E	ML
92520	209	A	ML	93036	118	F		94214	13	D	ML/WL	94621	229	E		99373	126	F	ML